READINGS IN THE
THEORY OF GRAMMAR

DATE DUE			
P Jul 6 '77			
Feb 17 '82			
Jul 7 '82			

READINGS IN THE THEORY OF GRAMMAR

FROM THE 17TH TO THE 20TH CENTURY

DIANE D. BORNSTEIN

Queens College
of the City University of New York

WINTHROP PUBLISHERS, INC.
Cambridge, Massachusetts

Library of Congress Cataloging in Publication Data

Main entry under title:
Readings in the theory of grammar.

Includes bibliographies.
1. English language — Grammar — Collected works.
2. Grammar, Comparative and general — Collected
works. 3. Linguistics — Collected works. I. Bornstein, Diane
PE1098.R4   425   76-3743
ISBN 0-87626-753-3

Selected acknowledgments are listed on page x.

425

R22

99525

Jan. 1977

© *1976 by Winthrop Publishers, Inc.*
17 Dunster Street, Cambridge, Massachusetts 02138

10   9   8   7   6   5   4   3   2   1

CONTENTS

PREFACE

The purpose of this book is to provide a history of the study of grammar, with emphasis on the study of English and on twentieth-century developments within the United States. The first chapter presents a historical overview, beginning with the Greeks and ending with generative semantics. The introductions to each section focus on the methodology and goals of the various theories. Most of the readings are complete articles or chapters from books that have been seminal in the development of grammatical theory.

This book grew out of the courses on modern theories of grammar that I have taught at Queens College. I would like to thank my students for the many learning experiences we have shared. I wish particularly to thank Marsha Deboer and Dena Poulos for reacting to the manuscript while it was in preparation, and Elizabeth Traugott, Edward Epstein, and Charles Dahlberg for the many helpful suggestions they have offered. I am very grateful to Mitchell Berson for helping me to proofread the manuscript.

D.D.B.

ACKNOWLEDGMENTS

p. 52   Homer C. House and Susan Emolyn Harman, *Descriptive English Grammar*, 2nd ed., © 1950, pp. 16-19. Reprinted by permission of Prentice-Hall, Inc., Englewood Cliffs, N.J.

p. 94   Elizabeth Traugott, "On the Notion 'Restructuring' in Historical Syntax," *Proceedings of the XIth International Congress of Linguistics,* 1972. Reprinted by permission of the author and Società editrice il Mulino, Bologna, Italy.

p. 122   From *Language: An Introduction to the Study of Speech* by Edward Sapir, copyright, 1921, by Harcourt Brace Jovanovich, Inc.; renewed, 1949, by Jean V. Sapir. Reprinted by permission of the publishers.

p. 137   From *Language* by Leonard Bloomfield. Copyright, 1933, by Holt, Rinehart and Winston, Inc. Copyright © 1961 by Leonard Bloomfield. Reprinted by permission of Holt, Rinehart and Winston.

p. 162   From *The Structure of English* by Charles Carpenter Fries, copyright, 1952, by Harcourt Brace Jovanovich, Inc. and reprinted with their permission.

p. 208   Morris Hale, "On the Bases of Phonology," from *The Structure of Language* by Jerry A. Fodor and Jerrold J. Katz, © 1964. Reprinted by permission of Prentice-Hall, Inc., Englewood Cliffs, N.J., and the Societa Italiana di Fisica.

p. 218   Reprinted from *The Theory of Syntax* by Noam Chomsky by permission of the M.I.T. Press, Cambridge, Massachusetts. © 1965 by Massachusetts Institute of Technology.

p. 241   Reprinted from *Psychology Today* Magazine, February 1968. Copyright © 1968 Ziff-Davis Publishing Company. All rights reserved.

p. 268   From *Irregularity in Syntax* by George Lakoff. Copyright © 1970 by Holt, Rinehart and Winston, Inc. Reprinted by permission of Holt, Rinehart and Winston.

p. 299   Reprinted by permission of Edicom N.V.

p. 333   Kenyon, John S., "Cultural Levels and Functional Varieties of English," *College English,* October 1948. Copyright © 1948 by the National Council of Teachers of English. Reprinted by permission of the publisher and the author.

p. 340   Joos, Martin, "Homeostasis in English Usage," *College Composition and Communication,* October 1962. Copyright © 1962 by the National Council of Teachers of English. Reprinted by permission of the publisher and the author.

READINGS IN THE
THEORY OF GRAMMAR

1 THE STUDY OF LANGUAGE

English belongs to a large group of languages known as the Indo-European language family. As far back as ancient times, two different methods of linguistic description were applied to languages belonging to this group. The earliest extant grammatical treatise on any Indo-European language is Panini's *Astādhyāyī*, a description of Sanskrit written in the fourth century B.C.[1] The Sanskrit grammatical tradition involved a detailed description of sounds and structure. The main component of Panini's grammar is an exhaustive statement of the rules of word formation of the Sanskrit language. There are also appendices giving a list of verbal roots, a list of similarly inflected words, and a list of the sounds of Sanskrit. The rules are expressed with great completeness and economy. Like the rules of modern transformational grammarians, they have to be applied in a set order. European languages were not described with similar precision until the late nineteenth century.

In Europe, speculation about language began with the Greeks. The Greek tradition leaned toward philosophic speculation and analysis based on meaning. The term *grammatikē* originally meant merely the understanding of letters, and problems we would think of as linguistic inquiries fell under the general heading of philosophy. Among the linguistically oriented questions considered by the Greeks was whether the relation between things and the words that named them was natural and necessary, or merely the result of human convention. Plato summarized the arguments in his dialogue, *Cratylus* (c. 358 B.C.), the earliest surviving document in Greek dealing with the subject of language. Cratylus and Heraclitus argue for the natural origin of words and for the reflection of the qualities of things in words. According to this position, there is something in the sound of a word that relates to the substance of the thing it signifies. In contrast,

[1]R. H. ROBINS, *A Short History of Linguistics* (Bloomington: Indiana Univ. Press, 1967), pp. 144–48.

Democritus and Hermogenes point out discrepancies between the sounds of words and the qualities of things, thereby arguing for the conventional or arbitrary origin of words. A word is just an arbitrary sound or group of sounds that comes to represent a particular thing. There is no connection between the two, although the relation may seem natural to speakers of a language once it has been established. As with most arguments regarding origins, the debate was rather futile, but it served a useful purpose in causing philosophers to analyze language more closely.

Cratylus raises a more significant issue, the problem of truth and falsehood in language: how can a sentence say something and yet say what is not so?[2] Aristotle takes up this problem in *De interpretatione, De anima*, and *Categories*. He considers the grammatical structure of sentences conveying truths and falsehoods as well as the logical or semantic structure of the truths and falsehoods themselves. Just as a sentence consists at least of a noun coupled with a verb, so the truth or falsehood conveyed by it consists of the *significatum* or sign of the noun coupled with that of the verb. These *significata* or signs are themselves neither true nor false. The intellectual comprehension of the signs does not involve believing. A proposition must contain at least a noun and a verb, but a grammatical sentence is not necessarily true. Judgments about grammatical correctness and truth should be made separately. Grammarians and philosophers are still wrestling with such questions regarding the relation of language and truth.

Consideration of these general philosophic questions led to a more precise analysis of language. The framework of grammatical description employed by the Greeks was that of the word and the paradigm. Unlike the Sanskrit grammarians, they did not often go below the word level. In *Cratylus* and *Sophistes*, Plato divided the sentence into nominal and verbal components, *ōnoma* and *rhēma*, which remained the primary grammatical distinction underlying syntactic analysis and word classification in all future linguistic description. In *Rhetorica*, Aristotle maintained this distinction but added a third class called *sȳndesmoi*, which included conjunctions, the article, and pronouns. Only *ōnoma* and *rhēma* were considered parts of speech in the full sense because they had meaning in isolation, whereas *sȳndesmoi* had only grammatical meaning. This distinction anticipated the division between full words and form words made by Henry Sweet (the late nineteenth- and early twentieth-century historical grammarian), as well as the analysis of words in terms of lexical and structural meaning made by Charles Fries (the twentieth-century structuralist). Modern thought is also anticipated by Aristotle's definition of a word in *De interpretatione* as a component of the sentence having a meaning of its own but not further divisible into meaningful units, which is close to the structuralists' definition of a word as a minimum free form. However, most Greek grammarians lacked Aristotle's scientific outlook and paid less attention to form.

[2] GILBERT RYLE, *Plato's Progress* (Cambridge: Cambridge Univ. Press, 1966), pp. 272–75, 282.

The Greek tradition of grammatical study was summarized and codified in the first century B.C. by an Alexandrian scholar named Dionysus Thrax in a treatise called the *Technē grammatikē* (the *Art of Grammar*). The Alexandrians were strongly conscious of their literary past and realized the divergence between their language and that of Homer. Seeing this change as decay, they felt that it was their task to find out how Greek should be written so as to fix it in an unchanging form. The desire to establish a constant classical form for a language has characterized the attitude of purists over the centuries. Following the practice of other Alexandrians, Dionysus drew his material from the written texts of accepted authors and defined grammar as the knowledge of the general usages of poets and prose writers:

> Grammar is the practical knowledge of the general usages of poets and prose writers. It has six parts: first, accurate reading with due regard to the prosodies; second, explanation of the literary expressions in the works; third, the provision of notes on phraseology and subject matter; fourth, the discovery of etymologies; fifth, the working out of analogical regularities; sixth, the appreciation of literary compositions, which is the noblest part of grammar.[3]

Dionysus did not see a grammar as a theoretical description of a language but as a tool that would lead to an appreciation of Greek literature. Consequently, his focus was on the formal, literary language. In analyzing the words within his texts, he discussed letters and syllables as well as the eight parts of speech: the noun, verb, participle, article, pronoun, preposition, adverb, and conjunction. These word classes were taken up by most later grammarians. In defining the classes, Dionysus used formal criteria, such as word endings and position in relation to other words, as well as meaning. His brief treatise became a standard textbook in ancient times and continued as such into the eighteenth century.

The Romans took over the grammatical system of the Greeks and adapted it to Latin with a minimum of alteration; thus they set a pattern for grammar studies in Europe.[4] In the case of Latin, the application of Greek theory did not create too much distortion since the language was fairly close to Greek. When the system that had been adapted to Latin was applied to the modern European languages, however, the results were less satisfactory. When the same pattern was applied to American Indian and Asian languages that did not belong to the Indo-European family, it did not work. This deficiency in the categories of traditional grammar led linguists to the conviction that each language must be analyzed and described in its own terms.

During Roman times, the only grammarian who really tested Greek categories before applying them to Latin was Varro, who lived in the first century B.C. He believed that the grammarian must discover regularities in the struc-

---

[3]ROBINS, trans., *Dionysii Thracii ars grammatica*, in *A Short History of Linguistics*, p. 31.
[4]R. H. ROBINS, *Ancient and Medieval Grammatical Theory in Europe* (Port Washington, N.Y.: Kennikat Press, 1951), pp. 49–67.

ture of language, not impose them. In his *De lingua Latina*, he classified words into four parts of speech, all based on form:

1. Nouns: words with case inflections
2. Verbs: words with tense forms
3. Participles: words with both case inflections and tense forms
4. Conjunctions and adverbs: words with neither case inflections nor tense forms

The treatise originally consisted of twenty-five volumes, but only books five through ten survive.

Varro's independence was not imitated by later Latin grammarians, whose attitudes resembled those of the Alexandrians. There was the same consciousness of a great literary past to be studied, and the same desire to preserve the purity of the language. This time the standard was set by the golden age of Cicero and Virgil. The most influential grammars of this period were written by Donatus (c. 400 A.D.) and Priscian (c. 500 A.D.). Donatus' treatise is a simplified work meant for students. Priscian's is an eighteen volume summary and compilation of earlier theories. He adopts the classification of the parts of speech used by Dionysus Thrax, but substitutes the interjection for the article since Latin had no article; he lists the noun, verb, participle, pronoun, preposition, adverb, conjunction, and interjection. In defining the categories, he does not follow any consistent principles but uses both meaning and formal criteria, a practice which is followed in later Latin grammars and in the early grammars of the vernacular languages that were based on them. Both Donatus and Priscian became favorite texts for teaching Latin grammar during the Middle Ages, with over a thousand manuscripts of Priscian's work testifying to its popularity.[5]

Priscian and Donatus formed the link between classical and medieval grammar studies. Latin and grammar formed an important part of the medieval curriculum. The liberal arts were divided into seven subjects and organized into the trivium (grammar, logic, rhetoric) and the quadrivium (music, arithmetic, geometry, astronomy). Since the study of grammar was necessary for the reading and writing of Latin, the universal language of learning, it formed the base of the curriculum. There was a school tradition and a more learned philosophical one. Many Latin grammars were compiled for students. The first one to be composed in England was written in Anglo-Saxon by Aelfric, Abbot of Eynsham (c. 1000). Like the other grammarians of this period, he based his work on Donatus and Priscian, abbreviating and simplifying their treatises to suit the needs of beginners. Aelfric claimed that his book would be suitable as an introduction to English grammar, thereby laying a foundation for the tradition of Latin-inspired English grammar.[6]

[5]Ibid., pp. 67–69.
[6]ROBINS, *Short History of Linguistics*, p. 71.

More speculative works were written by a group of scholars known as the *modistae* because they wrote treatises on *De modo significandi* (the modes of signifying). Their theory, called *grammatica speculativa* or speculative grammar, flourished from the late twelfth to the mid-fourteenth century.[7] An early member of the group was Peter Helias (c. 1150), a teacher at the University of Paris. He wrote a commentary on Priscian in which he sought philosophical explanations for the rules of grammar. A later work in this genre is Thomas of Erfurt's *Grammatica speculativa*, written in the early fourteenth century. The *modistae* believed that there was one universal grammar dependent on the structure of reality and human reason. This idea sounds similar to modern theories of linguistic universals; however, transformational grammarians seek these universals in human psychology, whereas the *modistae* sought the basis for a universal grammar in the external world. The *modistae* believed that language reflects reality, and that grammar provides clues to the nature of being. Therefore, the basis of their theory was metaphysical rather than psychological. Furthermore, they sought a univeral grammar in the study of logic and tended to identify logic with the categories of Latin. The dominance of Latin as the language of learning had a strong influence on medieval thinking regarding the nature of language.

A different variety of universal grammar was developed by the rationalist grammarians of the seventeenth century, particularly those associated with the French Port Royal schools. These religious and educational foundations, set up in 1637 and disbanded in 1661 because of political and religious strife, had a long-lasting influence on educational ideas.[8] The Port Royal grammar ascribed to Antoine Arnauld and Claude Lancelot was translated into English as *A General and Rational Grammar* in 1753.[9] The French version, reprinted during the eighteenth and nineteenth centuries, has been cited by Noam Chomsky as a precursor of transformational grammar.[10] The Port Royal grammarians were the successors of medieval scholastic grammarians, but they asserted the claims of human reason above authority and made the philosophy of Descartes the basis for their teaching. They believed that grammatical categories reflect universal elements of thought, with many of the same relations existing in all languages. Nevertheless, since these relations are often expressed differently, "the particular use of languages must be always consulted."[11] They did not confine their attention to the literary language but analyzed the differences between letters and

---

[7]ROBINS, *Short History of Linguistics*, pp. 74–90. Morton W. Bloomfield, Reviews of G. L. Bursill-Hall, *Speculative Grammars of the Middle Ages* (The Hague: Mouton, 1971), and Thomas of Erfurt, *Grammatica speculativa*, ed. G. L. Bursill-Hall (London: Longman, 1972), in *Speculum*, 49 (1974), 102–105.

[8]ROBINS, *Short History of Linguistics*, p. 123.

[9]ANTOINE ARNAULD AND CLAUDE LANCELOT, *A General and Rational Grammar* (London, 1753. Reprinted by Scolar Press, Yorkshire, England, 1968), p. 2.

[10]NOAM CHOMSKY, *Cartesian Linguistics* (N.Y.: Harper & Row, 1966).

[11]*A General and Rational Grammar*, p. 152.

sounds, and insisted that the speech forms of the living language should determine usage. Most writers on universal grammar paid more attention to literature, and sought linguistic universals in Latin rather than in human mental processes.

Many grammars of the vernacular languages were written during the Renaissance. By 1700, grammars had been printed for 61 languages including (in order of appearance) Spanish, Arabic, Hebrew, Italian, French, Czech, Portuguese, Tarascan, Inca, Nahuatl, Zapotec, Dutch, English, and Welsh. The first grammars of American Indian and Asiatic languages were not written significantly later than the first grammars of European languages. For example, grammars of four American Indian languages (Tarascan, Inca, Nahuatl, and Zapotec) were published before there were any grammars of English.

Most early grammars were written for pedagogical purposes rather than for scholarly use. In the case of the non-European languages, the grammars were usually written to teach missionaries the languages of the areas where they were assigned to work. When it came to the European languages, a common motive for grammar writing was to reform, purify, and standardize the literary language.[12] The first known grammar of English, published in 1586, is the *Bref Grammar for English* by William Bullokar, who was particularly interested in spelling reform.[13]

A desire to regulate the English language predominated during the eighteenth century. However, it was not the only attitude to be expressed. As far back as the eighteenth century, we find descriptive and prescriptive methods, liberal and conservative attitudes. The descriptive, liberal approach is found in Joseph Priestley's *Rudiments of English Grammar* (1761). Priestley, a chemist as well as a language scholar, was scientific and objective. He pointed out the many ways in which English differed from Latin, and criticized the use of Latin terminology as being "exceedingly awkward and absolutely superfluous."[14] Although he adapted the traditional parts of speech classification, substituting the adjective for the participle, he recognized its arbitrary nature. Priestley believed in a universal grammar but sought linguistic universals in human mental abilities rather than in logic or Latin. He was influenced by the Port Royal grammarians and quotes their work in his *Course of Lectures on the Theory of Language and Universal Grammar* (1762). Like the Port Royal grammarians, he did not allow general principles to mislead him in the analysis of his own language but considered usage and the "custom of speaking" the "only just standard of any language."[15]

---

[12]John Howland Rowe, "Sixteenth and Seventeenth Century Grammars," in *Studies in the History of Linguistics*, ed. D. Hymes (Bloomington: Indiana Univ. Press, 1974), pp. 361–79.

[13]Ibid., p. 363.

[14]Joseph Priestly, *The Rudiments of English Grammar* (London: J. & F. Rivington, 1772), p. vii.

[15]Ibid., p. ix.

The prescriptive, conservative approach is found in Robert Lowth's *Short Introduction to English Grammar* (1762). Lowth, a professor of poetry at Oxford University and later Bishop of London, had a bias in favor of older forms of the language. Having the same attitudes as the Alexandrians and the late Roman grammarians, he was conscious of a great literary past and wished to preserve older forms. Although he was aware of linguistic change, he saw it as corruption and wanted to keep the language in an unchanging form. To Lowth, the "golden age" of English was the Elizabethan period, two hundred years before his own time. He also believed that "the principal design of a grammar of any language is to teach us to express ourselves with propriety."[16] Therefore, his method was to prescribe rules regarding the proper use of English, illustrating them with correct and incorrect examples drawn from standard authors such as Shakespeare, Milton, Dryden, Addison, and Pope. Unlike Priestley, Lowth had little faith in the "custom of speaking," but sought proper forms in formal literary English and in logical analogies. Although he did not slavishly follow Latin categories, he was too fond of logical neatness. He asserted that "our best authors have committed gross mistakes, for want of a due knowledge of English Grammar, or at least of a proper attention to the rules of it."[17] This tendency to identify grammar with a set of abstract rules rather than with the patterns actually used by speakers and writers of the language has often gone along with the prescriptive approach.

Lowth's approach and attitudes came to dominate the school tradition in England and America. His work was first adapted for classroom use by Lindley Murray, an American lawyer who migrated to England after the Revolution. In 1795, Murray published his *English Grammar Adapted to the Different Classes of Learners*. It became the leading textbook in the field, going through at least fifty editions in its original form and over one hundred editions in an abridgment.[18] Many adaptations of it were published during the nineteenth century. Murray followed Lowth's prescriptive method, simplified it for classroom use, and added material dealing with spelling and punctuation. He focused attention on individual words by giving rules for parsing or identifying the parts of speech.

Together with the technique of parsing, school grammar developed a system of sentence analysis, which involved examining complete sentences and identifying major sentence elements, such as subjects, verbs, and objects. Diagrams were used to indicate sentence structure. This procedure was most fully worked out by Alonzo Reed and Brainerd Kellogg in *Work on English Grammar*

---

[16]ROBERT LOWTH, *A Short Introduction to English Grammar* (London: J. J. Tourneisin, 1794), p. xi.

[17]Ibid., p. 10.

[18]ROBERT C. POOLEY, *Grammar and Usage in Textbooks on English* (Madison, Wisc.: Univ. of Wisconsin, 1933), p. 24.

and Composition (1877), called *Higher Lessons in English* in later editions. They break up word order to show the relationship between principal and subordinate parts, such as nouns and adjectives, and to account for "understood" elements, such as the pronoun "you" in imperative sentences. This technique had possibilities, but it was limited to a narrow range of sentences that often illustrated outmoded prescriptive rules. As traditional grammar became simplified for classroom use, many of its refinements were lost. The exceptions and philosophic generalizations were omitted. Some of the arbitrary rules that remained had little to do with the living language. When they were relevant, they often applied mainly to formal literary English. Yet they were usually taught as if they accounted for, or should account for, the entire language.

While traditional grammar was being simplified for classroom use, more complex studies were being conducted by scholars who were interested in examining languages rather than in regulating them. The science of linguistics began in Europe in the late eighteenth century with the comparative study of the Indo-European family of languages. The first scholars in the field combined an interest in language with one in ancient history. Sir William Jones's "Third Anniversary Discourse on the Hindus," delivered to the Asiatic Society of Calcutta in 1786, had as much to do with Indian culture as it did with Sanskrit. Yet, in calling attention to the resemblances among Sanskrit, Greek, and Latin, it was instrumental in stimulating the study of the Indo-European languages. The following passage contains Jones's views regarding the common origin of Sanskrit, Greek, Latin, and other European languages:

> The Sanskrit language, whatever be its antiquity, is of a wonderful structure; more perfect than the Greek, more copious than the Latin, and more exquisitely refined than either, yet bearing to both of them a stronger affinity, both in the roots of verbs and in the forms of grammar, than could possibly have been produced by accident; so strong indeed, that no philologer could examine them all three, without believing them to have sprung from some common source, which, perhaps, no longer exists: there is a similar reason, though not quite so forcible, for supposing that both the Gothic and the Celtic, though blended with a very different idiom, had the same origin with the Sanskrit; and the old Persian might be added to the same family, if this were the place for discussing any question concerning the antiquities of Persia.[19]

Jones's observations and intuitions were confirmed in studies by later scholars. The common source he mentions has come to be called Indo-European, with its branches of Indian, Armenian, Iranian, Germanic, Balto-Slavic, Albanian, Celtic, Hellenic, and Italic.

During the nineteenth century, the historical point of view was first applied to language. Scholars came to realize that language was in a constant state of change, and that it had a history which could be traced through surviving docu-

---

[19]SIR WILLIAM JONES, "Third Anniversary Discourse on the Hindus," in *A Reader in Nineteenth-Century Historical Indo-European Linguistics*, ed. W. H. Lehmann (Bloomington: Indiana Univ. Press, 1967), p. 15.

nents. Franz Bopp helped to clarify the morphology of the Indo-European language in the various volumes of his *Comparative Grammar* (1833, 1857–61, 868–70). Yet he still gave a great deal of attention to external history and culture. A more linguistically oriented comparative grammar was the monograph of Rasmus Rask, "An Investigation Concerning the Source of the Old Northern or celandic Language" (1818), written for a contest sponsored by the Danish Academy of Sciences in 1811. Rask won the contest and made important contributions to linguistics with the facts he set forth and the methodology he employed. He demonstrated the relationship between Old Icelandic and the other Germanic languages as well as its more distant relation with the Slavonic languages, Lithuanian, Latin, and Greek. Rather than relying on vocabulary items, which are often adopted from other languages, he focused on inflectional systems and grammatical forms such as pronouns, which are rarely borrowed. He emphasized the need to examine the entire structure of languages in order to discover anything about their relationship. Rask also was the first to provide a systematic description of the consonant changes that characterize the Germanic languages.[20]

In the Preface to the second edition of his *Germanic Grammar* (1822), Jacob Grimm acknowledged his debt to Rask for the description of the consonant shift. In this comparative grammar of all the Germanic languages, Grimm presented the same facts as Rask, although he provided additional examples. More significantly, he developed a theory to account for the changes. He coined the term *Lautverschiebung* or sound shift and pointed out that a governing pattern was involved in the series of phonetic changes.[21] The phenomenon has come to be known as Grimm's Law or the first sound shift. Grimm also saw the pattern in a second sound shift, which occurred only in High German. According to the formulation, entire sets of consonant sounds shifted in the Germanic languages from their Indo-European pronunciation. In his study of *The Germanic Consonant Shifts* (1956), Jean Fourquet, the French structuralist, has suggested that the changes may have been initiated by a weakening in the habits of articulation. Once this began, a chain reaction took place that restructured the consonant system of the Germanic languages in order to preserve the pattern of contrasts.[22] The aspirated stops *bh, dh,* and *gh* (which became *ph* or *f, th,* and *h* in Greek and Latin) became the voiced stops *b, d,* and *g* in Germanic; the voiced stops *b, d,* and *g* changed to the voiceless stops *p, t,* and *k*; and the voiceless stops *p, t,* and *k* became the voiceless spirants *f, th,* and *h*. These correspondences enable us to relate a large number of words in the Germanic languages to words in other Indo-European languages, such as the following pairs in English (a member of the Germanic branch) and Latin (a member of the Italic branch and the ancestor

[20]OTTO JESPERSEN, *Language: Its Nature, Development, and Origin* (London: Allen & Unwin, 1922), pp. 36–40.
[21]JOHN WATERMAN, *Perspectives in Linguistics* (Chicago: Univ. of Chicago Press, 1963), pp. 20–30.
[22]Ibid., pp. 77–79.

of the modern Romance languages): tooth-*dens*, two-*duo*, kin-*genus*, fath‹ *pater*, fish-*piscis*, thou-*tū*, three-*trēs*, horn-*cornū*, hundred-*centum*. Grimm conception of the shifts as a pattern made a great impact on linguists in demc strating the regular, systematic nature of sound change.

Some exceptions were not covered by Grimm's formulation. A lar number of these exceptions were accounted for by Karl Verner in his essay, "/ Exception to the First Sound Shift" (1875). Verner showed that many exce tions could be explained by assuming the existence of variable stress in Ind European and early Germanic. Verner's article called attention to the importan‹ of the elements that were later to be called suprasegmentals: stress, pitch, qua tity, and juncture. It also supported the conviction that language change tak place regularly or systematically.[23]

A belief in the regularity of linguistic change characterized a group of la nineteenth-century linguists at Leipzig known as the *Junggrammatiker* or Ne grammarians. Members of their school included August Leskien, Karl Bru mann, Hermann Osthoff, Hermann Paul, and Eduard Sievers. Their centr principle regarding the regularity of sound change was first coined by Augu Leskien: "Sound laws have no exception."[24] This terminology was unfortunat for it caused a great deal of dispute. What it meant was that sounds change in regular manner which is not affected by nonphonetic factors.[25] The concept w; stated more moderately by Eduard Sievers in his *Foundations of Phonetic* (1901): "If somewhere under certain conditions a shift in the manner of articul: tion has occurred, the new manner of articulation must be applied without exce] tion in all instances which are subject to exactly the same conditions."[26] Th Neogrammarians' focus on the systematic nature of language led to importa advances in methodology. They believed that the chief factors in the history ‹ language were phonetic change and analogic change. An analogic change occu when a dominant pattern comes to supersede others, as when the "s" plural i English drove out other forms, with the exception of a few survivals such ‹ "feet," "geese," "oxen," and "children." Earlier scholars had looked upo such changes as corruptions and had used the term "false analogy." The Ne‹ grammarians pointed out that far from being a sign of decadence, analogical fo‹ mations represented a vital principle of language.[27] They also insisted on the im portance of speech and on the need to study contemporary language, includin dialects. In the Preface to his journal, *Morphological Investigations in th Sphere of the Indo-European Languages* (1878), Karl Brugmann called upon th linguist to step into "the clear air of tangible reality and of the present in order t get information about those things which gray theory can never reveal to him."[2]

[23]LEHMANN, *Reader*, p. 134.
[24]WATERMAN, *Perspectives in Linguistics*, p. 50.
[25]LEONARD BLOOMFIELD, *Language* (N.Y.: Holt, 1933), p. 354.
[26]LEHMANN, *Reader*, p. 266.
[27]JESPERSEN, *Language*, pp. 93–94.
[28]LEHMANN, *Reader*, p. 202.

One of the scholars who responded to Brugmann's challenge was William ight Whitney, an American professor of Sanskrit at Yale. Whitney did not fine himself to studies of the past but was interested in contemporary lan- ige and general principles of linguistics. When Whitney went to study in rmany, a mutually beneficial influence took place between him and the Neo- mmarians. Brugmann considered Whitney "the first to promulgate really ind essentials of language history free of any fanciful and disturbing tense."[29] In *Language and the Study of Language* (1867) and *The Life and owth of Language* (1874), Whitney discussed the forces that account for con- vatism and alteration in language. A language can change because it lives ty through the mouths of individuals who, for the most part, are unaware of torical content. Yet it tends to be stable since usage is mainly accepted by a nmunity of speakers. Whitney was influential because he tried to rise above : mass of details that had been accumulated in studies of comparative grammar d to make valid generalizations about the development of languages.

During the late nineteenth and early twentieth centuries, the historical point view was applied in studies of the modern languages. Studies of English in- ided Henry Sweet's *New English Grammar* (two vols., 1892–98), Henrik utsma's *Grammar of Late Modern English* (five vols., 1914–29), Etsko uisinga's *Handbook of Present-Day English* (three vols., 1925–32), George irme's *Grammar of the English Language* (two vols., 1931–35), and Otto spersen's *Modern English Grammar on Historical Principles* (seven vols., 09–49). These scholars were well acquainted with the historical development English and its dialects. Their reference points were Indo-European, the ermanic languages, and Old and Middle English. Although they used much of e terminology of traditional grammar, they did not follow its prescriptive point view. Rather than wanting to direct the language, they were interested in dis- vering where it had come from and where it was going. The historical gram- arian who departed most from traditional grammar was Otto Jespersen, a anish scholar. He discarded or modified a great deal of its terminology, which : considered too easy to confuse with logical or notional categories, and coined rms of his own when he found them necessary.

As scholars focused more on language and less on history, they came to cognize the need for two different types of study, called "synchronic" and diachronic." A synchronic study examines a language at a particular point in me, whereas a diachronic study traces its development through time. In *The hilosophy of Grammar* (1924), Jespersen points out that the view one gets when xamining the living language is different from the historical view. Irregular rms can be explained historically but are still irregular for the speakers of •day.[30] Most speakers view their language as a self-contained system and are naware of its history.

---

[29]ROMAN JAKOBSON, "The World Response to Whitney's Principles of Linguistic Science," in *hitney on Language*, ed. Michael Silverstein (Cambridge, Mass.: M.I.T. Press, 1971), p. xxvii.
[30]OTTO JESPERSEN, *The Philosophy of Grammar* (London: Allen & Unwin, 1924), p. 22.

The scholar who was most influential in separating diachronic and syn chronic studies was Ferdinand de Saussure. In insisting upon this separation, an in delineating the appropriate objects and goals of linguistics, he was instrumer tal in laying the foundation for descriptive or structural linguistics. As the grea theoretician of the new movement, he was the first to elaborate the structura principle into a well-defined theory.[31] Although he made important contribution to historical linguistics, such as his "Memoire on the Primitive System of Vow els in the Indo-European Languages" (1879), his major interest was in genera theory. His influence was exerted through his lectures at the University o Geneva and through a posthumous publication of his lecture notes, the *Course i General Linguistics* (1916). De Saussure set forth a number of important distinc tions and definitions regarding the nature of language, the most famous on being his distinction between "la langue" and "la parole": "la langue" is th system of conventions and signs that is shared by all members of a speech com munity and allows them to communicate; "la parole" is the speech of th individual.[32] This distinction enabled him to account for both the systematic na ture of language and individual variation. He believed that "la langue," the un derlying language system, is the proper object of linguistic study since it contain regular patterns. The structuralist wishes to discover and describe these patterns De Saussure's ideas were particularly influential in Europe, where the focus wa on general linguistic theory.

In America, the development of descriptive linguistics was closely con nected to work that was being done in anthropology. Linguists and an thropologists were trying to describe American Indian languages that had neve been written down and had no relation to the European languages. Procedure for field work and linguistic description were developed by Franz Boas, a profes sor of anthropology at Columbia University, in his *Handbook of American In dian Languages* (1911). His method was to set forth a detailed description of the phonology or sound system of a language and then to describe its morphology or use of grammatical forms, primarily at the word and phrase level. His object was to gain a knowledge of the phonetic processes of the American Indian languages and of the psychological foundations of their structure, particularly in regard to the distinctions of meaning made in their grammatical forms. In his Preface to the *Handbook*, Boas points out that such attempts were hindered in the past by the tendency to represent the grammars of Indian languages in a form analogous to that of the European grammars.[33] The result was a distortion or misrepresenta tion of the Indian languages. Even when observers did not try to fit the languages into a preconceived mold, they tended to think in terms of familiar categories and perceived sounds in accordance with the phonology of their own languages. This

[31]WATERMAN, *Perspectives in Linguistics*, p. 61.

[32]FERDINAND DE SAUSSURE, *Course in General Linguistics*, trans. Wade Baskin (N.Y.: Philosophical Library, 1959), pp. 9–13.

[33]FRANZ BOAS, *Handbook of American Indian Languages* (Washington, D.C.: Smithsonian Institution, Bureau of American Ethnology, Bulletin 40, 1911), I, v.

ind of unconscious bias was misleading since languages vary greatly in terms of
ie phonetic varieties of sounds that are united under one phoneme and the
roups of ideas that are expressed in words. Grammatical categories that are con-
idered essential in one language (such as number or gender) are lacking in
thers. Boas and his followers attempted to describe each language in its own
erms. The belief that each language should be analyzed in its own terms became
ne of the primary tenets of descriptive linguistics in America.

In contrast to Boas, who followed an inductive method and rejected general
neorizing, one of his students, Edward Sapir, was interested in deductive
heories and psychological explanations. He believed in describing each lan-
zuage in its own terms, and had little faith in conventional categories, such as the
iarts of speech. Nevertheless, he thought that basic categories (such as noun and
/erb) and basic grammatical processes (such as ordering of words) existed in all
ianguages, which were likely to have universal elements in their "great underly-
ng ground plans."[34] Grammar resulted from the human tendency toward
:conomy of thought and economy of speech; it is convenient to express analo-
zous concepts in analogous form. Yet no language system is always consistent:
'All grammars leak."[35] Sapir was particularly interested in the relations be-
.ween external grammatical and internal psychological processes.

This kind of theorizing was rejected by Leonard Bloomfield, who was interested in constructing a model of what goes on outside the minds of speakers
and hearers. Being under the influence of behavioral psychology, he used a
stimulus-response model to describe the communication process and wished to
confine linguistic description to observable phenomena. He also used a
stimulus-response model to describe language learning, emphasizing the role of
habit. Bloomfield insisted on the need to follow a mechanistic view of human
behavior and an inductive method in conducting linguistic research. His discussions in *Language* (1933) reveal a strong interest in the physical measurement of
speech and a reluctance to leave its safe domain. Nevertheless, he admits the
need to consider meaning in order to determine the distinctive features of a
language.[36] He was able to meet his own standards of rigor and objectivity most
successfully in dealing with phonology. Perhaps for this reason, he believed that
a description of a language should begin with phonology. His followers tried to
bring this same rigor into descriptions of morphology and syntax, and went even
further than Bloomfield in an attempt to exclude meaning from linguistic
analysis.

The post-Bloomfieldian descriptivists of the 1940s thought that it might be
possible to determine the forms of a language and the patterns by which they
combine without any reference to meaning.[37] Their aim was to separate grammar
and semantics completely. They also modified Bloomfield's treatment of

[34]EDWARD SAPIR, *Language* (N.Y.: Harcourt, 1921), p. 144.
[35]Ibid., p. 38
[36]BLOOMFIELD, *Language*, p. 77.
[37]CHARLES F. HOCKETT, *The State of the Art* (The Hague: Mouton, 1968), pp. 24–25.

phonology. Bloomfield concentrated on phonemic analysis at the word level. I followers, particularly Trager, Bloch, and Hockett, thought that phone analysis should determine all the features that serve to keep the utterances o language apart.[38] They wished to extend phonemic analysis beyond the w level. Such an analysis involved the consideration of stress, pitch, and junctu or degree of separation (called the suprasegmental phonemes). A detailed scription of English phonology that included these features of language was forth by George L. Trager and Henry Lee Smith, Jr. in *An Outline of Engl Structure* (first published in 1951). They focus upon the manner in which sou patterns signal grammatical patterns. This work shows how post-Bloomfieldi descriptivists tried to apply the assumptions and procedures that had been fruit. in dealing with phonology to grammar. A parallelism was worked out in cc cepts and technical terms.

The inductive, scientific methods of descriptive linguistics were brought the attention of teachers by Charles C. Fries. In his *American English Gramm* (1940), Fries conducted a survey that examined not the usages people thoug were correct, but the ones they actually used. He investigated a voluminó amount of correspondence, over two thousand complete letters and excerpts fro about one thousand more, written to the United States Government by peop classified as nearly illiterate, average, and educated. Only the usage of educat individuals (college graduates) was classified as standard. This usage was fou to contradict many of the rules that were being taught in the schools. Fries co cluded that school authorities were teaching "not 'standard' English realisticaï described, but a 'make-believe' correctness which contained some true forms real 'standard' English and many forms that had and have practically no currenc outside the classroom."[39] He called for new teaching practices based on actu English usage and a new grammar based on the findings of linguistics. *Th Structure of English* (1952) represents his attempt to provide such a gramma This time, recorded telephone conversations served as his data. His analysis w based on form and structure with as little reference to meaning as possible.

Descriptivists differed in their treatment of syntax. Item-and-proce grammars had been employed by early theorists such as Boas and Sapir. Th difference between two partially similar forms was described as a process, suc as vowel change or suffixation, which yielded one form out of the other. Iten and-arrangement grammars were later developed by Rulon Wells, Eugene Nid Charles Fries, Charles Hockett, and Zellig Harris. This method involved a enumeration of elements and the arrangements in which they occur. Immedia constituent analysis and phrase structure grammars were varieties of this mode During the 1950s, however, the model was challenged by some of the very peo ple who had been working on it. In a paper published in 1954, Hockett pointe

---

[38]Ibid., pp. 25–28.

[39]CHARLES C. FRIES, *American English Grammar* (N.Y.: Appleton-Century, 1940), p. 14.

t some of the weaknesses of an item-and-arrangement model and the strengths
an item-and-process model.[40] Harris proposed the concept of a process called
ransformation in papers published in 1952 and 1957.[41] The concept grew out
his development of discourse analysis, a method for analyzing samples of
nnected speech or writing that were entire texts rather than individual sen-
ces. He defined the transformation as a grammatical process that changes the
der of constituents within a sentence and can delete, substitute, or add ele-
nts. Transformations could account for relations between discontinuous ele-
nts, paraphrases such as actives and passives, and other grammatical
enomena that could not be adequately handled by the earlier methods of syn-
ctic analysis in descriptive linguistics.

The concept of the transformation was picked up from Harris by Noam
omsky, who was his student at the University of Pennsylvania. However,
omsky developed it within the framework of a new theory of language. He
me to feel that structural linguistics was going in the wrong direction in terms
its assumptions and methods. He was particularly critical of the emphasis on
bit in the explanation of language learning and the focus on the collection and
ssification of data. In *Syntactic Structures* (1957), his first challenge to the
guistics establishment, he pointed out that a language's "set of grammatical
ntences cannot be identified with any particular corpus of utterances obtained
the linguist in his field work" since the number of possible sentences within a
guage is infinite.[42] A person continually produces and understands new sen-
ces without consciously thinking about it. This creativity is taken for granted
such a great extent that we notice when someone repeats himself. Chomsky
phasizes the creative aspect of language use in many of his works, frequently
oting Wilhelm von Humboldt, a nineteenth-century linguist who saw language
a generative system that makes "infinite use of finite means." In *Language
d Mind* (1968) and "Language and the Mind" (1968), an essay based on the
ok, Chomsky focuses on the philosophical and psychological aspects of his
eory, identifying himself with the rationalist school of philosophy and the uni-
rsal grammarians of the seventeenth and eighteenth centuries.

Some features of transformational theory have remained fairly constant
nce its inception. A grammar is seen as a finite set of rules that can generate or
oduce the infinite number of sentences in a language. The rules relate mean-
gs, which are represented by a deep structure, to sounds or written symbols,
hich are represented by a surface structure. The transformational grammarian
ishes to study a native speaker's competence, his internalization of these rules,
ther than his actual performance. The distinction resembles the one made by

[40]CHARLES F. HOCKETT, "Two Models of Grammatical Description," *Word*, 10 (1954),
0–31.
[41]ZELLIG S. HARRIS, "Discourse Analysis," *Language*, 28 (1952), 1–30. Harris, "Co-
currence and Transformation in Linguistic Structure," *Language*, 33 (1957), 283–340.
[42]NOAM CHOMSKY, *Syntactic Structures* (The Hague: Mouton, 1957), p. 15.

de Saussure between "la langue" and "la parole," except the de Saussure thought in terms of segments of language and categories, whereas transfor mationalists are interested in rules for sentence formation. They wish to state explicitly and formally, the rules that will account for a native speaker's lin guistic intuition, and to express them in terms of a general theory that will also account for linguistic universals.

Although the aims and methods of transformational grammar have re mained constant, the details of the grammatical models that have been proposed have changed considerably. In *Syntactic Structures* (1957), a transformational grammar is said to consist of the following three parts:

1. Phrase structure rules
2. Transformational rules
3. Morphophonemic rules

Phrase structure rules are simple rewriting rules which allow for substitutions and for the expansion of grammatical categories. For example, $S \rightarrow NP + VP$ is a rewriting rule for a sentence (S) indicating that it consists of a noun phrase (NP) and a verb phrase (VP). Phrase structure rules were allowed to account for many features, including the selection of words. A transformational rule is de fined as one that operates on the structure of a given "string" or sentence, and converts it into a related structure. Morphophonemic rules account for the final written or spoken form of sentences. In this early model, negatives and interroga tives were considered optional transforms of declarative "kernel sentences." A kernel sentence was defined as one that involved the application only of phrase structure rules and of obligatory transformations, such as the agreement of sub ject and verb. Compound and complex sentences were rather loosely derived from double-base transformations that combined strings. Meaning was not con sidered at all.

During the 1960s, this model was revised considerably. The new features were incorporated into Chomsky's *Aspects of the Theory of Syntax* (1965). A grammar was now said to consist of the following three parts:

1. A syntactic component
2. A semantic component
3. A phonological component

The syntactic component in *Aspects* is much more complex than the one pre sented in *Syntactic Structures*. It is divided into a base and a transformational component. The base is further divided into a lexicon or word list, a set of phrase structure rules, and base transformational rules. Even the base was no longer a simple phrase structure grammar. Negatives, interrogatives, and compound or complex sentences were all incorporated into the base rules, doing away with the concepts of double-base transformations and kernel sentences. The property of recursiveness, the ability to expand structures and repeat a set of rules, was thus made a part of the base. The base was further complicated by the use of complex symbols to represent lexical categories or words. For instance, a noun was represented by features like [+ animate], [+ human], [+ count], etc. The representation of features was found to be necessary since such features determined the positions that words could fill. However, it resulted in a breakdown of the boundary between syntax and semantics and a certain amount of duplication in the syntactic and semantic components. The syntactic deep structure was said to account for all meaning. Lexical insertions (insertions of actual words) preceded grammatical transformations, which were said to be meaning preserving.

The issue of the relation between syntax and semantics has resulted in a split within the ranks of transformationalists. Followers of Chomsky, such as Jerrold Katz and Ray Jackendoff, assert that there is a separate semantic component in a transformational grammar whose role is mainly interpretive. This school is called *interpretive semantics*. In contrast, linguists who have developed the theory of *generative semantics* assert that syntax cannot be separated from semantics, and that the role of transformations is to relate semantic representations to surface structures. They deny the existence of an independent syntactic deep structure and a separate semantic component, recognizing instead an underlying semantic structure consisting of a series of predicates or propositions and noun phrases that are related to them. A grammar is seen as a single system of transformational rules that relates semantic structures to surface structures via intermediate stages. It is not assumed that lexical insertions (considered to be transformations) apply in a block, with no intervening nonlexical transformations. The grammar includes rules for combining semantic material into complex units or words. Therefore, a verb like ''jail'' can be decomposed into the deep verbs ''cause'' and ''be'' (in jail). The semantic constituents of words play a role in the syntactic structure of sentences. Leaders of the school of generative semantics include George Lakoff, John Ross, and James McCawley. Charles Fillmore and Paul and Carol Kiparsky have done important work within the framework of this theory. Generative semanticists consider not only rules of syntax, but also rules of appropriateness, presuppositions, and inferences. The theory has thus resulted in a focus on contexts and on the communicative function of language.

The question of contexts has also come to have an influence on studies of usage. Traditional grammar tended to elevate the formal literary language to a position of superiority above all other forms. However, the findings of linguistics have laid the basis for more liberal attitudes. It is now recognized that there are many varieties of language, all having legitimate functions in different social situations. The concept of ''functional variety'' has been developed by John Kenyon and Martin Joos. Nonstandard dialects have also come in for serious study. In *The Study of Nonstandard English* (1969), William Labov shows that these dialects are self-contained systems following their own sets of rules. Nevertheless, nonstandard dialects are closely related to the standard language. Style and class stratification of language are not independent. The same variables that are used in style shifting also distinguish cultural or social levels of English. The ability to vary style and to recognize the social value of different forms is part of an individual's competence. Studies of sociolinguists are beginning to take such factors into consideration, thus broadening the goals of linguistics to include the study of language in its entire cultural setting.

2 TRADITIONAL GRAMMAR

In early English use, the term "grammar" meant Latin grammar since Latin was the only language taught according to a formal grammatical system. "Grammar school" was the name given to a class of schools founded in the sixteenth century or earlier for the teaching of Latin.[1] Since the very word "grammar" was so closely tied to the study of Latin, it is not surprising that descriptions of Latin strongly influenced early descriptions of English. This influence made them more elaborate than they had to be since Latin is a synthetic language, that is, one that uses word endings to indicate a great deal of grammatical information. Nouns are inflected to show their functions within the sentence and have five case endings in the singular and plural: the nominative (subject), genitive (possessive), dative (indirect object), accusative (direct object), and ablative (location, means or instrument, and various other meanings). For example, the noun *fēmina* (woman) takes the following forms:

	Singular	Plural
Nom.	fēmin*a*	fēmin*ae*
Gen.	fēmin*ae*	fēmin*ārum*
Dat.	fēmin*ae*	fēmin*īs*
Acc.	fēmin*am*	fēmin*ās*
Abl.	fēmin*ā*	fēmin*īs*

In the sentence, "Vir occīdit fēminam" (The man killed the woman), the same party is the murderer even if the positions of the nouns are reversed: "Fēminam occīdit vir." The endings on the nouns determine case functions. In Modern English, case functions are indicated by word order and prepositions. The nouns cannot be reversed without a change of meaning (The woman killed the man).

In a synthetic language like Latin, individual words carry much more grammatical weight. Latin verbs are conjugated to show distinctions of person,

---

[1]*Oxford English Dictionary*, IV (1933), 344.

number, and tense. Different endings are used for the first, second, and third persons in the singular and plural; for the present, imperfect, future, perfect, pluperfect, and future perfect tenses; for the subjunctive and imperative moods; and for the passive voice in all of these tenses and moods. English was never this complex, although greater use was made of inflections during the Old English period. By the Early Modern period, however, when the first English grammars were written, English had become an analytic language, that is, one that relies mainly on word order and separate words such as prepositions and auxiliaries. Nevertheless, Latin patterns were used to describe English, even though the same form-changes did not exist in the two languages. Just as the Romans had taken over the system of the Greeks to describe Latin, so the writers of early English grammars took over the Latin system to describe English. This time, however, the results were less satisfactory since the differences between the two languages were much greater.

The first English grammars to have a wide influence were written during the eighteenth century. At that time, there was a strong desire to establish correct and precise rules for the use of English. The aspiring middle classes wanted a standard to follow. The neoclassicist writers of the late seventeenth and eighteenth centuries felt uncomfortable without rules and formal patterns. In his Dedication to *Troilus and Cressida* (1679), John Dryden stated that he tested doubtful passages in his writing by turning them into Latin. Dryden's comment reveals the tendency to rely on Latin, the strong interest in grammatical correctness, and the desire for a fixed standard that characterized the spirit of the time.

This desire for an authority led to a movement to establish an English academy on the model of the Italian Accademia della Crusca, founded in 1582, and the Académie Française, founded in 1635 under the auspices of Cardinal Richelieu. Dryden praised the French Academy and expressed his desire for an English academy in the Dedication to *Rival Ladies* (1664). In the same year, he became a member of a committee founded by the Royal Society to improve the English language. The group held only three or four meetings, but the idea of an academy lingered on. A proposal for an English academy was included by Daniel Defoe in his *Essay upon Projects* (1702). The establishment of an academy that might "fix the language forever" was recommended to the Lord High Treasurer of England by Jonathan Swift in his *Proposal for Correcting, Improving, and Ascertaining the English Tongue* (1712). However, such an institution was never established. Among the reasons were lack of a suitable patron, the demonstrable failure of the French and Italian academies to "fix" their languages, and the feeling that an authoritarian body of this kind would be against the spirit of English liberty. This last reason was the main objection of Samuel Johnson, which is ironic, since he came to be a kind of one-man academy for many people on the basis of his *Dictionary of the English Language* (1755).

Johnson's *Dictionary* was the first major one in English. Others had preceded it, such as the *New World of English Words* (1658) by Edward Phillips (John Milton's nephew), and the *Universal Etymological English Dictionary* (1721) by Nathaniel Bailey. Bailey's work was an important source for Johnson, but Johnson's became more popular and had a greater influence. Johnson was a conservative who adhered to a cyclical theory of language, similar to the gold-silver-bronze age model of Latin literature. Consequently, he believed that English should adhere to the "golden age" of its Germanic origins and should avoid unnecessary borrowing of Latin or French words. When he began the dictionary, he had hopes of being able to play a role in fixing the language, but he came to realize that such a goal was futile. Although he was conservative, he was an open-minded man with a sense of humor. This can be seen from his definition of a lexicographer as "a harmless drudge, that busies himself in tracing the original, and detailing the signification of words."[2] By the time Johnson had finished tracing all of his words, he was thoroughly aware of the inevitability of linguistic change.

Johnson's realistic attitude was not shared by most grammarians of the eighteenth century. Several conflicting theories of language were current. Some believed that language had been instituted directly by the deity and was dispersed at Babel. According to Lord Beattie in the *Theory of Language* (1787), this belief solves all difficulties regarding the origin of various languages. Others were not satisfied so easily.

A less mystical concept was that language follows a consistent, logical plan so as to mirror the reasoning processes assumed for the mind of man. This was the belief of the logical school of grammarians, who believed in a universal grammar. A prominent representative of this school in England was James Harris. In *Hermes or a Philosophical Inquiry Concerning Universal Grammar* (1751), Harris defines universal grammar as "that Grammar, which without regarding the several Idioms of particular languages, only respects those principles that are essential to them all."[3] Although such a belief was rejected by most linguists until the middle of the twentieth century, transformational grammarians have come to accept the idea of a universal grammar. In this respect, modern theoreticians have returned to the work of the rationalist school of the past.

An excellent presentation of universal grammar was the *Grammaire générale et raisonnée* by Antoine Arnauld and Claude Lancelot, members of the lay community that had established itself at the convent of Port Royal near Versailles. The French version was published at Paris in 1660 and at London in 1664. It was translated (probably by Thomas Nugent) into English as *A General*

---

[2]SAMUEL JOHNSON, *Dictionary of the English Language* (London, 1755), II, sig. 15I–4.
[3]JAMES HARRIS, *Hermes or a Philosophical Inquiry Concerning Universal Grammar* (London, 1751), p. x.

and Rational Grammar and published at London in 1753.[4] The Port Royal grammarians owed something to the *grammatica speculativa* of the Middle Ages for their views regarding universal grammar, but their approach was more psychological. They asserted the claims of human reason above authority and made the philosophy of Descartes the basis for their teaching. Like Descartes, they noted that human communication has a creative aspect which is absent in all animal communication. Man is able to take about 25 or 30 sounds and compose "that infinite variety of words, which tho' they have no natural resemblance to the operations of the mind, are yet the means of unfolding all its secrets."[5] The Port Royal grammarians believed that a knowledge of what passes in the mind is necessary to understand the foundation of grammar, for language is not merely a collection of physical properties but the link between thought and sound: "Words therefore may be defined, distinct and articulate sounds, made use of by men as signs, to express their thoughts."[6]

The rationalist outlook did not make the Port Royal grammarians squeeze languages into a single mold. They analyzed French and the other European languages in their own terms. For example, they pointed out that the vernacular languages do not have case endings but make use of particles and word order to express case relations. Nevertheless, case relations exist in all the languages. In their discussion of relative pronouns, they showed how sentences that include relative clauses or other kinds of phrases involve complex propositions. More than one sentence is expressed by the construction. For instance, the sentence "God who is invisible has created the world which is visible" includes three propositions: God is invisible; God has created the world; and the world is visible. The second proposition is the principal one, and the first and third are accessory. Transformational grammarians call accessory propositions of this kind embedded sentences. All languages can express complex propositions, but they do so in different ways. The Port Royal grammarians combined their interest in linguistic universals with a recognition of the patterns of individual languages, insisting that "the particular use of languages must be always consulted."[7] Moreover, they believed that the speech forms of the living language should determine usage.[8]

Most seventeenth- and eighteenth-century grammarians were not this scientific, neither in their attitude toward the living language nor in their search for linguistic universals. Rather than investigating human thought processes, they sought universals in the surface forms of Latin. Just as misleading as the analogies with Latin were the ones with logic. Language is often illogical and

---

[4]ANTOINE ARNAULD AND CLAUDE LANCELOT, *A General and Rational Grammar* (London, 1753. Reprinted Yorkshire, England: Scolar Press, 1968), pp. 1–2.
[5]Ibid., p. 22.
[6]Ibid., p. 22.
[7]Ibid., p. 152.
[8]Ibid., pp. 81–82.

irregular, but the prescriptive school of grammarians tried to establish rules on the basis of logic even when such principles went against established usage. When making authoritarian pronouncements, they appealed to reason or the "genius of the language," which frequently was a disguise for their own prejudices.

One of the few grammarians who adopted an objective, scientific attitude toward language was Joseph Priestley, better known as a chemist and as the discoverer of oxygen. Priestley transferred his scientific outlook to the realm of language. In his *Rudiments of English Grammar* (1761), we find the objective, descriptive approach of the modern linguist. He criticizes the use of "so much of the distribution and technical terms of the Latin grammar" in English, stating that they "could not possibly have entered into the head of any man who had not been previously acquainted with Latin." He points out the error of speaking of a future tense in English; we use the auxiliary "will" or "shall" with the verb to indicate future time, but there is no form change of the verb that serves as a future tense. Being thoroughly committed to the primacy of usage over authority or logic, he selects examples from his contemporaries so as to "see what is the real character and turn of the language at present." Furthermore, he is aware of the primacy of the spoken language and asserts that "the custom of speaking is the original and only just standard of any language." Priestley shared the fate of many men who are far ahead of their time. His work was ignored.

More in keeping with the spirit of the time was Robert Lowth's *Short Introduction to English Grammar* (1762). Lowth, a professor of poetry at Oxford and later Bishop of London, was a conservative who strongly favored older forms of the language. Like many other conservatives, he believed in the golden age theory of languages.[9] The contemporary language was seen as a corrupt variety of the noble form that had been used in the past. There was no agreement as to when the golden age had existed; it was variously placed in the reign of Queen Elizabeth, the Restoration, or the reign of Queen Anne. Most conservatives placed the golden age about one hundred years before their own time. Lowth, an archconservative, praised the example of Richard Hooker, whose *Of the Laws of Ecclesiastical Polity* was written in the 1590s — almost two hundred years earlier.

In spite of his authoritarian attitudes, Lowth was aware of the structure of English and rejected Latin analogies when they did not apply. He states that of all the European languages, English is "the most simple in its form and construction." English has only one variation in case (the possessive), no grammatical gender, no agreement of adjectives, and only about six or seven forms for the verb. In discussing verbs, he calls attention to the manner in which English makes use of "commodious little verbs," or auxiliaries, to indicate shades of

---

[9]STERLING A. LEONARD, *The Doctrine of Correctness in English Usage, 1700–1800* (Madison, Wisc: Univ. of Wisconsin, 1929), p. 127.

meaning. Lowth understood the structure of English but refused to accept the inevitability of linguistic change. He felt that the English language was deteriorating, and preferred the usage of older authors to that of his contemporaries. When usage conflicted with logic or with what he conceived of as universal principles of grammar, he often rejected usage. This kind of thinking led him to assert that "our best authors have committed gross mistakes, for want of a due knowledge of English Grammar." According to Lowth, the purpose of a grammar is "to teach us to express ourselves with propriety" and "to enable us to judge of every phrase and form of construction, whether it be right or not." He was particularly proud of his astuteness in pointing out errors. This negative attitude and the insistence on a single standard of correctness, identified with formal literary English, was typical of the prescriptive grammarians.

Prescriptivism was brought into the schools by Lindley Murray, who adapted Lowth's work for classroom use. Murray was an American lawyer who migrated to England after the Revolution and settled in Yorkshire. At the request of the teachers in a girls' school at York, he compiled his *English Grammar Adapted to the Different Classes of Learners* (1795). In 1797, he published two companion works, *English Exercises Adapted to Murray's English Grammar*, and the *Key to the Exercises Adapted to Murray's English Grammar*. These were followed by the *Abridgment of Murray's English Grammar* (1797), *English Exercises* (1802), and *An English Grammar in Two Volumes* (1814). Murray simplified Lowth's grammar and included material for classroom use on spelling, punctuation, and parsing, that is, classifying words into parts of speech and describing their functions. The dullness of his description of parsing suggests why generations of children came to hate grammar. The sample sentences show the attempts at moral inculcation that went along with instruction in grammar (this venerable practice went back to the teaching of Greek and Latin in ancient times). The commercial success of Murray's textbooks was phenomenal. They dominated the market in England and America, reaching a total of over 120 editions of 10,000 copies each; over 1,000,000 copies of his books were sold in America before 1850.[10]

Eighteenth-century attitudes and arbitrary rules, as codified and simplified by Murray, became fixed in nineteenth-century textbooks. Murray's works continued to be reprinted and adapted, as in Allen Fisk's *Murray's English Grammar Simplified* (1822). One of its early competitors was Samuel Kirkham's *English Grammar in Familiar Lectures* (1835). Kirkham admits the power of custom but does so most grudgingly and pays more attention to rules. In dealing with sentences, he uses the method of parsing or identification of parts of speech.

A different approach to sentence analysis was developed by Alonzo Reed and Brainerd Kellogg in *Higher Lessons in English* (1905), first published as *Work on English Grammar and Composition* (1877). They begin with complete

---

[10]ROBERT C. POOLEY, *Grammar and Usage in Textbooks on English* (Madison, Wisc.: Univ. of Wisconsin, 1933), p. 24.

sentences rather than individual words. According to their view, "the part of speech to which a word belongs is determined only by its function in the sentence, and inflections simply mark the offices and relations of words."[11] They break up word order to show the relation between principal and subordinate parts, such as nouns and adjectives, and to account for underlying or "understood" elements, such as the pronoun "you" in imperative sentences. The relations between parts of the sentence are shown in the famous Reed and Kellogg diagrams. The purpose of the diagrams is to enable the student to "look through the literary order and discover the logical order." The technique had possibilities, but it was confined to simple sentences that often illustrated outmoded prescriptive rules.

Prescriptivism still prevails in some textbooks of the twentieth century. For example, in House and Harmon's *Descriptive English Grammar* (1931 and 1950), the importance of usage is acknowledged, yet perfectly acceptable expressions such as "gym" for "gymnasium," are characterized as "barbarisms." Colloquial language is recognized but frowned upon. We are told that a colloquial expression cannot be regarded as standard until it becomes "universally used," which never happens.

These rules and attitudes hark back to the prescriptivism of the eighteenth century. Good usage is identified with formal literary style; thus the rules create the false impression that a single standard applies to all situations. Such attitudes are not necessarily connected with traditional grammar but can be applied to any theory. The best argument against linguistic authoritarianism is its futility. Samuel Johnson's famous line could well serve as an epigraph to all grammar textbooks: "To enchain syllables and to lash the wind are equally the undertakings of pride, unwilling to measure its desires by its strength."[12]

---

[11]ALONZO REED AND BRAINERD KELLOGG, *Higher Lessons in English* (New York: Maynard, Merrill & Co., 1903), p. vi.
[12]JOHNSON, *Dictionary*, I, sig. C-3.

A Proposal for Correcting, Improving, and Ascertaining the English Tongue

JONATHAN SWIFT

The Persons who are to undertake this Work, will have the Example of the French before them, to imitate where these have proceeded right, and to avoid their Mistakes. Beside the Grammar-part, wherein we are allowed to be very defective, they will observe many gross Improprieties, which however authorised by Practice, and grown familiar, ought to be discarded. They will find many Words that deserve to be utterly thrown out of our Language, many more to be corrected; and perhaps not a few, long since antiquated, which ought to be restored, on account of their Energy and Sound.

But what I have most at Heart is, that some Method should be thought on for ascertaining and fixing our Language for ever, after such Alterations are made in it as shall be thought requisite. For I am of Opinion, that it is better a Language should not be wholly perfect, than that it should be perpetually changing; and we must give over at one Time, or at length infallibly change for the worse: As the Romans did, when they began to quit their Simplicity of Style for affected Refinements; such as we meet in Tacitus and other Authors, which ended by degrees in many Barbarities, even before the Goths had invaded Italy.

The Fame of our Writers is usually confined to these two Islands, and it is hard it should be limited in Time, as much as Place, by the perpetual Variations of our Speech. It is Your Lordship's Observation, that if it were not for the Bible and Common Prayer Book in the vulgar Tongue, we should hardly be able to understand any Thing that was written among us an hundred Years ago: Which is certainly true: For those Books being perpetually read in Churches, have proved a kind of Standard for Language, especially to the common People. And I doubt whether the Alterations since introduced, have added much to the Beauty or Strength of the English Tongue, though they have taken off a great deal from that Simplicity, which is one of the greatest Perfections in any Language. You, My Lord, who are so conversant in the Sacred Writings, and so great a Judge of them in their Originals, will agree, that no Translation our Country ever yet produced, hath come up to that of the Old and New Testament: And by the many beautiful Passages, which I have often had the Honor to hear Your Lordship cite from

(from Jonathan Swift, *A Proposal for Correcting, Improving, and Ascertaining the English Tongue*, London, 1712, pp. 30–34.)

thence, I am persuaded that the Translators of the Bible were Masters of an English Style much fitter for that Work, than any we see in our present Writings, which I take to be owing to the Simplicity that runs through the whole. Then, as to the greatest part of our Liturgy, compiled long before the Translation of the Bible now in use, and little altered since; there seem to be in it as great strains of true sublime Eloquence, as are any where to be found in our Language; which every Man of good Taste will observe in the Communion Service, that of Burial, and other Parts.

But where I say, that I would have our Language, after it is duly correct, always to last; I do not mean that it should never be enlarged: Provided, that no Word which a Society shall give a Sanction to, be afterwards antiquated and exploded, they may have liberty to receive whatever new ones they shall find occasion for: Because then the old Books will yet be always valuable, according to their intrinsick Worth, and not thrown aside on account of unintelligible Words and Phrases, which appear harsh and uncouth, only because they are out of Fashion.

Preface to the Dictionary of the English Language

SAMUEL JOHNSON

It is the fate of those who toil at the lower employments of life, to be rather driven by the fear of evil, than attracted by the prospect of good; to be exposed to censure, without hope of praise; to be disgraced by miscarriage, or punished for neglect, where success would have been without applause, and diligence without reward.

Among these unhappy mortals is the writer of dictionaries; whom mankind have considered, not as the pupil, but the slave of science, the pionier of literature, doomed only to remove rubbish and clear obstructions from the paths of Learning and Genius, who press forward to conquest and glory, without bestowing a smile on the humble drudge that facilitates their progress. Every other authour may aspire to praise; the lexicographer can only hope to escape reproach, and even this negative recompense has been yet granted to very few.

I have, notwithstanding this discouragement, attempted a dictionary of the English language, which, while it was employed in the cultivation of every species of literature, has itself been hitherto neglected, suffered to spread, under the direction of chance, into wild exuberance, resigned to the tyranny of time and fashion, and exposed to the corruptions of ignorance, and caprices of innovation.

When I took the first survey of my undertaking, I found our speech copious without order, and energetick without rules: wherever I turned my view, there was perplexity to be disentangled, and confusion to be regulated; choice was to be made out of boundless variety, without any established principle of selection; adulterations were to be detected, without a settled test of purity; and modes of expression to be rejected or received, without the suffrages of any writers of classical reputation or acknowledged authority.

Having therefore no assistance but from general grammar, I applied myself to the perusal of our writers; and noting whatever might be of use to ascertain or illustrate any word or phrase, accumulated in time the materials of a dictionary, which, by degrees, I reduced to method, establishing to myself, in the progress of the work, such rules as experience and analogy suggested to me; experience, which practice and observation were continually increasing; and analogy, which, though in some words obscure, was evident in others.

(from Samuel Johnson, *Dictionary of the English Language*, London, 1755. Reprinted N.Y.: AMS Press, 1967, I, sigs. A-C.)

In adjusting the orthography, which has been to this time unsettled and fortuitous, I found it necessary to distinguish those irregularities that are inherent in our tongue, and perhaps coeval with it, from others which the ignorance or negligence of later writers has produced. Every language has its anomalies, which, though inconvenient, and in themselves once unnecessary, must be tolerated among the imperfections of human things, and which require only to be registered, that they may not be increased, and ascertained, that they may not be confounded: but every language has likewise its improprieties and absurdities, which it is the duty of the lexicographer to correct or proscribe. . . .

My purpose was to admit no testimony of living authours, that I might not be misled by partiality, and that none of my cotemporaries might have reason to complain; nor have I departed from this resolution, but when some performance of uncommon excellence excited my veneration, when my memory supplied me, from late books, with an example that was wanting, or when my heart, in the tenderness of friendship, solicited admission for a favorite name.

So far have I been from any care to grace my pages with modern decorations, that I have studiously endeavoured to collect examples and authorities from the writers before the Restoration, whose works I regard as the wells of English undefiled, as the pure sources of genuine diction. Our language, for almost a century, has, by the concurrence of many causes, been gradually departing from its original Teutonick character, and deviating towards a Gallick structure and phraseology, from which it ought to be our endeavour to recal it, by making our ancient volumes the ground-work of stile, admitting among the additions of later times, only such as may supply real deficiencies, such as are readily adopted by the genius of our tongue, and incorporate easily with our native idioms.

But as every language has a time of rudeness antecedent to perfection, as well as of false refinement and declension, I have been cautious lest my zeal for antiquity might drive me into times too remote, and croud my book with words now no longer understood. I have fixed Sidney's work for the boundary, beyond which I make few excursions. From the authours which rose in the time of Elizabeth, a speech might be formed adequate to all the purposes of use and elegance. If the language of theology were extracted from Hooker and the translation of the Bible; the terms of natural knowledge from Bacon; the phrases of policy, war, and navigation from Raleigh; the dialect of poetry and fiction from Spenser and Sidney; and the diction of common life from Shakespeare, few ideas would be lost to mankind, for want of English words, in which they might be expressed. . . .

The various syntactical structures occurring in the examples have been carefully noted; the licence or negligence with which many words have been hitherto used, has made our stile capricious and indeterminate; when the different combinations of the same word are exhibited together, the preference is readily given to propriety, and I have often endeavoured to direct the choice.

Thus have I laboured to settle the orthography, display the analogy, regulate the structures, and ascertain the signification of English words, to perform all the parts of a faithful lexicographer: but I have not always executed my own scheme, or satisfied my own expectations. The work, whatever proofs of diligence and attention it may exhibit, is yet capable of many improvements: the orthography which I recommend is still controvertible, the etymology which I adopt is uncertain, and perhaps frequently erroneous; the explanations are sometimes too much contracted, and sometimes too much diffused, the significations are distinguished rather with subtilty than skill, and the attention is harrassed with unnecessary minuteness.

The examples are too often injudiciously truncated, and perhaps sometimes, I hope very rarely, alleged in a mistaken sense; for in making this collection I trusted more to memory, than, in a state of disquiet and embarrassment, memory can contain, and purposed to supply at the review what was left incomplete in the first transcription.

Many terms appropriated to particular occupations, though necessary and significant, are undoubtedly omitted; and of the words most studiously considered and exemplified, many senses have escaped observation.

Yet these failures, however frequent, may admit extenuation and apology. To have attempted much is always laudable, even when the enterprize is above the strength that undertakes it: To rest below his own aim is incident to every one whose fancy is active, and whose views are comprehensive; nor is any man satisfied with himself because he has done much, but because he can conceive little. When first I engaged in this work, I resolved to leave neither words nor things unexamined, and pleased myself with a prospect of the hours which I should revel away in feasts of literature, the obscure recesses of northern learning, which I should enter and ransack, the treasures with which I expected every search into those neglected mines to reward my labour, and the triumph with which I should display my acquisitions to mankind. When I had thus enquired into the original of words, I resolved to show likewise my attention to things; to pierce deep into every science, to enquire the nature of every substance of which I inserted the name, to limit every idea by a definition strictly logical, and exhibit every production of art or nature in an accurate description, that my book might be in place of all other dictionaries whether appellative or technical. But these were the dreams of a poet doomed at last to wake a lexicographer. I soon found that it is too late to look for instruments, when the work calls for execution, and that whatever abilities I had brought to my task, with those I must finally perform it. To deliberate whenever I doubted, to enquire whenever I was ignorant, would have protracted the undertaking without end, and, perhaps, without much improvement; for I did not find by my first experiments, that what I had not of my own was easily to be obtained: I saw that one enquiry only gave occasion to another, that book referred to book, that to search was not always to find, and to find was not always to be informed; and that thus to persue perfection, was, like the first inhabitants of Arcadia, to chace the sun, which, when they had reached the hill where he seemed to rest, was still beheld at the same distance from them. . . .

That many terms of art and manufacture are omitted, must be frankly acknowledged; but for this defect I may boldly allege that it was unavoidable: I could not visit caverns to learn the miner's language, nor take a voyage to perfect my skill in the dialect of navigation, nor visit the warehouses of merchants, and shops of artificers, to gain the names of wares, tools, and operations, of which no mention is found in books; what favourable accident, or easy enquiry brought within my reach, has not been neglected; but it had been a hopeless labour to glean up words, by courting living information, and contesting with the sullenness of one, and the roughness of another. . . .

Nor are all words which are not found in the vocabulary, to be lamented as omissions. Of the laborious and mercantile part of the people, the diction is in a great measure casual and mutable; many of their terms are formed for some temporary or local convenience, and though current at certain times and places, are in others utterly unknown. This fugitive cant, which is always in a state of increase or decay, cannot be regarded as any part of the durable materials of a language, and therefore must be suffered to perish with other things unworthy of preservation.

Care will sometimes betray to the appearance of negligence. He that is catching opportunities which seldom occur, will suffer those to pass by unregarded, which he expects hourly to return; he that is searching for rare and remote things, will neglect those that are obvious and familiar: thus many of the most common and cursory words have been inserted with little illustration, because in gathering the authorities, I forebore to copy those which I thought likely to occur whenever they were wanted. It is remarkable that, in reviewing my collection, I found the word *sea* unexemplified.

Thus it happens, that in things difficult there is danger from ignorance, and in things easy from confidence; the mind, afraid of greatness, and disdainful of littleness, hastily withdraws herself from painful searches, and passes with scornful rapidity over tasks not adequate to her powers, sometimes too secure for caution, and again too anxious for vigorous effort; sometimes idle in a plain path, and sometimes distracted in labyrinths, and dissipated by different intentions.

A large work is difficult because it is large, even though all its parts might singly be performed with facility; where there are many things to be done, each must be allowed its share of time and labour, in the proportion only which it bears to the whole; nor can it be expected, that the stones which form the dome of a temple, should be squared and polished like the diamond of a ring.

Of the event of this work, for which, having laboured it with so much application, I cannot but have some degree of parental fondness, it is natural to form conjectures. Those who have been persuaded to think well of my design, require that it should fix our language, and put a stop to those alterations which time and chance have hitherto been suffered to make in it without opposition. With this consequence I will confess that I flattered myself for a while; but now begin to fear that I have indulged expectation which neither reason nor experience can justify. When we see men grow old and die at a certain time one after another, from century to century, we laugh at the elixir that promises to prolong life to a thousand years; and with equal justice may the lexicographer be derided, who being able to produce no example of a nation that has preserved their words and phrases from mutability, shall imagine that his dictionary can embalm his language, and secure it from corruption and decay, that it is in his power to change sublunary nature, or clear the world at once from folly, vanity, and affectation.

With this hope, however, academies have been instituted, to guard the avenues of their languages, to retain fugitives, and repulse intruders; but their vigilance and activity have hitherto been vain; sounds are too volatile and subtile for legal restraints; to enchain syllables, and to lash the wind, are equally the undertakings of pride, unwilling to measure its desires by its strength. . . .

Total and sudden transformations of a language seldom happen; conquests and migrations are now very rare; but there are other causes of change, which, though slow in their operation, and invisible in their progress, are perhaps as much superiour to human resistance, as the revolutions of the sky, or intumescence of the tide. Commerce, however necessary, however lucrative, as it depraves the manners, corrupts the language; they that have frequent intercourse with strangers, to whom they endeavour to accommodate themselves, must in time learn a mingled dialect, like the jargon which serves the traffickers on the Mediterranean and Indian coasts. This will not always be confined to the exchange, the warehouse, or the port, but will be communicated by degrees to other ranks of the people, and be at last incorporated with the current speech.

There are likewise internal causes equally forcible. The language most likely to continue long without alteration, would be that of a nation raised a little, and but a little, above barbarity, secluded from strangers, and totally employed in procuring the conveniences of life; either without books, or, like some of the Mahometan countries, with very few: men thus busied and unlearned, having only such words as common use requires, would perhaps long continue to express the same notions by the same signs. But no such constancy can be expected in a people polished by arts, and classed by subordination, where one part of the community is sustained and accommodated by the labour of the other. Those who have much leisure to think, will always be enlarging the stock of ideas, and every increase of knowledge, whether real or fancied, will produce new words, or combinations of words. When the mind is unchained from necessity, it will range after convenience; when it is left at large in the fields of speculation, it will shift opinions; as any custom is disused, the words that expressed it must perish with it; as any opinion grows popular, it will innovate speech in the same proportion as it alters practice.

As by the cultivation of various sciences, a language is amplified, it will be more furnished with words deflected from their original sense; the geometrician will talk of a courtier's zenith, or the excentrick virtue of a wild hero, and the physician of sanguine expectations and phlegmatick delays. Copiousness of speech will give opportunities to capricious choice, by which some words will be preferred, and others degraded; vicissitudes of fashion will enforce the use of new, or extend the signification of known terms. The tropes of poetry will make hourly encroachments, and the metaphorical will become the current sense: pronunciation will be varied by levity or ignorance, and the pen must at length comply with the tongue; illiterate writers will at one time or other, by publick infatuation, rise into renown, who, not knowing the original import of words, will use them with colloquial licentiousness, confound distinction, and forget propriety. As politeness increases, some expressions will be considered as too gross and vulgar for the delicate, others as too formal and ceremonious for the gay and airy; new phrases are therefore adopted, which must, for the same reasons, be in time dismissed. Swift, in his petty treatise on the English language, allows that new words must sometimes be introduced, but proposes that none should be suffered to become obsolete. But what makes a word obsolete, more than general agreement to forbear it? and how shall it be continued, when it conveys an offensive idea, or recalled again into the mouths of mankind, when it has once by disuse become unfamiliar and by unfamiliarity unpleasing? . . .

The great pest of speech is frequency of translation. No book was ever turned from one language into another, without imparting something of its native idiom; this is the most mischievous and comprehensive innovation; single words may enter by thousands, and the fabrick of the tongue continue the same, but new phraseology changes much at once; it alters not the single stones of the building, but the order of the columns. If an academy should be established for the cultivation of our stile, which I, who can never wish to see dependance multiplied, hope the spirit of English liberty will hinder or destroy, let them, instead of compiling grammars and dictionaries, endeavour, with all their influence, to stop the licence of translatours, whose idleness and ignorance, if it be suffered to proceed, will reduce us to babble a dialect of France.

If the changes that we fear be thus irresistible, what remains but to acquiesce with silence, as in the other insurmountable distresses of humanity? It remains that we retard what we cannot repel, that we palliate what we cannot cure. Life may be lengthened by care, though death cannot be ultimately defeated: tongues, like governments, have a natural tendency to degeneration; we have long preserved our constitution, let us make some struggles for our language.

A General and Rational Grammar

ANTOINE ARNAULD AND CLAUDE LANCELOT

CHAPTER I. THAT THE KNOWLEDGE OF WHAT PASSES IN THE MIND, IS NECESSARY, TO COMPREHEND THE FOUNDATION OF GRAMMAR: AND ON THIS DEPENDS THE DIVERSITY OF WORDS WHICH COMPOSE DISCOURSE

Hitherto we have treated of words, only with respect to their material part, and as they are common, at least in respect to the sound, to men and parrots. It remains now that we examine their spiritual part, which constitutes one of the most considerable advantages of man above all other animals, and is one of the most convincing arguments in favor of reason. This is the use we make of them to explain our thoughts, and the marvellous invention of composing out of 25 or 30 sounds that infinite variety of words, which tho' they have no natural resemblance to the operations of the mind, are yet the means of unfolding all its secrets, and of disclosing unto those who cannot see into our hearts, the variety of our thoughts, and our sentiments upon all manner of subjects.

Words therefore may be defined, distinct and articulate sounds, made use of by men as signs, to express their thoughts.

We cannot therefore perfectly understand the different sorts of significations, annexed to words, without first considering what passes in our minds, since words were invented only to communicate our thoughts.

'Tis the general doctrine of philosophers, that there are three operations of the mind: *Perception, Judgment,* and *Reasoning*.

Perception is no more than the simple apprehension or view which the understanding forms of the objects acting upon it, whether purely intellectual, as when I think of existence, duration, cogitation, God: or corporeal and material, as a square, a circle, a dog, a horse.

Judgment is, when we affirm, that the thing which we conceive or apprehend, is so, or not so: as for instance, When I understand what the *earth* is, and what *roundness* is, I affirm, that the *earth* is *round*.

Reasoning is, from two judgments to infer a third. As when having affirmed, that virtue is commendable, and that patience is a virtue, I draw an inference, that patience is commendable.

(from Antoine Arnauld and Claude Lancelot, *A General and Rational Grammar*, London, 1753. Reprinted Scolar Press, Yorkshire, England, 1968, pp. 21–24, 62–66.)

Hence it is plain, that the third operation of the mind is only an extension of the second. It will therefore suffice for our present subject, to take only the two first into our consideration, and as much of the first, as is comprized in the second. For men seldom mean to express their bare perceptions of things, but generally to convey their judgments concerning them.

The judgment, which we form of things, as when I say, *the earth is round,* is called a *proposition*; and therefore every proposition necessarily includes two terms, one called the *subject*, which is the thing of which the affirmation is; as *the earth*; and the other is called the *attribute*, which is the thing that is affirmed of the subject, as *round*: and moreover the connection between these two terms, namely the substantive verb, *is*.

Now, 'tis easy to see, that the two terms belong properly to the first operation of the mind, because that is what we conceive, and is the object of our thoughts; and the connexion belongs to the second, being properly the action of the mind, and the mode or manner of thinking.

Thus the greatest distinction of what passes in our minds, is to say, that we may consider the objects of our thoughts, and the form or manner of them, the chief of which is judgment. But we ought likewise to refer thither the conjunctions, disjunctions, and the like operations of the mind; as also all the other motions of the soul; as desires, commands, interrogations, etc.

Hence it follows, that men having occasion for signs to express what passes in the mind, the most general distinction of words must be this, that some signify the objects, and others the form or manner of our thoughts; tho' it frequently happens that they do not signify the manner alone, but in conjunction with the object, as we shall make appear hereafter.

The words of the first sort are those which are called *nouns, articles, pronouns, participles, prepositions,* and *adverbs.* Those of the second are, *verbs, conjunctions,* and *interjections.* Which are all derived by a necessary consequence from the natural manner of expressing our thoughts, as we shall soon demonstrate.

CHAPTER IX.   OF THE PRONOUN CALLED RELATIVE

There remains still another pronoun called relative, *qui, quae, quod, who,* or *which.* This pronoun relative has something common with other pronouns, and something particular.

It has something common in this, that it is used instead of a noun, and even more generally than all the other pronouns, being put for all persons. *I, who am a Christian: Thou, who art a Christian: He, who is a King.*

What it has particular, may be considered in two different manners.

The 1. is, that it always has a relation to another noun or pronoun called the antecedent; as, *God who is holy: God* is the antecedent of the relative *who.* But this antecedent is sometimes understood and not expressed, especially in Latin, as may be seen in the new method of learning the Latin tongue.

The 2. thing particular to the relative, and which I don't remember to have ever seen observed is, that the proposition into which it enters, (and which may be called accessary) may constitute part of the subject, or of the attribute of another proposition, which may be called principal.

This cannot be rightly understood, without recollecting what has been mentioned already in the commencement of this discourse: that in every proposition there is a subject, namely, that of which something is affirmed; and an attribute, that which is affirmed of something. But these two terms may be either simple, as when I say, *God is good*; or complex, as when I say, *an able magistrate is a man useful to the republic*. For that, of which I affirm in this last propositon, is not only *a magistrate*, but *an able magistrate*. And what I affirm is, that not only he is *a man*, but moreover, that he is *a man useful to the republic*. See what has been said on complex propositions, in the logic or art of thinking, part. 2. chap. 3. 4. 5. and 6.

This union of several terms in the subject and the attribute, is sometimes of such a nature, as not to hinder the proposition from being simple, when it contains no more than one judgment or affirmation, as when I say: *the valour of Achilles has been the cause of the taking of Troy*. Which always happens when of the two substantives, that enter into the subject or attribute of the proposition, one is governed by the other.

But at other times these propositions, whose subject or attribute are composed of several terms, include at least in the mind, several judgments, out of which so many propositions may be formed: as when I say; *the invisible God has created the visible world*; there are three judgments formed in my mind, all included in this proposition. For 1. I judge that *God is invisible*. 2. That *he has created the world*. 3. That *the world is visible*. And of those three propositions, the second is the principal and essential. But the first and third are accessary ones, which form but a part of the principal, the first constituting the subject, and the last the attribute.

Now these accessary propositions are frequently in the mind, without being expressed, as in the above mentioned example. But sometimes they are distinctly marked, and therein consists the use of the relative: As when I reduce the said example to these terms: *God who is invisible has created the world, which is visible*.

The property therefore of the relative consists in this, that the proposition, into which it enters, shall constitute a part of the subject, or of the attribute of another proposition.

But here we must observe; First, that when two nouns are joined together, one of which is not governed, but only is in concord with the other, either by apposition, as *urbs Roma*, or as an adjective, as *Deus sanctus*; especially if this adjective be a participle, *canis currens*: all these forms of speech include the relative in the sense, and may be resolved by the relative: *Urbs quae dicitur Roma, Deus qui est sanctus, Canis qui currit*. And it depends on the genius of languages to make use of either manner. Thus we find that in Latin the participle is generally used; *video canem currentem*; and in French the relative, *Je voy un chien qui court*.

Secondly, I have said that the proposition of the relative may make part of the subject or of the attribute of another proposition, which may be called the principal. For it never makes the intire subject, nor the intire attribute: but we must join with it the word, whose place the relative supplies, in order to make the subject intire, and some other word to make an intire attribute. For instance, when I say, *God who is invisible, is the creator of the world which is visible. Who is invisible* is not the intire subject of this proposition, but we must add *God*: And *which is visible* is not the whole attribute, but we must join *world*.

Thirdly, the relative may be also either the subject or part of the attribute of the accessary proposition. To be the subject, it must be in the nominative case, *qui creavit mundum*; *qui sanctus est*.

But when it happens to be in an oblique case, the genitive, dative, accusative: then it does not constitute the entire attribute of this accessary proposition, but only a part: *Deus quem amo, God whom I love*. The subject of the proposition is *ego*, and the verb makes the connexion and a part of the attribute, of which *quem* makes another part, as if it were, *ego amo quem*, or *ego sum amans quem*. And in like manner; *cujus cælum sedes est*: Which is just as if one were to say: *cælum est sedes cujus*.

And yet even on these occasions, the relative is always placed at the head of the proposition (tho' according to the sense it ought only to be at the end) unless it happens to be governed by a preposition. For the preposition generally precedes: *Deus a quo mundus est conditus, God by whom the world was created*.

The Rudiments of English Grammar

JOSEPH PRIESTLEY

I have retained the method of question and answer in the *Rudiments*, because I am still persuaded, it is both the most convenient for the master, and the most intelligible to the scholar. I have also been so far from departing from the simplicity of the plan of that short grammar, that I have made it, in some respects, still more simple; and I think it, on that account, more suitable to the genius of the English language. I own I am surprized to see so much of the distribution, and technical terms of the Latin grammar, retained in the grammar of our tongue; where they are exceedingly aukward, and absolutely superfluous; being such as could not possibly have entered into the head of any man, who had not been previously acquainted with Latin.

Indeed, this absurdity has, in some measure, gone out of fashion with us; but still so much of it is retained, in all the grammars that I have seen, as greatly injures the uniformity of the whole; and the very same reason that has induced several grammarians to go so far as they have done, should have induced them to go farther. A little reflection may, I think, suffice to convince any person, that we have no more business with a future tense in our language, than we have with the whole system of Latin moods and tenses; because we have no modification of our verbs to correspond to it; and if we had never heard of a future tense in some other language, we should no more have given a particular name to the combination of the verb with the auxiliary *shall* or *will*, than to those that are made with the auxiliaries *do*, *have*, *can*, *must*, or any other.

The only natural rule for the use of technical terms to express time, etc. is to apply them to distinguish the different modifications of words; and it seems wrong to confound the account of inflections, either with the grammatical uses of the combinations of words, of the order in which they are placed, or of the words which express relations, and which are equivalent to inflections in other languages.

Whenever this plain rule is departed from, with respect to any language whatever, the true symmetry of the grammar is lost, and it becomes clogged with superfluous terms and divisions. Thus we see the optative mood, and the perfect and pluperfect tenses of the passive voice, absurdly transferred from the Greek language into the Latin, where there were no modifications of verbs to corre-

(from Joseph Priestley, *The Rudiments of English Grammar*, London: J. & F. Rivington, 1772, Third Edition, pp. vi-xi, xviii-xix.)

spond to them. The authors of that distribution might, with the very same reason, have introduced the dual number into Latin; and *duo homines* would have made just as good a dual number, as *utinam amem* is an optative mood, or *amatus fui* a perfect tense. I cannot help flattering myself, that future grammarians will owe me some obligation, for introducing this uniform simplicity, so well suited to the genius of our language, into the English grammar.

It is possible I may be thought to have leaned too much from the Latin idiom, with respect to several particulars in the structure of our language; but I think it is evident, that all other grammarians have leaned too much to the analogies of that language, contrary to our modes of speaking, and to the analogies of other languages more like our own. It must be allowed, that the custom of speaking, is the original, and only just standard of any language. We see, in all grammars, that this is sufficient to establish a rule, even contrary to the strongest analogies of the language with itself. Must not this custom, therefore, be allowed to have some weight, in favour of those forms of speech, to which our best writers and speakers seem evidently prone; forms which are contrary to no analogy of the language with itself, and which have been disapproved by grammarians, only from certain abstract and arbitrary considerations, and when their decisions were not prompted by the genius of the language; which discovers itself in nothing more than in the general propensity of those who use it to certain modes of construction. I think, however, that I have not, in any case, seemed to favour what our grammarians will call an irregularity, but where the genius of the language, and not only single examples, but the general practice of those who write it, and the almost universal custom of those who speak it, have obliged me to do it. I also think I have seemed to favour those irregularities, no more than the degree of the propensity I have mentioned, when unchecked by a regard to arbitrary rules, in those who use the forms of speech I refer to, will authorize me.

If I have done any essential service to my native tongue, I think it will arise from my detecting in time a very great number of *gallicisms*, which have insinuated themselves into the style of many of our most justly admired writers; and which, in my opinion, tend greatly to injure the true idiom of the English language, being contrary to its most established analogies. I dare say, the collections I have made of this nature, will surprize many persons who are well acquainted with modern compositions. They surprize myself, now that I see them all together; and I even think, the writers themselves will be surprized, when they see them pointed out. For I do not suppose, that they designedly adopted those forms of speech, which are evidently French, but that they fell into them inadvertently, in consequence of being much conversant with French authors.

I think there will be an advantage in my having collected examples from *modern writings*, rather than from those of Swift, Addison, and others, who wrote about half a century ago, in what is generally called the classical period of our tongue. By this means we may see what is the real character and turn of the language at present; and by comparing it with the writings of preceding authors, we may better perceive which way it is tending, and what extreme we should most carefully guard against. . . .

Grammar may be compared to a treatise of Natural Philosophy; the one consisting of observations on the various changes, combinations, and mutual affections of words; and the other on those of the parts of nature; and were the language of men as uniform as the works of nature, the grammar of language would be as indisputable in its principles as the grammar of nature. But since good authors have adopted different forms of speech, and in a case which admits of no standard but that of custom, one authority may be of as much weight as another; the analogy of language is the only thing to which we can have recourse, to adjust these differences. For language, to answer the intent of it, which is to express our thoughts with certainty in an intercourse with one another, must be fixed and consistent with itself.

By an attention to these maxims hath this grammatical performance been conducted. The best and the most numerous authorities have been carefully followed. Where they have been contradictory, recourse hath been had to analogy, as the last resource. If this should decide for neither of two contrary practices, the thing must remain undecided, till all-governing custom shall declare in favour of the one or the other.

As to a public Academy, invested with authority to ascertain the use of words, which is a project that some persons are very sanguine in their expectations from, I think it not only unsuitable to the genius of a free nation, but in itself ill calculated to reform and fix a language. We need take no doubt but that the best forms of speech will, in time, establish themselves by their own superior excellence.

A Short Introduction to English Grammar

ROBERT LOWTH

The English Language hath been much cultivated during the last two hundred years. It hath been considerably polished and refined; its bounds have been greatly enlarged; its energy, variety, richness, and elegance, have been abundantly proved, by numberless trials, in verse and in prose, upon all subjects, and in every kind of style: but, whatever other improvements it may have received, it hath made no advances in Grammatical Accuracy. Hooker is one of the earliest writers, of considerable note, within the period above mentioned: let his writings be compared with the best of those of more modern date; and, I believe, it will be found, that in correctness, propriety, and purity of English style, he hath hardly been surpassed, or even equaled, by any of his successors.

It is now about fifty years, since Doctor Swift made a public remonstrance, addressed to the Earl of Oxford, then Lord Treasurer, concerning the imperfect State of our Language, alledging in particular, "that in many instances it offended against every part of Grammar." Swift must be allowed to have been a good judge of this matter; to which he was himself very attentive, both in his own writings, and in his remarks upon those of his friends: he is one of the most correct, and perhaps the best, of our prose writers. Indeed, the justness of this complaint, as far as I can find, hath never been questioned; and yet no effectual method hath hitherto been taken to redress the grievance, which was the object of it.

But let us consider, how, and in what extent, we are to understand this charge brought against the English Language: for the Author seems not to have explained himself with sufficient clearness and precision on this head. Does it mean, that the English Language, as it is spoken by the politest part of the nation, and as it stands in the writings of our most approved authors, often offends against every part of Grammar? Thus far, I am afraid, the charge is true. Or does it further imply, that our Language is in its nature irregular and capricious; not hitherto subject, nor easily reducible, to a System of rules? In this respect, I am persuaded, the charge is wholly without foundation.

The English Language is perhaps of all the present European Languages by much the most simple in its form and construction. Of all the antient Languages extant That is the most simple, which is undoubtedly the most antient; but even that Language itself does not equal the English in simplicity.

(from Robert Lowth, *A Short Introduction to English Grammar*, reprinted at Basil: J. J. Tourneisin, 1974, pp. iii-vii, x-xi, 7–8.)

The words of the English Language are perhaps subject to fewer variations from their original form, than those of any other. Its Substantives have but one variation of Case, nor have they any distinction of Gender, beside that which nature hath made. Its Adjectives admit of no change at all, except that which expresses the degrees of comparison. All the possible variations of the original form of the Verb are not above six or seven; whereas in many Languages they amount to some hundreds: and almost the whole business of Modes, Times, and Voices, is managed with great ease by the assistance of eight or nine commodious little Verbs, called from their use Auxiliaries. The Construction of this Language is so easy and obvious, that our Grammarians have thought it hardly worthwhile to give us any thing like a regular and systematical Syntax. The English Grammar, which hath been last presented to the public, and by the Person best qualified to have given us a perfect one, comprises the whole Syntax in ten lines: for this reason; "because our Language has so little inflexion, that its construction neither requires nor admits many rules." In truth, the easier any subject is in its own nature, the harder is it to make it more easy by explanation; and nothing is more unnecessary, and at the same time commonly more difficult, than to give a formal demonstration of a proposition almost self-evident.

It doth not then proceed from any peculiar irregularity or difficulty of our Language, that the general practice both of speaking and writing it is chargeable with inaccuracy. It is not the Language, but the Practice, that is in fault. The truth is, Grammar is very much neglected among us. . . .

It is with reason expected of every person of a liberal education, and it is indispensably required to every one who undertakes to inform or entertain the public, that he should be able to express himself with propriety and accuracy. It will evidently appear from these Notes, that our best authors have committed gross mistakes, for want of a due knowledge of English Grammar, or at least of a proper attention to the rules of it. The examples there given are such as occurred in reading, without any very curious or methodical examination: and they might easily have been much increased in number by any one who had leisure or phlegm enough to go through a regular course of reading with this particular view. However, I believe, they may be sufficient to answer the purpose intended; to evince the necessity of the Study of Grammar in our own Language; and to admonish those, who set up for authors among us, that they would do well to consider this part of Learning as an object not altogether beneath their regard.

The principal design of a Grammar of any Language is to teach us to express ourselves with propriety in that Language; and to enable us to judge of every phrase and form of construction, whether it be right or not. The plain way of doing this is, to lay down rules, and to illustrate them by examples. But, beside shewing what is right, the matter may be further explained by pointing out what is wrong. I will not take upon me to say, whether we have any Grammar, that sufficiently instructs us by rule and example; but I am sure we have none, that, in the manner here attempted, teaches us what is right by shewing what is wrong; though this perhaps may prove the more useful and effectual method of instruction. . . .

Words

Words are articulate sounds, used by common consent as signs of ideas or notions.

There are in English nine Sorts of Words, or, as they are commonly called, Parts of Speech.

1. The Article; prefixed to substantives, when they are common names of things, to point them out, and to show how far their signification extends.

2. The Substantive, or Noun; being the name of any thing conceived to subsist, or of which we have any notion.

3. The Pronoun; standing instead of the noun.

4. The Adjective; added to the noun to express the quality of it.

5. The Verb; or Word, by way of eminence, signifying to be, to do, or to suffer.

6. The Adverb; added to verbs, and also to adjectives and other adverbs, to express some circumstance belonging to them.

7. The Preposition; put before nouns and pronouns chiefly, to connect them with other words, and to show their relation to those words.

8. The Conjunction; connecting sentences together.

9. The Interjection; thrown in to express the affection of the speaker, though unnecessary with respect to the construction of the sentence.

English Grammar Adapted to the Different Classes of Learners

LINDLEY MURRAY

When the number and variety of English Grammars already published, and the ability with which some of them are written, are considered, little can be expected from a new compilation, besides a careful selection of the most useful matter, and some degree of improvement in the mode of adapting it to the understanding, and the gradual progress of learners. In these respects something, perhaps, may yet be done, for the ease and advantage of young persons.

In books designed for the instruction of youth, there is a medium to be observed, between treating the subject in so extensive and minute a manner, as to embarrass and confuse their minds, by offering too much at once for their comprehension; and, on the other hand, conducting it by such short and general precepts and observations, as convey to them no clear and precise information. A distribution of the parts, which is either defective or irregular, has also a tendency to perplex the young understanding, and to retard its knowledge of the principles of literature. A distinct general view, or outline, of all the essential parts of the study in which they are engaged; a gradual and judicious supply of this outline; and a due arrangement of the divisions, according to their natural order and connexion, appear to be among the best means of enlightening the minds of youth, and of facilitating their acquisition of knowledge. The Compiler of this work, at the same time that he has endeavoured to avoid a plan, which may be too concise or too extensive, defective in its parts or irregular in their disposition, has studied to render his subject sufficiently easy, intelligible, and comprehensive. He does not presume to have completely attained these objects. How far he has succeeded in the attempt, and wherein he has failed, must be referred to the determination of the judicious and candid reader.

The method which he has adopted, of exhibiting the performance in characters of different sizes, will, he trusts, be conducive to that gradual and regular procedure, which is so favourable to the business of instruction. The more important rules, definitions, and observations, and which are therefore the most proper to be committed to memory, are printed with a larger type; whilst rules and remarks that are of less consequence, that extend or diversify the general idea, or that serve as explanations, are contained in the smaller letter: these, or the chief of them, will be perused by the student to the greatest advantage, if

(from Lindley Murray, *English Grammar Adapted to the Different Classes of Learners*, N.Y.: McFarlane & Long, 1807, pp. iii-v, 186.)

postponed till the general system be completed. The use of notes and observations, in the common and detached manner, at the bottom of the page, would not, it is imagined, be so likely to attract the perusal of youth, or admit of so ample and regular an illustration, as a continued and uniform order of the several subjects. In adopting this mode, care has been taken to adjust it so that the whole may be perused in a connected progress, or the part contained in the larger character read in order by itself.

With respect to the definitions and rules, it may not be improper more particularly to observe, that, in selecting and forming them, it has been the Compiler's aim to render them as exact and comprehensive, and, at the same time, as intelligible to young minds, as the nature of the subject, and the difficulties attending it, would admit. In this attempt, he has sometimes been, unavoidably, induced to offer more for the scholar's memory, than he could otherwise have wished. But if he has tolerably succeeded in his design, the advantages to be derived from it, will, in the end, more than compensate the inconvenience. In regard to the notes and observations, he may add, that many of them are intended, not only to explain the subjects, and to illustrate them by comparative views, but also to invite the ingenious student to inquiry and reflection, and to prompt to a more enlarged, critical, and satisfactory research.

From the sentiment generally admitted, that a proper selection of faulty composition is more instructive to the young grammarian, than any rules and examples of propriety that can be given, the Compiler has been induced to pay peculiar attention to this part of the subject; and though the instances of false grammar, under the rules of Syntax, are numerous, it is hoped they will not be found too many, when their variety and usefulness are considered. . . .

On the utility and importance of the study of Grammar, and the principles of Composition, much might be advanced, for the encouragement of persons in early life, to apply themselves to this branch of learning; but as the limits of this Introduction will not allow of many observations on the subject, a few leading sentiments are all that can be admitted here with propriety. As words are the signs of our ideas, and the medium by which we perceive the sentiments of others, and communicate our own; and as signs exhibit the things which they are intended to represent, more or less accurately, according as their real or established conformity to those things, is more or less exact; it is evident, that in proportion to our knowledge of the nature and properties of words, of their relation to each other, and of their established connexion with the ideas to which they are applied, will be the certainty and ease, with which we transfuse our sentiments into the minds of one another; and that, without a competent knowledge of this kind, we shall frequently be in hazard of misunderstanding others, and of being misunderstood ourselves. It may indeed be justly asserted, that many of the differences in opinion amongst men, with the disputes, contentions, and alienations of heart, which have too often proceeded from such differences, have been occasioned by a want of proper skill in the connexion and meaning of words, and by a tenacious misapplication of language.

A PRAXIS
OR EXAMPLES OF GRAMMATICAL RESOLUTION

As we have finished the explanation of the different parts of speech, and the rules for forming them into sentences, it is now proper to give some examples of the manner in which the learners should be exercised, in order to prove their knowledge, and to render it familiar to them. This is called parsing. The nature of the subject, as well as the adaptation of it to learners, requires that it should be divided into two parts; viz. parsing, as it respects etymology alone; and parsing, as it respects both etymology and syntax.

Section 1.   Specimen of Etymological Parsing

"Virtue ennobles us."

Virtue is a common substantive of the third person, the singular number, and in the nominative case. (Decline the noun.) *Ennobles* is a regular verb active, indicative mood, present tense, and the third person singular. (Repeat the present tense, the imperfect tense, and the perfect participle.) *Us* is a personal pronoun, of the first person plural, and in the objective case. (Decline the pronoun.)

"Goodness will be rewarded."

Goodness is a common substantive, of the third person, the singular number, and in the nominative case. (Decline it.) *Will be rewarded* is a regular verb, in the passive voice, the indicative mood, the first future tense, and the third person singular. (Repeat the present tense, the imperfect tense, and the perfect participle.)

"Strive to improve."

Strive is an irregular verb neuter, in the imperative mood, and of the second person singular. (Repeat the present tense, etc.) *To improve* is a regular verb neuter, and in the infinitive mood. (Repeat the present tense, etc.)

English Grammar in Familiar Lectures

SAMUEL KIRKHAM

GRAMMAR

Grammar is the science of language.

Universal Grammar explains the principles which are common to all languages.

Particular Grammar applies those general principles to a particular language, modifying them according to its genius, and the established practice of the best speakers and writers by whom it is used. Hence,

The established practice of the best speakers and writers of any language, is the standard of grammatical accuracy in the use of that language.

By the phrase, *established practice,* is implied reputable, national, and present usage. A usage becomes *good* and *legal,* when it has been long and generally adopted.

The best speakers and writers, or such as may be considered good authority in the use of language, are those who are deservedly in high estimation: speakers, distinguished for their elocution and other literary attainments, and writers, eminent for correct taste, solid matter, and refined manner.

In the grammar of a *perfect* language, no rules should be admitted, but such as are founded on fixed principles, arising out of the genius of that language and the nature of things; but our language being *im*perfect, it becomes necessary, in a *practical* treatise, like this, to adopt some rules to direct us in the use of speech as regulated by *custom*. If we had a permanent and surer standard than capricious custom to regulate us in the transmission of thought, great inconvenience would be avoided. They, however, who introduce usages which depart from the analogy and philosophy of a language, are conspicuous among the number of those who form that language, and have power to control it.

Language is conventional, and not only invented, but, in its progressive advancement, *varied* for purposes of practical convenience. Hence it assumes any and every form which those who make use of it choose to give it. We are, therefore, as *rational* and *practical* grammarians, compelled to submit to the necessity of the case; to take the language as it *is*, and not as it *should be*, and bow to custom.

(from Samuel Kirkham, *English Grammar in Familiar Lectures*, N.Y.: William Hager & Co., 1835, pp. 17–19.)

Philosophical Grammar investigates and develops the principles of language, as founded in the nature of things and the original laws of thought. It also discusses the grounds of the classification of words, and explains those procedures which practical grammar lays down for our observance.

Practical Grammar adopts the most convenient classification of the words of a language, lays down a system of definitions and rules, founded on scientifick principles and good usage, illustrates their nature and design, and enforces their application.

Principle. A principle in grammar is a peculiar construction of the language, sanctioned by good usage.

Definition. A definition in grammar is a principle of language expressed in a definite form.

Rule. A rule describes the peculiar construction or circumstantial relation of words, which custom has established for our observance.

ENGLISH GRAMMAR

English Grammar is the art of speaking and writing the English language with propriety.

Grammar teaches us *how to use words in a proper manner*. The most important use of that faculty called speech, is, to convey our thoughts to others. If, therefore, we have a store of words, and even know what they signify, they will be of no real use to us unless we can also apply them to practice, and make them answer the purposes for which they were invented. *Grammar*, well understood, enables us to express our thoughts fully and clearly; and, consequently, in a manner which will defy the ingenuity of man to give our words any other meaning than that which we ourselves intend them to express. To be able to speak and write our vernacular tongue with accuracy and elegance is, certainly, a consideration of the highest moment.

Higher Lessons in English

ALONZO REED AND BRAINERD KELLOGG

To begin with the parts of speech is to begin with details and to disregard the higher unities, without which the details are scarcely intelligible. The part of speech to which a word belongs is determined only by its function in the sentence, and inflections simply mark the offices and relations of words. Unless the pupil has been systematically trained to discover the functions and relations of words as elements of an organic whole, his knowledge of the parts of speech is of little value. It is not because he cannot conjugate the verb or decline the pronoun that he falls into such errors as, "How many sounds *have* each of the vowels?," "Five years' interest *are* due," "She is older than *me*." He probably would not say, "each *have*," "interest *are*," "*me* am." One thoroughly familiar with the structure of the sentence will find little trouble in using correctly the few inflectional forms in English.

THE STUDY OF THE SENTENCE FOR THE LAWS OF DISCOURSE

Through the study of the sentence we not only arrive at an intelligent knowledge of the parts of speech and a correct use of grammatical forms, but we discover the laws of discourse in general. In the sentence the student should find the law of unity, of continuity, of proportion, of order. All good writing consists of good sentences properly joined. Since the sentence is the foundation or unit of discourse, it is all-important that the pupil should know the sentence. He should be able to put the principal and the subordinate parts in their proper relation: he should know the exact function of every element, its relation to other elements and its relation to the whole. He should know the sentence as the skillful engineer knows his engine, that, when there is a disorganization of parts, he may at once find the difficulty and the remedy for it.

THE STUDY OF THE SENTENCE FOR THE SAKE OF TRANSLATION

The laws of thought being the same for all nations, the logical analysis of the sentence is the same for all languages. When a student who has acquired a knowledge of the English sentence comes to the translation of a foreign language, he finds his work greatly simplified. If in a sentence of his own language

(from Alonzo Reed and Brainerd Kellogg, *Higher Lessons in English*, N.Y.: Maynard, Merrill & Co., 1903, pp. vi-ix.)

he sees only a mass of unorganized words, how much greater must be his confusion when this mass of words is in a foreign tongue! A study of the parts of speech is a far less important preparation for translation, since the declensions and conjugations in English do not conform to those of other languages. Teachers of the classics and of modern languages are beginning to appreciate these facts.

THE STUDY OF THE SENTENCE FOR DISCIPLINE

As a means of discipline nothing can compare with a training in the logical analysis of the sentence. To study thought through its outward form, the sentence, and to discover the fitness of the different parts of the expression to the parts of the thought, is to learn to think. It has been noticed that pupils thoroughly trained in the analysis and the construction of sentences come to their other studies with a decided advantage in mental power. These results can be obtained only by systematic and persistent work. Experienced teachers understand that a few weak lessons on the sentence at the beginning of a course and a few at the end can afford little discipline and little knowledge that will endure, nor can a knowledge of the sentence be gained by memorizing complicated rules and labored forms of analysis. To compel a pupil to wade through a page or two of such bewildering terms as ''complex adverbial element of the second class'' and ''compound prepositional adjective phrase,'' in order to comprehend a few simple functions, is grossly unjust; it is a substitution of form for content, of words for ideas.

SUBDIVISIONS AND MODIFICATIONS AFTER THE SENTENCE

Teachers familiar with text-books that group all grammatical instruction around the eight parts of speech, making eight independent units, will not, in the following lessons, find everything in its accustomed place. But, when it is remembered that the thread of connection unifying this work is the sentence, it will be seen that the lessons fall into their natural order of sequence. When, through the development of the sentence, all the offices of the different parts of speech are mastered, the most natural thing is to continue the work of classification and subdivide the parts of speech. The inflection of words, being distinct from their classification, makes a separate division of the work. If the chief end of grammar were to enable one to parse, we should not here depart from long-established precedent.

SENTENCES IN GROUPS — PARAGRAPHS

In tracing the growth of the sentence from the simplest to the most complex form, each element, as it is introduced, is illustrated by a large number of detached sentences, chosen with the utmost care as to thought and expression. These compel the pupil to confine his attention to one thing till he gets it well in hand. Paragraphs from literature are then selected to be used at intervals, with questions and suggestions to enforce principles already presented, and to prepare the way informally for the regular lessons that follow. The lessons on these selections are, however, made to take a much wider scope. They lead the pupil to discover how and why sentences are grouped into paragraphs, and how paragraphs are related to each other; they also lead him on to discover whatever is most worthy of imitation in the style of the several models presented.

THE USE OF THE DIAGRAM

In written analysis, the simple map, or diagram, found in the following lessons, will enable the pupil to present directly and vividly to the eye the exact function of every clause in the sentence, of every phrase in the clause, and of every word in the phrase — to picture the complete analysis of the sentence, with principal and subordinate parts in their proper relations. It is only by the aid of such a map, or picture, that the pupil can, at a single view, see the sentence as an organic whole made up of many parts performing various functions and standing in various relations. Without such map he must labor under the disadvantage of seeing all these things by piecemeal or in succession. But, if for any reason the teacher prefers not to use these diagrams, they may be omitted without causing the slightest break in the work. The plan of this book is in no way dependent on the use of the diagrams.

THE OBJECTIONS TO THE DIAGRAM

The fact that the pictorial diagram groups the parts of a sentence according to their offices and relations, and not in the order of speech, has been spoken of as a fault. It is, on the contrary, a merit, for it teaches the pupil to look through the literary order and discover the logical order. He thus learns what the literary order really is, and sees that this may be varied indefinitely, so long as the logical relations are kept clear.

The assertion that correct diagrams can be made mechanically is not borne out by the facts. It is easier to avoid precision in oral analysis than in written. The diagram drives the pupil to a most searching examination of the sentence, brings him face to face with every difficulty, and compels a decision on every point.

Descriptive English Grammar

HOMER C. HOUSE AND SUSAN E. HARMAN

Parts of speech are the divisions into which words are classified according to their functions in a sentence. Most grammarians recognize eight parts of speech in classifying all the words in the language which are used in connected discourse. Each part of speech has a special use (or part) in the make-up of the sentence of which it is a unit. The *noun* (the name of a person, place, or thing), the *pronoun* (a word substituting for a noun), and the *adjective* (a word qualifying a noun or pronoun) are generally associated with or thought to belong to the subject of the sentence or to substantives belonging to or relating to the subject. The *verb* (a word asserting action, being, or state of being) and the *adverb* (when a modifier of the verb) are felt to belong to the predicate of the sentence. The *preposition* ('a word placed before' to show relation between words) and the *conjunction* ('a yoking,' or connecting word) show relationship or connect units within the sentence. The *interjection* (an ejaculation, an exclamation) is used to show emotion.

The same word may belong to more than one part of speech, the classification depending upon the use of the word, not upon its form. *Love* may be a noun (*Love* rules the court), or a verb (*Love* your enemies). *In* may be a preposition (Duncan is *in* his grave), or an adverb (Come *in*). *For* may be a preposition (He came *for* the money), or a conjunction (Let another be judge, *for* I wish to enter the contest).

A group of words (phrase or clause) may serve as a single part of speech. The infinitive phrase, for example, may be a noun (*To lie* is wrong), or an adverb (He came *to see me*), or an adjective (I have an ax *to grind*). The gerund is always a verbal noun and the entire phrase of which it is a part is frequently used for a noun (I enjoy *playing baseball*; I cannot approve of *your going away*). Clauses may be used as nouns (I know *that you are my best friend*), as adverbs (I go *when I am invited*), or as adjectives (I like the suit *that you gave me*).

One part of speech may sometimes be converted into another by changing its form. An adjective by the addition of *-ness* or *-ty* may become a noun (*sweetness, purity*). Some nouns may become adjectives by adding *-ful* (*hopeful, cheerful*), or *-y* (*milky, fishy*), or *-ed* or *-d* (*talented, diseased*); or by adding other similar suffixes. The adjective may serve as a noun by ellipsis (The *good* die young; Take the *bitter* with the *sweet*). Some adjectives may become verbs by the addition of *-en* (*whiten, blacken, sweeten, thicken*), or adverbs by the addition of *-ly* (*slowly, rapidly*). The noun or pronoun in the possessive case may

(from Homer C. House and Susan E. Harman, *Descriptive English Grammar*, Englewood Cliffs, N.J.: Prentice-Hall, 1950, pp. 16–19.)

have the function of an adjective (The *boy's* hat; *My* coat). Other conversions of a similar nature will be treated more fully in the chapters devoted to the different parts of speech.

Usage is a term employed by linguists to classify speech habits or language peculiarities, to show what is or has been practiced at a given time by a stated group of users of a language. The term is frequently qualified to give us such expressions as *historical usage, Modern English usage, standard usage, current usage, British and American usage,* and so forth. The laws and rules of grammar are not always based upon historical facts or upon logic (as in mathematics and chemistry), but on current standard usage established by cultured and educated people whose influence is considered important.

Idioms and *idiomatic phrases* are terms used by grammarians, philologists, and lexicographers to explain or classify the unusual, the illogical, or the peculiar expressions in a language. Idiomatic expressions frequently defy grammatical analysis, and are, therefore, not easily translated into other words and phrases in the same language, or into other languages word for word without losing some of their highly specialized meaning. *Had better* in "You *had better* go at once" is an idiomatic expression. *It* in *"It* is snowing," *there* in "*There* is a loaf of bread on the table," and *How do you do*? in a formal salutation are all idiomatic expressions that occur very often in American English. When the terms *idiom* and *idiomatic* are used in this text, it is to be understood that they describe expressions that have been accepted through custom and usage as good English, even though these expressions may not always be used in such a way as to conform to the general and traditional rules of English grammar.

Solecism is a term used to describe a blunder in grammar or a construction not sanctioned by good usage. Any word or combination of words deviating from the idiom of the language or from the rules of syntax may be called a *solecism*; as, *He don't* for *He doesn't*, and *between you and I* for *between you and me*.

A *barbarism* is a word or phrase that is not in good use. It may be a newly coined word, a slang expression, a vulgarism, a provincialism, or any illiterate or unauthorized expression. *Ain't, orate, aviate, complected, gym, woozy, nowheres, attackted, unbeknownst,* and *irregardless* are all barbarisms, because these expressions are not used by cultured writers and speakers.

Colloquialisms are expressions used in ordinary conversation. They belong to the informal (popular or common) level of speech. Colloquial English admits words, phrases, forms, and constructions that would be out of place in formal oral or written speech. Because colloquial expressions without the aid of gestures, facial expressions, or tone of voice are often inexact, their use should be restricted to our informal communications. Colloquial English may include contractions, such as *I'll, you've, won't, shouldn't, can't,* and *don't*; or it may include such improprieties as *It is me; It is them; You are different than me*. When a colloquial expression becomes universally used, it may be regarded as standard English.

An *obsolete* expression is one that is no longer in use. An *archaic* expression is one that has the characteristics of a much earlier period and is on the way out of use. Any word is archaic if it is too old to be generally used. Poets frequently employ archaisms and thus prevent their becoming obsolete. Here are a few examples of obsolete or archaic English: *whilom, sikerly* (used by Chaucer for *surely*), *thilke* (for *that*), *methinks* (*it seems to me*), *hideth, wert, wast, quoth, thou, thy, thine, thee, ye, wrought* (for *worked*), *gotten, thrice, erstwhile, eftsoon*. To determine whether a word is obsolete or archaic, one must depend upon its classification in the standard dictionaries.

3 HISTORICAL GRAMMAR

Rather than trying to "enchain syllables," the historical grammarian attempts to trace their development through time. One of the first scholars to set forth the principles of historical linguistics was William Dwight Whitney, an American professor of Sanskrit at Yale University. Whitney's reputation was international: *Language and the Study of Language* (1867) was translated into German and Dutch; *The Life and Growth of Language* (1874) was translated into French, Italian, German, and Swedish. Whitney's works were so popular because he rose above the mass of details accumulated in studies of comparative grammar and made valid generalizations about language. He emphasized the fact that language is a system of arbitrary, conventional signs. The child learns these signs according to the usage of those around him. There is no necessary connection between race or nationality and language. Whitney gave a great deal of attention to the dynamics of language as it functions within a community. He recognized the existence of idiolects or individual dialects: there is no "absolute identity of dialect, down to the smallest details, among all the constituent members of a community."[1] There are degrees of cohesion among groups interacting by means of language. Groups that speak different regional or social dialects are potentially separate speech communities. The process of dialect and language formation is gradual and involves a balance between conservative and alterative forces. Tradition and group identity work toward stability. On the other hand, individual variation and changing conditions calling for new expressions operate toward change. Whitney emphasized the fact that a language does not have a life of its own. Every item of alteration goes back to some individual or group of individuals from whose example it won a wider currency. Changes are introduced more easily when they follow the established patterns of a language.

[1]WILLIAM DWIGHT WHITNEY, *Language and the Study of Language*, in *Whitney on Language*, ed. Michael Silverstein (Cambridge, Mass.: M.I.T. Press, 1971), p. 156.

In analyzing linguistic change, Whitney focused on words and morphology: "the history of language reposes on that of words."[2] He distinguished between material (roots and full words) and form (suffixes and prefixes). Full words can become formative elements, or words having mainly grammatical meaning. For example, in English the full word "like," originally the second element in compound adjectives such as "love-like," became the ending "ly," as in "lovely." The processes of combination and adaptation are constantly at work in the formation of language. In vocabulary development, restriction and specialization limit the meaning of some words, such as "fare" (*faran,* "to go" in Old English), while generalization extends the meaning of others, such as "knight" (*cniht,* "retainer" or "youth" in Old English). Whitney's method is illustrated by his analysis of the sentence from the Anglo-Saxon Gospels in Chapter III of *The Life and Growth of Language.* For the historical grammarian, the starting point for a study of English is Anglo-Saxon or the Germanic language group.

An early historical grammar of English was *A New English Grammar, Logical and Historical* (1892) by Henry Sweet. Sweet's grammar was new in view of the material included as well as his method of description. Since he considered a knowledge of Old and Middle English essential for an understanding of the language, he provided a brief history of English in which he discussed the different periods of the language, cognate languages, the invasion of England by the Germanic tribes, characteristics of Old English, the Danish invasions, the Norman Conquest, characteristics of Middle English, the rise of the London dialect, and Modern English. Each section of the grammar treats Old English, Middle English, and Modern English separately.

Sweet also provided a general discussion of linguistic change in which he dealt with the inevitability of change, sound changes, and changes in the meaning of words through generalization or specialization. He states that sound changes are regular but does not claim that they are without exception, as the Neogrammarians did. One sound change may be less general than another. He points out the importance of analogy in language change, which he defines as the influence exercised by the members of an association group on one another, as with the extension of the "s" plural form in English. A form may predominate either by being used in the greatest number of words or by being used in those words that are in most frequent use.

Sweet considers phonology "the indispensable foundation of all linguistic study." This attitude is not surprising since he was an eminent phonetician who helped to develop the International Phonetic Alphabet. He provides a detailed general discussion of phonetics, "the science of speech sounds," and discusses the phonology of Old English, Middle English, and Modern English in considerable detail. He frequently refers to differences between the literary and spoken language and variations that can be found in the dialects. His focus is on British

[2]Ibid., p. 25.

English, although he does mention the independent development of American English.

More attention is given to American English in George O. Curme's *Grammar of the English Language*, the first volume of which deals with *Syntax* (1931). Curme's examples range from Middle English to the colloquial speech and popular writing of his own day, even including quotations from magazines and newspapers. His method is illustrated by his discussion of the development of the second person pronouns. He shows the use of "thou" and "thee" to express singular number in Middle English, the loss of distinctions for number in standard English, and the emergence of "yous" and "you-all" in popular speech as a new expression of the plural in modern times. Curme seeks colloquialisms and examples of innovation rather than criticizing or ignoring these aspects of language. He takes many examples from novelists and dramatists since their writing is closest to popular speech. His recognition of the principle of functional variety is revealed in the Preface to *Syntax*, where he states that grammarians who present only one form of English do a great deal of harm by imparting erroneous ideas about language; it is natural for usage to vary according to the audience and the occasion.

Curme's interest in variation leads him into a detailed consideration of dialects. He points out that dialects can be innovative in some instances and conservative in others. The historical point of view is applied in his discussion of the manner in which American dialects reflect the settlement patterns and cultural tendencies of the colonial period. Although British English had a strong influence, life in the New World called forth a large number of new words and expressions. In view of Curme's admiration for popular speech and innovation, it is not surprising that he criticizes conservative grammarians who zealously defend the practices of the past but attack the new and unhallowed. Rather than seeing change as decay, Curme sees "constructive forces at work in the destruction of old grammatical forms." A language changes to meet the needs of the people who use it.

In their descriptions of the living, changing language, historical grammarians often felt constrained by traditional terminology. Otto Jespersen departed from this terminology most radically. He provided a detailed description of English phonology, morphology, and syntax in *A Modern English Grammar on Historical Principles* (seven vols., 1909–49. The seventh volume was completed by Niels Haislund and published posthumously). A briefer treatment can be found in Jespersen's *Essentials of English Grammar* (1933). The general principles of grammar that Jespersen came to believe in as a result of these studies are set forth in *The Philosophy of Grammar* (1924). He criticized the traditional division of words into parts of speech: "The division in the main goes back to the Greek and Latin grammarians with a few additions and modifications, but the definitions are very far from having attained the degree of exactitude found in Euclidean geometry. Most of the definitions given even in recent books are little better than sham definitions in which it is extremely easy to pick holes; nor has it been possible to come to a general arrangement as to what the distinction is to be based on — whether on form (and form changes), or on meaning, or on function in the sentence, or on all of these combined."[3] Yet he believed that it was impractical to throw out the entire system, and that it was useful to classify words. In classifying words, however, the grammarian should consider form and function, sound and signification, and should describe distinctions that exist only in the contemporary language. Jespersen adopts a scheme of classification that includes five parts of speech:

1. Substantives or nouns
2. Adjectives (in some respects, substantives and adjectives may be classed together as nouns)
3. Pronouns (including numbers and pronominal adverbs, such as "there," "then," "where," and "when")
4. Verbs
5. Particles (including adverbs, prepositions, conjunctions, and interjections)

Jespersen frankly admits the imprecise nature of the particle class, stating that it "may be negatively characterized as made up of all those words that cannot find any place in any of the first four classes."[4] Except for the comparative and superlative forms of adverbs, the words Jespersen categorizes as particles share the characteristic of having an invariable form. Placing adverbs and prepositions together enables him to show how words like "on" or "in" sometimes function by themselves, in which case they are usually called adverbs (as in "put your hat on"), and sometimes take an object, then being classified as prepositions (as in "put your hat on your head"). Placing prepositions and conjunctions together allows him to show that the conjunction can be viewed as a sentence preposition; the major difference between the two classifications is the nature of the complement. Prepositions take nouns or noun phrases as complements, whereas conjunctions take sentences ("after his arrival," where "after" is called a preposition, as opposed to "after he had arrived," where it is called a conjunction). Jespersen discusses the principle of functional shift, or how some words can function as more than one part of speech. Words should never be classified in isolation. Nevertheless, this does not invalidate the principle of word classes since a word has only one function in each use. Words that can be used as different parts of speech are called "grammatical homophones."

In dealing with the relations between words and word groups, Jespersen separates them into the ranks of primary, secondary, and tertiary: nouns are usually primary (as subjects and objects of sentences); verbs and adjectives, secondary (as predicates or modifiers); and particles, including adverbs, tertiary. He also deals with degrees of connection, which he calls "junction" and "nexus." Junction involves a single composite unit or idea, whereas nexus involves the

[3]OTTO JESPERSEN, *The Philosophy of Grammar* (N.Y.: Holt, 1924), p. 58.
[4]Ibid., p. 91.

connection of two units or ideas. In the phrases "the furiously barking dog" and "the dog barks furiously," the ranks of the words are the same: "dog" is primary, "barking" or "barks," secondary, and "furiously," tertiary. However, the connection between "barking" and "dog" is a juncture, forming a composite unit (a noun phrase), whereas the connection between "dog" and "barks" is a nexus, a joining of two units (subject and verb). Jespersen points out that subordinate members can be raised to a higher level and the type of connection altered.[5] Such changes are involved in the conversion of sentences into noun phrases (called "nominalization" by more recent grammarians). "The doctor arrived" can be changed into "the doctor's arrival," with the secondary member "arrived" becoming the primary "arrival," the nexus being turned into a juncture, and the entire phrase being made a part of another sentence: "The doctor's arrival brought about the patient's recovery." Nominalization thus allows for the expression of complex thoughts in concise language.

Jespersen's new terminology represents new ideas. Although he stayed within the framework of traditional grammar, he anticipated some of the insights of descriptive and transformational grammarians. His emphasis on form and actual usage anticipates the method of the descriptivists. For example, he insists on inquiring into the distinctions actually made by a language. Categories should not be posited because they exist in other languages or in earlier stages of the same language. On this basis, he recognizes cases only where there are changes in form: for the English noun, he identifies a common case and a genitive. Like the descriptivists, he recognizes the primacy of the spoken language.

Some of Jespersen's ideas anticipate those of the transformational grammarians. For instance, he states that linguistic phenomena may be regarded from without or within, either from the outward form or the inner meaning. In the first case, we take the sound and inquire into the meaning attached to it; in the second, we start from the signification and ask what formal expression it has found in the particular language we are dealing with.[6] This distinction resembles the one that is made between surface structure and deep structure in transformational grammar, although Jespersen does not explicitly propose the idea of separate levels. He also anticipates transformational theory in his emphasis on the creative aspect of language use. In the first chapter of *The Philosophy of Grammar*, he states that the child abstracts the system of the language from samples that he hears. Irregularities tend to be lost because they do not fit into the system. Most language consists of spontaneously created free expressions formed on patterns of the living language. Jespersen differs from most descriptivists and transformationalists, however, in that his presentations are less explicit and less abstract. He often focuses on language as a mode of expression and its immediate relation to human life.[7] Later grammarians focus more on the abstract underlying system.

[5]Ibid., p. 137.
[6]Ibid., p. 33.
[7]LEONARD BLOOMFIELD, Review of Otto Jespersen's *The Philosophy of Grammar*, in *JEGP*, 26 (1927), 444-46.

Besides focusing on the underlying system of languages, transformational grammarians have tried to account for historical change in terms of universal linguistic processes and the perceptual strategies and innate tendencies of the human mind. This philosophical, psychological approach is exemplified by Elizabeth Closs Traugott's article, "On the Notion 'Restructuring' in Historical Syntax." Restructuring involves radical change in language. Traugott defines it as "any modification that involves the reformulation of two or more rules or constraints." An example of restructuring would be the loss of cases in English, which affected rules regarding word order, prepositions, and markers of case.

Traugott calls attention to the important role played by children in the restructuring of language, since they construct their own grammars from the samples of language they hear. Possible parallels exist between language acquisition and language change. In both cases, we can see the operation of natural processes, such as segmentalization (giving phrasal expression to underlying structures to indicate things such as case, tense, mood, etc.), and syllable reduction. These natural processes also are reflected in the development of pidgins and creoles. Pidgins, non-native languages used by adults in addition to their native language, tend toward drastic simplification. Pidgin languages acquire native speakers when they are learned by the children of the adults who speak them. When a pidgin language becomes the native language of a speech community, it is called a "creole." In contrast to simplified pidgin languages, creole languages, which are developed by children, tend toward elaboration. Through the use of universal natural processes and their own perceptual strategies, children turn the severely limited pidgin language into a more complete natural language. Traugott's article shows how new insights regarding language acquisition and language change have grown out of applications of the theory of transformational grammar to historical studies.

The Life and Growth of Language

WILLIAM DWIGHT WHITNEY

CHAPTER III THE CONSERVATIVE AND ALTERATIVE FORCES IN LANGUAGE

We have seen in the foregoing chapter that the individual learns his language, obtaining the spoken signs of which it is made up by imitation from the lips of others, and shaping his conceptions in accordance with them. It is thus that every existing language is maintained in life; if this process of tradition, by teaching and learning, were to cease in any tongue upon earth, that tongue would at once become extinct.

But this is only one side of the life of language. If it were all, then each spoken dialect would remain the same from age to age. In virtue of it, each does, in fact, remain nearly the same; this is what maintains the prevailing identity of speech so long as the identity of the speaking community is maintained — aside from those great revolutions in their circumstances which now and then lead whole communities to adopt the speech of another people. This, then, is the grand conservative force in the history of language; if there were no disturbing and counteracting forces to interfere with its workings, every generation to the end of time would speak as its predecessors had done.

Such, however, as every one knows, is very far from being the case. All living language is in a condition of constant growth and change. It matters not to what part of the world we may go: if we can find for any existing speech a record of its predecessor at some time distant from it in the past, we shall perceive that the two are different — and more or less different, mainly in proportion to the distance of time that separates them. It is so with the Romanic tongues of southern Europe, as compared with their common progenitor the Latin; so with the modern dialects of India, as compared with the recorded forms of speech intermediate between them and the Sanskrit, or with the Sanskrit itself; and not less with the English of our day, as compared with that of other days. An English speaker even of only a century ago would find not a little in our every-day speech which he would understand with difficulty, or not at all; if we were to hear Shakespeare read aloud a scene from one of his own works, it would be in no small part unintelligible (by reason, especially, of the great difference between his pronunciation and ours); Chaucer's English (500 years ago) we master by dint of good solid application, and with considerable help from a glossary; and King Alfred's English (1000 years ago), which we call Anglo-Saxon, is not

(from William Dwight Whitney, *The Life and Growth of Language*, N.Y.: D. Appleton & Co., 1896, pp. 32–44.)

easier to us than German. All this, in spite of the fact that no one has gone about of set purpose to alter English speech, in any generation among the thirty or forty that have lived between us and Alfred, any more than in our own. Here, then, is another side of the life of language for us to deal with, and to explain, if we can. Life, here as elsewhere, appears to involve growth and change as an essential element; and the remarkable analogies which exist between the birth and growth and decay and extinction of a language and those of an organized being, or of a species, have been often enough noticed and dwelt upon: some have even inferred from them that language is an organism, and leads an organic life, governed by laws with which men cannot interfere.

Plainly, however, we should be overhasty in resorting to such an explanation until after mature inquiry and deliberation. There is no *prima facie* impossibility that language, if an institution of human device, and propagated by tradition, should change. Human institutions in general go down from generation to generation by a process of transmission like that of language, and they are all modified as they go. On the one hand, tradition is by its very nature imperfect and inaccurate. No one has ever yet been able to prevent what passes from mouth to ear from getting altered on the way. The child always commits blunders, of every kind, in his earlier attempts at speaking: if careful and well trained, he learns to correct them; but he is often careless and untrained. And all through the life-long process of learning one's "mother-tongue," one is liable to apprehend wrongly and to reproduce inexactly. On the other hand, although the child in his first stage of learning is more than satisfied to take what is set before him and use it as he best can, because his mental development is far short of that which it represents, and its acquisition is urging him on at his best rate of progress, the case does not always continue thus with him: by and by his mind has grown up, perhaps, to the full measure of that which his speech represents, and begins to exhibit its native and surplus force; it chafes against the imposed framework of current expression; it modifies a little its inherited instrument, in order to adapt this better to its own purposes. So, to have recourse to an obvious analogy, one may, by diligent study under instructors, have reached in some single department — as of natural science, mathematics, philosophy — the furthest limits of his predecessors' knowledge, and found them too strait for him; he adds new facts, draws new distinctions, establishes new relations, which the subsisting technical language of the department is incompetent to express; and there arises thus an absolute need of new expression, which must in some way or other be met; and it is met. Every language must prove itself able to signify what is in the minds of its speakers to express; if unequal to that, it would have to abdicate its office; it would no longer answer the purposes of a language. The sum of what all the individual speakers contribute to the common store of thought and knowledge by original work has to be worked into the "inner form" of their language along with and by means of some alteration in its outer form.

Here, then, at any rate, are two obvious forces, having their roots in human

action, and constantly operating toward the change of language; and it remains to
be seen whether there are any others, of a different character. Let us, then, proceed to examine the changes which actually go on in language, and which by
their sum and combined effect constitute its growth, and see what they will say as
to the force that brings them about.

And it will be well to begin with a concrete example, a specimen of altered
speech, which shall serve as a source of illustration, and as groundwork for a
classification of the kinds of linguistic change. The Frenchman would find his
best example in a parallel between a phrase of ancient Latin and its correspon-
dent in modern French, with intermediate forms from the older French; the German could trace a passage backward through the Middle to the Old High-
German, with hints of a yet remoter antiquity derived from the Gothic; to the
English speaker, nothing else is so available as a specimen of the oldest English,
or Anglo-Saxon, of a thousand years ago. Let us look, then, at a verse from the
Anglo-Saxon gospels, and compare it with its modern counterpart:

> Sē Hǣlend fōr on reste-dæg ofer æceras; sōthlīce his leorning-cnihtas hyn-
> grede, and hī ongunnon pluccian thā ear and etan.

No ordinary English reader, certainly, would understand this, or discover that it
is the equivalent of the following sentence of our modern version:

> Jesus went on the sabbath day through the corn; and his disciples were a
> hungered, and began to pluck the ears of corn to eat. (Matthew xii. 1.)

And yet, by translating it as literally as we can, we shall find that almost every
element in it is still good English, only disguised by changes of form and of
meaning. Thus:

> The Healing [one] fared on rest-day over [the] acres; soothly, his learning-
> knights [it] hungered, and they began [to] pluck the ears and eat.

Thus although, from one point of view, *and* and *his* are the only words in the
Anglo-Saxon passage which are the same also in the English — and not even
those really, since their former pronunciation was somewhat different from their
present — from another point of view everything is English excepting *sē*, "the,"
and *hī*, "they" — and even those, virtually; since they are cases of inflection of
the definite article and third personal pronoun, of which other cases (as *the, that,
they*, and *he, his, him*) are still in good use with us. Both the discordance and the
accordance are complete, according to the way in which we look at them. We
will proceed to examine the passage a little in detail, in order to understand better
the relations between the older and the newer form.

In the first place, their pronunciation is even more different than is indicated
by the written text. There are at least two sounds in the Anglo-Saxon which are
unknown in our present speech: namely, the *h* of *cnihtas*, which was nearly or
quite the same with the *ch* of the corresponding German word *knecht*, and the *y*

of *hyngrede*, which was the German *ü* and French *u*, an *u* (*oo*) sound with an *i* (*ee*) sound intimately combined with it. On the other hand, there are sounds in the English which were unknown to the Anglo-Saxon. Our so-called "short *o*," of *on*, was no ancient sound; nor was the "short *u*" of *begun, pluck*, which had then the vowel sound of *book* and *full*; nor was the "short *i*" of *his*, which was more like the French and German short *i*, not markedly different in quality from the true long *i*, our so-called "long *e*," or *ee* sound. All these are examples of the manifold changes of English pronunciation during the thousand years since Alfred — changes which have altered the whole aspect of our orthoepy and orthography. And others of them are illustrated in the passage: for instance, our *knight* and *eat* show protractions of the short vowels of *cniht* and *etan*, each typical of a whole class of cases; and the lengthened *i* has been changed into a diphthong, which we call "long *i*" simply because it has taken the place of our former long *i* (*ee*); while we call the real long *i* of *eat* by the false name of "long *e*" for the same reason.

Again, we may observe in the forms of many words the effects of a tendency toward abbreviation. *Reste* and *hyngrede* have lost with us their final *e*, which in Anglo-Saxon, as now in German and Italian, made an additional syllable. *Ongunnon, pluccian,* and *etan* have lost both vowel and consonant of a final syllable; and these syllables were the distinctive endings, in the first word of the plural verbal inflection (*ongan*, "I or he began," but *ongunnon*, "we or they began"), in the other two of the infinitive. In *æceras*, "acres," and *cnihtas*, "knights," though we have saved the final *s* of the plural ending, it no longer makes an additional syllable. And in *sōthlīce*, "soothly" (i.e. "truly, verily"), there is a yet more marked abbreviation, to which we shall presently return.

On the other hand, *ear*, "ears," and *fōr*, "fared," have been extended in modern time by the addition of other pronounced elements. It was the rule in Anglo-Saxon that a neuter noun of one syllable, if of long quantity, had no (nom. or accus.) plural ending. With us, every noun, of whatever gender or quantity (save a few exceptions, of which we need take no account here), takes *s* as its plural sign. As for *fōr*, the Anglo-Saxons conjugated *faran*, "fare," as they did *dragan*, "draw," and said *fōr*, "fared," like *droh*, "drew" (compare the corresponding German *fahren, fuhr* and *tragen, trug*) — that is to say, *faran* was to them a verb of the "irregular," or "old," or "strong" conjugation. But for a long time there has existed in English speech a tendency to work over such verbs, abandoning their irregularly varying inflection, and reducing them to accordance with the more numerous class of the "regularly" inflected, like *love, loved*; and *fare* is one of the many that have undergone this change. The process is quite analogous with that which has turned *ear* into *ears:* that is to say, a prevailing analogy has been extended to include cases formerly treated as exceptional.

In connection with *ear* comes to light another very striking difference between the ancient and modern English: the Anglo-Saxon had grammatical gender, like the Greek and Latin and German; it regarded *ear* as neuter, but *æcer* and *dæg* as masculine, and, for instance, *tunge*, "tongue," and *dæd*, "deed," as feminine; to us, who have abolished grammatical gender in favor of natural sex, all are alike neuter.

We turn now to consider a few points relative to the meaning of the words used. In *fōr* we find a marked difference of sense as well as of form. It is part of an old Germanic verb meaning "go," and is traceable even back into the earliest Indo-European, as the root *par*, "pass" (Sanskrit *párayâmi*, Greek περάω , Latin *ex-per-ior*); now it is quite obsolete in any such sense as this, and rather unusual even in that of "getting on," "making progress": "it *fared* ill with him." Again, *æcer* meant in Anglo-Saxon a "cultivated field," as does the German *acker* to the present day; and here, again, we have its very ancient correlatives in Sanskrit *ajra*, Greek αγρός , Latin *ager*; the restriction of the word to signify a field of certain fixed dimensions, taken as a unit of measure for fields in general, is something quite peculiar and recent. It is analogous with the like treatment of *rod* and *foot* and *grain*, and so on, except that in these cases we have saved the old meaning while adding the new.

Among the striking peculiarities of the Anglo-Saxon passage is its use of the words *Hælend*, "healing one," *reste-dæg*, "rest-day," and *leorning-cnihtas*, "learning-knights" (i.e. "youths under instruction"), in the sense respectively of "Savior," "sabbath," and "disciples." Though all composed of genuine old Germanic materials, they were nevertheless recent additions to the language. The introduction of Christianity had created a necessity for them. For the new idea of the Christian Creator and Father, the old word *god*, ennobled and inspired with a new meaning, answered English purposes well enough. But there was no current name applicable to the conception of one who saved men from their sins, making them whole or *hale;* and so the present participle of the verb *hælan*, "make hale, heal," was chosen to represent σωτήρ , and specialized into a proper name, a title for the one Savior. It is the same word which, in German, is still current as *Heiland*. *Reste-dæg*, as name for the sabbath, needs no word of explanation or comment. As for *leorning-cnihtas*, rendering *discipuli* and μαθηταί , its most striking characteristic, apart from its rather lumbering awkwardness. is the peculiar meaning which it implies in *cniht*, "knight." Between our *knight*, a word of high chivalric significance, and the German *knecht*, "servant, menial," is a long distance: both show a deviation, the one in an upward and the other in a downward direction, from the indifferent "youth, fellow," which lies at the bottom of the use of the word in our Anglo-Saxon compound.

But a not less noteworthy point in the history of these words is that in our later usage they have all become superseded by other terms, of foreign origin. The Anglo-Saxon did not, like our English, resort freely to foreign stores of expression for the supply of new needs. It was easier then to accept the new institutions of Christianity than new names for them. We have wonderfully changed all that; and in place of the three new Saxon names we have put other yet newer ones: two Latin-French, *disciple* and *savior*, and one Hebrew, *sabbath*. The substitution exemplifies a capital trait in English language-history.

Our attention being thus directed to the introduction of new elements into Anglo-Saxon, we will note another case or two of the same kind of linguistic change in another department. *Sōthlīce* is an adverb, answering to our "truly." We recognize in the first part of it our *sooth*, a word now almost obsolete — quite so, as far as ordinary use is concerned. Its second part, *līce*, is our *-ly*. But it is also a case-form (instrumental) of an adjective *līc*, our *like*, which was appended to the noun *sōth*, "truth," forming a compound adjective (or adjectival derivative) equivalent to *truth-like*, and completely analogous to *truthful*, from *truth* and *full*. Our adverbial ending *-ly*, then, by which most of our adverbs are made, and which to us is only a suffix, is really the product of alteration of a case-form of a compounded adjective, a word originally independent. Instead of using, like the modern German, the base or crude form of an adjective as adverb — that is to say, in the formal grammatical character of adaptedness to qualify a verb or adjective rather than a substantive — we have wrought out for that purpose a special form, of which the history of development may be followed step by step to its origin, and which is exclusively the property of our language among its kindred Germanic dialects.

A second case is brought before us in *hyngrede*. Its preterit ending *-de* is not, like the adverbial *-ly*, exclusively English; it is rather, like the adjective *līc*, a common Germanic possession. Without dwelling here at length upon its history, we will only observe that it is, like *līce*, traced back to an independent word, the preterit *did*, which was in remote Germanic time added to some verbal derivative, or other part of speech, to form a new style of past tense, when the yet older processes of preterit formation had become no longer manageable.

There are also changes of construction in our passage which ought not to pass without a moment's notice. The word *leorning-cnihtas* is object, not subject of *hyngrede*; and the construction is that peculiar one in which the impersonal verb, without expressed subject, takes before it as object the person affected by the action or feeling it signifies. This is still a familiar mode of expression in German, where one freely says *mich hungerte*, "me hungered" for "I hungered"; and even we have a trace of it, in the obsolescent *methinks*, German *mich dunkt* — that is, "it seems to me." Again, the infinitives *pluccian* and *etan*, being by origin verbal nouns, are directly dependent, as objects, on the transitive verb *ongunnon*. We make the same construction with some verbs: so, *he will pluck, he must eat, see him pluck, let him eat;* and even after *began* shortened to *'gan* it is allowed; but in the vast majority of cases we require the preposition *to* as "infinitive sign," saying "began *to* pluck and *to* eat." This preposition was not unknown in Anglo-Saxon; but it was used only where the connection pretty manifestly favored the insertion of such a connective; and the infinitive after it had a peculiar form: thus, *gōd to etanne*, "good unto eating," and so "good to eat." The *to* which at the period of our specimen-passage was a real word of relation has now become the stereotyped sign of a certain verbal form; it has no more independent value than the ending *-an* of *pluccian* and *etan* — which, indeed, it in a manner replaces; though not, like *-ly* and *-d,* combined with the word to which it belongs, its office is analogous with theirs.

We will notice but one thing more in the passage: the almost oblivion into which *sōth*, our *sooth*, has fallen. Only a small part of the great body of English speakers know that there is such a word; and no one but a poet, or an imitator of archaic style, ever uses it. We have put in place of it *true* and *truth*, which of old were more restricted to the expression of faithfulness, trustworthiness.

The brief sentence selected, we see, illustrates a very considerable variety of linguistic changes; in fact, there is hardly a possible mode of change which is not more or less distinctly brought to light by it. Such are, in general, the ways in which a language comes to be at a later period different from what it has been at an earlier. They are matters of individual detail; each item, or each class of accordant items, has its own time and occasion, and analogies, and secondary causes, and consequences; it is their sum and collective effect which make up the growth of language. If we are to understand how language grows, we must take them up and examine them in their individuality. This, then, is the subject which is now for some time to occupy us: an inquiry into the modes of linguistic change, and their causes, nearer and remoter.

We have already rudely made one classification of these linguistic changes, founded on the various purpose which they subserve: namely, into such as make new expression, being produced for the designation of conceptions before undesignated; and such as merely alter the form of old expression; or, into additions and alterations. It will, however, suit our purpose better to make a more external division, one depending upon the kind of change rather than upon its object. In carrying this out, it will be practicable to take everywhere sufficient notice of the object also.

We may distinguish, then:

I. Alterations of the old material of language; change of the words which are still retained as the substance of expression; and this of two kinds or sub-classes: 1. change in uttered form; 2. change in content or signification; the two, as we shall see, occurring either independently or in conjunction.

II. Losses of the old material of language, disappearance of what has been in use; and this also of two kinds: 1. loss of complete words; 2. loss of grammatical forms and distinctions.

III. Production of new material; additions to the old stock of a language, in the way of new words or new forms; external expansion of the resources of expression.

This classification is obviously exhaustive; there can be no change in any language which will not fall under one or other of the three classes here laid down.

A New English Grammar

HENRY SWEET

CHANGES IN LANGUAGE

The most important fact in the history of language is that it is always changing. Words, parts of words — inflections, derivative elements, etc. — word-groups, and sentences are always changing, both in form and meaning: the pronunciation of words changes, and their meaning changes; inflections change both in form and meaning; word-groups and sentences change their form in various ways — by altering the order of their words, by changes of stress and intonation — and are liable to change their meaning also, so that the meaning of the word-group or sentence can no longer be inferred from that of the words of which it is made up. These changes are inevitable.

Sound changes (phonetic changes, changes of pronunciation) are inevitable, because all speech sounds are the result of certain definite actions or positions of the organs of speech — tongue, lips, etc.; and the slightest deviation from the position which produces a sound alters that sound. Thus the vowel-sound expressed by *o* in *no* is produced by drawing back the tongue and narrowing the lip-opening; and if we draw back the tongue still more and raise it so as to make the mouth-passage narrower, and at the same time narrow the lip-opening by bringing the lips closer together, the sound passes by degrees into the *u* in *rule*; while if we open the lips and widen the mouth-passage, the sound of *o* passes into that of the *a* in *father*. Now in uttering a sound it is as impossible always to hit exactly the same position of the organs of speech as it would be always to hit the mark exactly in shooting with a bow or a gun. For this reason children never reproduce exactly the sounds they learn by imitation from their parents; and even when this deviation is so slight as to escape notice, it is liable to be increased in after-life by carelessness and laziness of pronunciation. But the initial deviation is often so marked that it can be expressed in writing, as when children in trying to imitate the sound of (þ) in *thin* make it into (f). We call sound-changes due to the tendencies of the organs of speech — such as the change of (o) into (u) or (a) — organic sound-changes; and we call changes due to defective imitation — such as that of (þ) into (f) — imitative sound changes. Organic and imitative sound-changes are both the result of something *in* the sound itself, and are therefore included under the common designation internal sound-changes. External sound-changes, on the other hand, have nothing to do with the nature of the

(from Henry Sweet, *A New English Grammar*, Oxford: Oxford Univ. Press, 1892, pp. 176–84.)

sound changed, but are the result of the influence of other words associated in some way — generally by similarity of meaning — with the words containing that sound, as in the change of *spake* into *spoke* by the influence of *spoken*.

The meanings of words change because the meaning of a word is always more or less vague, and we are always extending or narrowing (generalizing or specializing) the meanings of the words we use — often quite unconsciously. Thus in the present English the meaning of the word *morning* has been extended so as to include what in Scotland is still called the *forenoon*, the word *morning* originally denoting the time of day just after sunrise; but as the sun rises at different times at different seasons of the year, the distinction between *morning* and *forenoon* was always liable to be confused. We have an example of narrowing the meaning of a word in the modern English use of *deer* to signify one special kind of wild animal, while in Old English the word — in the form of *dēor* — meant "wild animal in general," being applied to foxes, wolves, etc., as well as deer; Shakespeare still uses the word in its older and more general meaning:

> But mice, and rats, and such small deer
> Have been Tom's food for seven long year.   (*King Lear*)

Of these processes, extension is the more important, especially that kind of extension known as metaphor, by which we use the name of a material object or an attribute to express some more abstract idea suggested by the original meaning of the word, as when we call a sly man a *fox*, or say that the sun is the *source of light and heat* on the analogy of *source of a river*, thus using the familiar word *source* to express the more abstract idea of "cause" or "origin." So also when we speak of a *bright idea* or *dark schemes*. It was mainly by the help of metaphor that primitive man was able to enlarge his originally scanty stock of words so as to find an expression for each new idea as it arose in his mind.

The use and meaning of inflections changes in the same way. Thus the genitive case in Modern English has not the same functions as in Old English. So also with derivative elements, etc.

Linguistic changes often take the form of the loss of sounds, sound-groups, parts of words, and complete words. By phonetic change a sound may be so weakened as to become almost inaudible, so that its dropping is almost inevitable. Sounds and syllables may be dropped because they are superfluous — because the word is intelligible without them, as when *examination* is shortened to *exam*. Words may drop out of sentences for the same reason.

The addition of a sound is generally only apparent when it is the result of organic change. Thus the change of (nr) into (ndr) in Modern English *thunder* from Old English *þunor*, genitive *þunres*, is really a change of the second half of the (n) into (d).

But sounds may be added to words, and words added to sentences by external influences.

Most of these changes of form and meaning are gradual in their operation —
especially the internal sound-changes — so that most of them are carried out unconsciously by those who speak the language, and are therefore beyond their
control. The speakers of a language cannot prevent it from changing; all they can
do is to retard the changes. These changes are the result of natural tendencies of
the organs of speech and of the human mind, and are therefore to a great extent
uniform in their operation. Thus if one child in a community says (fruu) instead
of *through*, we expect other children to do the same, because if one child finds it
easier to pronounce (f) than (þ), other children will probably find it easier too. So
also if one man gets into the habit of using a word which originally meant "wild
animal" in the sense of "deer," because deer are the most important wild animals in the place where he lives, it is natural to expect that most of his neigh-
bours will get into the same habit. Even when different changes of the same
sound, etc. are made by different speakers of the community, one change will
generally get the upper hand, either from having the majority of speakers on its
side, or because it is more convenient or easier to carry out.

Each linguistic change is regular in its operation. If the meaning of a word is
changed in one sentence, we expect to find it changed in all the other sentences in
which it occurs. So also if a sound is changed in one word, we expect to find it
changed in all other words. Thus, if we find that a child learning to speak makes
(þ) into (f) in the words *think* and *three*, we can assume with tolerable certainty
that it carries out the change in all the other words that contain a (þ). If — as is
generally the case — the change is the result of inability to form the sound (þ), it
is evident that it must be carried out with no exception. But one sound-change
may be less general than another. One child may change all (þ)'s into (f)'s, while
another may pronounce such words as *think* and *thing* correctly, while substituting (f) in *through* and *three*, that is, in the combination (þr). Again, a third child
might change *th* in *think* into one sound, and *th* in *through* into a different sound,
carrying out these changes in all the words containing (þ). We see then that the
same sound may undergo different changes under different circumstances — different combinations with other sounds, different positions in the word (initial,
etc.). Thus, to take an example from changes which have actually occurred in
English, we find that (k) has been dropped in the special combination *kn*, as in
know (nou), *knowledge*, but only when initial, the old *k* being kept in such a
word as *acknowledge*, where it is preceded by a vowel.

It sometimes happens that the same word changes in two or more different
ways, according to its surroundings. Thus in English the indefinite article *an*
drops its *n* before another word beginning with a consonant, as in *a man* compared with *an enemy*. When a word splits up in this way, the resulting forms are
called doublets.

Stress has a great influence on sound-change, and often gives rise to doublets. Thus in the Middle English of Chaucer *with* and *of* were pronounced with
final voiceless consonants (wiþ, of), but in the transition to Early Modern En-

glish the final consonants of these words became voiced when they were uttered with weak stress, the original sounds being preserved when they were uttered with strong stress, so that, for instance, *with* was pronounced (ωιð) in such a sentence as "I will go with you, not with him," and was pronounced (ωιþ) in such a sentence as "not *with* him, but *against* him." We call such pairs as (ωιþ, ωιð) stress-doublets. In the case of *an, a* and of strong and weak *with*, the differentiation of form is not accompanied by any differentiation of meaning and function, but in the case of Middle English *of* there has been differentiation in both ways. In Old and Middle English *of* was used in the sense of "of" and "off," but in Early Modern English the weak (ov) was gradually restricted to the less emphatic meaning, while the more marked adverbial meaning was appropriated by the strong (of), which was written *off* to distinguish it from the preposition *of* (ov). In the present English (of) has become (ɔf), and the two words — the adverb and preposition — have diverged so completely in form and meaning that the connection between them is forgotten. In fact *of* itself has split up into stress-doublets in the present English — the strong (ov) and the weak (əv, ə).

Such pairs as *whole* and *hale* — both from Old English *hāl*, "complete, healthy," are not organic doublets, but dialectal doublets, *whole* being the regular Standard English descendant of *hāl*, while *hale* is an importation from the Northern dialect of English, in which Old English *ā* appears regularly as *a*, instead of becoming *o*, as in the standard dialect.

EFFECTS OF CHANGE ON THE RELATIONS BETWEEN WORDS

It is evident that when two or more words resemble each other in form or meaning, or stand in any other relation to one another, these relations are liable to be modified by linguistic changes, which must further modify them in the direction either of convergence or divergence. If convergent changes are carried far enough, the result is the levelling of distinctions between the words. Thus in Modern English the two words *no* and *know* have been brought closer and closer together by convergent sound-change till at last they have been phonetically levelled under the common form (nou). We call such phonetically levelled pairs homonyms. Such homonyms as *bear* (the animal) and *to bear* show levelling in spelling as well as sound. Convergent change of meaning, if carried out as far as possible — to the point of levelling — results in a synonym. Thus *to buy* and *to purchase* are synonyms. Divergent change is most noticeable in doublets. Thus we have divergent sound-change in the Modern English *of, off*.

Linguistic changes have a great effect on association-groups. Convergent and divergent changes have directly opposite effects. Convergent changes form new association-groups, by bringing words into connection with one another which originally had little or nothing in common. Thus *buy* and *purchase* now form an association-group of a very intimate kind through having exactly the same meaning, but *purchase* originally meant "to pursue," and only gradually passed into its present meaning through that of "attain," "acquire," so that the two words were originally quite disassociated from one another in meaning as well as form.

Divergent changes tend to break up association-groups and to isolate the members of a group from one another. Thus in English words of foreign origin the addition of a derivative element often causes shifting of stress, as we see by comparing *photograph, photographer, photographic,* where the stress falls on a different syllable in each word, so that a vowel which is strong in one word is weak in another; and as weak vowels are often weakened to (ə) in English, the spoken forms of these words differ much more than their written forms would lead us to expect: (foutəgræf, fətogrəfer, foutəgræfik). As the consonant skeleton of these words remains unaltered together with their meaning, the shifting stress and the great difference in the vowels is not enough to break up the association-group, but merely loosens the connection between its members. In the case of *of* and *off*, where there has been change not only of form but of meaning, the association has been not only loosened, but completely broken, so that the two words are isolated from one another.

Isolation often leads to the creation of new grammatical categories. As we have seen, isolation is the essence of composition as opposed to mere word-grouping. So also the distinction between an idiom and an ordinary "general" sentence is that in the former the meaning of the whole is isolated from that of its elements. The development of proper names out of common nouns and adjectives is also a process of isolation: when the nickname or surname *Brown* or *Smith* was specially assigned to one particular man in a community, although there were perhaps other brown men and other smiths in it, isolation had begun; and when these appellations had become fixed family names, being given to the descendants of these men without regard to their complexion or trade, the isolation was complete as far as the meaning was concerned, so that the proper names *Brown* and *Smith* no longer had anything in common with the words *brown* and *smith* except in form, being partially isolated from them in form as well by the divergent use of the article, etc. The change of full-words into form-words, the use of nouns and adjectives as particles, etc. all go hand in hand with isolation. Thus the conjunction *because* appears in Middle English in the form of the group *bi cause þat*, "by the cause that," "through the cause that," but in Modern English it has been completely isolated from its elements *by* and *cause* not only by change of grammatical function, but also by the weakening of *bi* into *be* and the shortening of the vowel in the second syllable, formal isolation being carried still further in the careless colloquial pronunciation (koz).

Linguistic changes give rise to grammatical irregularities. The two main classes of changes that produce irregularities are convergent changes of meaning, and divergent sound-changes. What we call an "inflection" often consists of a number of different forms having distinct though similar meanings, which gradually converged so that they came to be identical in meaning and grammatical function. Thus the original reduplication in the preterite *held*, the vowel-change in *saw*, and the addition of *d* in *called*, all express the same grammatical function, although there can be no doubt that they each had a distinct meaning originally.

We can observe the effect of divergent sound-change in the variations of the preterite-ending *d* in *called*, *stopped* (stopt), and the accompanying vowel and consonant changes in such preterites as *kept*, *taught*, from *keep*, *teach*. Here the original unity has been broken up by purely phonetic changes.

Syntax

GEORGE O. CURME

PREFACE

The purpose of this volume is to present a systematic and rather full outline of English syntax based upon actual usage. The book contains the fruits of many years of earnest investigation. From the beginning of these studies the great *Oxford Dictionary* has been an unfailing source of inspiration and concrete help. The author owes much also to the large works of the foreign students of our language, the grammars of Jespersen, Poutsma, Kruisinga, Gustav Kruger, and Wendt, the first three written in English, the last two in German. Moreover, there is a considerable foreign literature in the form of monographs and articles in technical language journals. The author has learned much from the keen observations of these foreign scholars, who have sharp eyes for the peculiarities of our language. He has also made extensive use of the quotations gathered by them and the many other foreign workers in this field. In the same way he has availed himself of the materials gathered by English-speaking scholars. This book could not have been made without the aid of these great stores of fact. But to get a clear, independent view of present usage and its historical development, the author found it necessary to read widely for himself, in older English and in the present period, in British literature and, especially, in American literature, which has not been studied so generally as it deserves. Almost the entire important literature of the early part of the Modern English period has been read, in critical editions where such have appeared. Everywhere attention has been called to the loose structure of the English sentence at that time and to the subsequent development of our simple, terse, differentiated forms of expression — an eloquent testimony to the growing intellectual life of the English-speaking people. In the best literature of his own time the author has read so extensively that he feels that his findings have independent value. With his eyes constantly upon present usage, he has read a large number of recent novels, dramas, lectures, orations, speeches, letters, essays, histories, scientific treatises, poems, etc., from all parts of the English-speaking territory. It might seem at first glance that the novelists and dramatists are more fully represented than writers on the events of the day, politics, literature, history, science, etc., but in fact this, the calm, composed form of English speech, representing the higher unity of the language, has been very carefully studied and illustrative examples are given everywhere throughout the book, but usually without mention of the source since they represent common

(from George O. Curme, *Syntax*, N.Y.: D. C. Heath, 1931, pp. v-xi, 15–17).

normal usage. In the novel and the drama, however, we find the irregular beat of changeful life, varying widely in different provinces and social strata, and, moreover, often disturbed by the exciting influences of pressing events, changing moods, and passionate feeling. An attempt has been made to give at least a faint idea of this complex life so far as it has found an expression in our language.

On the other hand, the more dignified forms of expression have been carefully treated. Good English varies according to the occasion, just as our dress varies according to the occasion. Evening dress would be out of place in playing a football game. Loose colloquial English, as often described in this book, is frequently as appropriate as a loose-fitting garment in moments of relaxation. The lesser grammarians, who so generally present only one form of English, not only show their bad taste, but do a great deal of harm in that they impart erroneous ideas of language. In this book also the language of the common people is treated. It is here called "popular speech" since the common grammatical term "vulgar" has a disparaging meaning which arouses false conceptions. Popular English is an interesting study. On the one hand, it has retained characteristics of our greatest masters of English, which the literary language has discarded. On the other hand, quite forgetful of its old conservatism, it boldly faces the present with its new needs and hesitates not to give an expression to them, often, like our western pioneers, opening up paths to new and better things, going forward with faith in the present and the future. Those who always think of popular speech as ungrammatical should recall that our present literary grammar was originally the grammar of the common people of England. Who today would return to our older literary English? The common people will also in the future make contributions to our language. The author, however, does not desire to emphasize too much the importance of the common people. The expressive power of our language has for the most part come from the intellectual class. Left entirely to the common people the English language would soon deteriorate. On the other hand, intellectual struggles bring to language an undesirable abstractness and intricacy of expression, while the common people bring to it a refreshing concreteness and simplicity, which appeals also to people of culture and will influence them. Our American popular speech, in general, has not proved to be very productive. It has preserved in large measure the original British forms of expression. As, however, the various British dialects have been brought together on American soil, they have not been preserved intact, but have been curiously mingled. In sections where mountains, low swampy lands, and islands have isolated tracts of country the language is often peculiarly archaic. The Negroes as a result of social isolation have preserved many old forms of expression acquired in earlier days from the whites, who themselves often spoke archaic British dialect.

Diligent use has been made of every possible means to secure an accurate, reliable insight into existing conditions in all the different grades of English speech, both as to the actual fixed usage of today and as to present tendencies. Of course, the grades of our literary language have been put in the foreground. An earnest effort has been made to treat clearly the most difficult and most perplexing questions of literary English in order that those might receive practical help who are often in doubt as to how they should express themselves.

This book is not rich in details. It treats of the general principles of English expression. The attention is directed, not to words, but to the grammatical categories — the case forms, the nominative, genitive, dative, accusative, the prepositional phrase, the indicative, the subjunctive, the active, the passive, the word order, the clause formations, clauses with finite verb, and the newer, terser participial, gerundival, and infinitival clauses, etc. These categories are the means by which we present our thought in orderly fashion and with precision, and are intimately associated with the expression of our inner feeling. The story of the development of these categories constitutes the oldest and most reliable chapters in the history of the inner life of the English people. Serious efforts have been made everywhere throughout this book to penetrate into the original concrete meaning of these categories, in order to throw light upon the interesting early struggles of our people for a fuller expression of their inner life and to gain suggestions for their present struggles in this direction. In these excursions into older English the author in his quotations from the original sources always preserves the older form, usually in the original spelling, but in the case of writings still widely read, as the Bible and Shakespeare, the spelling has been modernized in conformity to present usage.

The author has not for a moment forgotten that English is a language without a central territory that regulates its use. It is spoken in many centers, which are becoming more and more real centers and are developing under peculiar circumstances. Hence, usage cannot be fixed in accordance with the standards of any particular center. In the erstwhile colonial centers, America, Ireland, etc., English, no longer in direct touch with the language of England, has not at all points developed in the same way. The development has proceeded unevenly in the different territories. There is no English colony or former colony that follows the British standard in every respect, so that English is characterized in every country by peculiarities of development; but as the differences are not in essential things, English is still an entity, a well-defined language with peculiar differences in the various countries. Except where something is said to the contrary, all descriptions of language in this book refer to the body of usage common to England and America. Where British and American English go different ways, each is described.

In early American English the prevailing type of expression was southern British, the language of the southern half of England and at the same time the literary language of the United Kingdom, so that at first the literary language of England and that of America had the same general character. In the eighteenth century came Scotch-Irish immigrants in large numbers, also many from the north of England. The speech of these newcomers was, of course, northern

British, a conservative form of English preserving older sounds and expressions. The new settlers naturally went to the newer parts of the country west of the old colonies. Their presence there in large numbers influenced American English in certain respects. While the younger, southern British form of English remained intact for the most part on the Atlantic seaboard and in large measure also in the south generally, the modified form of it, characterized by older, northern British features, became established everywhere in the north except along the Atlantic seaboard.

On the other hand, the new things and the new needs of the New World called forth a large number of new words and new expressions. Moreover, the abounding, freer life of the New World created a new slang. Even conservative Scotch-Irish had something new to offer — *will* in the first person of the future tense instead of literary *shall*. These differences in vocabulary and idiom will always distinguish the English speaking peoples, but will not separate them. They have already stood a severe test. Between 1620 and 1800 important changes took place in the grammatical structure of English, both in Great Britain and America, but instead of drifting apart in this period of marked changes these two branches of English, at all important points, developed harmoniously together. This was the result of the universal tendency in colonial days among Americans of culture to follow in speech the usage of the mother country. The colonies had little literature of their own and were largely dependent in matters of culture upon the Old World. If it had not been for this general tendency of American culture, the language of the New World might have drifted away from that of England, for, as can be seen by American popular speech, there is a very strong tendency for English on American soil to cling to the older forms of the language. About 1800 the structure of literary English had virtually attained its present form in both territories and was in both essentially the same. That since that date no syntactical changes of consequence have taken place in either branch indicates a remarkable solidarity of structure. The English speaking people are held together by their priceless common heritage — the English language in its higher forms in science and literature. Constant contact with these forces will keep the different peoples in touch with one another. The same English life pulsates everywhere, insuring in spite of the different conditions a similarity, if not a oneness, of evolution.

Definite unifying forces are now at work. We all feel that that is the best English which is most *expressive*, or most *simple*. These are the only principles that will be universally recognized. The drift towards simplicity is still strong and will continue strong. As many forms and concrete pictures have in the past disappeared, yielding to simpler modes of expression, so also will they continue to disappear in the future. We shall thus continue to lose and gain, lose in concreteness and gain in directness. Present tendencies point to the possible ultimate loss of several valuable forms, as *I, he, she, we, they* in certain categories, since these forms are exposed to the leveling influences of a powerful drift; but there is now, on the other hand, in careful language a strong tendency to express ourselves clearly, which prompts us to use these expressive old forms. Indeed, at the present time this tendency is, at this point, stronger than it has been for centuries. The desire to speak clearly and accurately is even leading us to create new forms for this purpose, as will be shown in this book. The territory is wide, but thinking people everywhere, even though not in actual contact with one another, will instinctively be guided by the same general principle, will choose that which is most expressive. Hence the author defends in this book the recommendations of conservative grammarians wherever they contend against the tendencies of the masses to disregard fine distinctions in the literary language already hallowed by long usage. On the other hand, the author often takes a stand against these conservative grammarians wherever they cling to the old simply because it is old and thus fail to recognize that English grammar is the stirring story of the English people's long and constant struggle to create a fuller and more accurate expression of their inner life.

This book has a good deal to say of these struggles, even the latest much censured ones, which find so little favor with conservative grammarians because they are new and violate rules that are sacred to them. In all ages, the things of long ago have found zealous and fanatical defenders, who are at the same time foes of the new and unhallowed. These new things of today, however, need no organized defense, for they are born of universal needs and will be supported by the resistless forces of life that created them. To the conservative grammarian all change is decay. Although he knows well that an old house often has to be torn down in part or as a whole in order that it may be rebuilt to suit modern conditions, he never sees the constructive forces at work in the destruction of old grammatical forms. He is fond of mourning over the loss of the subjunctive and the present slovenly use of the indicative. He hasn't the slightest insight into the fine constructive work of the last centuries in rebuilding the subjunctive. The present nicely differentiated use of the indicative and the newly created subjunctive, as presented in this book, is recommended for careful study to those who talk about the decay of our language. The English speaking people will chase after fads and eagerly employ the latest slang as long as it lives, for play is as necessary as work, but as long as it remains a great people it will strive unceasingly to find more convenient and more perfect forms of expression. It will do that as naturally as it breathes, and will continue to do it, so that grammarians shall occasionally have to *revise* the school grammars. The fads will pass away, but the constructive work will remain and go on. The author has spent his life in studying the growth and development of Germanic expression and has been very happy in his work. It is his ardent hope that he has presented in this book the subject of English expression in such a way that the reader may realize that English grammar is not a body of set, unchangeable rules, but a description of English expression, bequeathed to us by our forefathers, not to be piously preserved, but to be constantly used and adapted to our needs as they adapted it to their needs.

Thou, Thee, Ye, You

In Middle English, it was still possible to express the idea of number in the personal pronouns of the second person. In the singular, *thou* was used as subject and *thee* as dative and accusative object, while in the plural *ye* served as subject and *you* as dative and accusative object. These grammatical functions for *ye* and *you* were widely observed until the middle of the sixteenth century, and survive in the Biblical and higher poetical language of our time. In the fourteenth century, however, the form *you* — with reference to one or more — sometimes replaced *ye* in the subject relation in the usual intercourse of life, and later in the course of the sixteenth century became more common here than *ye*. Occasionally we find the opposite development in older English — *ye* was used instead of *you* in the object relation: "I do beseech *ye*" (*Julius Caesar*, III, i, 157). In older English, *ye* is thus not infrequently used in both the subject and the object relation, often in the form of *ee*: "D'*ee* (do *ee*) know this crucifix? (Middleton and Rowley, *The Spanish Gipsie*, III, iii, 40, A.D. 1661). "I commend me t'*ee*, sir" (Chapman, *The Gentleman Usher*, III, ii, 208, A.D. 1606). This usage survives in British dialect. The outcome of this development for the literary language is *you* for nominative, dative, and accusative. In Biblical language *ye* is now uniformly employed as nominative and *you* as dative and accusative, as can be seen in the present text of the King James Version of the Bible. In the original text of this version this usage was not so uniform, as there were in it a number of *you*'s where we now find *ye*. Both *ye* and *you* are here still always plural forms as originally.

The use of the plural forms *ye* and *you* for reference to one person is closely related to the use of the plural of majesty *we*. As a ruler often spoke of himself in the plural, others in addressing him felt that they should employ the plural form. After this model it became general in continental Europe to address by a plural form every individual of high rank in church and state. At last, plural form became a mark of politeness in general and was used in speaking to an equal as well as to a superior. This new usage arose in England in the thirteenth century under the influence of French, which here followed the continental Latin usage. The new polite form of addressing one person by the plurals *ye* and *you* did not at once displace the older usage of employing *thou* and *thee* here. For a long while the old and the new forms often alternated with each other, but gradually the new form was distinctly felt as more polite. Thus, in older English, the forms were often differentiated. *Thou* was used in familiar intercourse, and *you* employed as a polite form in formal relations. In Pecock's *Donet* (about A.D. 1449) the father, throughout the book, addresses his son by *thou* and *thee*, while the son out of deference uses *ye* and *you* to his father. The British dialects of the South and South Midland still distinguish between *thou* or *thee* used in intimate relation and *you* or *ye* (often written *ee*) employed in polite language in more formal intercourse. In the eighteenth century, Richardson in his *Pamela* lets Lady Davers use *thou* to her brother in moments of strong emotions and employ *thou* to Pamela in moments of anger and tenderness. This usage survives in British dialects.

In the standard prose English of the eighteenth century, *thou* and *thee* were entirely replaced by *you*, so that the form of polite address became general in the common intercourse of life, the one form *you* serving without distinction of rank or feeling for one or more persons and for the nominative, dative, and accusative relations. The lack of clearness here has called forth in the popular speech of America, Australia, and Ireland a plural ending for this form to indicate more than one, *yous* (or *youse* and in Ireland also *ye, yees, yez, yiz*): "He'll settle *yous* (you kids), *yous* guys." It is not unknown in British English. Horace Walpole in a letter to Miss Mary Berry, March 27, 1791, in speaking of her and her sister Agnes writes playfully: "I have been at White Pussy's (i.e., Lady Amherst's) this evening. She asked much after *yous*." This advantage, however, is sometimes lost through the popular tendency to simplify, i.e., to employ *yous* also as a singular: "So! At last I found *youse*." (cartoon in *Chicago Tribune*, Sept. 16, 1923).

In the southern states, *yóu all* is used as the plural of *you*: "He'll settle *yóu all*." The genitive *yóu all's* is also in use: "*yóu all's* business." *Yóu all* may be addressed to a single person provided the form is felt as a plural comprising a definite group of individuals: "Do *yóu all* (addressed to a clerk representing the different members of the firm) keep fresh eggs here?" (Alphonso Smith, *The Kit-Kat*, Vol. IX, p. 27). The *all* in *yóu all* is often reduced to *'ll*, as it is only weakly stressed: "Boys, I want *you'll* to stop that noise." (ib.) In the literary language *you áll* is used, but the stressed *all* indicates that the thought is different from the normal southern use of *yóu all*, which is simply a plural of *you*: "*You áll* are wrong," or "You are all wrong." In popular speech *you uns* is often used as the plural of *you*. The genitive is *you uns'*. In certain British dialects *you together* is used as plural of *you*. In the literary language and in ordinary colloquial speech we bring out the plural idea here by placing some plural noun after *you*: "you gentlemen," "you boys," "you kids," etc.

The older universal use of *thou* and *thee* in the singular and *ye* and *you* in the plural to all persons has survived in the higher forms of poetry and elevated diction, where the thoughts soar, but in the realistic forms of poetry the actual language of everyday city and country life holds almost complete sway, even where the thoughts rise somewhat from earth, the poet forgetting that the language of earth keeps us on earth: "Oh, when I was in love with *you*, Then I was clean and brave, And miles around the wonder grew, How well did I behave" (Housman, *A Shropshire Lad*, XVIII). Thus the old poetic forms, long used to elevate thought and feeling, are in our own time breaking down; it may be because the poetic elevation of thought and feeling that once gave them meaning is no longer present.

In older English, *thee* is sometimes seemingly used as a nominative subject, where in fact it may be an ethical dative: "Hear *thee* (possibly an ethical dative, but now felt as a nominative), Gratiano!'' (*Merchant of Venice*, II, ii, 189). This same form is also sometimes found in older English as a real nominative, perhaps after the analogy of *you*, which has one form for all the cases: "How agrees the devil and *thee* about thy soul?'' (Shakespeare, *I Henry IV*, I, ii, 127). "What hast *thee* done?'' (Marlowe, *Jew*, 1085, about A.D. 1590, ed. 1636). "If *thee* wilt walk with me, I'll show thee a better'' (words of a young Quaker to Benjamin Franklin, as quoted in Franklin's *Autobiography, Writings*, I, p. 255). This usage lingered much later in popular speech: "I know *thee* dost things as nobody 'ud do'' (George Eliot, *Adam Bede*, Ch. IV).

Thou and *thee* are still used by Quakers, often with the nominative form *thee* in connection with the third person of the verb: *"Thou art not* (or now more commonly *thee's not*) consistent.'' The Quaker address originally had a deep meaning in that it was used toward all men irrespective of rank, and hence emphasized their equality, but it has become a mere symbol of sect since society in general recognized this democratic principle by the employment of *you* without respect to social station.

The Philosophy of Grammar

OTTO JESPERSEN

CHAPTER I: LIVING GRAMMAR

Speaker and Hearer

The essence of language is human activity — activity on the part of one individual to make himself understood by another, and activity on the part of that other to understand what was in the mind of the first. These two individuals, the producer and the recipient of language, or as we may more conveniently call them, the speaker and the hearer, and their relations to one another, should never be lost sight of if we want to understand the nature of language and of that part of language which is dealt with in grammar. But in former times this was often overlooked, and words and forms were often treated as if they were things or natural objects with an existence of their own — a conception which may have been to a great extent fostered through a too exclusive preoccupation with written or printed words, but which is fundamentally false, as will easily be seen with a little reflexion.

If the two individuals, the producer and the recipient of language, are here spoken of as the speaker and the hearer respectively, this is in consideration of the fact that the spoken and heard word is the primary form for language, and of far greater importance than the secondary form used in writing (printing) and reading. This is evidently true for the countless ages in which mankind had not yet invented the art of writing or made only a sparing use of it; but even in our modern newspaper-ridden communities, the vast majority of us speak infinitely more than we write. At any rate we shall never be able to understand what language is and how it develops if we do not continually take into consideration first and foremost the activity of speaking and hearing, and if we forget for a moment that writing is only a substitute for speaking. A written word is mummified until someone imparts life to it by transposing it mentally into the corresponding spoken word.

The grammarian must be ever on his guard to avoid the pitfalls into which the ordinary spelling is apt to lead him. Let me give a few very elementary instances. The ending for the plural of substantives and for the third person singular of the present tense of verbs is in writing the same -s in such words as *ends, locks, rises*, but in reality we have three different endings, as seen when we transcribe them phonetically [endz, lɔks, raiziz]. Similarly the written ending -ed

(from Otto Jespersen, *The Philosophy of Grammar*, London: George Allen & Unwin, 1924, pp. 17–29.)

covers three different spoken endings in *sailed, locked, ended*, phonetically [seild, lɔkt, endid]. In the written language it looks as if the preterits *paid* and *said* were formed in the same way, but differently from *stayed*, but in reality *paid* and *stayed* are formed regularly [peid, steid], whereas *said* is irregular as having its vowel shortened [sed]. Where the written language recognizes only one word *there*, the spoken language distinguishes two both as to sound and signification (and grammatical import), as seen in the sentence "There [ð ə] were many people there [ð ɛ· ə]." Quantity, stress, and intonation, which are very inadequately, if at all, indicated in the usual spelling, play important parts in the grammar of the spoken language, and thus we are in many ways reminded of the important truth that grammar should deal in the first instance with sounds and only secondarily with letters.

Formulas and Free Expressions

If after these preliminary remarks we turn our attention to the psychological side of linguistic activity, it will be well at once to mention the important distinction between formulas or formular units and free expressions. Some things in language — in any language — are of the formula character; that is to say, no one can change anything in them. A phrase like "How do you do?" is entirely different from such a phrase as "I gave the boy a lump of sugar." In the former everything is fixed: you cannot even change the stress, saying "How *do* you do?" or make a pause between the words, and it is not usual nowadays as in former times to say "How does your father do?" or "How did you do?" Even though it may still be possible, after saying, "How do you do?" in the usual way to some of the people present, to alter the stress and say, "And how do *you* do, little Mary?" the phrase is for all practical purposes one unchanged and unchangeable formula. It is the same with "Good morning!," "Thank you," "Beg your pardon," and other similar expressions. One may indeed analyze such a formula and show that it consists of several words, but it is felt and handled as a unit, which may often mean something quite different from the meaning of the component words taken separately; "beg your pardon," for instance, often means "please repeat what you said, I did not catch it exactly"; "how do you do?" is no longer a question requiring an answer, etc.

It is easy to see that "I gave the boy a lump of sugar" is of a totally different order. Here it is possible to stress any of the essential words and to make a pause, for instance, after "boy," or to substitute "he" or "she" for "I," "lent" for "gave," "Tom" for "the boy," etc. One may insert "never" and make other alterations. While in handling formulas memory, or the repetition of what one has once learned, is everything, free expressions involve another kind of mental activity; they have to be created in each case anew by the speaker, who inserts the words that fit the particular situation. The sentence he thus creates may, or may not, be different in some one or more respects from anything he has ever heard or uttered before; that is of no importance for our inquiry. What is essential is that in pronouncing it he conforms to a certain pattern. No matter what words he inserts, he builds up the sentence in the same way, and even without any special grammatical training we feel that the two sentences

John gave Mary the apple,
My uncle lent the joiner five shillings,

are analogous, that is, they are made after the same pattern. In both we have the same type. The words that make up the sentences are variable, but the type is fixed.

Now, how do such types come into existence in the mind of a speaker? An infant is not taught the grammatical rule that the subject is to be placed first, or that the indirect object regularly precedes the direct object; and yet, without any grammatical instruction, from innumerable sentences heard and understood he will abstract some notion of their structure which is definite enough to guide him in framing sentences of his own, though it is difficult or impossible to state what that notion is except by means of technical terms like subject, verb, etc. And when the child is heard to use a sentence correctly constructed according to some definite type, neither he nor his hearers are able to tell whether it is something new he has created himself or simply a sentence which he has heard before in exactly the same shape. The only thing that matters is that he is understood, and this he will be if his sentence is in accordance with the speech habits of the community in which he happens to be living. Had he been a French child, he would have heard an infinite number of sentences like

Pierre donne une pomme à Jean,
Louise a donné sa poupee à sa soeur,

etc., and he would thus have been prepared to say, when occasion arose, something like

Il va donner un sou à ce pauvre enfant.

And had he been a German boy, he would have constructed the corresponding sentences according to another type still, with *dem* and *der* instead of the French à, etc. (Cf. *Language*, Ch. VII.)

If, then, free expressions are defined as expressions created on the spur of the moment after a certain type which has come into existence in the speaker's subconsciousness as a result of his having heard many sentences possessing some trait or traits in common, it follows that the distinction between them and formulas cannot always be discovered except through a fairly close analysis; to the hearer the two stand at first on the same footing, and accordingly formulas can and do play a great part in the formation of types in the minds of speakers, the more so as many of them are of very frequent occurrence. Let us take a few more examples.

"Long live the King!" Is this a formula or a free expression? It is impossible to frame an indefinite number of other sentences on the same pattern. Combinations such as "Late die the King!" or "Soon come the train!" are not used nowadays to express a wish. On the other hand, we may say "Long live the Queen" or "the President" or "Mr. Johnson." In other words, the type, in which an adverb is placed first, then a subjunctive, and lastly a subject, the whole being the expression of a wish, has totally gone out of the language as a living force. But those phrases which can still be used are a survival of that type, and the sentence "Long live the King" must therefore be analyzed as consisting of a formula "long live," which is living though the type is dead, + a subject which is variable. We accordingly have a sentence type whose use is much more restricted in our own days than it was in older English.

In a paper on ethics by J. Royce I find the principle laid down "Loyal is that loyally does." This is at once felt as unnatural, as the author has taken as a pattern the proverb "handsome is that handsome does" without any regard to the fact that whatever it was at the time when the sentence was first framed, it is now to all intents and purposes nothing but a formula, as shown by the use of *that* without any antecedent and by the word order.

The distinction between formulas and free expressions pervades all parts of grammar. Take morphology or accidence: here we have the same distinction with regard to flexional forms. The plural *eyen* was going out of use in the sixteenth century; now the form is dead, but once not only that word, but the type according to which it was formed, were living elements of the English language. The only surviving instance of a plural formed through the addition of *-en* to the singular is *oxen*, which is living as a formula, though its type is extinct. Meanwhile, *shoen, fone, eyen, kine* have been supplanted by *shoes, foes, eyes, cows*; that is, the plural of these words has been reshaped in accordance with the living type found in *kings, lines, stones*, etc. This type is now so universal that all new words have to conform to it: *bicycles, photos, kodaks, aeroplanes, hooligans, ions, stunts*, etc. When *eyes* was first uttered instead of *eyen*, it was an analogical formation on the type of the numerous words which already had *-s* in the plural. But now when a child says *eyes* for the first time, it is impossible to decide whether he is reproducing a plural form already heard, or whether he has learned only the singular *eye* and then has himself added *-s* (phonetically [z]) in accordance with the type he has deduced from numerous similar words. The result in either case would be the same. If it were not the fact that the result of the individual's free combination of existing elements is in the vast majority of instances identical with the traditional form, the life of any language would be hampered; a language would be a difficult thing to handle if its speakers had the burden imposed on them of remembering every little item separately.

It will be seen that in morphology what was above called a "type" is the same thing as the principle of what are generally called regular formations, while irregular forms are "formulas."

In the theory of word-formation it is customary to distinguish between productive and unproductive suffixes. An example of a productive suffix is *-ness*,
because it is possible to form new words like *weariness, closeness, perverseness*,
etc. On the contrary, *-lock* in *wedlock* is unproductive, and so is *-th* in *width*,
breadth, health, for Ruskin's attempt to construct a word *illth* on the analogy of
wealth has met with no success, and no other word with this ending seems to
have come into existence for several hundred years. This is a further application
of what we said above: the type adjective + *-ness* is still living, while *wedlock*
and the words mentioned in *-th* are now formulas of a type now extinct. But
when the word *width* originated, the type was alive. At that far-off time it was
possible to add the ending, which was then something like *-iþu*, to any adjective.
In the course of time, however, the ending dwindled down to the simple sound
þ(*th*), while the vowel of the first syllable was modified, with the consequence
that the suffix ceased to be productive, because it was impossible for an ordinary
man, who was not trained in historical grammar, to see that the pairs *long:length*,
broad:breadth, wide:width, deep:depth, whole:health, dear:dearth, represented
one and the same type of formation. These words were, accordingly, handed
down traditionally from generation to generation as units, that is, formulas, and
when the want was felt for a new "abstract noun" (I use here provisionally the
ordinary term for such words), it was no longer the ending *-th* that was resorted
to, but *-ness*, because that offered no difficulty, the adjective entering unchanged
into the combination.

With regard to compounds, similar considerations hold good. Take three
old compounds of *hus* "house," *husbonde, husþing, huswif*. These were formed
according to the usual type found in innumerable old compounds; the first fram-
ers of them conformed to the usual rules, and thus they were at first free expressions. But they were handed down as whole, indivisible words from generation
to generation, and accordingly underwent the usual sound changes; the long
vowel *u* was shortened, [s] became voiced [z] before voiced sounds, [þ] became
[t] after [s], [w] and [f] disappeared, and the vowels of the latter element were
obscured, the result being our present forms *husband, husting(s), hussy*, phonetically [hʌzbend, hʌstiŋz, hʌzi]. The tie, which at first was strong between these
words and *hus*, was gradually loosened, the more so because the long *u* had here
become a diphthong, *house*. And if there was a divergence in form, there was as
great a divergence in meaning, the result being that no one except the student of
etymology would ever dream of connecting *husband, hustings*, or *hussy* with
house. From the standpoint of the living speech of our own days the three words
are not compound words; they have, in the terminology here employed, become
formulas and are on a par with other disyllabic words of obscure or forgotten
origin, such as *sopha* or *cousin*.

With regard to *huswif* there are, however, different degrees of isolation
from *house* and *wife*. *Hussy* [hʌzi] in the sense "bad woman" has lost all connexion with both; but for the obsolete sense "needle case" old dictionaries record various forms showing conflicting tendencies: *huswife* [hʌzwaif], *hussif*

hʌzif], *hussive*; and then we have, in the sense of "manager of a house," *ousewife*, in which the form of both components is intact, but this appears to be a comparatively recent re-formation, not recognized, for instance, by Elphinston in 1765. Thus the tendency to make the old compound into a formula was counteracted more or less by the actual speech-instinct, which in some applications created it as a free expression: in other words, people would go on combining the two elements without regard to the existence of the formular compounds, which had become more or less petrified in sound and meaning. This phenomenon is far from rare: *grindstone* as a formula had become [grinstən] with the usual shortening of the vowel in both elements, but the result of a free combination has prevailed in the current pronunciation [graindstoun]; in *waistcoat* the new [weistkout] is beginning to be used instead of the formular [weskət]; *fearful* is given as sounding "ferful" by eighteenth-century orthoepists, but is now always [fiəful]. For other examples see MEG I, 4, 34 ff.

Something similar is seen in words that are not compounds. In Middle English we find short vowels in many comparatives: *deppre, grettre* as against *deep, great* (*greet*). Some of these comparatives became formulas and were handed down as such to new generations, the only surviving instances being *latter* and *utter*, which have preserved the short vowels because they were isolated from the positives *late* and *out* and acquired a somewhat modified meaning. But other comparatives were re-formed as free combinations, thus *deeper, greater*, and in the same way we have now *later* and *outer*, which are more intimately connected with *late* and *out* than *latter* and *utter* are.

Stress presents analogous phenomena. Children, of course, learn the accentuation as well as the sounds of each word: the whole of the pronunciation of a word is in so far a formular unit. But in some words there may be a conflict between two modes of accentuation, because words may in some instances be formed as free expressions by the speaker at the moment he wants them. Adjectives in *-able, -ible* as a rule have the stress on the fourth syllable from the ending in consequence of the rhythmic principle that the vowel which is separated by one (weak) syllable from the original stress is now stressed, thus *déspicable* (originally as in French *despicáble*), cómparable, lámentable, préferable, etc. In some of these the rhythmic principle places the stress on the same syllable as in the corresponding verb: *considerable, víolable*. But in others this is now so, and a free formation, in which the speaker was thinking of the verb and then would add *-able*, would lead to a different accentuation: the adjective corresponding to *accépt* was *ácceptable* in Shakespeare and some other poets, and this formula still survives in the reading of the Prayer Book, but otherwise it now is reshaped as *accéptable; refutable* was [réfjutəbl], but now it is more usual to say [rifjútəbl]; *réspectable* has given way to *respéctable*; Shakespeare's and Spencer's *détestable* has been supplanted by *detéstable*, which is Milton's form; in *admirable* the new [ədmáirəbl] has been less successful in supplanting [ǽdmirəbl], but in a great many adjectives analogy, i.e. free formation, has prevailed entirely: *agréeable, deplórable, remárkable, irresístible*. In words with other endings we have the same conflict: *cónfessor* and *conféssor*, *capítalist* and *cápitalist*, *demónstrative* and *démonstrative*, etc., sometimes with changes of meaning, the free formation following not only the accent, but also the signification of the word from which it is derived, while the formula has been more or less isolated. (Examples see MEG Ch. V.) The British *advertisement* [ədvə́tizment] shows the traditional formula; the American pronunciation [ǽdvətáizment] or [ǽdvətaizment] is a free formation on the basis of the verb.

The distinction between a formula and a free combination also affects word-order. One example may suffice: so long as *some* + *thing* is a free combination of two elements felt as such, another adjective may be inserted in the usual way: *some good thing*. But as soon as *something* has become a fixed formula, it is inseparable, and the adjective has to follow: *something good*. Compare also the difference between the old "They turned *each to other*" and the modern "they turned *to each other*."

The coalescence of originally separate elements into a formula is not always equally complete: in *breakfast* it is shown not only by the pronunciation [brekfəst] as against [breik fast], but also by forms like *he breakfasts*, *breakfasted* (formerly *breaks fast*, *broke fast*), but in *take place* the coalescence is not carried through to the same extent, and yet this must be recognized as a formula in the sense "come to happen," as it is impossible to treat it in the same way as *take* with another object, which in some combinations can be placed first (*a book he took*) and which can be made the subject in the passive (*the book was taken*), neither of which is possible in the case of *take place*.

Though it must be admitted that there are doubtful instances in which it is hard to tell whether we have a formula or not, the distinction here established between formulas and free combinations has been shown to pervade the whole domain of linguistic activity. A formula may be a whole sentence or a group of words, or it may be one word, or it may be only part of a word, — that is not important, but it must always be something which to the actual speech-instinct is a unit which cannot be further analyzed or decomposed in the way a free combination can. The type or pattern according to which a formula has been constructed, may be either an extinct one or a living one; but the type or pattern according to which a free expression is framed must as a matter of course be a living one; hence formulas may be regular or irregular, but free expressions always show a regular formation.

Grammatical Types

The way in which grammatical types or patterns are created in the minds of speaking children is really very wonderful, and in many cases we see curious effects on the history of languages. In German the prefix *ge-*, which at first could be added to any form of the verb to express completed action, has come to be specially associated with the past participle. In the verb *essen* there was, however, a natural fusion of the vowel of the prefix and the initial vowel of the verb itself, thus *gessen*; this was handed down as a formular unit and was no longer felt to contain the same prefix as *getrunken, gegangen, gesehn* and others; in a combination like *ich habe getrunken und gessen* it was then felt as if the latter form was incomplete, and *ge-* was added: *ich habe getrunken und gegessen*, which restored parallelism.

Grammatical habits may thus lead to what from one point of view may be termed redundancy. We see something similar with regard to the use of *it* in many cases. It became an invariable custom to have a subject before the verb, and therefore a sentence which did not contain a subject was felt to be incomplete. In former times no pronoun was felt to be necessary with verbs like Latin *pluit, ningit*, "it rains, it snows," etc.; thus Italian still has *piove, nevica*, but on the analogy of innumerable such expressions as *I come, he comes*, etc., the pronoun *it* was added in English, *it rains, it snows*, and correspondingly in French, German, Danish and other languages: *il pleut, es regnet, det regner*. It has been well remarked that the need for this pronoun was especially felt when it became the custom to express the difference between affirmation and question by means of word-order (*er kommt, kommt er?*), for now it would be possible in the same way to mark the difference between *es regnet* and *regnet es*?

Verbs like *rain, snow* had originally no subject, and as it would be hard even now to define logically what the subject *it* stands for and what it means, many scholars[1] look upon it as simply a grammatical device to make the sentence conform to the type most generally found. In other cases there is a real subject, yet we are led for some reason or other to insert the pronoun *it*. It is possible to say, for instance, "To find one's way in London is not easy," but more often we find it convenient not to introduce the infinitive at once; in which cases, however, we do not begin with the verb and say "Is not easy to find one's way in London," because we are accustomed to look upon sentences beginning with a verb as interrogative; so we say, "It is not easy," etc. In the same way it is possible to say, "That Newton was a great genius cannot be denied," but if we do not want to place the clause with *that* first we have to say, "It cannot be denied that Newton was a great genius." In these sentences *it* represents the following infinitive construction or clause, very much as in "He is a great scoundrel, that husband of hers" *he* represents the words *that husband of hers*. Cf. the colloquial: "It is perfectly wonderful the way in which he remembers things." It would be awkward to say "She made that he had committed many offences appear clearly" with the various grammatical elements arranged as in the usual construction of *make appear* ("She made his guilt appear clearly"): this awkwardness is evaded by using the representative *it* before the infinitive: *She made it appear clearly that he had committed many offences*. In this way many of the rules concerning the use of it are seen to be due on the one hand to the speaker's wish to conform to certain patterns of sentence construction found in innumerable sentences with other subjects or objects, and on the other hand to his wish

[1]Brugmann among others.

to avoid clumsy combinations which might even sometimes led to misunderstandings.

The rules for the use of the auxiliary *do* in interrogative sentences are to be explained in a similar way. The universal tendency is towards having the word-order Subject Verb, but there is a conflicting tendency to express a question by means of the inverted order Verb Subject, as in the obsolete "writes he?" (cf. German "Schreibt er?" and French "Écrit-il?"). Now many interrogative sentences had the word-order Auxiliary Subject Verb ("Can he write?," "Will he write?," "Has he written?," etc.), in which the really significant verb came after the subject just as in ordinary affirmative sentences: through the creation of the compromise form "Does he write?" the two conflicting tendencies were reconciled: from a formal point of view the verb, though an empty ~ e, preceded the subject to indicate the question, and from another point of view the subject preceded the real verb. But no auxiliary is required when the sentence has an interrogative pronoun as subject ("Who writes?") because the interrogatory pronoun is naturally put first, and so the sentence without any *does* conforms already to the universal pattern.[2]

Building up of Sentences

Apart from fixed formulas a sentence does not spring into a speaker's mind all at once, but is framed gradually as he goes on speaking. This is not always so conspicuous as in the following instance. I want to tell someone whom I met on a certain occasion, and I start by saying: "There I saw Tom Brown and Mrs. Hart and Miss Johnstone and Colonel Dutton. . . ." When I begin my enumeration I have not yet made up my mind how many I am going to mention or in what order, so I have to use *and* in each case. If, on the other hand, before beginning my story I know exactly whom I am going to mention, I leave out the *ands* except before the last name. There is another characteristic difference between the two modes of expression:

1. There I saw Tom Brown, and Mrs. Hart, and Miss Johnstone, and Colonel Dutton.
2. There I saw Tom Brown, Mrs. Hart, Miss Johnstone, and Colonel Dutton.

namely that in the former I pronounce each name with a falling tone, as if I were going to finish the sentence there, while in the latter all the names except the last have a rising tone. It is clear that the latter construction, which requires a comprehensive conception of the sentence as a whole, is more appropriate in the writ-

---

[2]Cf. *Language*, 357 f. The use of *do* in negative sentences is due to a similar compromise between the universal wish to have the negative placed before the verb and the special rule which places *not* after a verb: in *I do not say* it is placed after the verb which indicates tense, number, and person, but before the really important verb; cf. *Negation*, p. 10 f.

ten language, and the former in ordinary speech. But writers may occasionally resort to conversational style in this as well as in other respects. Defoe is one of the great examples of colloquial diction in English literature, and in him I find (*Robinson Crusoe*, 2. 178) "our God made the whole world, and you, and I, and all things," — where again the form "I" instead of *me* is characteristic of this style, in which sentences come into existence only step by step.

Many irregularities in syntax can be explained on the same principle, e.g. sentences like "Hee that rewards me, heaven reward him" (Sh.). When a writer uses the pronoun *thou*, he will have no difficulty in adding the proper ending *-st* to the verb if it follows immediately upon the pronoun; but if it does not he will be apt to forget it and use the form that is suitable to the *you* which may be at the back of his mind. Thus in Shakespeare (Tp. I. 2. 333) "Thou *stroakst* me, and *made* much of me." Byron apostrophizes Sulla (Ch. H. IV. 83): "Thou, who *didst* subdue Thy country's foes ere thou *wouldst* pause to feel The wrath of thy own wrongs, or reap the due of hoarded vengeance . . . thou who with thy frown *Annihilated* senates . . . thou *didst* lay down," etc. In Byron such transitions are not uncommon.

In a similar way the power of *if* to require a subjunctive is often exhausted when a second verb comes at some distance from the conjunction, as in Shakespeare (Hml. V. 2. 245), "If Hamlet from himselfe *be* tane away, And when he's not himselfe, *do's* wrong Laertes, Then Hamlet does it not"; (Meas. III. 2. 37) "If he *be* a whoremonger, and *comes* before him, he were as good go a mile on his errand"; Ruskin: "But if the mass of good things *be* inexhaustible, and there *are* horses for everybody, — why is not every beggar on horseback?"; Mrs. Ward: "A woman may chat with whomsoever she likes, provided it *be* a time of holiday, and she *is* not betraying her art."[3]

Anyone who will listen carefully to ordinary conversation will come across abundant evidence of the way in which sentences are built up gradually by the speaker, who will often in the course of the same sentence or period modify his original plan of presenting his ideas, hesitate, break off, and shunt on to a different track. In written and printed language this phenomenon, anakoluthia, is of course much rarer than in speech, though instances are well known to scholars. As an illustration I may be allowed to mention a passage in Shakespeare's *King Lear* (IV. 3. 19 ff.), which has baffled all commentators. It is given thus in the earliest quarto — the whole scene is omitted in the Folio:

Patience and sorrow strove,
Who should expresse her goodliest. You have seene,
Sun shine and raine at once, her smiles and teares,
Were like a better way those happie smilets,
That playd on her ripe lip seemed not to know,

[3]Other examples of this have been collected by C. Alphonso Smith, "The Short Circuit," in *Studies in English Syntax*, p. 39.

> What guests were in her eyes which parted thence,
> As pearles from diamonds dropt. In briefe,
> Sorow would be a raritie most beloued,
> If all could so become it.[4]

Some editors give up every attempt to make sense of lines 20–1, while others think the words *like a better way* corrupt, and try to emend in various ways ("Were link'd a better way," "Were like a better day," "Were like a better May," "Were like a wetter May," "Were like an April day," "Were like a bridal day," "Were like a bettering day," etc. — see the much fuller list in the Cambridge edition). But no emendation is necessary if we notice that the speaker here is a courtier fond of an affectedly refined style of expression. It is impossible for him to speak plainly and naturally in the two small scenes where we meet with him (Act III, sc. i., and here); he is constantly on the look-out for new similes and delighting in unexpected words and phrases. This, then, is the way in which I should read the passage in question, changing only the punctuation:

> You have seene
> Sunshine and rain at once; her smiles and tears
> Were like —

[pronounced in a rising tone, and with a small pause after *like*; he is trying to find a beautiful comparison, but does not succeed to his own satisfaction, and therefore says to himself, "No, I will put it differently."]

> — a better way:

[I have now found the best way beautifully to paint in words what I saw in Cordelia's face:]

> those happy smilets
> That play'd on her ripe lip seem'd not to know
> What guests were in her eyes[5]

My chief object in writing this chapter has been to make the reader realize that language is not exactly what a one-sided occupation with dictionaries and the usual grammars might lead us to think, but a set of habits, of habitual actions, and that each word and each sentence spoken is a complex action on the part of the speaker. The greater part of these actions are determined by what he has done previously in similar situations, and that again was determined chiefly by what he had habitually heard from others. But in each individual instance, apart from mere formulas, the speaker has to turn these habits to account to meet a new situation, to express what has not been expressed previously in every minute detail; therefore he cannot be a mere slave to habits, but has to vary them to suit

---

[4]I have changed *streme* into the obvious *strove*, and *seeme* into *seemed*, besides putting full stops after *goodliest* and *dropt*. On these points there is a general consensus among editors.
[5]Abridged from my article in *A Book of Homage to Shakespeare*, 1916, p. 481 ff.

varying needs — and this in course of time may lead to new turns and new habits; in other words, to new grammatical forms and usages. Grammar thus becomes a part of linguistic psychology or psychological linguistics; this, however, is not the only way in which the study of grammar stands in need of reshaping and supplementing if it is to avoid the besetting sins of so many grammarians, pedantry and dogmatism.

On the Notion "Restructuring" in Historical Syntax

ELIZABETH CLOSS TRAUGOTT

Syntax has been a kind of waif in the development of generative historical linguistics — a rather interesting phenomenon considering the emphasis until recently on syntax in transformational theory. This is doubtless in part a function of the enormous quantity of material one has to look at to get any notion at all of the facts of syntactic change. But it may also have been in part a function of difficulties with the transformational model — most things one could say were related more to the model than to language change itself. Arguments turned to such questions as whether the deep structure could change; and answers to such questions hinged on ideas about whether the deep structure is universal or not, on whether there is intrinsic ordering within a deep structure rule, and so forth. Another problem was the fact that little could be said about syntactic change without making reference to semantics, but it was not clear what status the semantic information had in a model of language change, considering its interpretive status in the synchronic model. Lakoff (1968), for example, demonstrated that much syntactic development of complements in Spanish from earlier Latin was a function not of changes in the transformational rules, but of changes in redundancy rules, redundancy rules that specified the scope of items, and which were at least in part dependent on semantic classes, such as verbs of ordering, verbs of saying, thinking and so forth. Some very suggestive work on causes of syntactic change has been done by Bever and Langendoen, who argue that perceptual strategies, in particular avoidance of potential "pernicious ambiguity," are an important factor in syntactic change (1971). Again, the emphasis is on meaning. Nearly everywhere one looks in syntactic change, meaning seems to play a part. Indeed, it may be that there is no such thing as "pure syntactic change" such as the rule re-ordering Klima (1965) posits, where reference is made exclusively to syntactic rules, and not at all to either semantic or phonological factors.

Now that semantics has once more become respectable, perhaps some of the problems of diachronic syntax can be resolved. What we need is a model of language with a semantic base that is unordered but nevertheless hierarchized. (The hierarchy would indicate, for instance, that temporal terms imply locatives, but not necessarily vice versa.) In this model syntax is the prephonological manifestation of the underlying semantic structure. The model, furthermore, is a compe-

(paper presented by Elizabeth Closs Traugott at the XIth International Congress of Linguistics, Bologna, August 28th - September 2nd, 1972, and published in the *Proceedings*, Vol. I, ed. Luigi Heilmann, pp. 922–28. Reprinted, with minor emendations, by permission of the author and of the publisher.)

tence model of our internalized ability to use language in context, and also to change the language. It is therefore a kind of generative semantic model with a dynamic dimension.

The present paper does not attempt to solve the problem of how to treat diachronic syntax. Rather, it is an exploration which attempts to draw together some disparate points of view which I feel must be taken into consideration before the subject can be seriously approached.

The particular topics I wish to touch on are:

1. What does the notion "restructuring" mean with reference to syntactic change?
2. How does restructuring come about? What is its relation to the often-made distinction between simplification and elaboration?
3. What is the relation of restructuring to natural processes?
4. What might natural processes be in syntax?
5. What insights do natural processes give us into the development of pidgins and creoles?

The notion of restructuring

It has been customary to speak of restructuring versus innovative additions to the grammar. In phonology, this idea has sometimes been highly constrained. King, for example, contrasts "*primary change* (change in the rule component)" with "*restructuring* (change in underlying representation)" (1969:39). This strong kind of differentiation is not too useful in syntax since the underlying representation presumably does not change, whether it is a universal syntactic deep structure, or a universal semantactic set of logical predicates (provided it is indeed universal). We can, however, clearly make use of the weaker definition, considering restructuring as any modification that involves the reformulation of two or more rules or constraints; and we can contrast it with the addition or modification of one rule or constraint that has no consequences elsewhere in the syntax.

For example, loss of cases in English clearly involves restructuring as it affects all the rules that have to do with specifying word-order, the function of prepositions, and the abstract markers of case. Anything that involves change of status in cyclical rules is also restructuring, but rules that come in, of the sort sometimes called "shallow structure" might not qualify as examples of restructuring — though one could well expect that such rules could change status and become fully integrated into the system.

How does restructuring come about; what is its relation to simplification and elaboration?

Generativists have on the whole accepted the principles laid down by Halle that restructuring, when it occurs, is largely brought about by children; hardly at all by adults: "a wholesale restructuring of his grammar is beyond the capabilities of the average adult'' (1962:64). Coupled with this hypothesis was another one carried over from the nineteenth century — that simplification, when it occurs, is brought about by children; adults only elaborate. Some linguists have taken these statements to be axiomatic, rather than empirical claims; furthermore, they have tended to view restructuring characteristically as simplification, innovation characteristically as elaboration. We need to keep an open mind about these inter-relationships if we are to get a clear idea of what is going on.

One way of getting at the problem is to reconsider simplification and elaboration. In the early days of generative diachronic studies, roughly the second half of the 60's, a great deal of work was done to prove that the main type of change was simplification. Simplification was demonstrated by means of comparing grammars called G_1 and G_2, G_1 being the adult's grammar, and G_2 being typically the child's (or later generation's) grammar at the stage when the child has virtually acquired its adult system. Outstanding work in this area was done by Kiparsky (especially 1965, 1968). But recently people have been calling the theory of simplification into question. I myself have claimed that at least in syntax the direction of change may well be elaboration (1969). A considerable number of people have been claiming similar things for phonological change, especially at the Chicago Meetings (e.g. Darden [1970] and Stampe [1969] who explicitly cite rule loss as rule blocking; depending on what general theory of language one holds, blocking may be regarded either as constraint, or as failure to add a constraint, but certainly not the simplification Kiparsky considered it to be).

My hypothesis is essentially this: simplification is a term that applies to comparative linguistics. If I compare G_1 and G_2 assuming G_1 is (a) prior to G_2 and (b) used by a different, presumably older speaker than G_2, then I may be able to say that G_2 is simpler than G_1. If G_1 and G_2 are far enough apart in time, say a generation or more, it is possible that G_2 will be simpler in certain respects. Nevertheless, it is questionable whether greater over-all systematic simplicity will be found, supposing, that is, one could test such a thing. Simplicity is obviously a function of what we compare. Middle Middle English was simpler than Early Middle English with respect to morphological case; but with respect to phrasal structures and word order it was more constrained, that is, less simple. Languages somehow balance themselves, and it is extremely questionable whether the balancing comes about solely or even primarily as a result of adult innovations. What we need is a theory that accounts adequately for this ability to balance in systematic, and it turns out often predictable, ways. The notion of simplification as the chief type of change does not answer satisfactorily to this problem especially when tied to the hypothesis that children simplify by restructuring, which is by definition systematic, but adults mainly elaborate by adding innovations that are by definition largely or completely non-systematic.

Doing comparative studies of adult G_1's and nearly adult G_2's is only one way of looking at historical linguistics and types of language change. Another way is to consider what goes on ontogenetically in the development of G_2 before the incipient adult stage, that is, in grammar construction before adulthood. In fact, if we were to take seriously the claim that children restructure we should immediately see something wrong with equating restructuring with simplification.

We must keep clearly in mind what we have always known but sometimes seem conveniently to forget — children do not restructure anybody else's grammar. They construct grammars, and as they do so their own grammar is restructured on the basis of their own system, of other people's output, and of universal principles. Andersen has pointed to the importance of these three sources of grammar-making in his studies of deductive and abductive change (1969, 1973). In addition children use perceptual strategies (Bever and Langendoen 1971; Kiparsky 1971; Slobin 1971) and, I shall argue, natural processes. In their first few years children make successive sets of radically different hypotheses, many of them more elaborate than those that preceded them; they expand their language-specific grammars and add constraints to them; after ten or so they do little but refine their already formulated grammar. As Chomsky (1969) and many others have shown, one can predict the order of entry of certain structures. Interesting questions arise about possible dependencies within the ordering, such that development of structure B may be dependent on the prior acquisition of structure A. For example, surface tense, and probably perception of a time-line, seem to be dependent on prior acquisition of aspect and the concept of temporal contour, and these are both dependent on perception of deixis or orientation from the moment of utterance (Ferreiro and Sinclair 1971; Sinclair 1971; Kurylowicz 1972). Similarly, Clark (1972) has demonstrated clear dependencies in the acquisition of locative terms like *in*, *on*, and *under*. In a recent study of the acquisition of causatives in English, Baron (1972) has suggested that the acquisition of causative *have* depends on prior acquisition of locative and possessive *have*, most particularly, of future possessive constructions such as *The girl will have her shoes polished*. What we also need is studies of possessive or causative expression, rather than of lexically-bound ones, but I would predict similar sorts of dependencies. Dependency might well explain why so much happens in such rapid succession developmentally, and why radically new hypotheses tend to reduce in number through the years. Acquisitional dependencies do not necessarily explain diachronic dependencies, but there certainly are interesting correlations. Benveniste (1968) has discussed the same type of dependencies in the diachronic development of *habere* in Latin as Baron found in the acquisitional material; the same sort of development occurred in the history of English. Language change does not always recapitulate language acquisition, but the parallels are too frequent to be ignored. Any account of language change must take them into consideration and therefore cannot be limited to comparative studies; it must also take ontogeny into account; if it does, simplification will no longer be considered the unmarked type of change.

It should be clear by now that simplification and elaboration are essentially properties of the language description, that is, of the metatheory, not of what a child or anyone else does. Restructuring too is nothing but a property of the metatheory — something we can say is the end-result of some process when we compare either two different generations' grammars, or different stages of the same person's grammar. Furthermore, restructuring cannot be equated with simplification; instead, it is the metatheoretic rule-change, along with its implications for the rest of the grammar, that is taken into account when one determines what is simplified on the one hand, what elaborated on the other.

What is the relation of restructuring to natural processes?

What I have said should sound familiar — it is much inspired by, though not exactly similar to, Stampe's view of natural processes as what actually occur in language acquisition and language change, as opposed to simplification, elaboration, markedness and so forth, which are functions of a linguist's grammatical description.

Stampe has argued that children are born with certain innate processes that would eventually lead them to simplify their phonology to "verbal pabulum" if unhindered. A child's task in acquiring the adult system is "to revise all aspects of the system which separate his pronunciation from the standard," and revision involves "suppression, limitation, and ordering" (1969:44). What is suppression, limitation, and ordering but the opposite of generalization? It is the development of constraints, the result of which is what linguists call elaboration. Phonetic change, Stampe points out, happens when children fail to suppress, order, and limit, and such failure often results in what I am calling comparative simplification; the failure is in itself, however, not a simplification, nor for that matter elaboration. Ontogenetically, nothing has happened.

Most linguists interested in natural processes have concerned themselves with phonology. Since natural processes are constraints on expressibility, phonologists have concentrated on articulatory phenomena, for example on claims such as: obstruents tend to be devoiced because of the oral constriction involved in pronunciation; but they also tend to assimilate to their surroundings, so a child has to resolve the conflict of the tendencies in intervocalic and similar "voicing" positions (Stampe 1969). It is, of course, an empirical issue whether non-phonological change has any resemblance to phonological change. It would certainly be a very interesting claim to say there is no resemblance. Having, however, seen no obvious proof of that claim, I take the weaker position that change is generalizable to the whole linguistic system, and therefore, if it is valid to talk about natural phonological processes, it should be valid to talk about natural syntactic ones too. Like phonological processes, they could be determined from evidence provided by language acquisition, typologies of language change, dialect variation, and so forth.

What are the kinds of natural processes that one can postulate with reference to syntax?

In syntax, as in phonology, natural processes involve constraints on expressibility, in this instance on the manifestation of unordered cognitive structures in an ordered, time-limited sequence. One kind of syntactic process, I hypothesize, is "segmentalization," the process of giving analytic or phrasal expression to underlying structures, including the functions of case, tense, mood, aspect, nominal classifiers, and so forth. This tendency is clearly manifested in language acquisition. To cite one personal example: my daughter, at the age of two and a half, consistently used *already* for past, presumably completed, action: *I already go, I already sleep*. This kind of segmentalization is also well known in a great number of languages. In the Indo-European group, and elsewhere, it seems to be interestingly heirarchized — mood is most typically segmentalized, aspect fairly often, tense not extensively (the discrepancies between aspect and tense segmentalization, incidentally, cast serious doubt on the hypothesis [McCawley 1971] that perfect is past embedded in present). There has been over a century of heated debate on the relation between analytic and synthetic languages. Only recently, Reighard once more suggested that there is an analytic-to-synthetic cycle (1971). The debate about the cyclic or non-cyclic nature of the change, or about which comes first seems to me to be centered on results, that is, on metatheoretic issues, not on natural processes. Reighard suggests that inflections may be lost because "as languages change, they prefer surface structures which allow separate representations of deep structure constituents. That is, attachment transformations get lost because they associate on the surface what is distinct in deep structure" (1971; 514). While much of what Reighard says is extremely valuable, especially what he says about the naturalness of pidgins and creoles, this particular kind of metaphorical language is very dangerous. I am sure he does not really believe grammars prefer certain states; nevertheless, his language could lead to an organic view of change that is patently unacceptable. It certainly leads to the idea of contradictory *syntactic* processes (loss or addition of attachment transformations). One thing suspicious about this is that it fails to explain why segmentalization involves phonologically unrelated forms in phrasal constructions — *comperivit* "he has understood" is eventually replaced by *compertum habet* — whereas desegmentalization involves phonologically related forms: *venire habes* "you have to come" is eventually replaced by *viendras* (Benveniste 1968). I would suggest that there is one consistent natural syntactic process involved in the segmentalization of tense, mood, and aspect, which lays out underlying structures in a sequence of morphemes, very largely in phrasal form. This should not be very surprising to anyone who argues for atomic predicates in the base; it seems, for example, to be implicit in Givón's work on syntactic change in Bantu and other languages (1971). There is also a consistent natural phonological process of syllable reduction which counteracts the syntactic segmentalization process and leads to the development of synthetic inflection. The cycle then is only the apparent result of certain processes. In any time span a cycle may appear to be operating, but in fact the processes are simultaneous, although presumably at one time one is dominant, at another time the other; exactly what motivates this change in dominance is an interesting question. It must presumably be bound up with conflicting tendencies between universals of language (which are constraints on language), natural processes (which are constraints on expressibility), and perceptual strategies (which are constraints on learnability); and furthermore it is bound up with systems of variables and movements toward maxima of systematic differentiation, and with varying types and degrees of external social pressure (Weinreich, Labov and Herzog 1968; Bailey, 1973).

What is the relation of natural processes to the development of pidgins and creoles?

Before closing, I would like to make another suggestion. I suspect that a lot of what has been said about pidgins and creoles being odd kinds of languages stems from confusions about simplification and elaboration of the type discussed above. And furthermore, I suspect that pidgins and creoles may tell us as much as language acquisition about natural processes. (By pidgins I mean non-native languages, by creoles native ones.)

Most linguists would probably no longer treat pidgins and creoles as non-languages, as deviations or "corruptions." Nevertheless, many are still clearly hesitant about exactly what they think their status is since it appears to them that pidgins, which are learned by adults, simplify, but creoles, which are developed by the adults' children, elaborate at remarkable speed — both violations of the Halle-Kiparsky principles. Let us reconsider the problem in the light of the proposals in this paper. Consider the typical pidgin situation as described by Whinnom (1971), for example a French trader and a Yoruba speaker. Each has native control over his own language. They meet, and if the right conditions prevail, they will speak a pidgin based on a language largely foreign to both, say English pidgin. This pidgin will clearly be grossly simpler than either French or Yoruba if compared to either. Nevertheless, in terms of the individual speakers, the pidgin is an addition to their system, hence can be viewed at least in part as an elaboration. It is not something entirely foreign to them, suggesting a change resulting in a sudden restructuring of the kind adults are not supposed to be able to make, but it is a grammar constructed on the basis of the speaker's native language, the addressee's output, and learned hypotheses about the pidgin. If we are ever to explain the similarities between pidgins in vastly different areas of the world, not even remotely subject to Portuguese influence, we have to refer to certain kinds of principles. It seems likely that we must hypothesize that there are certain universal natural processes at work. Samarin, indeed, has spoken of "universal intuitive notions of simplification" (1971:126); Ferguson, too, posits a "universal simplification process" to account for the remarkable similarities among distant pidgins and creoles, with special reference to the copula (1971:148). Both are referring to simplification as evidenced by comparative studies. I would like to suggest that what is happening is a partial return to innate natural processes; to this extent it is a return to a syntactically less constrained, hence a simpler system, similar to the one the speaker may once have had himself as a child; lexically, however, new constraints are being added. The high variability of pidgins could perhaps be partially accounted for in terms of the problem of returning to earlier processes that have been suppressed. All that is different, in this view, from normal adult language behavior is the utilization of natural processes usually blocked and constrained in various ways. And perhaps this revitalization will not seem so unfamiliar in everyday behavior when we consider the various kinds of so-called simplification we all use, with different sets of constraints, in varieties of speech like baby-talk and foreigner-talk, all through our lives. Of course, such a claim as this can only stand if there is evidence that pidgins show us the same types of processes as occur in language acquisition, or that pidgins in some sense reflect "basic universals." So far not enough has been done to either prove or disprove this hypothesis, though it is clear from a preliminary survey that the same sorts of segmentalization of tense, mood, and aspect occur in pidgins as in language acquisition and language change, and that they are hierarchized in similar ways — mood is most likely to be given surface expression, tense least likely, while aspect takes the middle position.

Creoles, too, can be thought of as following normal diachronic and acquisitional trends. Let us not forget that in some sense a child's language is, like a creole, a socially subordinate system moving toward a superordinate one. As I have said, children naturally constrain their own grammars and tend to develop total systems only insignificantly simpler or more elaborate than anybody else's. First or second generation creoles *do* seem, however, to elaborate extraordinarily fast; the question remains: Why? It is a characteristic of creoles to develop inflections and other phonologically reduced forms very rapidly, and also to develop more and more surface syntactic categories. A reasonable hypothesis for explaining this is that the different kinds of phonological and syntactic processes mentioned earlier are at work, leading to phonological desegmentalization and syntactic segmentalization at the same time. If so, what is going on ontogenetically is failure to block natural processes — exactly what we would expect when the input is a combination of a language as limited in surface representations as a pidgin, with the child's own hypotheses, universal natural processes, and perceptual strategies, and when there is little or no adult linguistic tradition to approximate to (for some recent discussions of the development of pidgins from creoles see Labov 1971; Kay and Sankoff, 1974; Sankoff and Laberge 1974).

In conclusion, any study of language must take all three dimensions — synchronic, diachronic, and acquisitional — into account and must touch on cognition, natural processes and perceptual strategies. This does not mean that synchrony, diachrony, and acquisition are the same thing; rather, it means that there is a heavy constraint on grammars of all types that the rules established are possible from each point of view, and not abstractions based on one point of view alone. Only then will we begin to be able to give a truly explanatory account of linguistic competence in general, and of the competence to restructure in particular.

REFERENCES

ANDERSEN, H. 1969. A Study in diachronic morphophonemics: the Ukrainian prefixes. *Language* 45: 807–830.

————. (1973). Abductive and deductive change. *Language* 49:765–793.

BAILEY, C. J. N. (1973). The patterning of language variation. In R. W. Bailey and J. L. Robinson, eds., *Varieties of present-day American English*. New York: Macmillan.

BARON, N. 1972. Language acquisition's role in diachrony. Paper given at the Second California Linguistics Conference, UCLA, May 1972.

BENVENISTE, E. 1968. Mutations of linguistic categories. In W. P. Lehmann and Y. Malkiel, eds., *Directions for historical linguistics*. Austin: University of Texas Press.

BEVER, T. G. AND D. T. LANGENDOEN. 1971. A dynamic model of the evolution of language. *Linguistic Inquiry* 2: 433–64.

CHOMSKY, C. 1969. *The acquisition of syntax in children from 5 to 10*. Cambridge, Mass.: MIT Press.

CLARK, E. V. 1972. Some perceptual factors in the acquisition of locative terms by young children. In *Papers from the eighth regional meeting of the Chicago Linguistic Society*.

DARDEN, B. J. 1970. The fronting of vowels after palatals in Slavic. *In Papers from the sixth regional meeting of the Chicago Linguistic Society*.

FERGUSON, C. A. 1971. Absence of copula and the notion of simplicity: a study of normal speech, baby talk, foreigner talk, and pidgins. In D. Hymes, ed., *Pidginization and creolization of languages*. London: Cambridge Univ. Press.

FERREIRO, E. AND H. SINCLAIR. 1971. Temporal relations in language. *International Journal of Psychology* 6:39–47.

GIVÓN, T. 1971. Historical syntax and synchronic morphology: an archaeologist's field trip. In *Papers from the seventh regional meeting of the Chicago Linguistic Society*.

HALLE, M. 1962. Phonology in a generative grammar. *Word* 18: 54–72.

KAY, P. AND G. SANKOFF. (1974). A language-universals approach to pidgins and creoles. In D. DeCamp and I. A. Hancock, eds., *Pidgins and creoles: current trends and prospects*. Georgetown University Press.

KING, R. D. 1969. *Historical linguistics and generative grammar*. Englewood Cliffs, N.J.: Prentice-Hall.

KIPARSKY, P. 1965. Phonological change. Ph.D. dissertation, MIT.

_____. 1968. Linguistic universals and linguistic change. In E. Bach and R. T. Harms, eds., *Universals in linguistic theory*. New York: Holt, Rinehart & Winston.

_____. 1971. Historical linguistics. In W. O. Dingwall, ed., *A survey of linguistic science*. Linguistics Program, University of Maryland.

KLIMA, E. 1965. Studies in diachronic syntax. Ph.D. dissertation, Harvard University.

KURYLOWICZ, J. 1972. The role of deictic elements in linguistic evolution. *Semiotica* 5: 174–83.

LABOV, W. 1971. On the adequacy of natural languages. I. The development of tense. Mimeo.

LAKOFF, R. 1968. *Abstract syntax and Latin complementation*. Cambridge, Mass.: MIT Press.

MCCAWLEY, J. D. 1971. Tense and time reference in English. In C. J. Fillmore and D. T. Langendoen, eds., *Studies in linguistic semantics*. New York: Holt, Rinehart & Winston.

REIGHARD, J. 1971. Some observations on syntactic change in verbs. In *Papers from the seventh regional meeting of the Chicago Linguistic Society*.

SAMARIN, W. 1971. Salient and substantive pidginization. In D. Hymes, ed., *Pidginization and creolization of languages*. London: Cambridge Univ. Press.

SANKOFF, G. AND S. LABERGE. 1974. On the acquisition of native speakers by a language. In D. DeCamp and I. A. Hancock, eds., *Pidgins and creoles: current trends and prospects*. Georgetown University Press.

SINCLAIR, H. 1971. Acquisition of language, linguistic theory and epistemology. Paper presented to Centre nationale de recherche scientifique, December 1971.

SLOBIN, D. 1971. Developmental psycholinguistics. In W. O. Dingwall, ed., *A survey of linguistic science*. Linguistics Program, University of Maryland.

STAMPE, D. 1969. The acquisition of phonetic representations, in R. I. Binnick et al., eds., *Papers from the fifth regional meeting of the Chicago Linguistic Society*.

_____. (forthcoming). On Chapter nine, part of a review of N. Chomsky and M. Halle, *The sound pattern of English*, by J. D. McCawley and D. Stampe, to appear in *IJAL*.

TRAUGOTT, E. C. 1969. Toward a theory of syntactic change. *Lingua* 23: 1–27.

TRAUGOTT, E. C. 1974. "Explorations in linguistic elaboration: language change, language acquisition, and the genesis of spatio-temporal terms," in J. M. Anderson and C. Jones, eds., *Proceedings of the First International Conference on Historical Linguistics*, September, 1973. North-Holland, Vol. I.

WEINREICH, U., W. LABOV, AND M. HERZOG. 1968. Empirical foundations for a theory of language change. In W. P. Lehmann and Y. Malkiel, eds. *Directions for historical linguistics*. Austin: Univ. of Texas Press.

WHINNOM, K. 1971. Linguistic hybridization and the "special case" of pidgins and creoles. In D. Hymes, ed., *Pidginization and creolization of languages*. London: Cambridge Univ. Press.

4 DESCRIPTIVE GRAMMAR

Although the language of a speech community is constantly undergoing change, the process is slow and usually is not perceptible to the speakers. If one examines a language during a relatively short period of time, it will appear to be a relatively stable system. Descriptive linguists wish to examine that system as it is perceived and employed by its users. Therefore, they do not consider historical changes or impose abstract theoretical categories, but try to arrive inductively at a description of the language in its own terms.

Ferdinand de Saussure was the great theoretician of the new movement of descriptive linguistics, and the first to set it apart from historical linguistics as a separate branch of study. He sharply distinguished between diachronic and synchronic studies. He believed that if one examined a language during a sufficiently short period of time, change would be so minimal that it could be disregarded, and one would be able to capture a "language state." Language states of different periods could then be related in diachronic or historical studies. Trying to do synchronic and diachronic studies simultaneously merely resulted in confusion. In Chapter III of the *Course in General Linguistics* (1916), he discusses the difficulty of determining the precise object of linguistics. Taken as a whole, speech is a many-sided, heterogeneous phenomenon that appears to have infinite variety. Yet beneath that variety is a complex, arbitrary system imposed upon the individual by society. De Saussure uses the term "la parole" for the speech of the individual and "la langue" for the underlying system, a collection of social conventions that allows individuals to communicate. It exists in the form of a sum of impressions deposited in the brain of each member of a speech community, almost like an internalized dictionary. "La langue" is the proper object of linguistic study since it contains regular patterns.

A language system is made up of linguistic signs, which are links between sounds (or the written forms that symbolize them) and meanings. De Saussure emphasizes the two-sided nature of linguistic signs; sounds alone are not significant. The method proposed for discovering signs is segmentation of the language into minimum units of sound (called phonemes) and meaning (called signs). De Saussure used the term "syntagm" for a linear sequence of signs.

De Saussure deals with language primarily at the word level. Words are broken up into simple signs or minimum units of meaning. He analyzes simple words, suffixes, prefixes, complex words, associative patterns among words (called paradigms), and syntagmatic or linear relationships. He omits most sentences from the realm of "la langue" and considers them to be part of "la parole" because he believed that they failed to meet the criterion of patterning: "If we picture to ourselves in their totality the sentences that could be uttered, their most striking characteristic is that in no way do they resemble each other."[1] The main method proposed for gathering data is introspection. This shows de Saussure's reliance on deduction. Although most descriptivists did not follow his method, it was a fruitful technique for him. Rulon Wells has pointed out that de Saussure's weaving of the general facts of linguistics into a fabric of premises and consequences was a method of discovery that led to many of his insights.[2]

De Saussure's theoretical bent was shared by Edward Sapir. In the introduction to *Language* (1921), Sapir states that he is concerned not with the concrete mechanisms and physical production of speech, but with the "function and form of the arbitrary systems of symbolism that we term languages."[3] Sapir was particularly interested in the psychological foundations of language. Even when dealing with phonology, the most physical aspect of language, he focuses on psychological tendencies. He states that in back of the purely objective system of sounds,

> there is a more restricted "inner" or "ideal" system which, while perhaps equally unconscious as a system to the naïve speaker, can far more readily than the other be brought to his consciousness as a finished pattern, a psychological mechanism. The inner sound system, overlaid though it may be by the mechanical or the irrelevant, is a real and an immensely important principle in the life of a language. It may persist as a pattern, involving number, relation, and functioning of phonetic elements, long after its phonetic content is changed.[4]

Sapir's view regarding an underlying phonological structure resembles the treatment of phonology that has been adopted in transformational grammar.

Sapir sees grammar as the result of the psychological tendency toward patterning and economy of expression. It is convenient to express analogous concepts in analogous forms. Yet no language is perfectly logical or consistent: "All

[1]Ferdinand de Saussure, *Course in General Linguistics*, trans. Wade Baskin (N.Y.: Philosophical Library, 1959), p. 106.

[2]Rulon Wells, "De Saussure's System of Linguistics," *Word*, 3 (1947), 25.

[3]Edward Sapir, *Language* (N.Y.: Harcourt, 1921), p. 11.

[4]Ibid., p. 55.

grammars leak."[5] Sapir's discussion of grammatical processes in Chapter 4 of *Language* shows both the irregular and regular nature of language. To a certain extent, languages are arbitrary, illogical, and idiosyncratic. There is no necessary relation between form and function, not even in the same language. For example, English expresses the negative idea by means of a prefix in "*un*kind" but by means of a suffix in "thought*less*." In order to illustrate the independence of form and function, he cites examples of multiple expressions of identical functions in a large number of European, Asian, and American Indian languages.

Nevertheless, he believes that all languages reveal a similar feeling for form, even though they tend to develop one or more grammatical processes at the expense of others. The basic grammatical processes are: word order, composition, affixation (including the use of prefixes, suffixes, and infixes), internal modification of the radical or root element, reduplication, and accentual differences in stress or pitch. Sapir analyzes the psychological bases of composition (the uniting into a single word of two or more radical elements), and reduplication (the repetition of all or part of the radical element). Sapir treats each language in its own terms and rejects classifications of words that are not based on form:

> A part of speech outside of the limitations of syntactic form is but a will o' the wisp. For this reason no logical scheme of the parts of speech — their number, nature, and necessary confines — is of the slightest interest to the linguist. Each language has its own scheme.[6]

Yet he believed that there were universal categories in languages, such as noun and verb, and that languages may share the same "great underlying ground plans."[7] These views are closer to those of the transformational grammarians than to those of most of the descriptivists of Sapir's time.

Theorizing about psychological tendencies and universal elements of language was rejected by Leonard Bloomfield. In the first chapter of *Language* (1933), he affirms: "The only useful generalizations about language are inductive generalizations. Features which we think ought to be universal may be absent from the very next language that becomes accessible."[8] Bloomfield wanted to turn linguistics into a rigorous science and confine the linguist to objective, measurable data in his investigations. When he referred to psychology in his later work, he used a behavioristic stimulus-response model, as in Chapter II of *Language*. According to this theory, all human mental processes are the result of external stimuli and bodily processes, either within the past or present. This is why he gives so much attention to physical phenomena in his analysis of an imagined act of speech. He demonstrates how the individual who receives a physical stimulus can get another person to fill his or her needs through a speech

---

[5]Ibid., p. 38.
[6]Ibid., p. 118–119.
[7]Ibid., p. 144.
[8]Leonard Bloomfield, *Language* (N.Y.: Holt, 1933), p. 20.

signal. This brings about the possibility of division of labor and cooperation in a human community.

Bloomfield also uses a stimulus-response model to account for language learning, emphasizing the role of habit and repetition. This is the weakest part of his theory since most of the sentences a person utters, even those of a young child, have never been heard before. He admits that the stimulus-response model does not explain very much about language but still believes that the linguist "must proceed exactly as if he held the materialistic view."[9]

Bloomfield considered the meaning of a speech utterance to be a combination of all the practical events preceding and following it. Since he defined meaning so broadly, it can be seen why he found it difficult to deal with. However, he recognized the role meaning plays in identifying the distinctive features of a language. In practical terms, he believed in referring to meaning as little as possible.

His discussion of the phoneme in Chapter V of *Language* demonstrates the necessity of allowing meaning into the picture. The study of language can be conducted without any reference to meaning only in the realm of phonetics or the physical measurement of speech sounds. As soon as we try to discover the speech sounds that are distinctive or functional in a language, we must have recourse to meaning. Distinctive features are the ones that are heard as "different" by speakers of a language, thereby functioning to signal differences in meaning. Bloomfield defines a phoneme as "a minimum unit of distinctive sound-feature." We can discover phonemes by contrasting words with ones that have similar sounds and altering parts of the word. For example, the [p] in *pin* is a phoneme since changing the first sound creates a new word (*fin, sin, tin*); the same is true of [i] and [n] (*pan, pen; pit, pig*). However, the different varieties of [p] that are pronounced in *pin, spin*, and *tip* are not phonemes in English since replacing one type of [p] with another will not result in a different word. Variants of a phoneme later came to be called "allophones."

Bloomfield believed that a description of a language should begin with phonology, including a list of phonemes and the combinations that occur. He considered vowels and consonants as the primary phonemes of English, stress and pitch as secondary. When the phonology of a language has been established, it is necessary to determine what meanings are attached to the phonetic forms. This phase of the description is called semantics, which includes grammar and the lexicon or dictionary. Grammar is defined as the "meaningful arrangements of forms in a language."[10] Within the field of grammar, he distinguishes between morphology and syntax, with the word as boundary. Morphology deals with constructions at the word level and below, whereas syntax deals with phrases and sentences. The morpheme is the minimum unit of meaning. It is defined as a simple linguistic form that "bears no partial phonetic-semantic resemblance to any other form" (*bird, play, -y*, and *-ing* are given as examples).[11]

[9]Ibid., p. 38.
[10]Ibid., p. 163.
[11]Ibid., p. 161.

Morphemes include free forms or words, and bound forms or prefixes and suffixes. A morphological description shows the way in which morphemes combine to form words.

Syntax deals with the manner in which words combine to form phrases. Bloomfield uses a method called *immediate constituent analysis*. Phrases and words are successively divided into immediate constituents until one arrives at the ultimate constituents or morphemes. Each division involves separating the construction into two parts. For example, the sentence "Poor John ran away" is divided as follows:

```
Poor John / ran away
poor / John
ran / away
a / way
```

The ultimate constituents are *poor, John, ran, a-, way*. Syntactic constructions are those in which none of the immediate constituents are in a bound form (all of the above examples would be syntactic constructions except "a / way"). Many of these concepts regarding phonology, morphology, and syntax were developed further by Bloomfield's followers.

Post-Bloomfieldian descriptivists tried to be even more objective and rigorous in their formulations and to get entirely away from reference to meaning.[12] Many of them considered grammar to be an autonomous set of patterns that was susceptible to analysis as though it had nothing to do with meaning; grammar was completely separated from semantics. The assumptions and procedures that had been fruitful in dealing with phonology were applied to grammar. Just as phonemes were considered the minimal elements in phonology, morphemes were called the minimal elements in grammar. Just as phonemes could appear in the guise of several allophones, morphemes were said to vary in shape. The term "allomorph" was proposed by Charles Hockett for morpheme alternants.[13] Examples of morpheme alternants are the irregular plurals for English nouns (men, mice, feet, oxen, children), which were classified as allomorphs of the plural {s} morpheme. The model of grammar was based on the one that had been designed for a phonological system.

All of these developments are exemplified by the *Outline of English Structure* by George L. Trager and Henry L. Smith, Jr. Hockett has stated that the watchword of the 1940's was *rigor*: "Precision of statement was far more important to us than whether anyone could understand us."[14] This comment may help to explain the style of the *Outline*. It is a detailed, technical description of English phonology and morphology written in a style that is "rigorous" but hard to read. Trager and Smith begin with an analysis of the phonology of American

---

[12]Charles F. Hockett, *The State of the Art* (The Hague: Mouton, 1968), pp. 24–29.
[13]Ibid., p. 28.
[14]Ibid., p. 27.

English, including a description of the allophones that exist in the various dialects: they list 9 vowel phonemes, 24 consonants, 4 degrees of stress, 4 levels of pitch, and 4 types of juncture, that is, degree of separation. The techniques that were applied to phonology are then applied to morphology: inspection of the data, substitution of items within a frame, and investigation of patterns of complementary distribution (variants of a morpheme are said to be in complementary distribution if they do not occur in the same environment; for example, if -en is a variant of the plural morpheme in English, we should expect to find *oxen* but not *oxes*. Each word takes only one form of the morpheme). Variants of a morpheme do not necessarily have phonetic similarity, as with the -en and -s plurals (i.e., *oxen, horses*). A morpheme is said to be "zero phonemically" when it does not appear in a word in the usual inflectional pattern, as with the plural forms *sheep* and *deer*, which are the same as the singular. *Morphophonemics* involves describing all the forms of the morphemes of a language, which are listed in a *lexicon* (corresponding to the dictionary). A statement of the sequences of morphemes that occur is called an *arrangement*; sequences that occur at the word level are dealt with under morphology, whereas those that include more than one word are considered under syntax.

Trager and Smith use the term grammar to cover phonology, morphology, and syntax, and insist on the separation of levels. Analysis at each level should be conducted without reference to meaning. Although it is convenient to refer to meaning as a shortcut, the theoretical basis of analysis should be the recognition of distributional patterns without recourse to meaning. Trager and Smith tried to establish their entire analysis, including syntax, on an objective, phonologic basis.

Subsequent experiments, particularly those conducted by Philip Lieberman, have shown that syntactic and semantic information influences what is heard. In conducting tests with trained linguists, Lieberman found that transcriptions varied by fifty percent when they heard a pure physical signal as opposed to the words of a sentence. When the linguists heard the complete speech signal, they were able to transcribe four degrees of stress. However, when they heard fixed vowels modulated with the fundamental frequency and amplitude contours of the original speech signal, they were unable to transcribe accurately more than two degrees of stress. Only seven percent of the secondary stresses and none of the tertiary stresses that were transcribed for the complete speech signal were transcribed under these conditions.[15] This experiment suggests that syntax influences phonology more than phonology influences syntax. Syntactic and semantic features help to determine what we hear.

In *The Structure of English*, Charles C. Fries attempts to provide a description of English grammar based on form and structure. His analysis is based on over 250,000 words of mechanically recorded telephone conversations that had

[15]Philip Lieberman, "On the Acoustic Basis of the Perception of Intonation by Linguists," *Word*, 21 (1965), 40–54.

taken place in a Midwestern college community. Throughout his book, he emphasizes the inability of traditional grammar, with its meaning-based definitions, to account for the patterns of the living language: "The more one works with the records of the actual speech of people, the more impossible it appears to describe the requirements of English sentences in terms of meaning content."[16] Consequently, he adopts Leonard Bloomfield's definition of a sentence, which has no reference to meaning: "It is evident that the sentences in any utterance are marked off by the mere fact that each sentence is an independent linguistic form, not included by virtue of any grammatical construction in any larger linguistic form."[17]

Fries does not exclude meaning from his analysis: "As a general principle I would insist that, in linguistic study and analysis, any use of meaning is unscientific whenever the fact of our knowing the meaning leads us to stop short of finding the precise formal signals that operate to convey that meaning."[18] Meaning should be consulted after there has been a thorough analysis of form and structure.

Fries distinguishes between the lexical meaning of an utterance, which consists of the definitions of separate words as a dictionary would record them, and the structural meaning, which consists of the information that is contributed by morphological and syntactic forms and patterns. The devices that signal structural meanings constitute the grammar of a language. The difference between the two kinds of meaning can be illustrated effectively by the use of nonsense words, as in "Jabberwocky" from *Through the Looking Glass*: "Somehow [said Alice], it seems to fill my head with ideas — only I don't exactly know what they are!"[19] The ideas that filled her head were the structure signals set up by the poem. Structure signals such as articles, word endings, and word order identify words as adjectives, nouns, and verbs even when their lexical meaning is not known.

Fries believes that a description of a language should begin with structure and form. He criticizes the procedure of traditional grammar, which starts with the total meaning of a sentence and then assigns names to parts of it (i.e., noun, verb, adjective, etc.). The definitions of the parts of speech are vague and slide from meaning (a noun is a name of a person, place, or thing) to function (an adjective modifies a noun). Furthermore, the definitions are not applied consistently. For example, *blue, yellow*, and *red* are names of colors, yet in the expressions *a blue tie, a yellow rose*, and *a red dress*, the color words are classified as adjectives because they "modify" nouns. Since the definitions of the noun and the adjective are not parallel but are based on meaning in one case and function in the other, a conflict arises. If classification is to be adequate, definitions must be

[16]Charles C. Fries, *The Structure of English* (N.Y.: Harcourt, 1952), p. 19.
[17]Bloomfield, *Language*, p. 170.
[18]Fries, *The Structure of English*, p. 8.
[19]Ibid., p. 70.

based on the same kind of criteria. Grammarians have always used formal criteria as well as the definitions. Fries proposes using formal criteria alone.

He constructs a series of simple sentences that serve as test frames, enabling him to classify the words that appear in his data through a process of substitution. In order to get away from traditional associations, he uses numbers rather than names to label the form classes of words. He identifies four major form classes (1 = nouns, 2 = verbs, 3 = adjectives, 4 = adverbs), which he calls parts of speech, and fifteen groups of function words. The function words belong to closed, limited classes, but they occur very frequently; among them are Group A, determiners (the, a / an, this / these, that / those, both, every, few, your, our, his, one, two), and Group B, auxiliaries (may, can, will, would, shall, should, must, have). The meaning of these words is primarily in the grammatical functions they express. They also serve as structure signals that identify the major form classes. For instance, determiners signal nouns, whereas auxiliaries come before main verbs.

Fries identifies the basic sentence patterns of English by examining the formal arrangements of words. He shows that sentence functions such as subject, direct object, indirect object, object complement, and predicate nominative are signaled by formal contrasts, primarily contrasts in arrangements of word order. He uses a series of sentence formulas to illustrate his point.[20] For example, the following sentence includes the functions of subject and predicate nominative:

(D = determiner, 1 = noun, 2b = verb of the "be" class, the letter exponent = whether the referents of two Class 1 words are the same or different)

$$D \quad 1^a \quad 2^b \quad D \quad 1^a$$

That woman is my teacher.

The next sentence includes the functions of subject and direct object:

(2d = a verb in the past tense or past participle form)

$$D \quad 1^a \quad 2d \quad D \quad 1^b$$

The dean approved the recommendations.

Fries shows that sentence functions such as subject, predicate nominative, and object can be identified by patterns of arrangement without reference to meaning.

In order to determine the levels of structure within the sentence, he uses immediate constituent analysis.[21] This process involves successive division of

[20]Ibid., pp. 189–201.
[21]Ibid., pp. 256–73.

parts of the sentence into two components. For example, the sentence "The recommending committee approved his promotion" would be divided as follows:

The	recommending	committee	approved	his	promotion

This kind of analysis reveals the hierarchical groupings of words within the sentence.

The procedures for analyzing syntax that were developed by descriptive linguists were most useful in dealing with simple sentences. When it came to more complicated sentences or ones that were paraphrases of each other, such as actives and passives, the methods proved to be inadequate. The descriptive models based on sentence patterns, immediate constituent analysis, and phrase structure were called item-and-arrangement grammars. During the early twentieth century, linguists such as Boas and Sapir had been interested in grammatical processes, but this line of inquiry was abandoned in favor of item-and-arrangement grammars. In the 1950s, however, some descriptivists again began to consider item-and-process grammars.[22] Zellig Harris developed the concept of a process called a *transformation* in the course of working out the technique of discourse analysis, a method for analyzing samples of connected speech or writing that were entire texts rather than individual sentences.[23] He defined the transformation as a grammatical process that changes the order of constituents within a sentence and can delete, substitute, or add elements. Transformations could account for relations between discontinuous elements, paraphrases such as actives and passives, and a whole range of grammatical phenomena that could not be adequately handled by the earlier methods of syntactic analysis in descriptive linguistics. The concept was developed further and led to a more powerful model of grammatical description.

[22]Charles F. Hockett, "Two Models of Grammatical Description," *Word*, 10 (1954), 210–31.

[23]Zellig S. Harris, "Discourse Analysis," *Language*, 28 (1952), 1–30. Harris, "Co-occurrence and Transformation in Linguistic Structure," *Language*, 33 (1957), 283–340.

Course in General Linguistics

FERDINAND DE SAUSSURE

CHAPTER III: THE OBJECT OF LINGUISTICS

Definition of Language

What is both the integral and concrete object of linguistics? The question is especially difficult; later we shall see why; where I wish merely to point up the difficulty.

Other sciences work with objects that are given in advance and that can then be considered from different viewpoints; but not linguistics. Someone pronounces the French word *nu* "bare": a superficial observer would be tempted to call the word a concrete linguistic object; but a more careful examination would reveal successively three or four quite different things, depending on whether the word is considered as a sound, as the expression of an idea, as the equivalent of Latin *nudum*, etc. Far from it being the object that antedates the viewpoint, it would seem that it is the viewpoint that creates the object; besides, nothing tells us in advance that one way of considering the fact in question takes precedence over the others or is in any way superior to them.

Moreover, regardless of the viewpoint that we adopt, the linguistic phenomenon always has two related sides, each deriving its values from the other. For example:

1. Articulated syllables are acoustical impressions perceived by the ear, but the sounds would not exist without the vocal organs; an *n*, for example, exists only by virtue of the relation between the two sides. We simply cannot reduce language to sound or detach sound from oral articulation; reciprocally, we cannot define the movements of the vocal organs without taking into account the acoustical impression.

2. But suppose that sound were a simple thing: would it constitute speech? No, it is only the instrument of thought; by itself, it has no existence. At this point a new and redoubtable relationship arises: a sound, a complex acoustical-vocal unit, combines in turn with an idea to form a complex physiological-psychological unit. But that is still not the complete picture.

3. Speech has both an individual and a social side, and we cannot conceive of one without the other. Besides:

(from Ferdinand de Saussure, *Course in General Linguistics*, trans. Wade Baskin, N.Y.: Philosophical Library, 1959, pp. 7–17.)

4. Speech always implies both an established system and an evolution; at every moment it is an existing institution and a product of the past. To distinguish between the system and its history, between what it is and what it was, seems very simple at first glance; actually the two things are so closely related that we can scarcely keep them apart. Would we simplify the question by studying the linguistic phenomenon in its earliest stages — if we began, for example, by studying the speech of children? No, for in dealing with speech, it is completely misleading to assume that the problem of early characteristics differs from the problem of permanent characteristics. We are left inside the vicious circle.

From whatever direction we approach the question, nowhere do we find the integral object of linguistics. Everywhere we are confronted with a dilemma: if we fix our attention on only one side of each problem, we run the risk of failing to perceive the dualities pointed out above; on the other hand, if we study speech from several viewpoints simultaneously, the object of linguistics appears to us as a confused mass of heterogeneous and unrelated things. Either procedure opens the door to several sciences — psychology, anthropology, normative grammar, philology, etc., which are distinct from linguistics, but which might claim speech, in view of the faulty method of linguistics, as one of their objects.

As I see it there is only one solution to all the foregoing difficulties: from the very outset we must put both feet on the ground of language and use language as the norm of all other manifestations of speech. Actually, among so many dualities, language alone seems to lend itself to independent definition and provide a fulcrum that satisfies the mind.

But what is language [*langue*]? It is not to be confused with human speech [*language*], of which it is only a definite part, though certainly an essential one. It is both a social product of the faculty of speech and a collection of necessary conventions that have been adopted by a social body to permit individuals to exercise that faculty. Taken as a whole, speech is many-sided and heterogeneous; straddling several areas simultaneously — physical, physiological, and psychological — it belongs both to the individual and to society; we cannot put it into any category of human facts, for we cannot discover its unity.

Language, on the contrary, is a self-contained whole and a principle of classification. As soon as we give language first place among the facts of speech, we introduce a natural order into a mass that lends itself to no other classification.

One might object to that principle of classification on the ground that since the use of speech is based on a natural faculty whereas language is something acquired and conventional, language should not take first place but should be subordinated to the natural instinct.

That objection is easily refuted.

First, no one has proved that speech, as it manifests itself when we speak, is entirely natural, i.e. that our vocal apparatus was designed for speaking just as our legs were designed for walking. Linguists are far from agreement on this point. For instance Whitney, to whom language is one of several social institutions, thinks that we use the vocal apparatus as the instrument of language purely through luck, for the sake of convenience: Men might just as well have chosen gestures and used visual symbols instead of acoustical symbols. Doubtless his thesis is too dogmatic; language is not similar in all respects to other social institutions; moreover, Whitney goes too far in saying that our choice happened to fall on the vocal organs; the choice was more or less imposed by nature. But on the essential point the American linguist is right: language is a convention, and the nature of the sign that is agreed upon does not matter. The question of the vocal apparatus obviously takes a secondary place in the problem of speech.

One definition of *articulated speech* might confirm that conclusion. In Latin, *articulus* means a member, part, or subdivision of a sequence; applied to speech, articulation designates, either the subdivision of a spoken chain into syllables or the subdivision of the chain of meanings into significant units; *gegliederte Sprache* is used in the second sense in German. Using the second definition, we can say that what is natural to mankind is not oral speech but the faculty of constructing a language, i.e. a system of distinct signs corresponding to distinct ideas.

Broca discovered that the faculty of speech is localized in the third left frontal convolution; his discovery has been used to substantiate the attribution of a natural quality to speech. But we know that the same part of the brain is the center of everything that has to do with speech, including writing. The preceding statements, together with observations that have been made in different cases of aphasia resulting from lesion of the centers of localization, seem to indicate: 1. that the various disorders of oral speech are bound up in a hundred ways with those of written speech; and 2. that what is lost in all cases of aphasia or agraphia is less the faculty of producing a given sound or writing a given sign than the ability to evoke by means of an instrument, regardless of what it is, the signs of a regular system of speech. The obvious implication is that beyond the functioning of the various organs there exists a more general faculty which governs signs and which would be the linguistic faculty proper. And this brings us to the same conclusion as above.

To give language first place in the study of speech, we can advance a final argument: the faculty of articulating words — whether it is natural or not — is exercised only with the help of the instrument created by a collectivity and provided for its use; therefore, to say that language gives unity to speech is not fanciful.

Place of Language in the Facts of Speech

In order to separate from the whole of speech the part that belongs to language, we must examine the individual act from which the speaking-circuit can be reconstructed. The act requires the presence of at least two persons; that is the minimum number necessary to complete the circuit. Suppose that two people, A and B, are conversing with each other:

Suppose that the opening of the circuit is in A's brain, where mental facts (concepts) are associated with representations of the linguistic sounds (sound-images) that are used for their expression. A given concept unlocks a corresponding sound-image in the brain; this purely *psychological* phenomenon is followed in turn by a *physiological* process: the brain transmits an impulse corresponding to the image to the organs used in producing sounds. Then the sound waves travel from the mouth of A to the ear of B: a purely *physical* process. Next, the circuit continues in B, but the order is reversed: from the ear to the brain, the physiological transmission of the sound-image; in the brain, the psychological association of the image with the corresponding concept. If B then speaks, the new act will follow — from his brain to A's — exactly the same course as the first act and pass through the same successive phases, which I shall diagram as follows:

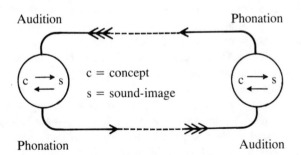

The preceding analysis does not purport to be complete. We might also single out the pure acoustical sensation, the identification of that sensation with the latent sound-image, the muscular image of phonation, etc. I have included only the elements thought to be essential, but the drawing brings out at a glance the distinction between the physical (sound waves), physiological (phonation and audition), and psychological parts (word-images and concepts). Indeed, we should not fail to note that the word-image stands apart from the sound itself and that it is just as psychological as the concept which is associated with it.

The circuit that I have outlined can be further divided into:

a. an outer part that includes the vibrations of the sounds which travel from the mouth to the ear, and an inner part that includes everything else;
b. a psychological and a nonpsychological part, the second including the physiological productions of the vocal organs as well as the physical facts that are outside the individual;
c. an active and a passive part: everything that goes from the associative center of the speaker to the ear of the listener is active, and everything that goes from the ear of the listener to his associative center is passive;
d. finally, everything that is active in the psychological part of the circuit is executive (c → s), and everything that is passive is receptive (s → c).

We should also add the associative and co-ordinating faculty that we find as soon as we leave isolated signs; this faculty plays the dominant role in the organization of language as a system.

But to understand clearly the role of the associative and co-ordinating faculty, we must leave the individual act, which is only the embryo of speech, and approach the social fact.

Among all the individuals that are linked together by speech, some sort of average will be set up: all will reproduce — not exactly of course, but approximately — the same signs united with the same concepts.

How does the social crystallization of language come about? Which parts of the circuit are involved? For all parts probably do not participate equally in it.

The nonpsychological part can be rejected from the outset. When we hear people speaking a language that we do not know, we perceive the sounds but remain outside the social fact because we do not understand them.

Neither is the psychological part of the circuit wholly responsible: the executive side is missing, for execution is never carried out by the collectivity. Execution is always individual, and the individual is always its master: I shall call the executive side *speaking* [*parole*].

Through the functioning of the receptive and co-ordinating faculties, impressions that are perceptibly the same for all are made on the minds of speakers. How can that social product be pictured in such a way that language will stand apart from everything else? If we could embrace the sum of word-images stored in the minds of all individuals, we could identify the social bond that constitutes language. It is a storehouse filled by the members of a given community through their active use of speaking, a grammatical system that has a potential existence in each brain, or, more specifically, in the brains of a group of individuals. For language is not complete in any speaker; it exists perfectly only within a collectivity.

In separating language from speaking we are at the same time separating: (1) what is social from what is individual; and (2) what is essential from what is accessory and more or less accidental.

Language is not a function of the speaker; it is a product that is passively assimilated by the individual. It never requires premeditation, and reflection enters in only for the purpose of classification, which we shall take up later.

Speaking, on the contrary, is an individual act. It is willful and intellectual. Within the act, we should distinguish between: (1) the combinations by which the speaker uses the language code for expressing his own thought; and (2) the psychophysical mechanism that allows him to exteriorize those combinations.

Note that I have defined things rather than words; these definitions are not endangered by certain ambiguous words that do not have identical meanings in different languages. For instance, German *Sprache* means both "language" and "speech"; *Rede* almost corresponds to "speaking" but adds the special connotation of "discourse." Latin *sermo* designates both "speech" and "speaking," while *lingua* means "language," etc. No word corresponds exactly to any of the notions specified above; that is why all definitions of words are made in vain; starting from words in defining things is a bad procedure.

To summarize, these are the characteristics of language:

1. Language is a well-defined object in the heterogeneous mass of speech facts. It can be localized in the limited segment of the speaking-circuit where an auditory image becomes associated with a concept. It is the social side of speech, outside the individual who can never create nor modify it by himself; it exists only by virtue of a sort of contract signed by the members of a community. Moreover, the individual must always serve an apprenticeship in order to learn the functioning of language; a child assimilates it only gradually. It is such a distinct thing that a man deprived of the use of speaking retains it provided that he understands the vocal signs that he hears.

2. Language, unlike speaking, is something that we can study separately. Although dead languages are no longer spoken, we can easily assimilate their linguistic organisms. We can dispense with the other elements of speech; indeed, the science of language is possible only if the other elements are excluded.

3. Whereas speech is heterogeneous, language, as defined, is homogeneous. It is a system of signs in which the only essential thing is the union of meanings and sound-images, and in which both parts of the sign are psychological.

4. Language is concrete, no less than speaking; and this is a help in our study of it. Linguistic signs, though basically psychological, are not abstractions; associations which bear the stamp of collective approval — and which added together constitute language — are realities that have their seat in the brain. Besides, linguistic signs are tangible; it is possible to reduce them to conventional written symbols, whereas it would be impossible to provide detailed photographs of acts of speaking [*actes de parole*]; the pronunciation of even the smallest word represents an infinite number of muscular movements that could be identified and put into graphic form only with great difficulty. In language, on the contrary,

there is only the sound-image, and the latter can be translated into a fixed visual image. For if we disregard the vast number of movements necessary for the realization of sound-images in speaking, we see that each sound-image is nothing more than the sum of a limited number of elements or phonemes that can in turn be called up by a corresponding number of written symbols. The very possibility of putting the things that relate to language into graphic form allows dictionaries and grammars to represent it accurately, for language is a storehouse of sound-images, and writing is the tangible form of those images.

Place of Language in Human Facts: Semiology

The foregoing characteristics of language reveal an even more important characteristic. Language, once its boundaries have been marked off within the speech data, can be classified among human phenomena, whereas speech cannot.

We have just seen that language is a social institution; but several features set it apart from other political, legal, etc. institutions. We must call in a new type of facts in order to illuminate the special nature of language.

Language is a system of signs that express ideas, and is therefore comparable to a system of writing, the alphabet of deaf-mutes, symbolic rites, polite formulas, military signals, etc. But it is the most important of all these systems.

A science that studies the life of signs within society is conceivable; it would be a part of social psychology and consequently of general psychology; I shall call it *semiology* (from Greek *sēmeîon*, "sign"). Semiology would show what constitutes signs, what laws govern them. Since the science does not yet exist, no one can say what it would be; but it has a right to existence, a place staked out in advance. Linguistics is only a part of the general science of semiology; the laws discovered by semiology will be applicable to linguistics, and the latter will circumscribe a well-defined area within the mass of anthropological facts.

To determine the exact place of semiology is the task of the psychologist. The task of the linguist is to find out what makes language a special system within the mass of semiological data. This issue will be taken up again later; here I wish merely to call attention to one thing: if I have succeeded in assigning linguistics a place among the sciences, it is because I have related it to semiology.

Why has semiology not yet been recognized as an independent science with its own object like all the other sciences? Linguists have been going around in circles: language, better than anything else, offers a basis for understanding the semiological problem; but language must, to put it correctly, be studied in itself; heretofore language has almost always been studied in connection with something else, from other viewpoints.

There is first of all the superficial notion of the general public: people see nothing more than a name-giving system in language, thereby prohibiting any research into its true nature.

Then there is the viewpoint of the psychologist, who studies the sign-mechanism in the individual; this is the easiest method, but it does not lead beyond individual execution and does not reach the sign, which is social.

Or even when signs are studied from a social viewpoint, only the traits that attach language to the other social institutions — those that are more or less voluntary — are emphasized; as a result, the goal is by-passed and the specific characteristics of semiological systems in general and of language in particular are completely ignored. For the distinguishing characteristic of the sign — but the one that is least apparent at first sight — is that in some way it always eludes the individual or social will.

In short, the characteristic that distinguishes semiological systems from all other institutions shows up clearly only in language where it manifests itself in the things which are studied least, and the necessity or specific value of a semiological science is therefore not clearly recognized. But to me the language problem is mainly semiological, and all developments derive their significance from that important fact. If we are to discover the true nature of language we must learn what it has in common with all other semiological systems; linguistic forces that seem very important at first glance (e.g., the role of the vocal apparatus) will receive only secondary consideration if they serve only to set language apart from the other systems. This procedure will do more than to clarify the linguistic problem. By studying rites, customs, etc. as signs, I believe that we shall throw new light on the facts and point up the need for including them in a science of semiology and explaining them by its laws.

Language

EDWARD SAPIR

CHAPTER IV: FORM IN LANGUAGE

Grammatical Processes

The question of form in language presents itself under two aspects. We may
either consider the formal methods employed by a language, its "grammatical
processes," or we may ascertain the distribution of concepts with reference to
formal expression. What are the formal patterns of the language? And what types
of concepts make up the content of these formal patterns? The two points of view
are quite distinct. The English word *unthinkingly* is, broadly speaking, formally
parallel to the word *reformers*, each being built up on a radical element which
may occur as an independent verb (*think, form*), this radical element being preceded by an element (*un-*, *re-*) that conveys a definite and fairly concrete significance but that cannot be used independently, and followed by two elements
(*-ing*, *-ly*, *-er*, *-s*) that limit the application of the radical concept in a relational
sense. This formal pattern — (b) + A + (c) + (d)[1] — is a characteristic feature
of the language. A countless number of functions may be expressed by it; in
other words, all the possible ideas conveyed by such prefixed and suffixed elements, while tending to fall into minor groups, do not necessarily form natural,
functional systems. There is no logical reason, for instance, why the numeral
function of *-s* should be formally expressed in a manner that is analogous to the
expression of the idea conveyed by *-ly*. It is perfectly conceivable that in another
language the concept of manner (*-ly*) may be treated according to an entirely different pattern from that of plurality. The former might have to be expressed by an
independent word (say, *thus unthinking*), the latter by a prefixed element (say,
plural[2]*-reformer*). There are, of course, an unlimited number of other possibilities. Even within the confines of English alone the relative independence of
form and function can be made obvious. Thus, the negative idea conveyed by
un- can be just as adequately expressed by a suffixed element (*-less*) in such a
word as *thoughtlessly*. Such a twofold formal expression of the negative function
would be inconceivable in certain languages, say Eskimo, where a suffixed element would alone be possible. Again, the plural notion conveyed by the *-s* of
reformers is just as definitely expressed in the word *geese*, where an utterly distinct method is employed. Furthermore, the principle of vocalic change

(from Edward Sapir, *Language*, N.Y.: Harcourt, pp. 57–81.)

---

[1]For the symbolism, see Chapter II.
[2]"Plural" is here a symbol for any prefix indicating plurality.

(*goose-geese*) is by no means confined to the expression of the idea of plurality; it may also function as an indicator of difference of time (e.g., *sing-sang*, *throw-threw*). But the expression in English of past time is not by any means always bound up with a change of vowel. In the great majority of cases the same idea is expressed by means of a distinct suffix (*die-d*, *work-ed*). Functionally, *died* and *sang* are analogous; so are *reformers* and *geese*. Formally, we must arrange these words quite otherwise. Both *die-d* and *re-form-er-s* employ the method of suffixing grammatical elements; both *sang* and *geese* have grammatical form by virtue of the fact that their vowels differ from the vowels of other words with which they are closely related in form and meaning (*goose; sing, sung*).

Every language possesses one or more formal methods for indicating the relation of a secondary concept to the main concept of the radical element. Some of these grammatical processes, like suffixing, are exceedingly widespread; others, like vocalic change, are less common but far from rare; still others, like accent and consonantal change, are somewhat exceptional as functional processes. Not all languages are as irregular as English in the assignment of functions to its stock of grammatical processes. As a rule, such basic concepts as those of plurality and time are rendered by means of one or other method alone, but the rule has so many exceptions that we cannot safely lay it down as a principle. Wherever we go we are impressed by the fact that pattern is one thing, the utilization of pattern quite another. A few further examples of the multiple expression of identical functions in other languages than English may help to make still more vivid this idea of the relative independence of form and function.

In Hebrew, as in other Semitic languages, the verbal idea as such is expressed by three, less often by two or four, characteristic consonants. Thus, the group *sh-m-r* expresses the idea of "guarding," the group *g-n-b* that of "stealing," *n-t-n* that of "giving." Naturally these consonantal sequences are merely abstracted from the actual forms. The consonants are held together in different forms by characteristic vowels that vary according to the idea that it is desired to express. Prefixed and suffixed elements are also frequently used. The method of internal vocalic change is exemplified in *shamar* "he has guarded," *shomer* "guarding," *shamur* "being guarded," *shmor* "(to) guard." Analogously, *ganab* "he has stolen," *goneb* "stealing", *ganub* "being stolen," *gnob* "(to) steal." But not all infinitives are formed according to the type of *shmor* and *gnob* or of other types of internal vowel change. Certain verbs suffix a *t*-element for the infinitive, e.g. *ten-eth* "to give," *heyo-th* "to be." Again, the pronominal ideas may be expressed by independent words (e.g., *anoki* "I"), by prefixed elements (e.g., *e-shmor* "I shall guard"), or by suffixed elements (e.g., *shamar-ti* "I have guarded"). In Nass, an Indian language of British Columbia, plurals are formed by four distinct methods. Most nouns (and verbs) are reduplicated in the plural, that is, part of the radical element is repeated, e.g., *gyat* "person," *gyigyat* "people." A second method is the use of certain characteristic prefixes, e.g., *an'on* "hand," *ka-an'on* "hands;" *wai* "one paddles," *lu-wai* "several paddle." Still other plurals are formed by means of internal vowel change, e.g., *gwula* "cloak," *gwila* "cloaks." Finally, a fourth class of plurals is constituted by such nouns as suffix a grammatical element, e.g., *waky* "brother," *wakykw* "brothers."

From such groups of examples as these — and they might be multiplied *ad nauseam* — we cannot but conclude that linguistic form may and should be studied as types of patterning, apart from the associated functions. We are the more justified in this procedure as all languages evince a curious instinct for the development of one or more particular grammatical processes at the expense of others, tending always to lose sight of any explicit functional value that the process may have had in the first instance, delighting, it would seem, in the sheer play of its means of expression. It does not matter that in such a case as the English *goose-geese, foul-defile, sing-sang-sung* we can prove that we are dealing with historically distinct processes, that the vocalic alternation of *sing* and *sang*, for instance, is centuries older as a specific type of grammatical process than the outwardly parallel one of *goose* and *geese*. It remains true that there is (or was) an inherent tendency in English, at the time such forms as *geese* came into being, for the utilization of vocalic change as a significant linguistic method. Failing the precedent set by such already existing types of vocalic alternation as *sing-sang-sung*, it is highly doubtful if the detailed conditions that brought about the evolution of forms like *teeth* and *geese* from *tooth* and *goose* would have been potent enough to allow acceptance of these new types of plural formation as psychologically possible. This feeling for form as such, freely expanding along predetermined lines and greatly inhibited in certain directions by the lack of controlling types of patterning, should be more clearly understood than it seems to be. A general survey of many diverse types of languages is needed to give us the proper perspective on this point. We saw in the preceding chapter that every language has an inner phonetic system of definite pattern. We now learn that it has also a definite feeling for patterning on the level of grammatical formation. Both of these submerged and powerfully controlling impulses to definite form operate as such, regardless of the need for expressing particular groups of concepts. It goes without saying that these impulses can find realization only in concrete functional expression. We must say something to be able to say it in a certain manner.

Let us now take up a little more systematically, however briefly, the various grammatical processes that linguistic research has established. They may be grouped into six main types: word order; composition; affixation, including the use of prefixes, suffixes, and infixes; internal modification of the radical or grammatical element, whether this affects a vowel or a consonant; reduplication; and accentual differences, whether dynamic (stress) or tonal (pitch). There are also special quantitative processes, like vocalic lengthening or shortening, and consonantal doubling, but these may be looked upon as particular sub-types of the process of internal modification. Possibly still other formal types exist, but they are not likely to be of importance in a general survey. It is important to bear in mind that a linguistic phenomenon cannot be looked upon as illustrating a definite "process" unless it has an inherent functional value. The consonantal change in English, for instance, of *book-s* and *bag-s* (*s* in the former, *z* in the latter) is of no functional significance. It is a purely external, mechanical change induced by the presence of a preceding voiceless consonant, *k*, in the former case, of a voiced consonant, *g*, in the latter. This mechanical alternation is objectively the same as that between the noun *house* and the verb *to house*. In the latter case, however, it has an important grammatical function, that of transforming a noun into a verb. The two alternations belong, then, to entirely different psychological categories. Only the latter is a true illustration of consonantal modification as a grammatical process.

The simplest, at least the most economical, method of conveying some sort of grammatical notion is to juxtapose two or more words in a definite sequence without making any attempt by inherent modification of these words to establish a connection between them. Let us put down two simple English words at random, say *sing praise*. This conveys no finished thought in English, nor does it clearly establish a relation between the idea of singing and that of praising. Nevertheless, it is psychologically impossible to hear or see the two words juxtaposed without straining to give them some measure of coherent significance. The attempt is not likely to yield an entirely satisfactory result, but what is significant is that as soon as two or more radical concepts are put before the human mind in immediate sequence it strives to bind them together with connecting values of some sort. In the case of *sing praise* different individuals are likely to arrive at different provisional results. Some of the latent possibilities of the juxtaposition, expressed in currently satisfying form, are: *sing praise* (to him)!, or *singing praise, praise expressed in a song*, or *to sing and praise*, or *one who sings a song of praise* (compare such English compounds as *killjoy*, i.e., *one who kills joy*), or *he sings a song of praise* (to him). The theoretical possibilities in the way of rounding out these two concepts into a significant group of concepts or even into a finished thought are indefinitely numerous. None of them will quite work in English, but there are numerous languages where one or other of these amplifying processes is habitual. It depends entirely on the genius of the particular language what function is inherently involved in a given sequence of words.

Some languages, like Latin, express practically all relations by means of modifications within the body of the word itself. In these, sequence is apt to be a rhetorical rather than a strictly grammatical principle. Whether I say in Latin *hominem femina videt* or *femina hominem videt* or *hominem videt femina* or *videt femina hominem* makes little or no difference beyond, possibly, a rhetorical or stylistic one. *The woman sees the man* is the identical significance of each of these sentences. In Chinook, an Indian language of the Columbia River, one can be equally free, for the relation between the verb and the two nouns is as inherently fixed as in Latin. The difference between the two languages is that, while Latin allows the nouns to establish their relation to each other and to the verb,

Chinook lays the formal burden entirely on the verb, the full content of which is more or less adequately rendered by *she-him-sees*. Eliminate the Latin case suffixes (*-a* and *-em*) and the Chinook pronominal prefixes (*she-him-*) and we cannot afford to be so indifferent to our word order. We need to husband our resources. In other words, word order takes on a real functional value. Latin and Chinook are at one extreme. Such languages as Chinese, Siamese, and Annamite, in which each and every word, if it is to function properly, falls into its assigned place, are at the other extreme. But the majority of languages fall between these two extremes. In English, for instance, it may make little grammatical difference whether I say *yesterday the man saw the dog* or *the man saw the dog yesterday*, but it is not a matter of indifference whether I say *yesterday the man saw the dog* or *yesterday the dog saw the man*, or whether I say *he is here* or *is he here*? In the one case, of the latter group of examples, the vital distinction of subject and object depends entirely on the placing of certain words of the sentence, in the latter a slight difference of sequence makes all the different between statement and question. It goes without saying that in these cases the English principle of word order is as potent a means of expression as is the Latin use of case suffixes or of an interrogative particle. There is here no question of functional poverty, but of formal economy.

We have already seen something of the process of composition, the uniting into a single word of two or more radical elements. Psychologically this process is closely allied to that of word order in so far as the relation between the elements is implied, not explicitly stated. It differs from the mere juxtaposition of words in the sentence in that the compounded elements are felt as constituting but parts of a single word-organism. Such languages as Chinese and English, in which the principle of rigid sequence is well developed, tend not infrequently also to the development of compound words. It is but a step from such a Chinese word sequence as *jin tak* "man virtue," i.e., "the virtue of men," to such more conventionalized and psychologically unified juxtapositions as *t'ien tsz* "heaven son," i.e., "emperor," or *shui fu* "water man," i.e., "water carrier." In the latter case we may as well frankly write *shui-fu* as a single word, the meaning of the compound as a whole being as divergent from the precise etymological values of its component elements as is that of our English word *typewriter* from the merely combined values of *type* and *writer*. In English the unity of the word *typewriter* is further safeguarded by a predominant accent on the first syllable and by the possibility of adding such a suffixed element as the plural *-s* to the whole word. Chinese also unifies its compounds by means of stress. However, then, in its ultimate origins the process of composition may go back to typical sequences of words in the sentence, it is now, for the most part, a specialized method of expressing relations. French has as rigid a word order as English but dovs not possess anything like its power of compounding words into more complex units. On the other hand, classical Greek, in spite of its relative freedom in the placing of words, has a very considerable bent for the formation of compound terms.

It is curious to observe how greatly languages differ in their ability to make use of the process of composition. One would have thought on general principles that so simple a device as gives us our *typewriter* and *blackbird* and hosts of other words would be an all but universal grammatical process. Such is not the case. There are a great many languages, like Eskimo and Nootka and, aside from paltry exceptions, the Semitic languages, that cannot compound radical elements. What is even stranger is the fact that many of these languages are not in the least averse to complex word formations, but may on the contrary effect a synthesis that far surpasses the utmost that Greek and Sanskrit are capable of. Such a Nootka word, for instance, as "when, as they say, he had been absent for four days" might be expected to embody at least three radical elements corresponding to the concepts of "absent," "four," and "day." As a matter of fact the Nootka word is utterly incapable of composition in our sense. It is invariably built up out of a single radical element and a greater or less number of suffixed elements, some of which may have as concrete a significance as the radical element itself. In the particular case we have cited the radical element conveys the idea of "four," the notions of "day" and "absent" being expressed by suffixes that are as inseparable from the radical nucleus of the word as is an English element like *-er* from the *sing* or *hunt* of such words as *singer* and *hunter*. The tendency to word synthesis is, then, by no means the same thing as the tendency to compounding radical elements, though the latter is not infrequently a ready means for the synthetic tendency to work with.

There is a bewildering variety of types of composition. These types vary according to function, the nature of the compounded elements, and order. In a great many languages composition is confined to what we may call the delimiting function, that is, of the two or more compounded elements one is given a more precisely qualified significance by the others, which contribute nothing to the formal build of the sentence. In English, for instance, such compounded elements as *red* in *redcoat* or *over* in *overlook* merely modify the significance of the dominant *coat* or *look* without in any way sharing, as such, in the predication that is expressed by the sentence. Some languages, however, such as Iroquois and Nahuatl,[3] employ the method of composition for much heavier work than this. In Iroquois, for instance, the composition of a noun, in its radical form, with a following verb is a typical method of expressing case relations, particularly of the subject or object. *I-meat-eat*, for instance, is the regular Iroquois method of expressing the sentence *I am eating meat*. In other languages similar forms may express local or instrumental or still other relations. Such English forms as *killjoy* and *marplot* also illustrate the compounding of a verb and a noun, but the resulting word has a strictly nominal, not a verbal, function. We cannot say *he marplots*. Some languages allow the composition of all or nearly all types of elements. Paiute, for instance, may compound noun with noun, adjective with noun, verb with noun to make a noun, noun with verb to make a verb, adverb

---

[3]The language of the Aztecs, still spoken in large parts of Mexico.

with verb, verb with verb. Yana, an Indian language of California, can freely compound noun with noun and verb with noun, but not verb with verb. On the other hand, Iroquois can compound only noun with verb, never noun and noun as in English or verb and verb as in so many other languages. Finally, each language has its characteristic types of order of composition. In English the qualifying element regularly precedes; in certain other languages it follows. Sometimes both types are used in the same language, as in Yana, where "beef" is "bitter-venison" but "deer-liver" is expressed by "liver-deer." The compounded object of a verb precedes the verbal element in Paiute, Nahuatl, and Iroquois, follows it in Yana, Tsimshian,[4] and the Algonkin languages.

Of all grammatical processes affixing is incomparably the most frequently employed. There are languages, like Chinese and Siamese, that make no grammatical use of elements that do not at the same time possess an independent value as radical elements, but such languages are uncommon. Of the three types of affixing — the use of prefixes, suffixes, and infixes — suffixing is much the commonest. Indeed, it is a fair guess that suffixes do more of the formative work of language than all other methods combined. It is worth noting that there are not a few affixing languages that make absolutely no use of prefixed elements but possess a complex apparatus of suffixes. Such are Turkish, Hottentot, Eskimo, Nootka, and Yana. Some of these, like the three last mentioned, have hundreds of suffixed elements, many of them of a concreteness of significance that would demand expression in the vast majority of languages by means of radical elements. The reverse case, the use of prefixed elements to the complete exclusion of suffixes, is far less common. A good example is Khmer (or Cambodgian), spoken in French Cochin-China, though even here there are obscure traces of old suffixes that have ceased to function as such and are now felt to form part of the radical element.

A considerable majority of known languages are prefixing and suffixing at one and the same time, but the relative importance of the two groups of affixed elements naturally varies enormously. In some languages, such as Latin and Russian, the suffixes alone relate the word to the rest of the sentence, the prefixes being confined to the expression of such ideas as delimit the concrete significance of the radical element without influencing its bearing in the proposition. A Latin form like *remittebantur* "they were being sent back" may serve as an illustration of this type of distribution of elements. The prefixed element *re-*"back" merely qualifies to a certain extent the inherent significance of the radical element *mitt-* "send," while the suffixes *-eba-, -nt-,* and *-ur* convey the less concrete, more strictly formal, notions of time, person, plurality, and passivity.

On the other hand, there are languages, like the Bantu group of Africa or the Athabaskan languages[5] of North America, in which the grammatically sig-

---

[4]An Indian language of British Columbia closely related to the Nass already cited.
[5]Including such languages as Navaho, Apache, Hupa, Carrier, Chipewyan, Loucheux.

nificant elements precede, those that follow the radical element forming a relatively dispensable class. The Hupa word *te-s-e-ya-te* "I will go," for example, consists of a radical element *-ya-* "to go," three essential prefixes and a formally subsidiary suffix. The element *te-* indicates that the act takes place here and there in space or continuously over space; practically, it has no clear-cut significance apart from such verb stems as it is customary to connect it with. The second prefixed element *-s-*, is even less easy to define. All we can say is that it is used in verb forms of "definite" time and that it marks action as in progress rather than as beginning or coming to an end. The third prefix, *-e-*, is a pronominal element, "I," which can be used only in "definite" tenses. It is highly important to understand that the use of *-e-* is conditional on that of *-s-* or of certain alternative prefixes and that *te-* also is in practice linked with *-s-*. The group *te-s-e-ya* is a firmly knit grammatical unit. The suffix *-te*, which indicates the future, is no more necessary to its formal balance than is the prefixed *re-* of the Latin word; it is not an element that is capable of standing alone but its function is materially delimiting rather than strictly formal.[6]

It is not always, however, that we can clearly set off the suffixes of a language as a group against its prefixes. In probably the majority of languages that use both types of affixes each group has both delimiting and formal or relational functions. The most that we can say is that a language tends to express similar functions in either the one or the other manner. If a certain verb expresses a certain tense by suffixing, the probability is strong that it expresses its other tenses in an analogous fashion and that, indeed, all verbs have suffixed tense elements. Similarly, we normally expect to find the pronominal elements, so far as they are included in the verb at all, either consistently prefixed or suffixed. But these rules are far from absolute. We have already seen that Hebrew prefixes its pronominal elements in certain cases, suffixes them in others. In Chimariko, an Indian language of California, the position of the pronominal affixes depends on the verb; they are prefixed for certain verbs, suffixed for others.

It will not be necessary to give many further examples of prefixing and suffixing. One of each category will suffice to illustrate their formative possibilities. The idea expressed in English by the sentence *I came to give it to her* is rendered in Chinook[7] by *i-n-i-a-l-u-d-am*. This word — and it is a thoroughly unified word with a clear-cut accent on the first *a* — consists of a radical element, *-d-* "to give," six functionally distinct, if phonetically frail, prefixed elements, and

---

[6]This may seem surprising to an English reader. We generally think of time as a function that is appropriately expressed in a purely formal manner. This notion is due to the bias that Latin grammar has given us. As a matter of fact the English future (*I shall go*) is not expressed by affixing at all; moreover, it may be expressed by the present, as in *tomorrow I leave this place*, where the temporal function is inherent in the independent adverb. Though in lesser degree, the Hupa *-te* is as irrelevant to the vital word as is *tomorrow* to the grammatical "feel" of *I leave*.

[7]Wishram dialect.

[8]Really "him," but Chinook, like Latin or French, possesses grammatical gender. An object may be referred to as "he," "she," or "it," according to the characteristic form of its noun.

a suffix. Of the prefixes, *i*- indicates recently past time; *n*-, the pronominal subject "I"; *-i-*, the pronominal object "it";[8] *-a-*, the second pronominal object "her"; *-l-*, a prepositional element indicating that the preceding pronominal prefix is to be understood as an indirect object (-her-to-, "to her"); and *-u-*, an element that it is not easy to define satisfactorily but which, on the whole, indicates movement away from the speaker. The suffixed *-am* modifies the verbal content in a local sense; it adds to the notion conveyed by the radical element that of "arriving" or "going (or coming) for that particular purpose." It is obvious that in Chinook, as in Hupa, the greater part of the grammatical machinery resides in the prefixes rather than in the suffixes.

A reverse case, one in which the grammatically significant elements cluster, as in Latin, at the end of the word is yielded by Fox, one of the better known Algonkin languages of the Mississippi Valley. We may take the form *eh-kiwi-n-a-m-oht-ati-wa-ch(i)* "then they together kept (him) in flight from them." The radical element here is *kiwi*-, a verb stem indicating the general notion of "indefinite movement round about, here and there." The prefixed element *eh*- is hardly more than an adverbial particle indicating temporal subordination; it may be conveniently rendered as "then." Of the seven suffixes included in this highly wrought word, *-n*- seems to be merely a phonetic element serving to connect the verb stem with the following *-a-*;[9] *-a*- is a "secondary stem"[10] denoting the idea of "flight, to flee"; *-m*- denotes causality with reference to an animate object;[11] *-o(ht)*- indicates activity done for the subject (the so-called "middle" or "medio-passive" voice of Greek); *-(a)ti*- is a reciprocal element, "one another"; *-wa-ch(i)* is the third person animate plural (*-wa*-, plural; *-chi*, more properly personal) of so-called "conjunctive" forms. The word may be translated more literally (and yet only approximately as to grammatical feeling) as "then they (animate) caused some animate being to wander about in flight from one another of themselves." Eskimo, Nootka, Yana, and other languages have similarly complex arrays of suffixed elements, though the functions performed by them and their principles of combination differ widely.

We have reserved the very curious type of affixation known as "infixing" for separate illustration. It is utterly unknown in English, unless we consider the *-n*- of *stand* (contrast *stood*) as an infixed element. The earlier Indo-European languages, such as Latin, Greek and Sanskrit, made a fairly considerable use of

[9]This analysis is doubtful. It is likely that *-n*- possesses a function that still remains to be ascertained. The Algonkin languages are unusually complex and present many unsolved problems of detail.

[10]"Secondary stems" are elements which are suffixes from a formal point of view, never appearing without the support of a true radical element, but whose function is as concrete, to all intents and purposes, as that of the radical element itself. Secondary verb stems of this type are characteristic of the Algonkin languages and of Yana.

[11]In the Algonkin languages all persons and things are conceived of as either animate or inanimate, just as in Latin or German they are conceived of as masculine, feminine, or neuter.

infixed nasals to differentiate the present tense of a certain class of verbs from other forms (contrast Latin *vinc-o* "I conquer" with *vic-i* "I conquered"; Greek *lamban-o* "I take" with *e-lab-on* "I took"). There are, however, more striking examples of the process, examples in which it has assumed a more clearly defined function than in these Latin and Greek cases. It is particularly prevalent in many languages of southeastern Asia and of the Malay archipelago. Good examples from Khmer (Cambodgian) are *tmeu* "one who walks" and *daneu* "walking" (verbal noun), both derived from *deu* "to walk." Further examples may be quoted from Bontoc Igorot, a Filipino language. Thus, an infixed *-in-* conveys the idea of the product of an accomplished action, e.g., *kayu* "wood," *kinayu* "gathered wood." Infixes are also freely used in the Bontoc Igorot verb. Thus, an infixed *-um-* is characteristic of many intransitive verbs with personal pronominal suffixes, e.g., *sad-* "to wait," *sumid-ak* "I wait"; *kineg* "silent," *kuminek-ak* "I am silent." In other verbs it indicates futurity, e.g., *tengao-* "to celebrate a holiday," *tumengao-ak* "I shall have a holiday." The past tense is frequently indicated by an infixed *-in-*; if there is already an infixed *-um-*, the two elements combine to *-in-m*, e.g., *kinminek-ak* "I am silent." Obviously the infixing process has in this (and related) languages the same vitality that is possessed by the commoner prefixes and suffixes of other languages. The process is also found in a number of aboriginal American languages. The Yana plural is sometimes formed by an infixed element, e.g., *k'uruwi* "medicine-men," *k'uwi* "medicine-man"; in Chinook an infixed *-l-* is used in certain verbs to indicate repeated activity, e.g., *ksik-ludelk* "she keeps looking at him," *iksik-lutk* "she looked at him" (radical element *-tk*). A peculiarly interesting type of infixation is found in the Siouan languages, in which certain verbs insert the pronominal elements into the very body of the radical element, e.g., Sioux *cheti* "to build a fire," *chewati* "I build a fire"; *shuta* "to miss," *shuunta-pi* "we miss."

A subsidiary but by no means unimportant grammatical process is that of internal vocalic or consonantal change. In some languages, as in English (*sing, sang, sung, song; goose, geese*), the former of these has become one of the major methods of indicating fundamental changes of grammatical function. At any rate, the process is alive enough to lead our children into untrodden ways. We all know of the growing youngster who speaks of having *brung* something, on the analogy of such forms as *sung* and *flung*. In Hebrew, as we have seen, vocalic change is of even greater significance than in English. What is true of Hebrew is of course true of all other Semitic languages. A few examples of so-called "broken" plurals from Arabic[12] will supplement the Hebrew verb forms that I have given in another connection. The noun *balad* "place" has the plural *bilad*;[13] *gild* "hide" forms the plural *gulud*; *ragil* "man," the plural *rigal*;

---

[12]Egyptian dialect.

[13]There are changes of accent and vocalic quantity in these forms as well, but the requirements of simplicity force us to neglect them.

shibbak "window," the plural *shababik*. Very similar phenomena are illustrated by the Hamitic languages of Northern Africa, e.g., Shilh[14] *izbil* "hair," plural *izbel*; *a-slem* "fish," plural *i-slim-en*; *sn* "to know," *sen* "to be knowing"; *rmi* "to become tired," *rumni* "to be tired"; *ttss*[15] "to fall asleep," *ttoss* "to sleep." Strikingly similar to English and Greek alternations of the type *sing—sang* and *leip-o* "I leave," *leloip-a* "I have left," are such Somali[16] cases as *al* "I am," *il* "I was"; *i-dah-a* "I say," *i-di* "I said," *deh* "say!"

Vocalic change is of great significance also in a number of American Indian languages. In the Athabaskan group many verbs change the quality or quantity of the vowel of the radical element as it changes its tense or mode. The Navaho verb for "I put (grain) into a receptacle" is *bi-hi-sh-ja*, in which *-ja* is the radical element; the past tense, *bi-hi-ja'*, has a long *a*-vowel, followed by the "glottal stop"; the future is *bi-h-de-sh-ji* with complete change of vowel. In other types of Navaho verbs the vocalic changes follow different lines, e.g., *yah-a-ni-ye* "you carry (a pack) into (a stable)"; past, *yah-i-ni-yin* (with long *i* in *-yin*; *-n* is here used to indicate nasalization); future, *yah-a-di-yehl* (with long *e*). In another Indian language, Yokuts,[17] vocalic modifications affect both noun and verb forms. Thus, *buchong* "son" forms the plural *bochang-i* (contrast the objective *buchong-a*); *enash* "grandfather," the plural *inash-a*; the verb *engtyim* "to sleep" forms the continuative *ingetym-ad* "to be sleeping" and the past *ingetym-ash*.

Consonantal change as a functional process is probably far less common than vocalic modifications, but it is not exactly rare. There is an interesting group of cases in English, certain nouns and corresponding verbs differing solely in that the final consonant is voiceless or voiced. Examples are *wreath* (with *th* as in *think*) but *to wreathe* (with *th* as in *then*); *house*, but *to house* (with *s* pronounced like *z*). That we have a distinct feeling for the interchange as a means of distinguishing the noun from the verb is indicated by the extension of the principle by many Americans to such a noun as *rise* (e.g., *the rise of democracy*) — pronounced like *rice* — in contrast to the verb *to rise* (*s* like *z*).

In the Celtic languages the initial consonants undergo several types of change according to the grammatical relation that subsists between the word itself and the preceding word. Thus, in modern Irish, a word like *bo* "ox" may, under the appropriate circumstances, take the forms *bho* (pronounce *wo*) or *mo* (e.g., *an bo*, "the ox," as a subject, but *tir na mo*, "land of the oxen," as a possessive plural). In the verb the principle has as one of its most striking consequences the "aspiration" of initial consonants in the past tense. If a verb begins with *t*, say, it changes the *t* to *th* (now pronounced *h*) in forms of the past; if it

---

[14]A Berber language of Morocco.

[15]Some of the Berber languages allow consonantal combinations that seem unpronounceable to us.

[16]One of the Hamitic languages of eastern Africa.

[17]Spoken in the south-central part of California.

begins with *g*, the consonant changes, in analogous forms, to *gh* (pronounced like a voiced spirant[19] *g* or like *y*, according to the nature of the following vowel. In modern Irish the principle of consonantal change, which began in the oldest period of the language as a secondary consequence of certain phonetic conditions, has become one of the primary grammatical processes of the language.

Perhaps as remarkable as these Irish phenomena are the consonantal interchanges of Ful, an African language of the Soudan. Here we find that all nouns belonging to the personal class form the plural by changing their initial *g*, *j*, *d*, *b*, *k*, *ch*, and *p* to *y* (or *w*), *y*, *r*, *w*, *h*, *s*, and *f* respectively; e.g., *jim-o* "companion," *yim'-be* "companions"; *pio-o* "beater," *fio'-be* "beaters." Curiously enough, nouns that belong to the class of things form their singular and plural in exactly reverse fashion, e.g., *yola-re* "grass-grown place," *jola-je* "grass-grown places"; *fitan-du* "soul," *pital-i* "souls." In Nootka, to refer to but one other language in which the process is found, the *t* or *tl*[18] of many verbal suffixes becomes *hl* in forms denoting repetition, e.g., *hita'-ato* "to fall out," *hita'-ahl* "to keep falling out"; *mat-achisht-utl* "to fly on to the water," *mat-achisht-ohl* "to keep flying on to the water." Further, the *hl* of certain elements changes to a peculiar *h*-sound in plural forms, e.g., *yak-ohl* "sore-faced," *yak-oh* "sore-faced (people)."

Nothing is more natural than the prevalence of reduplication, in other words, the repetition of all or part of the radical element. The process is generally employed, with self-evident symbolism, to indicate such concepts as distribution, plurality, repetition, customary activity, increase of size, added intensity, continuance. Even in English it is not unknown, though it is not generally accounted one of the typical formative devices of our language. Such words as *goody-goody* and *to pooh-pooh* have become accepted as part of our normal vocabulary, but the method of duplication may on occasion be used more freely than is indicated by such stereotyped examples. Such locutions as *a big big man* or *Let it cool till it's thick thick* are far more common, especially in the speech of women and children, than our linguistic text-books would lead one to suppose. In a class by themselves are the really enormous number of words, many of them sound-imitative or contemptuous in psychological tone, that consist of duplications with either change of the vowel or change of the initial consonant — words of the type *sing-song, riff-raff, wishy-washy, harum-skarum, roly-poly*. Words of this type are all but universal. Such examples as the Russian *Chudo-Yudo* (a dragon), the Chinese *ping-pang* "rattling of rain on the roof,"[19] the Tibetan *kyang-kyong* "lazy," and the Manchu *porpon parpan* "blear-eyed" are curiously reminiscent, both in form and in psychology, of words nearer home. But it can hardly be said that the duplicative process is of a distinctively grammatical significance in English. We must turn to other languages for illustration. Such cases as Hottentot *go-go* "to look at carefully" (from *go* "to see"), Somali

---

[18]These orthographies are but makeshifts for simple sounds.
[19]Whence our *ping-pong*.

fen-fen "to gnaw at on all sides" (from *fen* "to gnaw at"), Chinook *iwi iwi* "to look about carefully, to examine" (from *iwi* "to appear"), or Tsimshian *am'am* "several (are) good" (from *am* "good") do not depart from the natural and fundamental range of significance of the process. A more abstract function is illustrated in Ewe,[20] in which both infinitive and verbal adjectives are formed from verbs by duplication; e.g., *yi* "to go," *yiyi* "to go, act of going"; *wo* "to do," *wowo*[21] "done"; *mawomawo* "not to do" (with both duplicated verb stem and duplicated negative particle). Causative duplications are characteristic of Hottentot, e.g., *gam-gam*[22] "to cause to tell" (from *gam* "to tell"). Or the process may be used to derive verbs from nouns, as in Hottentot *khoe-khoe* "to talk Hottentot" (from *khoe-b* "man, Hottentot"), or as in Kwakiutl *metmat* "to eat clams" (radical element *met-* "clam").

The most characteristic examples of reduplication are such as repeat only part of the radical element. It would be possible to demonstrate the existence of a vast number of formal types of such partial duplication, according to whether the process makes use of one or more of the radical consonants, preserves or weakens or alters the radical vowel, or affects the beginning, the middle, or the end of the radical element. The functions are even more exuberantly developed than with simple duplication, though the basic notion, at least in origin, is nearly always one of repetition or continuance. Examples illustrating this fundamental function can be quoted from all parts of the globe. Initially reduplicating are, for instance, Shilh *ggen* "to be sleeping" (from *gen* "to sleep"); Ful *pepeu'-do* "liar" (i.e., "one who always lies"), plural *fefeu'-be* (from *fewa* "to lie"); Bontoc Igorot *anak* "child," *ananak* "children"; *kamu-ek* "I hasten," *kakamu-ek* "I hasten more"; Tsimshian *gyad* "person," *gyigyad* "people"; Nass *gyibayuk* "to fly," *gyigyibayuk* "one who is flying." Psychologically comparable, but with the reduplication at the end, are Somali *ur* "body," plural *urar*; Hausa *suna* "name," plural *sunana-ki*; Washo[23] *gusu* "buffalo," *gususu* "buffaloes"; Takelma[24] *himi-d-* "to talk to," *himim-d-* "to be accustomed to talk to." Even more commonly than simple duplication, this partial duplication of the radical element has taken on in many languages functions that seem in no way related to the idea of increase. The best known examples are probably the initial reduplication of our older Indo-European languages, which helps to form the perfect tense of many verbs (e.g., Sanskrit *dadarsha* "I have seen," Greek *leloipa* "I have left," Latin *tetigi* "I have touched," Gothic *lelot* "I have let"). In Nootka reduplication of the radical element is often employed in association with certain suffixes; e.g., *hluch-* "woman" forms *hluhluch'-ituhl* "to dream of a woman," *hluhluch-k'-ok* "resembling a woman." Psychologically similar to

---

[20]An African language of the Guinea Coast.

[21]In the verbal adjective the tone of the second syllable differs from that of the first.

[22]Initial "click" omitted.

[23]An Indian language of Nevada.

[24]An Indian language of Oregon.

the Greek and Latin examples are many Takelma cases of verbs that exhibit two forms of the stem, one employed in the present or past, the other in the future and in certain modes and verbal derivatives. The former has final reduplication, which is absent in the latter; e.g., *al-yebeb-i'n* "I show (or showed) to him," *al-yeb-in* "I shall show him."

We come now to the subtlest of all grammatical processes, variations in accent, whether of stress or pitch. The chief difficulty in isolating accent as a functional process is that it is so often combined with alternations in vocalic quantity or quality or complicated by the presence of affixed elements that its grammatical value appears as a secondary rather than as a primary feature. In Greek, for instance, it is characteristic of true verbal forms that they throw the accent back as far as the general accentual rules will permit, while nouns may be more freely accented. There is thus a striking accentual difference between a verbal form like *eluthemen* "we were released," accented on the second syllable of the word, and its participual derivative *lutheis* "released," accented on the last. The presence of the characteristic verbal elements *e-* and *-men* in the first case and of the nominal *-s* in the second tends to obscure the inherent value of the accentual alternation. This value comes out very neatly in such English doublets as *to refund* and *a refund, to extract* and *an extract, to come down* and *a come down, to lack luster* and *lack-luster eyes*, in which the difference between the verb and the noun is entirely a matter of changing stress. In the Athabaskan languages there are not infrequently significant alternations of accent, as in Navaho *ta-di-gis* "you wash yourself" (accented on the second syllable), *ta-di-gis* "he washes himself" (accented on the first).[25]

Pitch accent may be as functional as stress and is perhaps more often so. The mere fact, however, that pitch variations are phonetically essential to the language, as in Chinese (e.g., *feng* "wind" with a level tone, *feng* "to serve" with a falling tone) or as in classical Greek (e.g., *lab-on* "having taken" with a simple or high tone on the suffixed participial *-on, gunaik-on* "of women" with a compound or falling tone on the case suffix *-on*) does not necessarily constitute a functional, or perhaps we had better say grammatical, use of pitch. In such cases the pitch is merely inherent in the radical element or affix, as any vowel or consonant might be. It is different with such Chinese alternations as *chung* (level) "middle" and *chung* (falling) "to hit the middle"; *mai* (rising) "to buy" and *mai* (falling) "to sell"; *pei* (falling) "back" and *pei* (level) "to carry on the back." Examples of this type are not exactly common in Chinese and the language cannot be said to possess at present a definite feeling for tonal differences as symbolic of the distinction between noun and verb.

There are languages, however, in which such differences are of the most fundamental grammatical importance. They are particularly common in the Soudan. In Ewe, for instance, there are formed from *subo* "to serve" two redup-

---

[25]It is unlikely, however, that these Athabaskan alternations are primarily tonal in character.

licated forms, an infinitive *subosubo* "to serve," with a low tone on the first two syllables and a high tone on the last two, and an adjectival *subo-subo* "serving" in which all the syllables have a high tone. Even more striking are cases furnished by Shilluk, one of the languages of the headwaters of the Nile. The plural of the noun often differs in tone from the singular, e.g., *yit* (high) "ear" but *yit* (low) "ears." In the pronoun three forms may be distinguished by tone alone; *e* "he" has a high tone and is subjective, *-e* "him" (e.g., *a chwol-e* "he called him") has a low tone and is objective, *-e* "his" (e.g., *wod-e* "his house") has a middle tone and is possessive. From the verbal element *gwed-* "to write" are formed *gwed-o* "(he) writes" with a low tone, the passive *gwet* "(it was) written" with a falling tone, the imperative *gwet* "write!" with a rising tone, and the verbal noun *gwet* "writing" with a middle tone. In aboriginal America also pitch accent is known to occur as a grammatical process. A good example of such a pitch language is Tlingit, spoken by the Indians of the southern coast of Alaska. In this language many verbs vary the tone of the radical element according to tense; *hun* "to sell," *sin* "to hide," *tin* "to see," and numerous other radical elements, if low-toned refer to past time, if high-toned, to the future. Another type of function is illustrated by the Takelma forms *hel* "song," with falling pitch, but *hel* "sing!" with a rising inflection; parallel to these forms are *sel* (falling) "black paint," *sel* (rising) "paint it!" All in all it is clear that pitch accent, like stress and vocalic or consonantal modifications, is far less infrequently employed as a grammatical process than our own habits of speech would prepare us to believe possible.

Language

LEONARD BLOOMFIELD

CHAPTER II: THE USE OF LANGUAGE

2.1. The most difficult step in the study of language is the first step. Again and again, scholarship has approached the study of language without actually entering upon it. Linguistic science arose from relatively practical preoccupations, such as the use of writing, the study of literature and especially of older records, and the prescription of elegant speech, but people can spend any amount of time on these things without actually entering upon linguistic study. As the individual student is likely to repeat the delays of history, we may do well to speak these matters, so as to distinguish them from the subject of our study.

Writing is not language, but merely a way of recording language by means of visible marks. In some countries, such as China, Egypt, and Mesopotamia, writing was practised thousands of years ago, but to most of the languages that are spoken today it has been applied either in relatively recent times or not at all. Moreover, until the days of printing, literacy was confined to a very few people. All languages were spoken through nearly all of their history by people who did not read or write; the languages of such peoples are just as stable, regular, and rich as the languages of literate nations. A language is the same no matter what system of writing may be used to record it, just as a person is the same no matter how you take his picture. The Japanese have three systems of writing and are developing a fourth. When the Turks, in 1928, adopted the Latin alphabet in place of the Arabic, they went on talking in just the same way as before. In order to study writing, we must know something about language, but the reverse is not true. To be sure, we get our information about the speech of past times largely from written records — and for this reason we shall, in another connection, study the history of writing — but we find this to be a handicap. We have to use great care in interpreting the written symbols into terms of actual speech; often we fail in this, and always we should prefer to have the audible word.

Literature, whether presented in spoken form or, as is now our custom, in writing, consists of beautiful or otherwise notable utterances. The student of literature observes the utterances of certain persons (say, of a Shakespeare) and concerns himself with the content and with the unusual features of form. The interest of the philologist is even broader, for he is concerned with the cultural significance and background of what he reads. The linguist, on the other hand, studies the language of all persons alike; the individual features in which the lan-

(from Leonard Bloomfield, *Language*, N.Y.: 1933, pp. 21–41, 74–79.)

guage of a great writer differs from the ordinary speech of his time and place, interest the linguist no more than do the individual features of any other person's speech, and much less than do the features that are common to all speakers.

The discrimination of elegant or "correct" speech is a by-product of certain social conditions. The linguist has to observe it as he observes other linguistic phenomena. The fact that speakers label a speech-form as "good" or "correct," or else as "bad" or "incorrect," is merely a part of the linguist's data concerning this speech-form. Needless to say, it does not permit him to ignore part of his material or to falsify his records: he observes all speech-forms impartially. It is part of his task to find out under what circumstances the speakers label a form in one way or the other, and, in the case of each particular form, why they label it as they do: why, for example, many people say that *ain't* is "bad" and *am not* is "good." This is only one of the problems of linguistics, and since it is not a fundamental one, it can be attacked only after many other things are known. Strangely enough, people without linguistic training devote a great deal of effort to futile discussions of this topic without progressing to the study of language, which alone could give them the key.

A student of writing, of literature or philology, or of correct speech, if he were persistent and methodical enough, might realize, after some waste of effort, that he had better first study language and then return to these problems. We can save ourselves this detour by turning at once to the observation of normal speech. We begin by observing an act of speech-utterance under very simple circumstances.

2.2. Suppose that Jack and Jill are walking down a lane. Jill is hungry. She sees an apple in a tree. She makes a noise with her larynx, tongue, and lips. Jack vaults the fence, climbs the tree, takes the apple, brings it to Jill, and places it in her hand. Jill eats the apple.

This succession of events could be studied in many ways, but we, who are studying language, will naturally distinguish between the *act of speech* and the other occurrences, which we shall call *practical events*. Viewed in this way, the incident consists of three parts, in order of time:

A. Practical events preceding the act of speech
B. Speech
C. Practical events following the act of speech

We shall examine first the practical events, A and C. The events in A concern mainly the speaker, Jill. She was hungry; that is, some of her muscles were contracting, and some fluids were being secreted, especially in her stomach. Perhaps she was also thirsty: her tongue and throat were dry. The light-waves reflected from the red apple struck her eyes. She saw Jack by her side. Her past dealings with Jack should now enter into the picture; let us suppose that they consisted in some ordinary relation, like that of brother and sister or that of husband and wife. All these events, which precede Jill's speech and concern her, we call the *speaker's stimulus*.

We turn now to C, the practical events which came after Jill's speech. These concern mainly the hearer, Jack, and consist of his fetching the apple and giving it to Jill. The practical events which follow the speech and concern the hearer, we call the *hearer's response*. The events which follow the speech concern also Jill, and this in a very important way: *she gets the apple into her grasp and eats it*.

It is evident at once that our whole story depends upon some of the more remote conditions connected with A and C. Not every Jack and Jill would behave like these. If Jill were bashful or if she had had bad experiences of Jack, she might be hungry and see the apple and still say nothing; if Jack were ill disposed toward her, he might not fetch her the apple, even though she asked for it. The occurrence of a speech (and, as we shall see, the wording of it) and the whole course of practical events before and after it, depend upon the entire life-history of the speaker and of the hearer. We shall assume in the present case, that all these *predisposing factors* were such as to produce the story as we have told it. Supposing this, we want to know what part the speech-utterance (B) played in this story.

If Jill had been alone, she might have been just as hungry and thirsty and might have seen the same apple. If she had sufficient strength and skill to get over the fence and climb the tree, she could get hold of the apple and eat it; if not, she would have to stay hungry. The lone Jill is in much the same position as the speechless animal. If the animal is hungry and sees or smells food, it moves toward the food; whether the animal succeeds in getting the food, depends upon its strength and skill. The state of hunger and the sight or smell of the food are the *stimulus* (which we symbolize by S) and the movements toward the food are the *reaction* (which we symbolize by R). The lone Jill and the speechless animal act in only one way, namely.

$$S \longrightarrow R$$

If this works, they get the food; if it does not work — if they are not strong or skillful enough to get the food by the actions R — they must stay hungry.

Of course, it is important for Jill's welfare that she get the apple. In most instances it is not a matter of life and death, though sometimes it is; in the long run, however, the Jill (or the animal) that gets the food has far better chances of surviving and populating the earth. Therefore, any arrangement which adds to Jill's chances of getting the apple, is enormously valuable for her. The speaking Jill in our story availed herself of just such an arrangement. She had, to begin with, the same chance of getting the apple as had the lone Jill or the speechless animal. In addition to this, however, the speaking Jill had a further chance which the others did not share. Instead of struggling with the fence and the tree, she made a few small movements in her throat and mouth, which produced a little noise. At once, Jack began to make the reactions for her; he performed actions that were beyond Jill's strength, and in the end Jill got the apple. *Language enables one person to make a reaction (R) when another person has the stimulus (S).*

In the ideal case, within a group of people who speak to each other, each person has at his disposal the strength and skill of every person in the group. The more these persons differ as to special skills, the wider a range of power does each one person control. Only one person needs to be a good climber, since he can get fruit for all the rest; only one needs to be a good fisherman, since he can supply the others with fish. *The division of labor, and, with it, the whole working of human society, is due to language.*

2.3.   We have yet to examine B, the speech-event in our story. This, of course, is the part of the story with which we, as students of language, are chiefly concerned. In all of our work we are observing B; A and C concern us only because of their connection with B. Thanks to the sciences of physiology and physics, we know enough about the speech-event to see that it consists of three parts:

(B1) The speaker, Jill, moved her vocal chords (two little muscles inside the adam's-apple), her lower jaw, her tongue, and so on, in a way which forced the air into the form of sound-waves. These movements of the speaker are a reaction to the stimulus S. Instead of performing the *practical* (or *handling*) reaction R — namely, starting realistically off to get hold of the apple — she performed these vocal movements, a *speech* (or *substitute*) reaction, which we shall symbolize by a small letter r. In sum, then, Jill, as a speaking person, has not one but two ways of reacting to a stimulus:

$$S \longrightarrow R \quad \text{(practical reaction)}$$
$$S \longrightarrow r \quad \text{(linguistic substitute reaction)}$$

In the present case she performed the latter.

(B2) The sound-waves in the air in Jill's mouth set the surrounding air into a similar wave-motion.

(B3) These sound-waves in the air struck Jack's ear-drums and set them vibrating, with an effect on Jack's nerves: Jack *heard* the speech. This hearing acted as a stimulus on Jack: we saw him running and fetching the apple and placing it in Jill's grasp, much as if Jill's hunger-and-apple stimulus had been acting on him. An observer from another planet, who did not know that there was such a thing as human speech, would have to conclude that somewhere in Jack's body there was a sense-organ which told him, "Jill is hungry and sees an apple up there." In short, Jack, as a speaking person, reacts to two kinds of stimuli: *practical* stimuli of the type S (such as hunger and the sight of food) and *speech* (or *substitute*) stimuli, certain vibrations in his ear-drums, which we shall symbolize by a small letter s. When we see Jack doing anything (fetching an apple, say), his action may be due not only, as are an animal's actions, to a practical stimulus (such as hunger in his stomach, or the sight of an apple), but, just as often, to a speech-stimulus. His actions, R, may be prompted, not by one, but by two kinds of proddings:

$$\text{(practical stimulus)} \quad S \longrightarrow R$$
$$\text{(linguistic substitute stimulus)} \quad s \longrightarrow R$$

It is evident that the connection between Jill's vocal movements (B1) and Jack's hearing (B3) is subject to very little uncertainty or variation, since it is merely a matter of sound-waves passing through the air (B2). If we represent this connection by a dotted line, then we can symbolize the two human ways of responding to a stimulus by these two diagrams:

speechless reaction: S——————→ R
reaction mediated by speech: S———→ r . . . s———→R

The difference between the two types is evident. The speechless reaction occurs always in the same person as does the stimulus; the person who gets the stimulus is the only one who can make the response. The response, accordingly, is limited to whatever actions the receiver of the stimulus can make. In contrast with this, the reaction mediated by speech may occur in a person who did not get the practical stimulus; the person who gets a stimulus can prompt another person to make a response, and this other person may be able to do things which the speaker cannot. The arrows in our diagrams represent the sequence of events within one person's body — a sequence of events which we think is due to some property of the nervous system. Therefore the speechless reaction can take place only in the body which received the stimulus. In the reaction mediated by speech, on the other hand, there is the link, represented by a dotted line, which consists of sound-waves in the air: the reaction mediated by speech can take place in the body of any person who hears the speech; the possibilities of reaction are enormously increased, since different hearers may be capable of a tremendous variety of acts. *The gap between the bodies of the speaker and the hearer — the discontinuity of the two nervous systems — is bridged by the sound-waves.*

The important things, biologically, are the same in both the speechless and the speaking occurrence, namely S (the hunger and sight of the food) and R (movements which get the food or fail to get it). These are the *practical* phase of the affair. The speech-occurrence, s . . . r, is merely a means by which S and R may occur in different individuals. The normal human being is interested only in S and R; though he uses speech, and thrives by it, he pays no attention to it. Saying the word *apple* or hearing it said, appeases no one's hunger. It, along with the rest of speech, is only a way of getting one's fellow-men to help. As students of language, however, we are concerned precisely with the speech event (s . . . r), worthless in itself, but a means to great ends. We distinguish between language, the subject of our study, and *real* or *practical* events, stimuli and reactions. When anything apparently unimportant turns out to be closely connected with more important things, we say that it has, after all, a "meaning"; namely, it "means" these more important things. Accordingly, we say that speech-utterance, trivial and unimportant in itself, is important because it has a *meaning*: the meaning consists of the important things with which the speech-utterance (B) is connected, namely the practical events (A and C).

2.4.   Up to a certain point, some animals respond to each other's stimuli. Evidently the marvelous co-ordination in a group of ants or bees must be due to some form of interaction. Sounds as a means for this are common enough: crickets, for instance, call other crickets by *stridulation*, noisily rubbing the leg against the body. Some animals, like man, use *vocal* noises. Birds produce sound-waves by means of the *syrinx*, a pair of reed-like organs at the head of the lungs. The higher mammals have a *larynx*, a box of cartilage (in man called the adam's-apple) at the top of the wind-pipe. Inside the larynx, at the right and left, two shelf-like muscles run along the walls; when these muscles, the *vocal chords*, are stretched taut, the outgoing breath sets them into a regular vibration which produces sound. This sound we call the *voice*.

Human speech differs from the signal-like actions of animals, even of those which use the voice, by its great differentiation. Dogs, for instance, make only two or three kinds of noise — say, barking, growling, and whining: a dog can set another dog acting by means of only these few different signals. Parrots can make a great many kinds of noise, but apparently do not make different responses to different sounds. Man utters many kinds of vocal noise and makes use of the variety: under certain types of stimuli he produces certain vocal sounds, and his fellows, hearing these same sounds, make the appropriate response. To put it briefly, in human speech, different sounds have different meanings. To study this co-ordination of certain sounds with certain meanings is to study language.

This co-ordination makes it possible for man to interact with great precision. When we tell someone, for instance, the address of a house he has never seen, we are doing something which no animal can do. Not only has each person at his service the abilities of many other persons, but this co-operation is very precise. The extent and accuracy of this working-together is the measure of success of our social organization. The term *society* or *social organism* is not a metaphor. A human social group is really a unit of a higher order than a single animal, just as a many-celled animal is a unit of a higher order than a single cell. The single cells in the many-celled animal co-operate by means of such arrangements as the nervous system; the individuals in a human society co-operate by means of sound-waves.

The different ways in which we profit by language are so obvious that we need mention only a few. We can *relay* communication. When some farmers or traders say *We want a bridge over this stream*, this news may pass through a town meeting, a state legislature, a bureau of roads, an engineering staff, and a contractor's office, running through many speakers and many relays of speech, until at last, in response to the farmers' original stimulus, a corps of workmen make the actual (practical) response movements of putting up a bridge. Closely connected with the relay character of speech is its *abstraction*. The relays of speech, between the practical stimulus and the practical response, have no immediate practical effect. Therefore they can be put into all kinds of forms, provided only one changes them back correctly before proceeding to the final, practical response. The engineer who plans the bridge does not have to handle the actual beams and girders; he works merely with speech-forms (such as numbers in calculation); if he makes a mistake, he does not destroy any materials; he need only replace the ill-chosen speech-form (say, a wrong figure) by a suitable one before he begins the actual building. In this lies the value of *talking to oneself* or *thinking*. As children, we talk to ourselves aloud, but, under the correction of our elders, we soon learn to suppress the sound-producing movements and replace them by very slight inaudible ones: we "think in words." The usefulness of thinking can be illustrated by the process of counting. Our ability to estimate numbers without using speech, is extremely limited, as anyone may see by glancing, say, at a row of books on a shelf. To say that two sets of objects "have the same number" means that if we take one object from the first set and place it next to one object of the second set, and keep on doing this without using any object more than once, we shall have no unpaired objects left over. Now, we cannot always do this. The objects may be too heavy to move, or they may be in different parts of the world, or they may exist at different times (as, say, a flock of sheep before and after a storm). Here language steps in. The numerals *one, two, three, four*, and so on, are simply a series of words which we have learned to say in a fixed order, as substitutes for the above-described process. Using them, we can "count" any set of objects by placing them into one-to-one correspondence (as mathematicians call it) with the number-words, saying *one* for one of the objects, *two* for another, *three* for the next, and so on, taking care to use each object only once, until the objects of the set are exhausted. Suppose 'that when we had said *nineteen*, there were no more objects left. Thereafter, at any time or place, we can decide whether any set of objects has the same number as this first set, by merely repeating the counting process with the new set. Mathematics, the ideal use of language, consists merely of elaborations of this process. The use of numbers is the simplest and clearest case of the usefulness of talking to oneself, but there are many others. We think before we act.

2.5. The particular speech-sounds which people utter under particular stimuli, differ among different groups of men; mankind speaks many languages. A group of people who use the same system of speech-signals is a *speech-community*. Obviously, the value of language depends upon people's using it in the same way. Every member of the social group must upon suitable occasion utter the proper speech-sounds and, when he hears another utter these speech-sounds, must make the proper response. He must speak intelligibly and must understand what others say. This holds good for even the least civilized communities; wherever we find man, he speaks.

Every child that is born into a group acquires these habits of speech and response in the first years of his life. This is doubtless the greatest intellectual feat any one of us is ever required to perform. Exactly how children learn to speak is not known; the process seems to be something like this:

1. Under various stimuli the child utters and repeats vocal sounds. This seems to be an inherited trait. Suppose he makes a noise which we may represent

as *da*, although, of course, the actual movements and the resultant sounds differ from any that are used in conventional English speech. The sound-vibrations strike the child's ear-drums while he keeps repeating the movements. This results in a habit: whenever a similar sound strikes his ear, he is likely to make these same mouth-movements, repeating the sound *da*. This babbling trains him to reproduce vocal sounds which strike his ear.

2. Some person, say the mother, utters in the child's presence a sound which resembles one of the child's babbling syllables. For instance, she says *doll*. When these sounds strike the child's ear, his habit (1) comes into play and he utters his nearest babbling syllable, *da*. We say that he is beginning to "imitate." Grown-ups seem to have observed this everywhere, for every language seems to contain certain nursery-words which resemble a child's babbling — words like *mama*, *dada*: doubtless these got their vogue because children easily learn to repeat them.

3. The mother, of course, uses her words when the appropriate stimulus is present. She says *doll* when she is actually showing or giving the infant his doll. The sight and handling of the doll and the hearing and saying of the word *doll* (that is, *da*) occur repeatedly together, until the child forms a new habit: the sight and feel of the doll suffice to make him say *da*. He has now the use of a word. To the adults it may not sound like any of their words, but this is due merely to its imperfection. It is not likely that children ever invent a word.

4. The habit of saying *da* at sight of the doll gives rise to further habits. Suppose, for instance, that day after day the child is given his doll (and says *da*, *da*, *da*) immediately after his bath. He has now a habit of saying *da*, *da* after his bath; that is, if one day the mother forgets to give him the doll, he may nevertheless cry *da*, *da* after his bath. "He is asking for his doll," says the mother, and she is right, since doubtless an adult's "asking for" or "wanting" things is only a more complicated type of the same situation. The child has now embarked upon *abstract* or *displaced* speech: he names a thing even when that thing is not present.

5. The child's speech is perfected by its results. If he says *da*, *da* well enough, his elders understand him; that is, they give him his doll. When this happens, the sight and feel of the doll act as an additional stimulus, and the child repeats and practises his successful version of the word. On the other hand, if he says his *da*, *da* imperfectly — that is, at great variance from the adults' conventional form *doll*, — then his elders are not stimulated to give him the doll. Instead of getting the added stimulus of seeing and handling the doll, the child is now subject to other distracting stimuli, or perhaps, in the unaccustomed situation of having no doll after his bath, he goes into a tantrum which disorders his recent impressions. In short, his more perfect attempts at speech are likely to be fortified by repetition, and his failures to be wiped out in confusion. This process never stops. At a much later stage, if he says *Daddy bringed it*, he merely gets a disappointing answer such as *No! You must say "Daddy brought it"*; but if he

says *Daddy brought it*, he is likely to hear the form over again: *Yes, Daddy brought it*, and to get a favorable practical response.

At the same time and by the same process, the child learns also to act the part of a hearer. While he is handling the doll he hears himself say *da, da* and his mother say *doll*. After a time, hearing the sound may suffice to make him handle the doll. The mother will say *Wave your hand to Daddy*, when the child is doing this of his own accord or while she is holding up the child's arm and waving it for him. The child forms habits of acting in conventional ways when he hears speech.

This twofold character of the speech-habits becomes more and more unified, since the two phases always occur together. In each case where the child learns the connection S ──────→ r (for instance, to say *doll* when he sees his doll), he learns also the connection s ──────→ R (for instance, to reach for his doll or handle it when he hears the word *doll*). After he has learned a number of such twofold sets, he develops a habit by which one type always involves the other: as soon as he learns to speak a new word, he is also able to respond to it when he hears others speak it, and, vice versa, as soon as he learns how to respond to some new word, he is usually able, also, to speak it on proper occasion. The latter transference seems to be the more difficult of the two; in later life, we find that a speaker understands many speech-forms which he seldom or never employs in his own speech.

2.6.   The happenings which in our diagram are represented by a dotted line, are fairly well understood. The speaker's vocal chords, tongue, lips, and so on, interfere with the stream of his outgoing breath, in such a way as to produce sound-waves; these waves are propagated through the air and strike the hearer's ear-drums, which then vibrate in unison. The happenings, however, which we have represented by arrows, are very obscure. We do not understand the mechanism which makes people say certain things in certain situations, or the mechanism which makes them respond appropriately when these speech-sounds strike their ear-drums. Evidently these mechanisms are a phase of our general equipment for responding to stimuli, be they speech sounds or others. These mechanisms are studied in physiology and, especially, in psychology. To study them in their special bearing on language, is to study the psychology of speech, *linguistic psychology*. In the division of scientific labor, the linguist deals only with the speech signal (r . . . . s); he is not competent to deal with problems of physiology or psychology. The findings of the linguist, who studies the speech-signal, will be all the more valuable for the psychologist if they are not distorted by any prepossessions about psychology. We have seen that many of the older linguists ignored this; they vitiated or skimped their reports by trying to state everything in terms of some psychological theory. We shall all the more surely avoid this fault, however, if we survey a few of the more obvious phases of the psychology of language.

The mechanism which governs speech must be very complex and delicate.

Even if we know a great deal about a speaker and about the immediate stimuli which are acting upon him, we usually cannot predict whether he will speak or what he will say. We took our story of Jack and Jill as something known to us, after the fact. Had we been present, we could not have foretold whether Jill would say anything when she saw the apple, or, in case she did speak, what words she would utter. Even supposing she asked for the apple, we could not foretell whether she would preface her request by saying *I'm hungry* or whether she would say *please* or whether she would say *I want that apple* or *Get me that apple* or *I was just wishing I had an apple*, and so on: the possibilities are almost infinite. This enormous variability has led to two theories about human conduct, including speech.

The *mentalistic* theory, which is by far the older, and still prevails both in the popular view and among men of science, supposes that the variability of human conduct is due to the interference of some non-physical factor, a *spirit* or *will* or *mind* (Greek *psyche*, hence the term psychology) that is present in every human being. This spirit, according to the mentalistic view, is entirely different from material things and accordingly follows some other kind of causation or perhaps none at all. Whether Jill will speak or what words she will use, depends, then, upon some act of her mind or will, and, as this mind or will does not follow the patterns of succession (cause-and-effect sequences) of the material world, we cannot foretell her actions.

The *materialistic* (or, better, *mechanistic*) theory supposes that the variability of human conduct, including speech, is due only to the fact that the human body is a very complex system. Human actions, according to the materialistic view, are part of cause-and-effect sequences exactly like those which we observe, say in the study of physics or chemistry. However, the human body is so complex a structure that even a relatively simple change, such as, say, the impingement on the retina of light-waves from a red apple, may set off some very complicated chain of consequences, and a very slight difference in the state of the body may result in a great difference in its response to the light-waves. We could foretell a person's actions (for instance, whether a certain stimulus will lead him to speak, and, if so, the exact words he will utter), only if we knew the exact structure of his body at the moment, or, what comes to the same thing, if we knew the exact make-up of his organism at some early stage — say at birth or before — and then had a record of every change in that organism, including every stimulus that had ever affected the organism.

The part of the human body responsible for this delicate and variable adjustment, is the nervous system. The nervous system is a very complex conducting mechanism, which makes it possible for a change in one part of the body (a stimulus, say, in the eye) to result in a change in some other part (a response, say, of reaching with the arm, or of moving the vocal chords and tongue). Further, it is clear that the nervous system is changed, for a time or even permanently, by this very process of conduction: our responses depend very largely upon our earlier dealings with the same or similar stimuli. Whether Jill will speak depends largely on her liking for apples and on her past experience of Jack. We remember and acquire habits and learn. The nervous system is evidently a trigger-mechanism: a very slight change may set the match to a large store of explosive material. To take the case that interests us, only so can we explain the fact that large-scale movements like Jack's fetching the apple, are set off by very slight changes, such as the minute thrumming of air-waves on his ear-drum.

The working of the nervous system is not accessible to observation from without, and the person himself has no sense-organs (such as he has, for instance, for the working of the muscles in his hand) with which he himself could observe what goes on in his nerves. Therefore the psychologist must resort to indirect methods of approach.

2.7. One such method is experiment. The psychologist submits numbers of people to carefully prearranged stimuli under the simplest conditions, and records their responses. Usually he also asks these persons to "introspect," — that is, to describe as much as possible of what goes on inside them when they get the stimulus. At this point psychologists often go astray for want of linguistic knowledge. It is a mistake, for instance, to suppose that language enables a person to observe things for which he has no sense-organs, such as the workings of his own nervous system. An observer's only advantage in reporting what goes on inside him is that he can report stimulations which an outsider cannot detect — say, a pain in his eye or a tickling in his throat. Even here, we must not forget that language is a matter of training and habit; a person may be unable to report some stimulations, simply because his stock of speech-habits provides no formula; this is the case with many of our less useful adventures, such as smaller goings-on in our internal organs. Often the very structure of our body leads to a false report; we show the physician exactly the spot where we feel a pain, and he finds the injury some distance away, at a point which his experience may teach him to locate at once from our false description. In this respect many psychologists go astray by actually training their observers to use a set of technical terms for obscure stimuli and then attaching significance to the observer's use of these terms.

Abnormal conditions in which speech is disturbed, seem to reflect general maladjustments or lesions and to throw no light on the particular mechanism of language. *Stuttering* is probably due to imperfect specialization of the two cerebral hemispheres: in the normal speaker the left hemisphere (or, if he is left-handed, the right hemisphere) dominates more delicate actions, such as those of speech; in the stutterer this one-sided specialization is incomplete. Imperfect production of specific sounds (*stammering*), where it is not due to anatomical defects in the organs of speech, seems to result from similar maladjustments. Head-wounds and diseases which injure the brain often result in *aphasia*, disturbances in the manner of making speech-responses and in responding to speech. Dr. Henry Head, who had unusually good opportunities for the study of aphasia in wounded soldiers, recognizes four types.

Type 1 reacts well to other people's speech, and in milder cases, uses words for the proper objects, but mispronounces or confuses his words; in extreme cases, the sufferer can say little more than *yes* and *no*. A patient reports, with some difficulty: "I know it's not . . . the correct . . . pronunciation . . . I don't always . . . *corret* it . . . because I shouldn't get it right . . . in five or six times . . . unless someone says it for me." In a more serious case, the patient, when asked his name, answers *Honus* instead of Thomas, and says *erst* for "first" and *hend* for "second."

Type 2 reacts fairly well to simple speech, and pronounces appropriate words and short phrases, but not in the conventional constructions; he may talk an unintelligible jargon, although each word is correct enough. To the question, "Have you played any games?" a patient answers: "Played games, yes, played one, daytime, garden." He says, "Get out, lay down, go to sleep, sometimes goes away. If sit in kitchen, moving about working, makes me getting worse on it." He comments, "Funny thing, this worse, that sort of thing," and by way of explanation, writes down the words *as* and *at*. We shall see later that the structure of normal language forces us to distinguish between lexical and grammatical habits of speech; the latter are disturbed in these patients.

Type 3 reacts with difficulty to the names of objects, and has trouble in finding the right words, especially names of things. His pronunciation and arrangement are good, but he has to use ingenious circumlocutions for the words he cannot find. For "scissors" a patient says "what you cut with"; for "black" he says: "people who are dead, — the other people who are not dead, have this color." He may use the wrong word, as *button* for "scissors." The words lost are chiefly the names of concrete objects. This state seems like an exaggeration of many normal persons' difficulty in recalling people's names and the designations of objects, especially under preoccupation, excitement, or fatigue.

Type 4 often does not respond correctly to the speech of others; he has no trouble in uttering single words, but he cannot finish a connected speech. It is significant that these patients suffer from apraxia; they cannot find their way about and are confused by being set, say, on the opposite side of the street. One patient reports: "I don't seem to understand all you say, and then I forget what I've got to do." Another patient says: "When at table, I am very slow in picking out the object, say the milk-jug, which I want. I don't spot it at once . . . I see them all, but I don't spot them. When I want the salt or the pepper or a spoon, I suddenly tumble to its presence." The disturbance of speech appears in this answer of a patient: "Oh, yes! I know the difference between the Nurse and the Sister by the dress: Sister blue; Nurse — oh! I get muddled, just ordinary nurse's clothes, white, blue . . ."

Ever since 1861, when Broca showed that damage to the third frontal convolution in the left hemisphere of the brain was accompanied by aphasia, there has been dispute as to whether "Broca's center" and other regions of the cortex act as specific centers for the activity of speech. Head finds some correlation between different points of lesion and each of his four types of aphasia. The demonstrable functional identifications of cortical areas always concern some specific organ: an injury in one area of the brain is accompanied by paralysis of the right foot, an injury in another area by failure to respond to stimulation in the left-hand side of the retina, and so on. Now, speech is a very complex activity, in which stimulation of every kind leads to highly specific movements of the throat and mouth; these last, moreover, are not, in a physiologic sense, "organs of speech," for they serve biologically earlier uses in man and in speechless animals. Many injuries to the nervous system, accordingly, will interfere with speech, and different injuries will result in different kinds of difficulty, but the points of the cortex are surely not correlated with specific socially significant features of speech, such as words or syntax; this appears plainly from the fluctuating and contradictory results of the search for various kinds of "speech centers." We may expect the physiologist to get better results when he looks for correlations between points of the cortex and specific physiologic activities concerned in speech, such as the movement of special muscles or the transmission of kinesthetic stimuli from the larynx and tongue. The error of seeking correlations between anatomically defined parts of the nervous system and socially defined activities appears clearly when we see some physiologists looking for a "visual word-center" which is to control reading and writing: one might as well look for a specific brain-center for telegraphy or automobile-driving or the use of any modern invention. Physiologically, language is not a unit of function, but consists of a great many activities, whose union into a single far-reaching complex of habits results from repeated stimulations during the individual's early life.

2.8. Another way of studying human responses is to observe them in the mass. Some actions are highly variable in each person, but fairly constant in large groups of persons. We cannot predict whether any particular unmarried adult will marry during the next twelve months, or which particular persons will commit suicide, or which ones will get into prison, but, given a large enough community, and the figures for past years (and perhaps certain other data, such as those which concern economic conditions), statisticians can foretell the number of marriages, suicides, convictions for crime, and so on, which will take place. If we found it possible and worth while to register every speech-utterance in a large community, we should doubtless be able to foretell how many times any given utterance such as *Good-morning* or *I love you* or *How much are oranges today*? would be spoken within a fixed number of days. A detailed study of this kind would tell us a great deal, especially about the changes that are constantly going on in every language.

However, there is another and simpler way of studying human action in the mass: the study of conventional actions. When we go to a strange country, we soon learn many established modes of action, such as the system of currency and of weights and measures, the rules of the road (does one keep to the right, as in America and Germany, or to the left, as in England and Sweden?), good manners, hours for meals, and so on. The traveler does not gather statistics: a very few observations put him on the track, and these are confirmed or corrected by further experience. Here the linguist is in a fortunate position: in no other respect are the activities of a group as rigidly standardized as in the forms of language. Large groups of people make up all their utterances out of the same stock of lexical forms and grammatical constructions. A linguistic observer therefore can describe the speech-habits of a community without resorting to statistics. Needless to say, he must work conscientiously and, in particular, he must record every form he can find and not try to excuse himself from this task by appealing to the reader's common sense or to the structure of some other language or to some psychological theory, and, above all, he must not select or distort the facts according to his views of what the speakers ought to be saying. Aside from its intrinsic value for the study of language, a relevant and unprejudiced description of this kind, serves as a document of major importance for psychology. The danger here lies in mentalistic views of psychology, which may tempt the observer to appeal to purely spiritual standards instead of reporting the facts. To say, for instance, that combinations of words which are "felt to be" compounds have only a single high stress (e.g. *blackbird* as opposed to *black bird*), is to tell exactly nothing, since we have no way of determining what the speakers may "feel": the observer's task was to tell us, by some tangible criterion, or, if he found none, by a list, which combinations of words are pronounced with a single high stress. A worker who accepts the materialistic hypothesis in psychology is under no such temptation; it may be stated as a principle that in all sciences like linguistics, which observe some specific type of human activity, the worker must proceed exactly as if he held the materialistic view. This practical effectiveness is one of the strongest considerations in favor of scientific materialism.

The observer who, by this mass-observation, gives us a statement of the speech-habits of a community, can tell us nothing about the changes which are going on in the language of this as of every community. These changes could be observed only by means of genuinely statistical observation through a considerable length of time; for want of this, we are ignorant of many matters concerning linguistic change. In this respect, too, the science of language is fortunate, however, because comparative and geographical methods of study, again through mass-observation, supply a good deal of what we should hope to get from statistics. The fortunate position of our science in these matters is due to the fact that language is the simplest and most fundamental of our social (that is, peculiarly human) activities. In another direction, however, the study of linguistic change profits by a mere accident, namely by the existence of written records of speech of the past.

2.9.   The stimulus which calls forth speech, leads also to some other reactions. Some of these are not visible from the outside; these are muscular and glandular actions which are of no immediate importance to the speaker's fellow-men. Others are important handling responses, such as locomotion or the displacement of objects. Still other responses are visible, but not directly important; they do not change the lay-out of things, but they do, along with speech, serve as stimuli to the hearer. These actions are facial expression, mimicry, tone of voice (in so far as it is not prescribed by the conventions of the language), insignificant handling of objects (such as fiddling with a rubber band), and, above all, *gesture*.

Gesture accompanies all speech; in kind and in amount, it differs with the individual speaker, but to a large extent it is governed by social convention. Italians use more gesture than English-speaking people; in our civilization people of the privileged class gesticulate least. To some extent, individual gestures are conventional and differ for different communities. In saying good-by we wave the hand with palm outward; Neapolitans wave it with the back outward.

Most gestures scarcely go beyond an obvious pointing and picturing. American Indians of plains or woodland tribes will accompany a story by unobtrusive gestures, foreign to us, but quite intelligible: the hand, palm in, thumb up, is held just under the eyes to represent spying; a fist is slapped into a palm for a shot; two fingers imitate a man walking, and four the running of a horse. Even where gestures are symbolic, they go little beyond the obvious, as when one points back over one's shoulder to indicate past time.

Some communities have a *gesture language* which upon occasion they use instead of speech. Such gesture languages have been observed among the lower-class Neapolitans, among Trappist monks (who have made a vow of silence), among the Indians of our western plains (where tribes of different language met in commerce and war), and among groups of deaf-mutes.

It seems certain that these gesture languages are merely developments of ordinary gestures and that any and all complicated or not immediately intelligible gestures are based on the conventions of ordinary speech. Even such an obvious transference as pointing backward to indicate past time, is probably due to a linguistic habit of using the same word for "in the rear" and "in the past." Whatever may be the origins of the two, gesture has so long played a secondary role under the dominance of language that it has lost all traces of independent character. Tales about peoples whose language is so defective that it has to be eked out by gesture, are pure myths. Doubtless the production of vocal sound by animals, out of which language has grown, originated as a response-movement (say, contraction of the diaphragm and constriction of the throat) which happened to produce noise. It seems certain, however, that in the further development, language always ran ahead of gesture.

If one gestures by moving some object so as to leave a trace on another object, one has entered upon marking and drawing. This kind of reaction has the value of leaving a permanent mark, which may serve as a stimulus repeatedly and even after intervals of time and can be transported to stimulate persons far away. For this reason, doubtless, many peoples attribute magic power to drawings, apart from their esthetic value, which is still with us.

In some parts of the world drawing has developed into writing. The details of this process will concern us later; the point of interest here is that the action of tracing an outline becomes subordinate to language: drawing a particular set of lines becomes attached, as an accompaniment or substitute, to the utterance of a particular linguistic form.

The art of symbolizing particular forms of speech by means of particular visible marks adds a great deal to the effective uses of language. A speaker can be heard only a short ways and only for an instant or two. A written record can be carried to any place and preserved for any length of time. We can see more things at one time than we can hear, and we can deal better with visible things: charts, diagrams, written calculations, and similar devices, enable us to deal with very complex matters. The speech-stimuli of distant people, and especially of persons in the past, are available to us through writing. This makes possible an accumulation of knowledge. The man of science (but not always the amateur) surveys the results of earlier students and applies his energies at the point where they left off. Instead of always starting over again from the beginning, science progresses cumulatively and with acceleration. It has been said that, as we preserve more and more records of more and more speech-reactions of highly gifted and highly specialized individuals, we approach, as an ideal limit, a condition where all the events in the universe, past, present, and future, are reduced (in a symbolic form to which any reader may react) to the dimensions of a large library. It is no wonder that the discovery of printing, which manifolds a written record to any desired number of copies, brought about, in all our manner of living, a revolution which has been under way for some centuries and is still in full swing.

There is no need of dilating upon the significance of other means for recording, transmitting, and multiplying speech, such as the telegraph, telephone, phonograph, and radio. Their importance for the simpler uses of language is obvious, as in the use of wireless telegraphy in cases of shipwreck.

In the long run, anything which adds to the viability of language has also an indirect but more pervasive effect. Even acts of speech that do not prompt any particular immediate response, may change the predisposition of the hearer for further responses: a beautiful poem, for instance, may make the hearer more sensitive to later stimuli. This general refinement and intensification of human response requires a great deal of linguistic interaction. Education or culture, or whatever name we choose to give it, depends upon the repetition and publication of a vast amount of speech.

CHAPTER V: THE PHONEME

5.1. In Chapter II we distinguished three successive events in an act of speech: A, the speaker's situation; B, his utterance of speech-sound and its impingement on the hearer's ear-drums; and C, the hearer's response. Of these three types of events, A and C include all the situations that may prompt a person to speak and all the actions which a hearer may perform in response; in sum, A and C make up the world in which we live. On the other hand, B, the speech-sound, is merely a means which enables us to respond to situations that would otherwise leave us unaffected, or to respond more accurately to situations that otherwise might prompt less useful responses. In principle, the student of language is concerned only with the actual speech (B); the study of speakers' situations and hearers' responses (A and C) is equivalent to the sum total of human knowledge. If we had an accurate knowledge of every speaker's situation and of every hearer's response — and this would make us little short of omniscient — we could simply register these two facts as the *meaning* (A-C) of any given speech-utterance (B), and neatly separate our study from all other domains of knowledge. The fact that speech-utterances themselves often play a part in the situation of a speaker and in the response of a hearer, might complicate things, but this difficulty would not be serious. Linguistics, on this ideal plane, would consist of two main investigations: *phonetics*, in which we studied the speech-event without reference to its meaning, investigating only the sound-producing movements of the speaker, the sound-waves, and the action of the hearer's ear-drum, and *semantics*, in which we studied the relation of these features to the features of meaning, showing that a certain type of speech-sound was uttered in certain types of situations and led the hearer to perform certain types of response.

Actually, however, our knowledge of the world in which we live is so imperfect that we can rarely make accurate statements about the meaning of a speech-form. The situations (A) which lead to an utterance, and the hearer's responses (C), include many things that have not been mastered by science. Even if we knew much more than we do about the external world, we should still have to reckon with the predispositions of the speaker and the hearer. We cannot foretell whether, in a given situation, a person will speak, or if so, what words he will use, and we cannot foretell how he will respond to a given speech.

It is true that we are concerned not so much with each individual as with the whole community. We do not inquire into the minute nervous processes of a person who utters, say the word *apple*, but content ourselves rather with determining that, by and large, for all members of the community, the word *apple* means a certain kind of fruit. However, as soon as we try to deal accurately with this matter, we find that the agreement of the community is far from perfect, and that every person uses speech-forms in a unique way.

The study of language can be conducted without special assumptions only so long as we pay no attention to the meaning of what is spoken. This phase of language study is known as *phonetics* (*experimental phonetics, laboratory phonetics*). The phonetician can study either the sound-producing movements of the speaker (*physiological phonetics*) or the resulting sound-waves (*physical* or *acoustic phonetics*); we have as yet no means for studying the action of the hearer's ear-drum.

Physiological phonetics begins with inspection. The *laryngoscope*, for instance, is a mirror-device which enables an observer to see another person's (or his own) vocal chords. Like other devices of the sort, it interferes with normal speech and can serve only for very limited phases of observation. The x-ray does good service where its limitations can be overcome; tongue-positions can be photographed, for instance, if one lays a thin metal strip or chain along the upper surface of the tongue. Other devices give a transferred record. For instance, a false palate covered with coloring-matter is put into the mouth; after the speaker utters a sound, the places where the tongue has touched the palate are recognizable by the removal of the coloring-matter. In most devices of this sort a bulb is attached to some part of the speaker's vocal organs, say to the adam's-apple; the mechanism transforms the movement into up-and-down movements of a pen-point which touches a strip of paper. The strip of paper is kept moving at an even rate of speed, so that the up-and-down movement of the pen-point appears on the paper as a wavy line. This recording device is called a *kymograph*. In acoustic phonetics one secures imprints of the sound-waves. Records of this kind are familiar to us in the form of phonograph-disks; phoneticians have not yet succeeded in analyzing most features of such records.

A considerable part of our information about speech-sounds is due to the methods we have just outlined. However, laboratory phonetics does not enable us to connect speech-sounds with meanings; it studies speech-sounds only as muscular movements or as disturbances in the air, without regard to their use in communication. On this plane we find that speech-sounds are infinitely complex and infinitely varied.

Even a short speech is continuous: it consists of an unbroken succession of movements and sound-waves. No matter into how many successive parts we break up our record for purposes of minute study, an even finer analysis is always conceivable. A speech-utterance is what mathematicians call a *continuum*; it can be viewed as consisting of any desired number of successive parts.

Speech-utterances are infinitely varied. Everyday experience tells us that different persons speak differently, for we can recognize people by their voices. The phonetician finds that no two utterances are exactly alike.

Evidently the working of language is due to a resemblance between successive utterances. Utterances which in ordinary life we describe as consisting of "the same" speech-forms — say, successive utterances of the sentence *I'm hungry* — evidently contain some constant features of sound-wave, common to all utterances of this "same" speech-form. Only on this assumption can we account for our ordinary use of language. The phonetician, however, cannot make sure of these constant features, as long as he ignores the meaning of what is said. Suppose, for instance, that he had records of an utterance which we could identify as representing the syllable *man*, spoken on two different pitch-schemes. If the language of these utterances were English, we should say that both contained the same speech-form, namely, the word *man*, but if the language were Chinese, the two records might represent two different speech-forms, since in Chinese differences of pitch-schemes are connected with different meanings: the word *man* with a high rising pitch, for instance means "deceive," and the word *man* with a falling pitch means "slow." As long as we pay no attention to meanings, we cannot decide whether two uttered forms are "the same" or "different." The phonetician cannot tell us which features are significant for communication and which features are immaterial. A feature which is significant in some languages or dialects, may be indifferent in others.

5.3.   The fact that two utterances of the syllable *man* with different pitch-schemes are "the same" speech-form in English, but "different" speech-forms in Chinese, shows us that the working of language depends upon our habitually and conventionally discriminating some features of sound and ignoring all others. The features of sound in any utterance, as they might be recorded in the laboratory, are the *gross acoustic features* of this utterance. Part of the gross acoustic features are indifferent (*non-distinctive*), and only a part are connected with meanings and essential to communications (*distinctive*). The difference between distinctive and non-distinctive features of sound lies entirely in the habit of the speakers. A feature that is distinctive in one language, may be non-distinctive in another language.

Since we can recognize the distinctive features of an utterance only when we know the meaning, we cannot identify them on the plane of pure phonetics. We know that the difference between the English forms *man* and *men* is distinctive, because we know from ordinary life that these two forms are used under different circumstances. It is possible that some science other than linguistics may define this difference in accurate terms, providing even for the case where we use *man* for more than one individual (*man wants but little here below*). In any case, however, this difference cannot be recognized by purely phonetic observation: the difference between the vowel sounds of *man* and *men* is in some languages non-distinctive.

To recognize the distinctive features of a language, we must leave the ground of pure phonetics and act as though science had progressed far enough to identify all the situations and responses that make up the meaning of speech-forms. In the case of our own language, we trust to our everyday knowledge to tell us whether speech-forms are "the same" or "different." Thus, we find that the word *man* spoken on various pitch-schemes is in English still "the same" word, with one and the same meaning, but that *man* and *men* (or *pan* and *pen*) are "different" words, with different meanings. In the case of a strange language we have to learn such things by trial and error, or to obtain the meanings from someone that knows the language.

The study of *significant* speech-sounds is *phonology* or *practical phonetics*. Phonology involves the consideration of meanings. The meanings of speech-forms could be scientifically defined only if all branches of science, including especially, psychology and physiology, were close to perfection. Until that time, phonology and, with it, all the semantic phase of language study, rests upon an assumption, the fundamental assumption of linguistics: we must assume that *in every speech-community some utterances are alike in form and meaning*.

5.4.   A moderate amount of experimenting will show that the significant features of a speech-form are limited in number. In this respect, the significant features contrast with the gross acoustic features, which, as we have seen, form a continuous whole and can be subdivided into any desired number of parts. In order to recognize the distinctive features of forms in our own language, we need only determine which features of sound are "different" for purposes of communication. Suppose, for instance, that we start with the word *pin*: a few experiments in saying words out loud soon reveal the following resemblances and differences:

> 1. *pin* ends with the same sound as *fin, sin, tin*, but begins differently; this kind of resemblance is familiar to us because of our tradition of using end-rime in verse;
> 2. *pin* contains the sound of *in*, but adds something at the beginning;
> 3. *pin* ends with the same sound as *man, sun, hen*, but the resemblance is smaller than in (1) and (2);
> 4. *pin* begins with the same sound as *pig, pill, pit*, but ends differently;
> 5. *pin* begins with the same sound as *pat, push, peg*, but the resemblance is smaller than in (4);
> 6. *pin* begins and ends like *pen, pan, pun*, but the middle part is different;
> 7. *pin* begins and ends differently from *dig, fish, mill*, but the middle part is the same.

In this way, we can find forms which partially resemble *pin*, by altering any one of *three* parts of the word. We can alter first one and then a second of the three parts and still have a partial resemblance: if we alter the first part and then the second, we get a series like *pin - tin - tan*; if we alter the first part and then the third, we get a series like *pin - tin- tick*; if we alter the second part and then the third, we get a series like *pin - pan - pack*: And if we alter all three parts, no resemblance is left, as in *pin - tin - tan - tack*.

Further experiment fails to reveal any more replaceable parts in the word *pin*: we conclude that the distinctive features of this word are three indivisible units. Each of these units occurs also in other combinations, but cannot be further analyzed by partial resemblances: each of the three is *a minimum unit of distinctive sound-feature, a phoneme*. Thus we say that the word *pin* consists of three phonemes: the first of these occurs also in *pet, pack, push*, and many other words; the second also in *fig, hit, miss*, and many other words; the third also in *tan, run, hen*, and many other words. In the case of *pin* our alphabetic writing represents the three phonemes by three letters, *p, i*, and *n*, but our conventions of writing are a poor guide; in the word *thick*, for instance, our writing represents the first phoneme by the two-letter group *th* and the third by the two-letter group *ck*.

A little practice will enable the observer to recognize a phoneme even when it appears in different parts of words, as *pin, apple, mop*. Sometimes our stock of words does not readily bring out the resemblances and differences. For instance, the word *then* evidently consists of three phonemes, but (especially under the influence of our way of writing) we might question whether the initial phoneme was or was not the same as in *thick*; once we hit upon the pair *thigh* and *thy*, or upon *mouth* and *mouthe*, we see that they are different.

An Outline of English Structure

GEORGE L. TRAGER AND HENRY LEE SMITH, JR.

The phonemes of English have been shown to be the following:

vowels: /i e æ ɨ ə a u o ɔ/;
consonants: /p t k b d g c j f θ s š v ð z ž m n ŋ l r w
      y h/;
stresses: /ˊ ˆ ˋ ˇ/;
internal juncture: /+/;
pitches: /¹ ² ³ ⁴/;
terminal junctures: / | ‖ #/;

MORPHEMICS

When the phonological analysis of a language has been made, the next point to consider is what use one can make of it for further analysis. It is taken for granted that further analysis is necessary and possible: knowing the phonological system of a language does not tell us anything about the way the phonological units are used. Saying this does not, however, lead to the conclusion that we are then immediately to become concerned with the "meaning" of the linguistic material. It simply means that we have to look for further structural systems on levels other than the phonological.

Inspection of the linguistic material shows immediately that similar sequences or combinations of phonemes keep recurring. The recurrences exhibit patterns of occurrence and distribution. And from time to time recurrent gaps in distribution are noted. We say then that the analysis we are now going to do, the *Morphemics* of the language, deals with the recurring patterned partials in utterances. These partials are made up of one or more phonemes. The distributional gaps are often found to pattern as if they were themselves partials with phonemic content, and are then set up as zero-elements.

The recurring partials, including zero-elements, are the *Morphemes* of a language. They are determined by processes parallel to those used in phonology: inspection, commutation within a frame, complementary distribution. There is, however, no criterion parallel to that of phonetic similarity, for phonemic similarity is not a necessary basis for classifying morphemes: different morphemes may be homonymous, or the variants of one morpheme may have very different phonemic shapes, or some variants may be zero phonemically; illustrations will be given below.

(from George L. Trager and Henry Lee Smith, Jr., *An Outline of English Structure*. Washington, D.C.: American Council of Learned Societies, 1957, pp. 50, 53–57. Reprinted by permission of Intext Educational Publishers).

The morphemic analysis should be based on the fullest possible phonological statement in order to be complete. It is true that incomplete morphemic analyses can be made from phonologically inadequate data, or even in the absence of such data; but all such analyses are defective in direct proportion to the amount of phonological analysis omitted. In these terms, all existing morphemic analyses are defective, being based on traditional writing systems, or on phonemic statements that disregard or omit systematic and complete treatment of all or part of the accentual, junctural, and intonational phenomena. This is not to say that in the actual procedure of analyzing a language there is not a constant going back and forth between phonology and morphemics, with refinements and corrections being made in either direction. But the analyst must at all times be aware of the level-differences, and the systematic presentation must always be made in terms of the logical sequence, in one linear order, with the levels carefully distinguished.

In the present state of morphemic analysis it is often convenient to use the meanings of utterance fractions as a general guide and short-cut to the identification of morphemes. This is especially so in the case of languages that are more or less well known to the analyst, as has been true for most morphemic work done up to now. When we are confronted, however, with a language that we know little about in terms of the relation of the linguistic behavior of the speakers to the rest of their cultural behavior, it becomes clear that meaning can be of little help as a guide. The theoretical basis of the analysis then becomes evident: it consists of the recognition of the recurrences and distributions of similar patterns and sequences. The analyst must therefore constantly keep in mind this theoretical basis, and must be aware that his hunches about what goes with what are really short-cut conclusions about distributional facts.

Morphemes may have variants in different situations. These are the *Allomorphs*. The statement of all the forms of the morphemes of a language is the *Morphophonemics*. The statement of the sequences of morphemes that occur is the *Arrangement* (also called *Tactics*). In English, as in many other languages, it is found to be convenient to dichotomize morphemes into bases and all others (see below), and then to treat morpheme sequences that involve only one base under one heading — *Morphology*, and those that involve more than one base under another — *Syntax*. The term *Grammar* can be used to include the whole of the analysis of a language — phonology and morphemics. One of the concomitants of the morphophonemics is a list of all the morphemes of a language — the *Lexicon*.

A full presentation would begin with the recording of the behavior events — the actually occurring allomorphs, in their several phonemic forms. These would then be classified and arranged by the morphophonemic relationships into the lexicon. Then would follow the statement of the arrangements. No such full grammar is attempted here. The purpose is to present enough material for discussion to illustrate the procedures and techniques involved.

Examination of the language shows that English morphemes may be classified as follows on the basis of their phonological make-up and their role in morphology or syntax.

Segmental morphemes: consist of vowels and/or consonants (including semivowels) in normal transition; zero allomorphs are included here. Segmental morphemes are the basis of the morphological structure.

Suprasegmental morphemes: consist of sequences of stress phonemes with or without plus junctures; or of sequences of pitch phonemes with a terminal juncture. There are no zero allomorphs here. Some suprasegmental morphemes enter into morphological structures; most of them, however, are in the realm of syntax.

Segmental morphemes are divided into two types: *Bases* and *Suffixes*. Bases come first in a morpheme-complex. The number of bases is large, and the list cannot be exhaustively stated. English bases are the part of the structure usually described as having the "meaning" of the item. Bases are classifiable further by whether they do or do not combine with suffixes; and if they do, by the suffix-sets that enter into the combinations. Certain bases in English of limited distribution occur principally as the first item of a multibase sequence: they are usually called prefixes, but as their functioning is different from that of affixes as a whole, the term *Pre-Base* is here preferred. Examples of bases follow ($\sqrt{}$ is read "morpheme"; base morphemes are shown with a terminal hyphen): $\sqrt{}$mehn-, $\sqrt{}$huw-, $\sqrt{}$gud-, $\sqrt{}$duw-, $\sqrt{}$in-, $\sqrt{}$ænd-, $\sqrt{}$næw-, $\sqrt{}$ow-; pre-bases are: $\sqrt{}$bɨ-, $\sqrt{}$ə-, $\sqrt{}$diy-, $\sqrt{}$mis-, $\sqrt{}$kan-, etc. (these can be exhaustively listed).

Suffixes are of at least two kinds: *Final* (or inflectional), and *Non-final* (or derivational). They follow bases. Non-final suffixes form *Stems* from bases; stems behave with final suffixes as do bases, so that a stem is an extended base, consisting of a base followed by one or more non-final suffixes. Final suffixes are added to bases and stems in sets; these sets, or inflections, are the basis for classifying bases and stems into the so-called "parts of speech." The sets of inflected or derived forms of a base are *Paradigms*. All suffixes can be exhaustively listed; examples of non-final suffixes are: $\sqrt{}$-nɨs-, $\sqrt{}$-ər-, $\sqrt{}$-ɨtiy-, $\sqrt{}$-hud-, $\sqrt{}$dəm-, $\sqrt{}$eyšən-; of final suffixes: $\sqrt{}$-z, $\sqrt{}$-s, $\sqrt{}$-ɨz, $\sqrt{}$-d, $\sqrt{}$-iŋ, etc.

Suprasegmental morphemes consisting of patterns of stress, with the possibility of including plus junctures, are called *Superfixes*. Those consisting of pitches and a terminal juncture are called *Intonation Patterns*.

English superfixes always contain one — and only one — primary stress. In addition they may contain one or more plus junctures, and one or more stresses other than primary.

A morpheme-complex consisting of a single base, its accompanying suffixes (if any), and a superfix, is called a (*Morphemic*) *Word*. This is the primary unit of morphology as contrasted with morphemics as a whole, whose unit is the morpheme, or with syntax, where the unit is the *Morphemic Phrase*.

A morphemic phrase consists of two or more bases, with their suffixes, and a superfix. But it must be noted that the bases in a phrase have to be considered as words first, in order to make the analysis of the phrase. That is, one cannot simply consider the phrase as a sequence of bases (with or without suffixes), and a superfix, because the phrase superfix is found to be statable always in terms of the morphological nature of the included words and as an element superseding their superfixes in accordance with regular correlations. On the addition of an intonation pattern to a phrase we get a *Morphemic Clause*; this is wholly in the realm of syntax. Intonation patterns always contain at least one pitch phoneme, and end in one of the terminal junctures.

There is a hierarchy of relationship and analytical primacy in these various kinds of morphemes: intonation patterns depend for their scope and exact form on the phrase-superfixes; the phrase-superfixes depend on the word-superfixes; the word-superfixes depend on the base-and-suffix combinations.

Examples of superfixes as such are: $\sqrt{\dot{-}}$ in *go*, $\sqrt{\dot{-}\tilde{}}$ in *under*, $\sqrt{\acute{}+}$ in *black-bird*, $\sqrt{\hat{+}\; \maltese}$ in *Do it now*, etc. Examples of intonation patterns, for the segmental and superfixal filling-in of which see 1.8, are: $\sqrt{}^{2\;3\;1}\#$, $\sqrt{}^{3\;2}\|$, $\sqrt{}^{3}\|$, $\sqrt{}^{2\;4\;1}\#$, etc.

Examples of words can now be given. The symbol & is read "combined with," → means "results in," $\overset{w}{\sqrt{}}$ means "morphemic word." *Man* has the formula: $\sqrt{}$ mehn- & $\sqrt{\dot{-}}\overset{w}{\sqrt{}}$méhn; *taker* is: $\sqrt{}$ teyk- & $\sqrt{}$-ər- & $\sqrt{\dot{-}}\tilde{}\rightarrow\overset{w}{\sqrt{}}$téykər; *slynesses* is: $\sqrt{}$slay- & $\sqrt{}$-nɨs- & $\sqrt{}$-iz & $\sqrt{\dot{-}}+\tilde{\;}\rightarrow\overset{w}{\sqrt{}}$ sláy+nɨsiz (or the superfix may be $\sqrt{\dot{-}}\tilde{\;}$ giving $\overset{w}{\sqrt{}}$sláynɨsiz).

Examples of phrases are ($^{ps}\sqrt{}$ means "phrase-superfix": these are also written without hyphens under the primary stress, in contrast with word super-fixes which have a hyphen; $^{p}\sqrt{}$ means "phrase"): *take her* is $\overset{w}{\sqrt{}}$téyk & $\overset{w}{\sqrt{}}$hǝhr & $^{ps}\sqrt{\hat{+}}\rightarrow{}^{p}\sqrt{}$téyk + hǝhr; or the superfix may be $^{ps}\sqrt{\hat{+}}$, giving $^{p}\sqrt{}$têyk + hǝhr; or it may be $^{ps}\sqrt{\dot{-}\tilde{}}$, giving $^{p}\sqrt{}$téykǝr. These with intonation patterns ($^{i}\sqrt{}$) become clauses ($^{c}\sqrt{}$): $^{p}\sqrt{}$téyk + hǝhr + $^{i}\sqrt{}^{3\;1}\#\rightarrow{}^{c}\sqrt{}^{3}$ téyk + hǝhr $^{1}\#$; $^{p}\sqrt{}$têyk + hǝhr & $^{i}\sqrt{}^{2\;3\;1}\#\rightarrow{}^{c}\sqrt{}^{2}$têyk + hǝhr$^{1}\#$; $^{p}\sqrt{}$téyker & $\sqrt{}^{3\;1}\#\rightarrow{}^{c}\sqrt{}^{3}$téykǝr$^{1}\#$.

Other intonation patterns may occur, of course, with this phrase.

The Structure of English

CHARLES C. FRIES

CHAPTER V: PARTS OF SPEECH

A number of examples given in the preceding chapter were used to demonstrate the fact that, in English, some type of structural ambiguity results whenever an utterance consists of certain important form-classes or parts of speech without clear markers. The markers that distinguish these important parts of speech in English are therefore of primary importance in our description of the patterns of the devices that signal structural meanings — a description which will be made in terms of the selection of these parts of speech and the formal arrangements in which they occur. What parts of speech, then, can we — or, rather, must we — recognize in English for a basic description of our utterances, and what are the special markers of these parts of speech?

All the conventional school grammars deal extensively with the "parts of speech," usually given as eight in number, and explained in definitions that have become traditional. It has often been assumed that these eight parts of speech — noun, pronoun, adjective, verb, adverb, preposition, conjunction, interjection — are basic classifications that can be applied to the "words" of all languages[1] and that the traditional definitions furnish an adequate set of criteria by which to make the classification.

As a matter of fact our common school grammars of English have not always used eight parts of speech. Some have named ten, making the "article" and the "participle" separate classes.[2] Some have included the "adjective" under the name "noun" and have given as subclasses of "nouns" the "noun substantive" and the "noun adjective."[3] Others have insisted that "interjections" are not "parts of speech" but "sentence words." Some of the early Greek grammarians recognized only three parts of speech, ὄνομα (names), ῥῆμα (sayings), and συνδέομαι (joinings or linkings). The Latin grammarian,

(from Charles C. Fries, *The Structure of English*, New York: Harcourt, 1952, pp. 65–86.)

[1]"The distinctions between the various parts of speech . . . are distinctions in thought, not merely in words." John Stuart Mill, *Rectorial Address at St. Andrews*, 1867.

[2]See Goold Brown, *The Grammar of English Grammars* (10th ed., New York, 1868), pp. 220–23.

[3]"How mony partyse of speche ben þer? viii. Wych viii? Nowne, pronowne, verbe, aduerbe, partycypull, coniunccion, preposicion, and interieccion. . . . How mony maner of nownys ben there? ii. Wyche ii? Nowne substantyfe & nowne adiectyfe." From Douce Ms. 103 (fifteenth century). Text printed in *PMLA*, 50 (1935), 1012–32.

"Nouns are distinguished into two sorts, called noun substantives and noun adjectives." William Ward, *A Practical Grammar of the English Language* (London, 1765), p. 324.

Varro, distinguished four parts of speech: 1. words with cases (nouns), 2. words with tenses (verbs), 3. words with both cases and tenses (participles), 4. words with neither cases nor tenses (particles). The current conventional classification of words into the particular eight parts of speech now common seems to have begun with Joseph Priestley and to have been generally accepted in the grammars since 1850.[4] We cannot assume without question that the eight parts of speech thus inherited from the past will be the most satisfactory or the essential classification of the form-classes of present-day English, but will instead examine anew the functioning units in our collection of utterances, with a view to establishing the minimum number of different groups needed for a basic description of the signals of the most important structural meanings.

Unfortunately we cannot use as the starting point of our examination the traditional definitions of the parts of speech. What is a "noun," for example? The usual definition is that "a noun is the name of a person, place, or thing." But *blue* is the "name" of a color, as is *yellow* or *red*, and yet, in the expressions *a blue tie, a yellow rose, a red dress* we do not call *blue* and *yellow* and *red* "nouns." We do call *red* a noun in the sentence *this red is the shade I want. Run* is the "name" of an action, as is *jump* or *arrive. Up* is the "name" of a direction, as is *down* or *across*. In spite of the fact that these words are all "names" and thus fit the definition given for a noun they are not called nouns in such expressions as "We *ran* home," "They were looking *up* into the sky," "The acid made the fiber *red*." The definition as it stands — that "A noun is a name" — does not furnish all the criteria necessary to exclude from this group many words which our grammars in actual practice classify in other parts of speech.

In the expressions *a blue tie, a yellow rose, a red dress*, the words *blue, yellow*, and *red*, in spite of the fact that according to their meanings they are "names" of colors, are called "adjectives," because the adjective is defined as "A word that modifies a noun or a pronoun." A large part of the difficulty here lies in the fact that the two definitions — the definition of the noun and the definition of the adjective — are not parallel. The one for the noun, that "a noun is a name," attempts to classify these words according to their *lexical meanings*; the one for the adjective, that "an adjective is a word that modifies a noun or a pronoun," attempts to classify the words according to their *function in a particular sentence*. The basis of definition slides from meaning to function. For the purposes of adequate classification, the definitions of the various classes must consider the same kind of criteria.

Even with the usual definition of an adjective the criteria are not always consistently applied. Many grammars will not classify *boy's* as an adjective in *the boy's hat*, nor *his* as an adjective in *his hat*, in spite of the fact that both these words, *boy's* and *his*, "modify" the word *hat*, and thus fit the definition. *Boy's*

---

[4] "I shall adopt the usual distribution of words into eight classes. . . . All the innovations I have made hath been to throw out the Participle and substitute the Adjective, as more evidently a part of sp⌐⌐h." Joseph Priestley, *Rudiments of English Grammar* (London, 1769; 1st ed. 1761), p. 3.

is usually called "noun in the possessive case," and *his*, a "possessive pronoun," or a "pronoun in the possessive case." Here again, criteria that are not included in the definition — in this case certain formal characteristics — are used in practice to exclude from the classification items that fit the definition.

The common definition for a pronoun presents even more difficulty. "A pronoun is a word used instead of a noun." But just what kind of substitution is to be called "pronoun" in the following examples? In the sentence *John and James brought their letters of recommendation* there should be no question that *John* and *James*, as the names for two persons, are nouns. In the following series of words "substituted for these two nouns" just which are to be called pronouns and why?

John and James
The two boys
The undersigned
A few
The two
Two   }   brought their letters of recommendation.
A couple
Several
Some
Both
These
They

A slightly different kind of series, substituted for the noun *Wednesday* in the sentence *Wednesday is the time to see him*, presents the same problem. Which of the following substitutes are "pronouns"?

Wednesday
Tomorrow
Today
Next week
Later   }   is the time to see him.
Now
When
This
That
It

Obviously even in the usual procedure of classifying words into "parts of speech" — noun, adjective, pronoun — the criteria indicated in the definitions, that "names" are nouns, that "modifiers of nouns" are adjectives, and that "substitutes for nouns" are pronouns, do not include all that is actually used, and these definitions, therefore, cannot provide the basis for our approach here. We cannot use "lexical" meaning as the basis for the definition of some classes, "function in the sentence" for others, and "formal characteristics" for still others. We must find, as the basis for our grouping into parts of speech, a set of criteria that can be consistently applied.

Two problems then confront us:

1. We have concluded above that the structural signals of English consist of arrangements, not of words as words, but of words as parts of speech. We should be able, then, to express our descriptions of the patterns that signal structural meanings in terms of formulas with the various parts of speech as the units. Our first problem, then, is to discover just how many different kinds of these functioning units the formulas for English require, and precisely what they are.

2. We have insisted that unless these functioning units, these parts of speech, are clearly marked, are identifiable in an utterance, some type of structural ambiguity will result. The ambiguity of the following utterances, for example, arises because of the uncertainty of the kind of functioning unit of each of the italic words:

> *Ship sails* today
> *Time flies*
> The dogs looked *longer* than the cat
> Avoid infection by *killing* germs

The conventional definitions do not provide the necessary criteria. Our second problem is to discover just what the criteria are that the users of the language actually employ to identify the necessary various form-class units when they give and receive the signals of structural meaning.

You will remember Alice's experience with the poem of the Jabberwocky:[5]

> Twas brillig, and the slithy toves
> Did gyre and gimble in the wabe;
> All mimsy were the borogoves
> And the mome raths outgrabe. . . .

> "Somehow [she said], it seems to fill my head with ideas — only I don't exactly know what they are!"

What are the "ideas" she gets and how are they stimulated? All the words that one expects to have clearly definable meaning content are nonsense, but any speaker of English will recognize at once the frames in which these words appear.

---

[5]For the suggestion of this type of use of nonsense words, I am indebted to Prof. Aileen Traver Kitchin. I had used algebraic symbols for words but not with the success she has attained with "Jabberwocky" material.

Twas _____, and the _____y _____s
Did _____ and _____ in the _____;
All _____y were the _____s,
And the _____ _____s _____.

The "ideas" which the verse stimulates are without doubt the structural meanings for which the framework contains the signals. Most of these nonsense words have clearly marked functions in frames that constitute familiar structural patterns. These "ideas" seem vague to the ordinary speaker because in the practical use of language he is accustomed to dealing only with total meanings to which lexical content contributes the elements of which he is conscious.

For the Jabberwocky verse certain familiar words of the frame in which the nonsense appeared furnished important clues to the structures; but such clues are often unnecessary. One need not know the lexical meaning of any word in the following:

1. Woggles ugged diggles
2. Uggs woggled diggs
3. Woggs diggled uggles

If we assume that these utterances are using the structural signals of English, then at once we know a great deal about these sequences. We would know that *woggles* and *uggs* and *woggs* are "thing" words of some kind; that in each case there is more than one of these "things," and that they at some time in the past performed certain "actions"; and that these actions were directed toward other "things," *diggles, diggs,* and *uggles.*

As speakers of English, given the three utterances above, we should not hesitate to make such new utterances as the following:

4. A woggle ugged a diggle
5. An ugg woggles diggs
6. A diggled woggle ugged a woggled diggle

We would know that *woggles* and *uggs* and *woggs* are "thing" words, in sentences 1, 2, 3, because they are treated as English treats "thing" words — by the "positions" they occupy in the utterances and the forms they have, in contrast with other positions and forms. We would know that *ugged* and *woggled* and *diggled* are "action" words in these same sentences because they are treated as English treats "action" words — by the "positions" they occupy and the forms they have, in contrast with the positions and forms of the other "words."

We would make the new utterances 4, 5, 6 with confidence because in these we simply proceed to continue to treat the various units of the utterances in accord with the formal devices which constitute the grammar of English. For all of this it has not been necessary to know the meaning of a single word. As native speakers of English we have learned to use certain formal clues by which we identify the various kinds of units in our structures. The process is wholly unconscious unless some failure attracts attention; — just as unconscious as our responses to sight clues with the muscular adjustments of balancing when we walk.

The game of baseball, again, may provide a more satisfactory illustration. Like any other game that results in "winners," baseball consists of a system of contrastive patterns which give significance to an infinite variety of specific actions. The "strike" is one of the basic patterns. One cannot really play baseball without being able to recognize and deal with a "strike" immediately, unconsciously, as a conditioned reflex. One cannot define a strike with any simple statement that will furnish much help to a beginner. It is true that all strikes are the "same" in baseball. But that "sameness" is not physical identity; it is not even physical likeness with an area of tolerance. All strikes are alike in baseball only in the sense that they have the same functional significance. We cannot then hope to find in strikes physical boundaries of an objective likeness common to all. We can only enumerate the very diverse kinds of contrasts that constitute the criteria for determining whether any particular throwing by a pitcher is to be assigned to the pattern of a strike for the batter, i.e.:

1. Did the ball pass over the plate or not?
2. If the ball passed over the plate was it, in height, between the shoulders and the knees of the particular batter?
3. If the ball passed outside or inside the plate, or was higher than the shoulders or lower than the knees of the particular batter then "at bat," did the batter attempt to hit it with his bat and miss?
4. If the batter hit the ball and it fell to the ground outside the playing "diamond," did the batter have less than two strikes against him?
5. If the batter hit the ball very slightly so that the ball did not rise above the level of his head, and if the batter already had two strikes against him, did the catcher catch and hold the ball?

A part of speech in English, like the strike in baseball, is a functioning pattern. It cannot be defined by means of a simple statement. There is no single characteristic that all the examples of one part of speech must have in the utterances of English. All the instances of one part of speech are the "same" only in the sense that in the structural patterns of English each has the same functional significance.

This does not mean that in analyzing our sentences we must first determine the function of a word and then assign it the name of one of the parts of speech. Each part of speech like the strike in baseball is marked off from other parts of speech by a set of formal contrasts which we learn to use unconsciously as we learn our language. The patterns of our parts of speech as functioning units are complex just as the patterns of the game of baseball are complex. But in spite of the complexity of the structure of the game of baseball and the variety of the criteria by which the different specific actions are assigned to significant patterns, boys ten years of age learn not only to play the game skillfully, but also to apply consciously, as well as to discuss vigorously, the intricate criteria by which widely differing actions have the same structural significance.

As indicated above, if we are native speakers of English, we have learned to use and react to the contrasts that mark our functioning parts of speech. As speakers we are not accustomed to describe them and we find it difficult to know exactly what they are. If we have studied the conventional grammar of the schools we find it doubly difficult because the channelling of our thinking by the traditional material leads away from the descriptive approach.

. . .

In the rest of this chapter we shall sketch the procedure used here in the attempt to discover inductively from the recorded materials what these various contrasts were.

We concluded that the signals of structural meaning in English consisted primarily of patterns of arrangment of classes of words which we have called form-classes, or parts of speech. We have assumed here that all words that could occupy the same "set of positions" in the patterns of English single free utterances must belong to the same part of speech. We assumed then that if we took first our minimum free utterances as test frames we could find all the words from our materials that would fit into each significant position without a change of the structural meaning. It was not necessary for us to define the structural meaning nor to indicate the structural significance of any particular "position"; we simply had to make certain whether with each substitution, the structural meaning was the same as that of our first example or different from it.[6] After using the minimum free utterances we tested the resulting lists in the "positions" that appeared in the single free utterances that were not minimum but expanded in various ways.[7]

[6]The use of the technique of substitution in investigation always demands control of certain features of "meaning." The investigator must, in some way, either through an informant or by using his own knowledge, control enough of a particular kind of meaning to determine whether the frame is the "same" or "different" after any substitution is made. In the substitution process used here a knowledge of the lexical meanings of the words is unnecessary; a control of the structural meaning of each frame used is essential. See also my discussion in *Meaning and Linguistic Analysis*. Of course, the object of our search here is not the meaning but the strictly formal features which make a difference in the "meaning."

For a brief statement of some of the problems in the process of substitution see Zellig Harris, "From Morpheme to Utterance," *Language*, XXII (1946), 161–65.

[7]The necessity of testing "same" or "different" in "expanded" structures will appear from the following illustration from another problem. In the minimum structures *the boy laughed at the man* and *the boy called up the man*, the expressions *laughed at* and *called up* seem structurally alike. The first however can be expanded with *vigorously* between *laughed* and *at*, as *the boy laughed vigorously at the man*; the second cannot. The second can be shifted to *the boy called the man up*; the first could not appear with this order.

The minimum free utterance test frames that formed the basis of our examination were the following:

Frame A
> The concert was good (always)

Frame B
> The clerk remembered the tax (suddenly)

Frame C
> The team went there

We started with the minimum free utterance *the concert was good* as our first test frame and set out to find in our materials all the words that could be substituted for the word *concert* with no change of structural meaning. The words of this list we called Class 1 words.[8] When we repeated this process for each of the significant positions in all the structural frames we found in our materials, we had a large number of examples of each of the parts of speech we must recognize for present-day English.

Words of Class 1[9]

Frame A
> The concert was good
> > food
> > coffee
> > taste
> > container
> > difference
> > privacy
> > family
> > company [guests]

---

[8] I include here not the complete list of all the words from our materials but only a hundred examples of the various forms that occurred. The order of the words in the list here follows the order in which they occurred in the materials. These words are to be taken only in the particular lexical meaning they have in the recorded utterances from which they were gathered. Whenever some question seems probable concerning that meaning a brief gloss is given in brackets. There are often other lexical meanings of these words that do not fit in the particular frame used. We were not attempting to classify words in isolation but examples of words from actual utterances in which the selection of a particular lexical meaning is identified. These words in their particular meanings were grouped into classes by testing them in the frames used here. As they stand in the lists they are always to be considered as belonging in their special "position" in the frames that have been used to test them. All the examples in the lists are taken from the recorded materials and thus appeared there in "positions" that formed part of the testing.

[9] Ninety-nine examples from the total list follow: meal, water, sugar, list, time, cooker, charcoal, stuff, temperature, trouble, heating [of a house], eating [at a particular boarding-house], combination, business [of a particular corporation], thing, variation, thought, moisture, green [of a particular shade], boiling [as a process of sterilization], home, delivery, intrusion, reference [name for

The process of substitution in one position in our first frame provided a large list of items that for English structure are the same kind of functioning unit — our first class. Mindful of the diversity of the "strike," we did not assume that this particular frame would provide for all of Class 1, nor that it was a complete test. Such words as *meals, reports,* and *lessons* required an adjustment in certain word forms. These words without the "s" endings[10] did fit the frame as it stood.

> The meal was good
>> report
>> lesson

But with the "s" ending another word, *were*, occurred in similar minimum utterances instead of *was*.

> The meals were good
>> reports
>> lessons

The adjusted frame provided for many more words in our list and also for one subgrouping of the words in Class 1.

> The _____ was good
>> _____s were

Many of the words with these "s" endings appeared in the materials in situations similar to those of our frame but without the preceding word *the*. Our frame then could be adjusted as follows:

> Class 1
> (The) _____ is/was good
>> _____s are/were
>> Coffee is good
>> Sugar is good
>> Reports were good

---

recommendation], possibility, examination [set of questions], afternoon [as a time for meeting], convenience, expense, course, positive [photographic print], sixth, upstairs [of a new house], introduction [of a book], assembly [meeting], lounge [room in a residence hall], building [edifice], fun, abstract [of title to a property], deed [document showing ownership], summer [season], commissioner [public officer], direction [administration], teaching [process of instruction], supervisor, picture, hose [for garden], spray [mixture for treating plants], construction [of a house], memorandum, annoyance, inquiry [method of examination], width [dimension], length, specification [giving of details], floor, weather, fall [season], luncheon, reason [particular basis for an action], difficulty, history [subject of study], dance [particular pattern of steps], arrangement, management [administrative direction], catering [providing food], location, shape, report [certificate of school grades], idea, sun [sunshine], corn, use, kind, husband, note, street, appointment [engagement for meeting], English [language used], permanent [hair-curling], garage [auto service shop], price, shingling [roofing material installed], painting [process], machinery, name, cutter, wife, foot, care, washing [process], laundry [soiled clothes for washing or clothes that have been washed], place, service [of church], office [place of work], institute, training [process of teaching], woman, facility [a mechanical convenience].

[10]The expression "s" ending means, of course, the sounds [s], [z], or [iz], which constitute inflectional signs of a plural number.

The word *the*, although it accompanied all the words of our original list, and, when present, served as one of the markers of Class 1, is not a necessary accompaniment of all Class 1 words. We can thus take the adjusted frame and find the words which do not use the marker *the*, but which must also be included in Class 1. As we shall see later there are other subdivisions within this general class and some other kinds of words that must be included; but, for the present, we can insist that we have here a body of words that belong to the same part of speech by virtue of the fact that they can all fill this particular position in this minimum free utterance. They are all Class 1 words.

The words of our list also fitted into other positions in other minimum and expanded free utterances. The various "positions" in which a part of speech can stand in our sentences constitute its functions or uses. All the words of this particular list could appear in the positions indicated in the following minimum frames:

Frame B

The	clerk[11]	remembered the	tax
	husband		food
	supervisor		coffee
	woman		container
			difference
			family

Frame C

The team	went there
husband	
woman	
supervisor	

It is not enough for our purpose to say that a Class 1 word is any word that can fill certain positions in the structure of our sentences, even if we enumerate all these positions. We want to know what the special characteristics of these words are that make them recognizably different from the words used in other positions. To discover these characteristics we need to explore these other positions.[12] Significant formal characteristics of each class will appear then in the contrasts of one class with another. Before proceeding further with Class 1 words, therefore, we need a general view of the other major parts of speech in present-day English.

---

[11]Although structurally any Class 1 word may be used in this position, only certain subgroups (those for which *he* or *she* can be a substitute) would commonly occur with (i.e., be lexically compatible with) such a Class 2 word as *remembered*.

[12]It is probably unnecessary to point out that the "positions" used here are absolute order positions only in the minimum free utterances. In general they are significant structural positions. Ultimately the proof of the identity of particular positions in expanded structures rests upon the facts of "same" or "different" responses by native speakers. These are observed responses, not those elicited by direct question concerning "same" or "different."

Words of Class 2

Again we proceed with the process of substitution. To be consistent we use the same test frames we have already tried for Class 1 words, but seek substitutions in another "position." The words that fit this position we have called Class 2 words.

Frame A	Class 1	Class 2
(The)_____		is/was good
_____s		are/were
		seems/seemed
		seem
		sounds/sounded
		sound
		feels/felt
		feel
		becomes/became
		become

The particular words from our materials that could fit into this position of this particular frame were very few.

For the next frame, however, a great many more appeared.[13]

Frame B	Class 1	Class 2	Class 3
(The)_____		remembered (the)	_____
_____s		wanted	_____s
		saw	
		discussed	
		suggested	
		understood	
		signed	
		preferred	
		stopped	
		straightened	

---

[13]Ninety-eight examples from the total list are the following:

1. Those that fitted into the frame without any correlation with the presence or absence of an "s" ending on the Class 1 word: felt, arranged, ironed, worked, dried, included, started, applied, asked, needed, deposited, collected, mentioned, cleared, delivered, removed, decided, billed, reimbursed, worked [operated], made, isolated, turned, pleased, painted, bought, planned, consulted, called, thanked, wore, appreciated, touched, complicated, reported, contracted [shortened], knocked, handled, assumed, inconvenienced, lost, burned, sold, ordered, addressed, finished, invited, forgot, tested, produced.

2. Those that fitted into the frame with a correlation of an "s" or no "s" ending on the Class 1 word: sees, tells, knows, has, makes, gets, includes, believes, owes, wants, means, decides, follows, offers, leaves, shields, accept, change, try, guess, know, see, allow, specify, borrow, use, work, help, find, watch, apply, recommend, embarrass, convince, imagine, settle, purchase, forward [send on], order, like, expect, bring, separate, run [operate], mow, correct, give, doubt.

Frame C	Class 1	Class 2
(The)_____		went there
		came
		ran
		started
		moved
		walked
		lived
		worked
		met
		talked

All the words on this list can occupy the same structural position in our test frames. The separation of the test frames is significant only for subgroupings of these words. They are all Class 2 words.

Words of Class 3

For Class 3 words we again take our original sentences and explore another position:

Frame A	Class 1	Class 2	Class 3
(The)_____		is/was	good
_____s		are/were	

Here we are concerned with all the words that are structurally like *good*. Because we found that the absolute order position of *good* in this frame permitted the overlapping of several kinds of structural units as shown by confusion in the decisions of "same" and "different" from informants, we used a double position for the test of Class 3 words. To be accepted as belonging to Class 3 a word had to be one that could fit both in the position after the Class 2 word and also between *the* and the Class 1 word.

	Class	Class	Class	Class
(The)_____		_____	is/was	_____
		_____s	are/were	
	large			large
	necessary			necessary
	foreign			foreign
	new			new
	empty			empty
	hard			hard
	best			best
	lower			lower

All of the words of this list[14] belong in a single part-of-speech class. They can all be substituted in these significant positions in our test frame — they are all Class 3.

Words of Class 4

For the next large class of words we shall take those that can be substituted in the position following the three already explored.

Frame A

	Class 3	Class 1	Class 2	Class 3	Class 4
(The)	_____	_____ _____s	is/was are/were	_____	there here always then sometimes suddenly soon now generally lately

Frame B

	Class 1	Class 2	Class 1	Class 4
(The)	_____ _____s	remembered (the)	_____	clearly sufficiently especially repeatedly soon then suddenly later always

[14] A hundred examples of the words from the total list of this group are the following: English, educational, general, eighth, elite, small, regular, usable, short, fine, long, ready, great, good, straight, particular, last, personal, first, right [correct], supplementary, big, earlier, final, quick, greater, better, oral, low, glad, principal, high, free, whole, little, public, shut, pink, sure, essential, clear, anxious, separate, red, commercial, vigorous, complete, singular, important, permanent, intimate, vivid, real, full, awful, nice, later, convenient, busy, drunk, excellent, difficult, probable, outstanding, technical, easy, confident, open, strong, sufficient, outside, higher, clean, kind, weak, hot, tentative, slightest, physical, serious, close, religious, possible, international, different, broad, white, hostile, welcome, ordinary, afraid, domestic, wide, heavy, young, valuable, least, lost, younger, unsightly.

Frame C

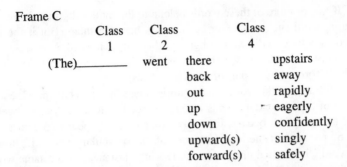

We have called the words of this list[15] Class 4 words although the need for making subgroups in this class becomes immediately apparent when we attempt to explore the other positions in which the Class 4 words can operate. Although there is considerable overlapping in the positions the words of our list can occupy, there are also positions in which large groups naturally fit, from which other groups are excluded. Here it will be sufficient to point out the three subgroups that show themselves when we attempt to use several of these words to-

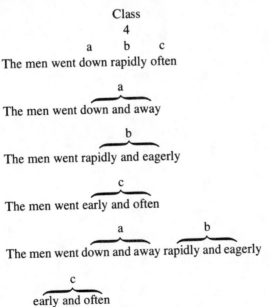

[15]Other examples of words that fit these positions of our frames are the following: usually, often, frequently, seldom, downward, over, under, through, across, easily, tentatively, suspiciously, awhile, last, next, brokenly, religiously, inconveniently, personally, principally, technically, artistically, conveniently, confidently, completely, definitely, directly, absolutely, cheaply, luxuriously, surely, closely, perfectly, somewhere, anywhere, everywhere, longer, privately, sadly, idly, crazily, openly, recently, finally, meanwhile, hourly, annually, once, twice, again, vigorously, first, increasingly.

gether. If two or more of these words belong to the same subgroup then a formal connecting word such as *and* or *but* appears between them. But if the two or more words belong to different subgroups then no such word occurs.

For the present, however, we shall consider all these words as belonging to a single large form-class or part of speech — Class 4.

The full lists of the words that comprise these four parts of speech contain a large part of the vocabulary items of our recorded materials. If each "word" is counted every time it occurs, then these four parts of speech contain approximately 67 per cent of the total instances of the vocabulary items. If, however, each "word" is counted only once and repeated instances of the same word ignored, then, in the material of 1,000 different words, the percentage of the total vocabulary in these four parts of speech is over 93 per cent. In other words our utterances consist primarily of arrangements of these four parts of speech. These utterances contain also, however, a body of other words, comparatively few in actual number of items, but used very frequently. The next chapter will explore the various kinds of these "other words."

5 TRANSFORMATIONAL GRAMMAR

The goals, methods, and assumptions of transformational grammarians differ from those of descriptive linguists. Descriptivists believe that the proper object of linguistic study is the spoken language. In order to analyze it, they collect a large number of spoken samples and classify their material, beginning with the sound system and working up to syntax. They work with sentences that have been produced by native speakers of a language, using a mainly inductive method.

In contrast, transformationalists believe that the proper object of linguistic study is the knowledge that native speakers possess which enables them to produce and understand sentences. This knowledge is called "competence," whereas the individual's use of this knowledge in an act of communication is called "performance." The distinction resembles the one that de Saussure made between "la langue" and "la parole," but de Saussure viewed "la langue" in terms of segments of language and categories, whereas transformationalists define competence in terms of the rules that a native speaker follows in producing and understanding sentences. In transformational grammar, the term "rule" is used not for a precept set down by an external authority but for a principle that is unconsciously yet regularly followed in the production and interpretation of sentences. Transformationalists are interested in constructing a grammar that will account for linguistic competence. In constructing the grammar, they rely heavily on deduction and intuition, although the results are tested against actual samples of language. Furthermore, they insist that rules be stated in explicit form, with no appeal to intuition. When criticized for their reliance on deduction and intuition, they point out that all scientists rely on such mental processes in the formulation of hypotheses. Experimentation involves the testing of hypotheses.

Taking syntax as the most basic level of language, and the sentence as the basic unit, transformationalists try to state the rules that will account for a native speaker's intuitive knowledge of his language and his ability to produce an infinite number of sentences. The speaker is not conscious of the rules and could not formulate them himself, but they account for his linguistic intuition (his ability to judge sentences as grammatical, ungrammatical, ambiguous, or synonymous) as well as his linguistic creativity (his ability to produce and interpret an infinite number of sentences that he has never heard before).

The rules of transformational grammar are stated in terms of symbols and techniques that have been borrowed from mathematics. Zellig Harris had begun to apply mathematical and logical techniques of analysis to language.[1] Noam Chomsky studied linguistics under the direction of Harris at the University of Pennsylvania and was influenced by his work. However, Chomsky came to feel that structural linguistics was going in the wrong direction in terms of its assumptions and methods. He was particularly critical of the structuralists' emphasis on habit in their explanation of language learning, and the focus on the collection and classification of data.

Chomsky was interested in the psychological processes that account for language use and tried to construct models that would represent them. In constructing these models, he drew upon his knowledge of logic and mathematics, taking concepts from communication theory, finite automata theory, and recursive function theory and applying them to natural languages.[2] He was interested in generative systems (procedures by which a mathematician starts with basic postulates and can generate an infinite number of proofs) and thought that languages might be generated from a few basic principles in a similar manner.

Chomsky first challenged the linguistics establishment when he made known his views in *Syntactic Structures* (1957). He followed the structuralists in maintaining that phonology and syntax should be described as purely formal systems without reference to meaning, or semantics. However, he disagreed with the methods and goals of the structuralists, pointing out that the grammatical sentences of a language cannot be identified "with any particular corpus of utterances obtained by the linguist in his field work."[3] Therefore, focusing on the collection and classification of data is futile. The linguist should attempt to formulate the rules or principles that enable a native speaker to produce and understand an infinite number of sentences. Chomsky describes a grammar as "a device of some sort for producing the sentences of the language under analysis."[4] The term "device" is not used in a physical or mechanistic sense but abstractly, without reference to the actual physical or psychological properties that might implement the "device" in the human mind. The rules of a grammar should generate, or "produce," structural descriptions for all the grammatical sentences of a language and no ungrammatical ones, and should be able to show why a

---

[1]Zellig Harris, "Co-occurrence and Transformation in Linguistic Structure," *Language*, 33 (1957), 283–340.

[2]John Lyons, *Noam Chomsky* (N.Y.: Viking, 1970), p. 69.

[3]Noam Chomsky, *Syntactic Structures* (The Hague: Mouton, 1957), p. 15.

[4]Ibid., p. 11.

native speaker would consider a sentence to be ungrammatical. In constructing the rules, the linguist may refer to intuition. This was a departure from the structuralists' emphasis on external, observable data. Chomsky also departed from the structuralists in seeking rules that underlie all languages; universal grammar had been scorned for several centuries.

Chomsky establishes the case for transformational grammar by investigating several other models of linguistic description and showing their inferiority. First, he investigates a finite state model from communication theory, called a "finite state Markov process." This model he is able to dismiss very quickly, since English or any other natural language is not a finite state language. The number of possible sentences within a language is infinite, even though the language operates with a finite number of elements (sounds, words, etc.). In the course of discussing this model, he shows that a grammar of a natural language must have a recursive device, something that will allow for the expansion and repetition of structures.

Chomsky next investigates a phrase structure grammar. A phrase structure grammar provides rewriting rules for the expansion of constituents (such as sentence, noun phrase, verb phrase). The procedure is similar to the one that is followed in immediate constituent analysis, except that rewriting rules produce or generate sentences. In immediate constituent analysis, one has to start with the sentence. The following rewriting rules are given in Chapter 4 of *Syntactic Structures*:

$$
\begin{aligned}
\text{Sentence} &\longrightarrow \text{NP} + \text{VP} \\
\text{NP} &\longrightarrow \text{T} + \text{N} \\
\text{VP} &\longrightarrow \text{Verb} + \text{NP} \\
\text{T} &\longrightarrow \text{the} \\
\text{N} &\longrightarrow \text{man, ball, etc.} \\
\text{Verb} &\longrightarrow \text{hit, took, etc.}
\end{aligned}
$$

T + N + Verb + T + N
the + man + hit + the + ball

(NP = noun phrase, VP = verb phrase, T = article or determiner, N = noun)

A derivation of a sentence consists of the substitutions that result from the application of the rewriting rules. One rule is applied at a time. The derivation can be represented in a phrase marker or a branching tree diagram:

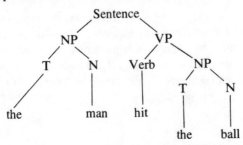

The last line of the derivation is called a terminal string.

Phrase structure grammars are more powerful models of description than finite-state grammars since they can account for an infinite number of sentences. Nevertheless, they have serious limitations. They deal with only one element and one rule at a time. In processes such as conjunction, one must consider the entire sentence in order to determine whether the process can apply. Constituents must be identical in order to allow deletion and conjunction to take place, as in the following example:

The scene - of the movie - was in Chicago.
The scene - of the play - was in Chicago.
The scene of the movie and of the play was in Chicago.

Operations such as conjunction refer to two distinct sentences. There is no economical way to incorporate such a double reference into a phrase structure grammar. Furthermore, a phrase structure grammar cannot economically describe processes such as inversion, substitution, relations between sentences that are paraphrases of each other such as actives and passives, and relations between discontinuous elements. All of these processes and relations can be described more effectively in a transformational grammar.

Chomsky defines a grammatical transformation as a rule that "operates on a given string . . . with a given constituent structure and converts it into a new string with a new derived constituent structure."[5] A string is a sentence that has not gone through obligatory transformations, such as the agreement of subject and verb. A transformation requires a string with a particular structure. For example, the passive transformation operates on a sentence with a direct object. It takes a sentence such as "John admires sincerity" and converts it to "Sincerity is admired by John." The noun phrases are reversed, "by" is added before the noun phrase that was the subject of the active sentence, a form of "be" is added, and the main verb is put into past participle form. These are the kinds of changes that are brought about by transformations.

In *Syntactic Structures*, a transformational grammar is said to consist of the following three parts:

1. Phrase structure rules
2. Transformational rules
3. Morphophonemic rules

Phrase structure rules or rewriting rules account for the expansion of grammatical categories and for substitutions, including the selection of words. Transformational rules must be applied in a particular order. Some are considered obligatory, such as the agreement of subject and verb, whereas others are considered optional. "Kernel sentences" are defined as "the set of sentences that are

[5]Ibid., p. 44.

produced when we apply obligatory transformations to the terminal strings of the [Σ, F] grammar" (the phrase structure grammar).[6] Kernels are simple, declarative, active sentences. Chomsky points out that traditional grammarians followed a correct linguistic intuition in beginning the grammar of English with the study of declarative "actor-action" sentences and simple grammatical relations, such as subject-predicate or verb-object. In *Syntactic Structures*, negatives and interrogatives are considered to be optional transformations of declarative kernel sentences. For example, the negative sentence "They can't come" is described as an optional transformation of the kernel sentence "They can come"; the question "Can they arrive?" is analyzed as an optional transformation of the kernel sentence, "They can arrive." Complex or compound sentences are formed by means of optional double-base transformations that combine two strings. For instance, the sentence "I found the boy studying in the library" is derived from the pair of terminal strings that underlie the simple kernel sentences, "I found the boy," and "The boy is studying in the library." The final written or spoken form of the sentence is determined by morphophonemic rules.

The transformationalists' interest in more abstract rules of grammatical description led to a new treatment of phonology. Structural linguists described phonological segments as indivisible entities called "phonemes." An alternative system had been worked out by linguists belonging to the Prague School in Czechoslovakia.[7] Their system was further developed by Roman Jakobson, who introduced it to linguists in the United States. Jakobson considers phonological segments as bundles of distinctive features or significant qualities that are present in various sounds. The system emphasizes acoustic rather than articulatory features, although both types are considered. Many sounds are voiced, many are consonantal (the flow of air is impeded in some way), and many are continuants (the flow of air is not stopped). Every sound can be characterized by the presence or absence of these and other features. For example, the sound [p] can be indicated in a distinctive feature representation as follows:

$$[p]$$

$$
\begin{bmatrix}
+ & \text{consonant} \\
- & \text{vocalic} \\
- & \text{continuant} \\
- & \text{nasal} \\
- & \text{voice} \\
- & \text{back}
\end{bmatrix}
$$

Such an arrangement of distinctive phonological features is called a "feature matrix." The total number of distinctive features is only about fifteen. Since these fifteen attributes have been found sufficient to characterize phonological

---

[6]Ibid., p. 45.
[7]Manfred Bierwisch, *Modern Linguistics* (The Hague: Mouton, 1971), pp. 22–27.

segments in all the languages to which they have been applied, it seems likely that they are linguistic universals.

In his article "On the Bases of Phonology," Morris Halle shows how the distinctive feature system reveals similarities among sounds that are not apparent when phonological segments are analyzed as indivisible entities. Distinctive feature analysis enables us to divide the sounds of English into four categories:

1. Vowels, which are vocalic and nonconsonantal
2. Liquids (r and l), which are vocalic and consonantal
3. Consonants, which are nonvocalic and consonantal
4. Glides (h, w, and y), which are nonvocalic and nonconsonantal

Vocalic sounds are produced with an open oral cavity, whereas nonvocalic sounds are produced with an oral cavity that is narrowed at least to the point of producing an obstruction. Consonantal sounds are produced with contact in the oral cavity, whereas nonconsonantal sounds are produced with lesser degrees of narrowing. The division of sounds into vowels, liquids, consonants, and glides on the basis of distinctive features is more precise than the traditional one of vowels and consonants. Halle gives rules for the combinations of vowels (V), consonants (C), liquids (L), and glides (H) that can occur at the beginning of English morphemes or words.

The distinctive feature system allows for cross-classification and enables us to show that sounds have many features in common. Those sounds that share the most features form natural classes. For example, the liquids [r] and [l] form a natural class since they are the only sounds that have the features [+ consonant] and [+ vocalic]; they differ in that [r] is [− anterior] and [l] is [+ anterior]. A consonant has the feature [+ anterior] if the obstruction in the oral cavity is at the gum ridge or farther forward. Two sounds are different if they differ by at least one feature. Another natural class of sounds is that of the sibilants, [s, z, š, ž, č, ǰ], since these are the only ones that share the features "nongrave" and "strident." Nongrave sounds are articulated with a narrowing in the central region of the oral cavity. Strident sounds are produced with an obstruction that is not complete closure but which is narrow enough to cause considerable noisiness as the air is forced out of an opening.

The concept of "natural class" helps us to describe phonological rules. For instance, in the formation of the plural in English, [iz] is added to the sibilants, [s] is added to words ending with consonants that have the feature [− voice], and [z] is added to words ending with vowels or consonants that have the feature [+ voice]. Natural classes defined by distinctive features provide a basis for meaningful generalizations about the sound system.

In the phonological rules for the generation of sentences, morphemes are directly represented by their distinctive features. For example, the word "mail" [mel] would be represented as follows:

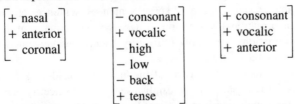

When phonetic transcriptions or letters are used in this system, they function as abbreviations for bundles of features. Since morphemes are represented directly in terms of their distinctive features, the phoneme is no longer considered a separate entity or a separate level of language, as it is in structural grammar. Moreover, structural grammar treats phonology as the basic level of language. In transformational grammar, phonology is seen as dependent upon syntax. Phonological rules merely assign sound to an abstract syntactic structure. This is why the phonological component of the grammar is said to be interpretive.

During the early 1960s, a great deal of work was done on the syntactic component of the grammar. Chomsky set forth these changes and summarized a good deal of the research that had been done in *Aspects of the Theory of Syntax* (1965). The model of a grammar that is presented in this work is often referred to as the Standard Theory. In *Aspects*, a grammar is said to consist of the following three components:

1. a Syntactic component
2. a Semantic component (a new feature)
3. a Phonological component

The syntactic component is more complex than the one that had been presented earlier. Chomsky states that for each sentence, the syntactic component must specify a deep structure that determines its semantic interpretation, and a surface structure that determines its phonetic interpretation. Both the phonetic and the semantic components are said to be purely interpretive. All meaning resides in the deep structure, and words are selected before transformations take place. Transformations are therefore said to be meaning-preserving. The syntactic component contains a base and a transformational component. The base is further divided into a lexicon, a set of phrase structure rules, and base transformational rules.

Many of the earlier optional transformations, such as the ones for questions and negatives, were made obligatory and incorporated into the base rules. Now only stylistic transformations (such as the passive) were said to be optional. Furthermore, double-base transformations were done away with. The option of beginning a new sentence, or the property of recursiveness, was written into the base rules. Since the base rules incorporated phrase structure rewriting rules and transformational rules, the base could no longer be considered a simple phrase structure grammar. The concept of kernel sentences (sentences produced without optional transformations) was no longer necessary since many of the former optional transformations were now obligatory. Sentences generated by the base rules were called basic strings.

Chomsky illustrates the scope of the base by considering what traditional grammar has to say about a simple English sentence ("Sincerity may frighten the boy"), and then analyzing it in terms of transformational grammar. The rewriting or phrase structure rules define the grammatical relations in the deep structure, which are illustrated by the phrase marker or the branching tree diagram. The sentence is represented by category symbols (S, NP, VP, Aux), and formatives, which are further divided into lexical items (sincerity, frighten, boy) and grammatical items (there are none in this sentence, but they would include markers for the perfect, progressive, etc.). Chomsky suggests that at least some category symbols are probably linguistic universals. The methods of transformational grammar enable him to formulate explicit rules for the notions of traditional grammar. Moreover, these techniques provide more information for complicated sentences in which a word can have multiple functions and be part of more than one sentence. For example, in the sentence "Bill persuaded John to leave," "John" is simultaneously the object of "persuade" and the subject of "leave." This can be illustrated by the phrase marker for the sentence:

```
                    S
                  /   \
              NP        VP
              |        /  \
              N       V    NP
              |       |   /  \
             Bill  persuade N    S
                          |   /  \
                        John NP   VP
                             |    |
                             N    V
                             |    |
                           John  leave
```

Traditional grammar provides names only for grammatical functions (i.e., subject, object) at the higher level of the sentence.

One of the problems that had been revealed in regard to traditional categories, particularly in Robert B. Lees's *The Grammar of English Nominalizations* (1960), was that the usual classifications for verbs and nouns were too broad. English verbs can be divided into the copula (*be*), linking verbs (*seem, become*), intransitive verbs (*walk, sleep*), pseudo-intransitive verbs (verbs that allow for omission of the object, such as *steal* and *drive*), transitive verbs (*see, hit*), verbs that can take two objects (*buy, teach*), stative or nonaction verbs (*know, understand*), and verbs that cannot occur in the passive or with manner adverbials, which Lees calls "middle verbs" (*have, cost, resemble*).[8]

Nouns can be characterized in terms of shared features, such as whether they are proper or common (*John, boy*), concrete or abstract (*book, truth*), countable or non-countable (*pebble, sand*), human or nonhuman (*boy, cat*), animate or inanimate (*dog, car*). A method for specifying features and for dealing with cross-classification was required. Linguists working on these problems recognized the usefulness of distinctive feature analysis and applied the system to the classification of various syntactic and semantic properties of nouns and verbs. Lexical categories were analyzed as complex symbols, each one being a set of specified features. For example, the noun "boy" can be represented in a distinctive feature matrix as the following complex symbol:

$$
\text{boy}
$$

$$
\begin{bmatrix}
+ \text{ noun} \\
+ \text{ common} \\
+ \text{ concrete} \\
+ \text{ count} \\
+ \text{ human} \\
+ \text{ male}
\end{bmatrix}
$$

Redundant features, or those implied by the presence of others, are generally omitted. In the above matrix, the feature [+ human] implies [+ animate], so the latter feature can be left out. The use of "plus-or-minus" notation simplifies exposition. The term "common" has its traditional meaning, whereas "abstract" is represented as [− concrete]. Many of the terms that are employed go back to traditional grammar.

Earlier descriptions of a language in structural and transformational grammar had avoided any reference to semantics. Semantic properties were allowed into syntactic analysis since they determined the positions that words could fill. According to the system used in *Aspects*, nouns are chosen first in terms of context-free selectional rules. Verbs are then chosen by means of context-sensitive rules. Selectional restrictions determine which verbs can go with which nouns, but metaphorical or poetic language often involves a violation of selectional restrictions. For example, the verbs "sputter," "mutter," and "say" require a human subject. When in "Rhapsody on a Windy Night," T. S. Eliot says,

---

[8]Robert B. Lees, *The Grammar of English Nominalizations* (The Hague: Mouton, 1966), pp. 1–20.

> The street-lamp sputtered,
> The street-lamp muttered,
> The street-lamp said,
> "Regard that woman"[9]

he makes the street-lamp seem like a human being by using verbs that require a human subject. Thus, the concept of selectional restrictions is useful for explaining extensions of the normal grammatical patterns of the language as well as its usual rules.

Unless a writer is deliberately violating normal patterns, the nouns and verbs that are chosen for a particular sentence must match up in terms of their features. Restrictions that relate to the features of words are called "selectional restrictions," whereas those that relate to grammatical categories (such as NP, V, Adj) are called "strict subcategorization restrictions." Violation of strict subcategorization restrictions usually results in more deviant sentences than violation of selectional restrictions. For instance, the verb "please" takes an animate object. Using an adjective in the position of the object instead of a noun (a violation of a strict subcategorization restriction) produces a less grammatical sentence than using an inanimate noun (a violation of a selectional restriction):

> *Mary pleases green.
> *Mary pleases the desk.

(The asterisk indicates an ungrammatical sentence.)

The distinction between selectional restrictions and strict subcategorization restrictions enables us to introduce the concept of degree of grammaticality. All errors do not have the same effect. Some incorrect sentences are less grammatical than others. Subcategorization rules enable us explicitly to account for a native speaker's intuitions regarding grammaticality, one of the goals of transformational grammar.

The development of rules for subcategorization demanded more and more attention to semantic features. A certain amount of duplication was involved since semantic features were being dealt with by the syntactic component. The boundary between syntax and semantics was breaking down. Chomsky acknowledges this fact in *Aspects*, stating that "the interrelation of semantic and syntactic rules is by no means a settled issue," and that "there is quite a range of possibilities that deserve serious exploration."[10] Those possibilities were to be explored with great intensity in the following years.

The preceding discussion has focused on the grammatical model presented in *Aspects*. Chomsky also gives a considerable amount of attention to philosophical and psychological issues. He asserts that transformational theory is

---

[9]T. S. Eliot, *Collected Poems* (N.Y.: Harcourt, 1963), p. 16.

[10]Noam Chomsky, *Aspects of the Theory of Syntax* (Cambridge, Mass.: M.I.T. Press, 1965), p. 159.

mentalistic since it is concerned with discovering a mental reality underlying actual behavior. Rather than trying to explain his position in terms of modern empiricism, he criticizes an overly strong attachment to empiricism and points out the roots of his theory in the rationalist philosophy and universal grammar of the seventeenth and eighteenth centuries. Rationalism versus empiricism is an important theme in *Language and Mind* (1968, based on lectures delivered at Berkeley in 1967) and in "Language and the Mind," an article based on the book. In this article, Chomsky characterizes the major positions that have developed in regard to the acquisition of knowledge as rationalism and empiricism. Rationalist theories are marked by the importance they assign to central processes and organizing principles in perception, and to innate ideas and principles in learning. In contrast, the empiricist approach has stressed the role of experience and control by environmental factors. Chomsky places himself firmly in the camp of the rationalists. At several points in the article, he quotes Wilhelm von Humboldt, a nineteenth-century linguist who saw language as a generative system that makes "infinite use of finite means." Chomsky points out that the deep structure of a language is a highly abstract entity that is not represented directly in the form of a speech signal. Furthermore, children construct a grammar or a "theory" of their language from very faulty data. One can explain the highly complex, creative linguistic behavior of human beings only by concluding that it is determined by intrinsic properties of mental organization. He cites evidence from experimental psychology to support his point of view. However, many psychologists believe that Chomsky goes too far in postulating a language-specific learning device, and are inclined to explain language learning in terms of more general cognitive processes.

Chomsky's views regarding innate ideas and the organization of the human mind have caused considerable debate among psychologists and philosophers. In the field of linguistics, debate has centered around the nature of deep structure and the relation between syntax and semantics. The model of a grammar presented in *Aspects of the Theory of Syntax* has been challenged in several ways, and Chomsky himself has revised it in subsequent publications. In *Studies on Semantics in Generative Grammar* (1972), he no longer claims that all meaning resides in the deep structure. Items such as focus, presupposition, reference, and the scope of logical elements (including quantifiers such as "many" and "few") are said to be determined somewhat by surface structure.[11] The semantic component relates both the deep structure and the surface structure to a semantic representation. However, the grammatical relations expressed in a sentence are inherent in the syntactic deep structure. A separate semantic component with a purely interpretive role is still assumed. Since the *Aspects* model had come to be

[11]Noam Chomsky, *Studies on Semantics in Generative Grammar* (Mouton: The Hague, 1972), p. 113.

called the Standard Theory, Chomsky calls his current version the Extended Standard Theory.

One of the features of the *Aspects* model that has been criticized is its handling of grammatical relations or functions, such as subject and object. In *Aspects* grammatical functions are defined as relations among category symbols within the underlying phrase-markers provided by the base. For example, the subject of a sentence is defined as a noun phrase (NP) that is immediately dominated by (directly attached to) the category symbol representing a sentence (S); the object is defined as a noun phrase (NP) that is immediately dominated by a verb phrase (VP).

In "Toward a Modern Theory of Case" (1966), Charles J. Fillmore questions the deep-structure validity of the notions "subject" and "object," and proposes a new way to handle grammatical relations in the deep structure. The details of his analysis have changed since he wrote the article, but he still accepts a model based on case. In this article, Fillmore regards each simple sentence in a language as made up of a verb and a collection of nouns in various "cases" in the deep structure, where they occur together with prepositions. Each noun + preposition combination is dominated by a category label, such as objective, dative, locative, instrumental, and agentive. These categories correspond to the traditional notion of cases. The derivation of a sentence begins with a proposition, which includes the verb and all of its associated noun phrases. Once one of the noun phrases is selected as subject, the remaining proposition corresponds to the traditional predicate.

This method of analysis has several advantages. The distinction between noun phrases and prepositional phrases disappears, since all noun phrases have a preposition in the deep structure. The model can show the deep-structure similarities among different historical stages of a language. For instance, Old English used case endings to indicate grammatical functions whereas Modern English uses prepositions (Old English *wordum*, Modern English *with words*). What is most interesting from the standpoint of universal grammar, the model points out underlying similarities among synthetic and analytic languages (those that use inflections to indicate a great deal of grammatical information and those that rely on separate words). It shows that where synthetic languages use case endings to express certain functional relations, an analytic language such as Modern English uses prepositions. It also relates cross-language or inter-language differences in lexical structure. Fillmore proposes that the words "kill" and "die" have the same underlying semantic representation; however, "die" requires an animate subject that actually has an objective function, whereas "kill" takes an instrumental or agentive subject: *The dog died*; *a stone or a man killed the dog*. Fillmore's positing of an underlying semantic representation differing in content from the words that appear in the surface structure brings him into the realm of generative semantics.

The theory of generative semantics is an outgrowth of transformational grammar that developed through an attempt on the part of Fillmore, Postal,

Lakoff, Ross, McCawley, and others to apply the methodology of transformational grammar to an increasing body of data. They found that the dichotomy between syntax and semantics did not hold up. The new theory has been developed within the framework of transformational grammar. Generative semanticists accept the goal of accounting for the linguistic intuition of a native speaker of a language in terms of formal rules and a general theory, and they accept the concept of a nonsurface syntactic structure. However, they have come to believe that syntax cannot be separated from semantics, and that the role of transformations is to relate semantic representations to surface structures. They deny the existence of a separate syntactic deep structure, recognizing instead an underlying semantic representation. The underlying structure includes predicates expressing events, states, or actions, and noun phrases that are related to them. A grammar is seen to include not only rules of syntax, but also "rules of application" involving such things as presuppositions, conditions of appropriateness, and inferences. Generative semantics has thus progressed from a syntactically-based, language-internal view of grammar to one that is semantically based and concerned with problems of context and conditions of social interaction.[12]

George Lakoff has been one of the leaders of the generative semanticists. His dissertation, *On the Nature of Syntactic Irregularity* (1965, published in 1970 as *Irregularity in Syntax*), was the first extensive work that led to the current split within the ranks of transformationalists and laid the foundations for the development of generative semantics.[13] One of Lakoff's innovations was his attempt to construct a more universal base and reduce the number of categories. He showed that although adjectives and verbs behave differently in the surface structure, they share many similarities in underlying structure, and should both be treated as members of a single category labeled V. This treatment of verbs and adjectives led to the rejection of a large number of category symbols in generative semantics.

Lakoff describes the theory in his article, "On Generative Semantics."[14] The highly technical language of the article might give the impression that generative semanticists are involved even more than earlier transformationalists in abstract mathematical theory. Though their terminology is complex, this is not the case, as can be seen when the symbols of the formulas are interpreted. A semantic representation (SR) of a sentence is defined as SR = (P_1, PR, Top, F, . . .): P_1 is the phrase marker, which represents the grammatical structure; *PR* stands for the presuppositions assumed by the speaker; *Top* indicates the topic that is under discussion; and F represents the focus, the constituent containing new information. These categories allow for the symbolization of contextual factors that are independent of the grammatical structure of the sentence.

---

[12] Elizabeth Closs Traugott, Review of *Irregularity in Syntax* by George Lakoff, in *Language*, 50 (1974), 166–67.

[13] Ibid., p. 161.

[14] George Lakoff, "On Generative Semantics," in *Semantics*, eds. Danny D. Steinberg and Leon A. Jakobovits (Cambridge: Cambridge Univ. Press, 1971), pp. 232–96.

The theory of generative semantics permits a variety of options that were not available in earlier versions of transformational grammar. For example, it is not assumed that lexical insertions apply in a block, with no intervening nonlexical transformations. The possibility that lexical insertions and nonlexical transformations may be interspersed is left open. If one assumes that lexical insertions do not apply in a block, and do not precede all grammatical transformations, the concept of a separate level of syntactic deep structure as defined in *Aspects* is no longer valid. According to the *Aspects* model, lexical insertions have to precede all grammatical transformations. Although the theory allows for a transformational cycle in the sense of *Aspects* (so that a sequence of cyclical rules applies from the bottom up, from the lowest sentence to the highest) the concept of directionality has no significance. One could just as well say that the cycle applies downward, from the surface structure to the semantic representation. The description of the semantic component that went along with the *Aspects* model involved semantic projection rules, a new kind of rule. According to Lakoff, one of the most important innovations of generative semantics is the claim that semantic representations and syntactic phrase markers involve the same kind of rules; there exist no separate semantic projection rules but only transformations. He criticizes the belief in "autonomous syntax," and affirms that there is a continuum between syntax and semantics.

The type of analysis that results from the theory of generative semantics can be seen in James McCawley's article, "On Identifying the Remains of Deceased Clauses." McCawley views a grammar as "a single system of rules that relate semantic structures to surface structures via intermediate stages." The grammar includes not only deletion, movement, and copying rules, but also rules that combine semantic material into complex units and lexical insertion rules. Since lexical insertion rules do not necessarily precede deletion rules, either words or semantic material can be removed in deletion transformations. McCawley argues that the simple object of "want" in sentences such as "Max wants a lollipop" results from the deletion of an embedded clause ("Max wants Max to have a lollipop"). Depending upon the sentence, the verb that is deleted in the subordinate clause appears to be "have," "get," "obtain," or "receive." These cases involve the deletion of a single verb and can be handled within the framework of the *Aspects* model of transformational grammar. However, other cases exist that must be analyzed not in terms of deletion, but in terms of the incorporation of material into the meaning of a semantically complex verb. An example is the sentence, "The sheriff of Nottingham jailed Robin Hood for four years"; "for four years" applies to the time Robin Hood was in jail rather than to the act of jailing. Therefore, the sentence must be broken down into "the sheriff of Nottingham caused something" and "Robin Hood was in jail for four years," with the adverbial phrase "for four years" applying to the verb "be." The surface verb "jail" incorporates the deep verbs "cause" and "be." In this sentence, the semantic features of the surface verb play a role in the deep structure, which suggests that a boundary between syntax and semantics does not exist.

In their article entitled "Fact," Paul and Carol Kiparsky demonstrate the interrelationship between syntax and semantics by showing the role played by presuppositions of the speaker in sentences that have complements. They analyze the syntactic behavior of nonfactive and factive predicates that take sentences as complements. With nonfactives such as "likely," "possible," and "seems," the speaker does not assume the truth of the embedded sentence. With factives such as "significant," "odd," and "tragic," the speaker presupposes that the embedded sentence expresses a true proposition and makes some assertion about that proposition. The speaker does not have to assert the truth of what he is saying. Factivity depends on presupposition. This description of factivity would not hold up if the speaker were lying, but in that case he would be using the resources of the language to create a misleading impression about his presuppositions.

The Kiparskys show that factives and nonfactives differ in regard to the constructions they can assume. The semantic difference between them is correlated with syntactic differences. For example, only factive predicates allow a full range of gerundial constructions (It is significant that he was found guilty = His being found guilty is significant). On the other hand, only nonfactives allow the initial noun phrase of the embedded sentence to become the subject of the main clause, converting the remainder of the embedded sentence into an infinitive phrase (It is likely that he will accomplish even more = He is likely to accomplish even more). The different syntactic behavior of factive and nonfactive predicates is based on a semantic difference, the presuppositions of the speaker. Therefore, these predicates must have a different deep structure, which should include presuppositions. The deep structure is represented by the use of pairs of tree diagrams given for both the syntactic object (the sentence) and the semantic object (the proposition with its related presuppositions). This paper presents a strong argument for the interrelationship of syntax and semantics, and shows how generative semantics is expanding the study of grammar through the consideration of contexts.

Syntactic Structures

NOAM CHOMSKY

CHAPTER I: INTRODUCTION

Syntax is the study of the principles and processes by which sentences are constructed in particular languages. Syntactic investigation of a given language has
as its goal the construction of a grammar that can be viewed as a device of some
sort for producing the sentences of the language under analysis. More generally,
linguists must be concerned with the problem of determining the fundamental
underlying properties of successful grammars. The ultimate outcome of these investigations should be a theory of linguistic structure in which the descriptive
devices utilized in particular grammars are presented and studied abstractly, with
no specific reference to particular languages. One function of this theory is to
provide a general method for selecting a grammar for each language, given a
corpus of sentences of this language.

   The central notion in linguistic theory is that of "linguistic level." A linguistic level, such as phonemics, morphology, phrase structure, is essentially a set
of descriptive devices that are made available for the construction of grammars; it
constitutes a certain method for representing utterances. We can determine the
adequacy of a linguistic theory by developing rigorously and precisely the form
of grammar corresponding to the set of levels contained within this theory, and
then investigating the possibility of constructing simple and revealing grammars
of this form for natural languages. We shall study several different conceptions
of linguistic structure in this manner, considering a succession of linguistic levels
of increasing complexity which correspond to more and more powerful modes of
grammatical description; and we shall attempt to show that linguistic theory must
contain at least these levels if it is to provide, in particular, a satisfactory grammar of English. Finally, we shall suggest that this purely formal investigation of
the structure of language has certain interesting implications for semantic
studies.

CHAPTER II: THE INDEPENDENCE OF GRAMMAR

2.1.   From now on I will consider a *language* to be a set (finite or infinite) of
sentences, each finite in length and constructed out of a finite set of elements. All
natural languages in their spoken or written form are languages in this sense,

(from Noam Chomsky, *Syntactic Structures*, The Hague: Mouton, 1957, pp. 11–12, 13–17,
34–48.)

since each natural language has a finite number of phonemes (or letters in its alphabet) and each sentence is representable as a finite sequence of these phonemes (or letters), though there are infinitely many sentences. Similarly, the set of "sentences" of some formalized system of mathematics can be considered a language. The fundamental aim in the linguistic analysis of a language L is to separate the *grammatical* sequences which are the sentences of L from the *ungrammatical* sequences which are not sentences of L and to study the structure of the grammatical sequences. The grammar of L will thus be a device that generates all of the grammatical sequences of L and none of the ungrammatical ones. One way to test the adequacy of a grammar proposed for L is to determine whether or not the sequences that it generates are actually grammatical, i.e., acceptable to a native speaker, etc. We can take certain steps toward providing a behavioral criterion for grammaticalness so that this test of adequacy can be carried out. For the purposes of this discussion, however, suppose that we assume intuitive knowledge of the grammatical sentences of English and ask what sort of grammar will be able to do the job of producing these in some effective and illuminating way. We thus face a familiar task of explication of some intuitive concept — in this case, the concept "grammatical in English," and more generally, the concept "grammatical."

Notice that in order to set the aims of grammar significantly it is sufficient to assume a partial knowledge of sentences and non-sentences. That is, we may assume for this discussion that certain sequences of phonemes are definitely sentences, and that certain other sequences are definitely non-sentences. In many intermediate cases we shall be prepared to let the grammar itself decide, when the grammar is set up in the simplest way so that it includes the clear sentences and excludes the clear non-sentences. This is a familiar feature of explication.[1] A certain number of clear cases, then will provide us with a criterion of adequacy for any particular grammar. For a single language, taken in isolation, this provides only a weak test of adequacy, since many different grammars may handle the clear cases properly. This can be generalized to a very strong condition, however, if we insist that the clear cases be handled properly for *each* language by grammars all of which are constructed by the same method. That is, each grammar is related to the corpus of sentences in the language it describes in a way fixed in advance for all grammars by a given linguistic theory. We then have a very strong test of adequacy for a linguistic theory that attempts to give a general explanation for the notion "grammatical sentence" in terms of "observed

[1]Cf., for example, N. Goodman, *The Structure of Appearance* (Cambridge, 1951), pp. 5–6. Notice that to meet the aims of grammar, given a linguistic theory, it is sufficient to have a partial knowledge of the sentences (i.e., a corpus) of the language, since a linguistic theory will state the relation between the set of observed sentences and the set of grammatical sentences; i.e., it will define "grammatical sentence" in terms of "observed sentence," certain properties of the observed sentences, and certain properties of grammars. To use Quine's formulation, a linguistic theory will give a general explanation for what "could" be in language on the basis of "what *is* plus *simplicity* of the laws whereby we describe and extrapolate what is." (W. V. Quine, *From a logical point of view* [Cambridge, 1953], p. 54).

sentence,'' and for the set of grammars constructed in accordance with such a theory. It is furthermore a reasonable requirement, since we are interested not only in particular languages, but also in the general nature of Language. There is a great deal more that can be said about this crucial topic, but this would take us too far afield.

2.2   On what basis do we actually go about separating grammatical sequences from ungrammatical sequences? I shall not attempt to give a complete answer to this question here, but I would like to point out that several answers that immediately suggest themselves could not be correct. First, it is obvious that the set of grammatical sentences cannot be identified with any particular corpus of utterances obtained by the linguist in his field work. Any grammar of a language will *project* the finite and somewhat accidental corpus of observed utterances to a set (presumably infinite) of grammatical utterances. In this respect, a grammar mirrors the behavior of the speaker who, on the basis of a finite and accidental experience with language, can produce or understand an indefinite number of new sentences. Indeed, any explication of the notion "grammatical in L" (i.e., any characterization of "grammatical in L" in terms of "observed utterance of L") can be thought of as offering an explanation for this fundamental aspect of linguistic behavior.

2.3.   Second, the notion "grammatical" cannot be identified with "meaningful" or "significant" in any semantic sense. Sentences (1) and (2) are equally nonsensical, but any speaker of English will recognize that only the former is grammatical.

1. Colorless green ideas sleep furiously.
2. Furiously sleep ideas green colorless.

Similarly, there is no semantic reason to prefer (3) to (5) or (4) to (6), but only (3) and (4) are grammatical sentences of English.

3. Have you a book on modern music?
4. The book seems interesting.
5. Read you a book on modern music?
6. The child seems sleeping.

Such examples suggest that any search for a semantically based definition of "grammaticalness" will be futile. We shall see, in fact, that there are deep structural reasons for distinguishing (3) and (4) from (5) and (6); but before we are able to find an explanation for such facts as these we shall have to carry the theory of syntactic structure a good deal beyond its familiar limits.

2.4.   Third, the notion "grammatical in English" cannot be identified in any way with the notion "high order of statistical approximation of English." It is fair to assume that neither sentence (1) nor (2) (nor indeed any part of these sentences) has ever occurred in an English discourse. Hence, in any statistical model for grammaticalness, these sentences will be ruled out on identical grounds as equally "remote" from English. Yet (1), though nonsensical, is grammatical, while (2) is not. Presented with these sentences, a speaker of English will read (1) with a normal sentence intonation, but he will read (2) with a falling intonation on each word: in fact, with just the intonation pattern given to any sequence of unrelated words. He treats each word in (2) as a separate phrase. Similarly, he will be able to recall (1) much more easily than (2), to learn it much more quickly, etc. Yet he may never have heard or seen any pair of words from these sentences joined in actual discourse. To choose another example, in the context "I saw a fragile ___," the words "whale" and "of" may have equal (i.e., zero) frequency in the past linguistic experience of a speaker who will immediately recognize that one of these substitutions, but not the other, gives a grammatical sentence. We cannot, of course, appeal to the fact that sentences such as (1) "might" be uttered in some sufficiently far-fetched context, while (2) would never be, since the basis for this differentiation between (1) and (2) is precisely what we are interested in determining.

Evidently, one's ability to produce and recognize grammatical utterances is not based on notions of statistical approximation and the like. The custom of calling grammatical sentences those that "can occur," or those that are "possible" has been responsible for some confusion here. It is natural to understand "possible" as meaning "highly probable" and to assume that the linguist's sharp distinction between grammatical and ungrammatical[2] is motivated by a feeling that since the "reality" of language is too complex to be described completely, he must content himself with a schematized version replacing "zero probability, and all extremely low probabilities, by *impossible*, and all higher probabilities by *possible*."[3] We see, however, that this idea is quite incorrect, and that a structural analysis cannot be understood as a schematic summary developed by sharpening the blurred edges in the full statistical picture. If we rank the sequences of a given length in order of statistical approximation to English, we will find both grammatical and ungrammatical sequences scattered throughout the list; there appears to be no particular relation between order of approximation and grammaticalness. Despite the undeniable interest and importance of semantic and statistical studies of language, they appear to have no direct relevance to the problem of determining or characterizing the set of grammatical utterances. I think that we are forced to conclude that grammar is autonomous and

---

[2]Below we shall suggest that this sharp distinction may be modified in favor of a notion of levels of grammaticalness. But this has no bearing on the point at issue here. Thus (1) and (2) will be at different levels of grammaticalness even if (1) is assigned a lower degree of grammaticalness than, say, (3) and (4); but they will be at the same level of statistical remoteness from English. The same is true of an indefinite number of similar pairs.

[3]C. F. Hockett, *A manual of phonology* (Baltimore, 1955), p. 10.

independent of meaning, and that probabilistic models give no particular insight into some of the basic problems of syntactic structure.[4]

CHAPTER V   LIMITATIONS OF PHRASE STRUCTURE DESCRIPTION

5.1.   We have discussed two models for the structure of language, a communication theoretic model based on a conception of language as a Markov process and corresponding, in a sense, to the minimal linguistic theory, and a phrase structure model based on immediate constituent analysis. We have seen that the first is surely inadequate for the purposes of grammar, and that the second is more powerful than the first, and does not fail in the same way. Of course there are languages (in our general sense) that cannot be described in terms of phrase structure, but I do not know whether or not English is itself literally outside the range of such analysis. However, I think that there are other grounds for rejecting the theory of phrase structure as inadequate for the purposes of linguistic description.

The strongest possible proof of the inadequacy of a linguistic theory is to show that it literally cannot apply to some natural language. A weaker, but perfectly sufficient demonstration of inadequacy would be to show that the theory can apply only clumsily; that is, to show that any grammar that can be constructed in terms of this theory will be extremely complex, *ad hoc*, and "unrevealing," that certain very simple ways of describing grammatical sentences cannot be accommodated within the associated forms of grammar, and that certain fundamental formal properties of natural language cannot be utilized to simplify grammars. We can gather a good deal of evidence of this sort in favor of the thesis that the form of grammar described above, and the conception of linguistic theory that underlies it, are fundamentally inadequate.

[4]We return to the question of the relation between semantics and syntax [later], where we argue that this relation can only be studied after the syntactic structure has been determined on independent grounds. I think that much the same thing is true of the relation between syntactic and statistical studies of language. Given the grammar of a language, one can study the use of the language statistically in various ways: and the development of probabilistic models for the use of language (as distinct from the syntactic structure of language) can be quite rewarding. Cf. B. Mandelbrot, "Structure formelle des textes et communication: deux études," *Word* 10. 1–27 (1954). H. A. Simon, "On a class of skew distribution functions," *Biometrika* 42. 425–40 (1955).

One might seek to develop a more elaborate relation between statistical and syntactic structure than the simple order of approximation model we have rejected. I would certainly not care to argue that any such relation is unthinkable, but I know of no suggestion to this effect that does not have obvious flaws. Notice, in particular, that for any n, we can find a string whose first n words may occur as the beginning of a grammatical sentence S_1 and whose last n words may occur as the ending of some grammatical sentence S_2, but where S_1 must be distinct from S_2. For example, consider the sequences of the form, "the man who . . . are here," where . . . may be a verb phrase of arbitrary length. Notice also that we can have new but perfectly grammatical sequences of word classes, e.g., a sequence of adjectives longer than any ever before produced in the context "I saw a ____ house." Various attempts to explain the grammatical-ungrammatical distinction, as in the case of (1), (2), on the basis of frequency of sentence type, order of approximation of word class sequences, etc., will run afoul of numerous facts like these.

The only way to test the adequacy of our present apparatus is to attempt to apply it directly to the description of English sentences. As soon as we consider any sentences beyond the simplest type, and in particular, when we attempt to define some order among the rules that produce these sentences, we find that we run into numerous difficulties and complications. To give substance to this claim would require a large expenditure of effort and space, and I can only assert here that this can be shown fairly convincingly.[1] Instead of undertaking this rather arduous and ambitious course here, I shall limit myself to sketching a few simple cases in which considerable improvement is possible over grammars of the form $[\Sigma, F]$. In section 8* I shall suggest an independent method of demonstrating the inadequacy of constituent analysis as a means of describing English sentence structure.

5.2   One of the most productive processes for forming new sentences is the process of conjunction. If we have two sentences $Z + X + W$ and $Z + Y + W$, and if X and Y are actually constituents of these sentences, we can generally form a new sentence $Z - X + Y - W$. For example, from the sentences (20 a-b) we can form the new sentence (21).

20. a. The scene-of the movie-was in Chicago.
     b. The scene-of the play-was in Chicago.
21. The scene-of the movie and of the play-was in Chicago.

If X and Y are, however, not constituents, we generally cannot do this.[2] For example we cannot form (23) from (22 a-b).

---

[1] See my *The logical structure of linguistic theory* for detailed analysis of this problem.

[2] (21) and (23) are extreme cases in which there is no question about the possibility of conjunction. There are many less clear cases. For example, it is obvious that "John enjoyed the book and liked the play" (a string of the form NP − VP + and + VP) is a perfectly good sentence, but many would question the grammaticalness of, e.g., "John enjoyed and my friend liked the play" (a string of the form NP + Verb + and + Verb − NP). The latter sentence, in which conjunction crosses over constituent boundaries, is much less natural than the alternative, "John enjoyed the play and my friend liked it," but there is no preferable alternative to the former. Such sentences with conjunction crossing constituent boundaries are also, in general, marked by special phonemic features such as extra long pauses (in our example, between "liked" and "the"), contrastive stress and intonation, failure to reduce vowels and drop final consonants in rapid speech, etc. Such features normally mark the reading of non-grammatical strings. The most reasonable way to describe this situation would seem to be by a description of the following kind: to form fully grammatical sentences by conjunction, it is necessary to conjoin single constituents; if we conjoin pairs of constituents, and these are major constituents (i.e., "high up" in the diagram (15)), the resulting sentences are semigrammatical; the more completely we violate constituent structure by conjunction, the less grammatical is the resulting sentence. This description requires that we generalize the grammatical-ungrammatical dichotomy, developing a notion of degree of grammaticalness. It is immaterial to our discussion, however, whether we decide to exclude such sentences as "John enjoyed and my friend liked the play" as ungrammatical, whether we include them as semigrammatical, or whether we include them as fully grammatical but with special phonemic features. In any event they form a class of utterances distinct from "John enjoyed the play and liked the book," etc., where constituent structure is preserved perfectly; and our conclusion that the rule for conjunction must make explicit reference to constituent structure therefore stands, since this distinction will have to be pointed out in the grammar.

[*Not included in this selection−ed.]

22. a. The-liner sailed down the-river.
    b. The-tugboat chugged up the-river.
23. The-liner sailed down the and tugboat chugged up the-river.

Similarly, if X and Y are both constituents, but are constituents of different kinds (i.e., if in the diagram of the form (15) they each have a single origin, but this origin is labelled differently), then we cannot in general form a new sentence by conjunction. For example, we cannot form (25) from (24 a-b).*

24. a. The scene-of the movie-was in Chicago.
    b. The scene-that I wrote-was in Chicago.
25. The scene-of the movie and that I wrote-was in Chicago.

In fact, the possibility of conjunction offers one of the best criteria for the initial determination of phrase structure. We can simplify the description of conjunction if we try to set up constituents in such a way that the following rule will hold:

26. If S_1 and S_2 are grammatical sentences, and S_1 differs from S_2 only in that X appears in S_1 where Y appears in S_2 (i.e., $S_1 = . . X . .$ and $S_2 = . . Y . .$), and X and Y are constituents of the same type in S_1 and S_2, respectively, then S_3 is a sentence, where S_3 is the result of replacing X by X + and + Y in S_1 (i.e., $S_3 = . . X + and + Y . .$).

Even though additional qualification is necessary here, the grammar is enormously simplified if we set up constituents in such a way that (26) holds even approximately. That is, it is easier to state the distribution of "and" by means of qualifications on this rule than to do so directly without such a rule. But we now face the following difficulty: we cannot incorporate the rule (26) or anything like it in a grammar [Σ, F] of phrase structure, because of certain fundamental limitations on such grammars. The essential property of rule (26) is that in order to apply it to sentences S_1 and S_2 to form the new sentence S_3 we must know not only the actual form of S_1 and S_2 but also their constituent structure — we must know not only the final shape of these sentences, but also their "history of derivation." But each rule X → Y of the grammar [Σ, F] applies or fails to apply to a given string by virtue of the actual substance of this string. The question of how this string gradually assumed this form is irrelevant. If the string contains X as a substring, the rule X → Y can apply to it; if not, the rule cannot apply.

We can put this somewhat differently. The grammar [Σ, F] can also be regarded as a very elementary process that generates sentences not from "left to

[*Not included in this selection: see Ch. 4, p. 27 of the original text–ed.]

right'' but from "top to bottom." Suppose that we have the following grammar of phrase structure:

27. Σ : Sentence

$$F: \quad X_1 \rightarrow Y_1$$

$$X_{11} \rightarrow Y_{11}$$

Then we can represent this grammar as a machine with a finite number of internal states, including an initial and a final state. In its initial state it can produce only the element *Sentence*, thereby moving into a new state. It can then produce any string Y_i such that Sentence $\rightarrow Y_i$ is one of the rules of F in (27), again moving into a new state. Suppose that Y_i is the string . . . X_i . . . Then the machine can produce the string . . . Y_j . . . by "applying" the rule $X_j \rightarrow Y_j$. The machine proceeds in this way from state to state until it finally produces a terminal string: it is now in the final state. The machine thus produces derivations. The important point is that the state of the machine is completely determined by the string it has just produced (i.e., by the last step of the derivation); more specifically, the state is determined by the subset of "left-hand" elements X_i of F which are contained in this last-produced string. But rule (26) requires a more powerful machine, which can "look back" to earlier strings in the derivation in order to determine how to produce the next step in the derivation.

Rule (26) is also fundamentally new in a different sense. It makes essential reference to two distinct sentences S_1 and S_2, but in grammars of the [Σ, F] type, there is no way to incorporate such double reference. The fact that rule (26) cannot be incorporated into the grammar of phrase structure indicates that even if this form for grammar is not literally inapplicable to English, it is certainly inadequate in the weaker but sufficient sense considered above. This rule leads to a considerable simplification of the grammar; in fact, it provides one of the best criteria for determining how to set up constituents. We shall see that there are many other rules of the same general type as (26) which play the same dual role.

5.3.   In the grammar (13) we gave only one way of analyzing the element *Verb*, namely, as *hit* (cf. 13vi).* But even with the verbal root fixed (let us say, as *take*), there are many other forms that this element can assume, e.g., *takes, has + taken, will + take, has + been + taken, is + being + taken*, etc. The study of these "auxiliary verbs" turns out to be quite crucial in the development of English grammar. We shall see that their behavior is very regular and simply describable when observed from a point of view that is quite different from that developed above, though it appears to be quite complex if we attempt to incorporate these phrases directly into a [Σ, F] grammar.

[*Not included in this selection: see Ch. 4, p. 26 of the original text–ed.]

Consider first the auxiliaries that appear unstressed; for example, "has" in "John has read the book" but not *"does"* in "John *does* read books."[3] We can state the occurrence of these auxiliaries in declarative sentences by adding to the grammar (13) the following rules:

28.　i.　Verb → Aux + V

　　ii.　V → hit, take, walk, read, etc.

　　iii.　Aux → C (M) (have + en) (be + ing) (be + en)

　　iv.　M → will, can, may, shall, must

29.　i.　$C \rightarrow \begin{cases} S \text{ in the context NP sing} \\ \emptyset \text{ in the context NP}_e \\ \text{past} \end{cases}$ [4]

　　ii.　Let *Af* stand for any of the affixes, *past, S, $\emptyset$, en, ing*. Let *v* stand for any *M* or *V*, or *have* or *be* (i.e., for any non-affix in the phrase *Verb*).
Then: Af + v → v + Af #,
where # is interpreted as word boundary.[5]

　　iii.　Replace + by # except in the context v — Af.
Insert # initially and finally.

The interpretation of the notations in (28iii) is as follows: we must choose the element C, and we may choose zero or more of the parenthesized elements in the given order. In (29i) we may develop C into any of three morphemes, observing the contextual restrictions given. As an example of the application of these rules, we construct a derivation in the style of (14), omitting the initial steps.

30.　the + man + verb + the + book　　　　from 13i-v

　　the + man + Aux + V + the + book　　28i

　　the + man + Aux + read + the + book　28ii

　　the + man + C + have + en + be + ing + read
　　+ the + book

　　　　　　　　　　　　　　　　　　　　28iii — we
　　　　　　　　　　　　select the elements C, have + en
　　　　　　　　　　　　and be + ing.

　　the + man + s + have + en + be + ing + read
　　+ the + book　　　　　　　　　　　29i

　　the + man + have + s # be + en # read + ing #
　　the + book　　　　　　　　　　　29ii —three times

　　#the #man #have + s #be + en #read + ing #the #book#
　　　　　　　　　　　　　　　　29iii

---

[3]We return to the stressed auxiliary "do" below, in sec. 7.1 (45)–(47)–[Not included in this selection: see Ch. 7, p. 65 of the original text–ed.]

[4]We assume here that (13ii) has been extended in the manner of fn. 3, above, or something similar.

[5]If we were formulating the theory of grammar more carefully, we would interpret # as the concatenation operator on the level of words, while + is the concatenation operator on the level of

The morphophonemic rules (19),* etc., will convert the last line of this derivation into:

31. the man has been reading the book

in phonemic transcription. Similarly, every other auxiliary verb phrase can be generated. We return later to the question of further restrictions that must be placed on these rules so that only grammatical sequences can be generated. Note, incidentally, that the morphophonemic rules will have to include such rules as: will + S → will, will + past → would. These rules can be dropped if we rewrite (28iii) so that either C or M, but not both, can be selected. But now the forms *would, could, might, should* must be added to (28iv), and certain "sequence of tense" statements become more complex. It is immaterial to our further discussion which of these alternative analyses is adopted. Several other minor revisions are possible.

Notice that in order to apply (29i) in (30) we had to use the fact that *the +man* is a singular noun phrase *NP sing*. That is, we had to refer back to some earlier step in the derivation in order to determine the constituent structure of *the + man*. (The alternative of ordering (29i) and the rule that develops *NP sing* into *the + man* in such a way that (29i) must precede the latter is not possible, for a variety of reasons, some of which appear below). Hence, (29i), just like (26), goes beyond the elementary Markovian character of grammars of phrase structure, and cannot be incorporated within the [Σ, F] grammar.

Rule (29ii) violates the requirements of [Σ, F] grammars even more severely. It also requires reference to constituent structure (i.e., past history of derivation) and in addition, we have no way to express the required inversion within the terms of phrase structure. Note that this rule is useful elsewhere in the grammar, at least in the case where *Af* is *ing*. Thus the morphemes *to* and *ing* play a very similar role within the noun phrase in that they convert verb phrases into noun phrases, giving, e.g.,

32. to prove that theorem $\left.\right\}$ was difficult
    proving that theorem

etc. We can exploit this parallel by adding to the grammar (13) the rule

33. NP → $\left\{ \begin{array}{c} ing \\ to \end{array} \right\}$ VP

The rule (29ii) will then convert *ing + prove + that + theorem* into *proving that + theorem*. A more detailed analysis of the *VP* shows that this parallel extends much further than this, in fact.

---

phrase structure. (29) would then be part of the definition of a mapping which carries certain objects on the level of phrase structure (essentially, diagrams of the form (15)) into strings of words. See my *The logical structure of linguistic theory* for a more careful formulation.

[*Not included in this selection: see Ch. 4, p. 32–ed.]

The reader can easily determine that to duplicate the effect of (28iii) and (29) without going beyond the bounds of a system [Σ, F] of phrase structure, it would be necessary to give a fairly complex statement. Once again, as in the case of conjunction, we see that significant simplification of the grammar is possible if we are permitted to formulate rules of a more complex type than those that correspond to a system of immediate constituent analysis. By allowing ourselves the freedom of (29ii) we have been able to state the constituency of the auxiliary phrase in (28iii) without regard to the interdependence of its elements, and it is always easier to describe a sequence of independent elements than a sequence of mutually dependent ones. To put the same thing differently, in the auxiliary verb phrase we really have discontinuous elements — e.g., in (30), the elements *have* . . *en* and *be* . . *ing*. But discontinuities cannot be handled within [Σ, F] grammars.[6] In (28iii) we treated these elements as continuous, and we introduced the discontinuity by the very simple additional rule (29ii). We shall see below, that this analysis of the element *Verb* serves as the basis for a far-reaching and extremely simple analysis of several important features of English syntax.

5.4.   As a third example of the inadequacy of the conceptions of phrase structure, consider the case of the active-passive relation. Passive sentences are formed by selecting the element *be + en* in rule (28iii). But there are heavy restrictions on this element that make it unique among the elements of the auxiliary phrase. For one thing, *be + en* can be selected only if the following *V* is transitive (e.g., *was + eaten* is permitted, but not *was + occurred*); but with a few exceptions the other elements of the auxiliary phrase can occur freely with verbs. Furthermore, *be + en* cannot be selected if the verb *V* is followed by a noun phrase, as in (30) (e.g., we cannot in general have NP + is + V + en + NP, even when V is transitive — we cannot have "lunch is eaten John"). Furthermore, if V is transitive and is followed by the prepositional phrase *by + NP*, then we *must* select *be + en* (we can have "lunch is eaten by John" but not "John is eating by lunch," etc.). Finally, note that in elaborating (13) into a

---

[6]We might attempt to extend the notions of phrase structure to account for discontinuities. It has been pointed out several times that fairly serious difficulties arise in any systematic attempt to pursue this course. Cf. my "System of syntactic analysis," *Journal of Symbolic Logic* 18.242–56 (1953); C. F. Hockett, "A formal statement of morphemic analysis," *Studies in Linguistics* 10.27–39 (1952); idem, "Two models of grammatical description," *Linguistics Today, Word* 10.210–33 (1954). Similarly, one might seek to remedy some of the other deficiencies of [Σ, F] grammars by a more complex account of phrase structure. I think that such an approach is ill-advised, and that it can only lead to the development of *ad hoc* and fruitless elaborations. It appears to be the case that the notions of phrase structure are quite adequate for a small part of the language and that the rest of the language can be derived by repeated application of a rather simple set of transformations to the strings given by the phrase structure grammar. If we were to attempt to extend phrase structure grammar to cover the entire language directly, we would lose the simplicity of the limited phrase structure grammar and of the transformational development. This approach would miss the main point of level construction . . . namely, to rebuild the vast complexity of the actual language more elegantly and systematically by extracting the contribution to this complexity of several linguistic levels, each of which is simple in itself.

full-fledged grammar we will have to place many restrictions on the choice of V in terms of subject and object in order to permit such sentences as: "John admires sincerity," "sincerity frightens John," "John plays golf," "John drinks wine," while excluding the "inverse" non-sentences,[7] "sincerity admires John," "John frightens sincerity," "golf plays John," "wine drinks John." But this whole network of restrictions fails completely when we choose $be + en$ as part of the auxiliary verb. In fact, in this case the same selectional dependencies hold, but in the opposite order. That is, for every sentence $NP_1 - V - NP_2$ we can have a corresponding sentence $NP_2 - is + Ven - by + NP_1$. If we try to include passives directly in the grammar (13), we shall have to restate all of these restrictions in the opposite order for the case in which $be + en$ is chosen as part of the auxiliary verb. This inelegant duplication, as well as the special restrictions involving the element $be + en$, can be avoided only if we deliberately exclude passives from the grammar of phrase structure, and reintroduce them by a rule such as:

34. If S_1 is a grammatical sentence of the form

    $NP_1 - Aux - V - NP_2,$

    then the corresponding string of the form

    $NP_2 - Aux + be + en - V - by + NP_1$

    is also a grammatical sentence.

We can now drop the element $be + en$ and all of the special restrictions associated with it, from (28iii). The fact that $be + en$ requires a transitive verb, that it cannot occur before $V + NP$, that it must occur before $V + by + NP$ (where V is transitive), that it inverts the order of the surrounding noun phrases, is in each case an automatic consequence of rule (34). This rule thus leads to a considerable simplification of the grammar. But (34) is well beyond the limits of $[\Sigma, F]$ grammars. Like (29ii), it requires reference to the constituent structure of the string to which it applies and it carries out an inversion on this string in a structurally determined manner.

5.5   We have discussed three rules (26), (29), (34) which materially simplify the description of English but which cannot be incorporated into a $[\Sigma, F]$ grammar. There are a great many other rules of this type, a few of which we shall discuss below. By further study of the limitations of phrase structure grammars with respect to English we can show quite conclusively that these grammars will

---

[7]Here too we might make use of a notion of levels of grammaticalness as suggested in footnote 2. Thus "sincerity admires John," though clearly less grammatical than "John admires sincerity," is certainly more grammatical than "of admires John." I believe that a workable notion of degree of grammaticalness can be developed in purely formal terms (cf. by *The logical structure of linguistic theory*), but this goes beyond the bounds of the present discussion.

be so hopelessly complex that they will be without interest unless we incorporate such rules.

If we examine carefully the implications of these supplementary rules, however, we see that they lead to an entirely new conception of linguistic structure. Let us call each such rule a "grammatical transformation." A grammatical transformation T operates on a given string (or, as in the case of (26), on a set of strings) with a given constituent structure and converts it into a new string with a new derived constituent structure. To show exactly *how* this operation is performed requires a rather elaborate study which would go far beyond the scope of these remarks, but we can in fact develop a certain fairly complex but reasonably natural algebra of transformations having the properties that we apparently require for grammatical description.[8]

From these few examples we can already detect some of the essential properties of a transformational grammar. For one thing, it is clear that we must define an order of application on these transformations. The passive transformation (34), for example, must apply *before* (29). It must precede (29i), in particular, so that the verbal element in the resulting sentence will have the same number as the new grammatical subject of the passive sentence. And it must precede (29ii) so that the latter rule will apply properly to the new inserted element *be + en*. (In discussing the question of whether or not (29i) can be fitted into a [Σ, F] grammar, we mentioned that this rule could not be required to apply before the rule analyzing *NP sing* into *the + man*, etc. One reason for this is now obvious — (29i) must apply after (34), but (34) must apply after the analysis of *NP sing*, or we will not have the proper selectional relations between the subject and verb and the verb and "agent" in the passive.)

Secondly, note that certain transformations are *obligatory*, whereas others are only *optional*. For example, (29) must be applied to every derivation, or the result will simply not be a sentence.[9] But (34), the passive transformation, may or may not be applied in any particular case. Either way the result is a sentence. Hence (29) is an obligatory transformation and (34) is an optional transformation.

This distinction between obligatory and optional transformations leads us to set up a fundamental distinction among the sentences of the language. Suppose that we have a grammar G with a [Σ, F] part and a transformational part, and suppose that the transformational part has certain obligatory transformations and certain optional ones. Then we define the *kernel* of the language (in terms of the

[8]See my "Three models for the description of language" for a brief account of transformations, and *The logical structure of linguistic theory* and *Transformational Analysis* for a detailed development of transformational algebra and transformational grammars. See Z. S. Harris, "Co-occurrence and Transformations in linguistic structure," *Language* 33.283–340 (1957), for a somewhat different approach to transformational analysis.

[9]But of the three parts of (29i), only the third is obligatory. That is, *past* may occur after *NP sing* or *NP pl*. Whenever we have an element such as C in (29i) which must be developed, but perhaps in several alternative ways, we can order the alternatives and make each one but the last optional, and the last, obligatory.

grammar G) as the set of sentences that are produced when we apply obligatory transformations to the terminal strings of the [Σ, F] grammar. The transformational part of the grammar will be set up in such a way that transformations can apply to kernel sentences (more correctly, to the forms that underlie kernel sentences — i.e., to terminal strings of the [Σ, F] part of the grammar) or to prior transforms. Thus every sentence of the language will either belong to the kernel or will be derived from the strings underlying one or more kernel sentences by a sequence of one or more transformations.

From these considerations we are led to a picture of grammars as possessing a natural tripartite arrangement. Corresponding to the level of phrase structure, a grammar has a sequence of rules of the form $X \rightarrow Y$, and corresponding to lower levels it has a sequence of morphophonemic rules of the same basic form. Linking these two sequences, it has a sequence of transformational rules. Thus the grammar will look something like this:

35. $\quad$ Σ: $\quad$ Sentence

$$F: \quad \left. \begin{array}{l} X_1 \rightarrow Y_1 \\ \qquad \cdot \\ \qquad \cdot \\ X_n \rightarrow Y_n \end{array} \right\} \text{Phrase structure}$$

$$\left. \begin{array}{l} T_1 \\ \quad \cdot \\ \quad \cdot \\ T_j \end{array} \right\} \text{Transformational structure}$$

$$\left. \begin{array}{l} Z_1 \rightarrow W_1 \\ \qquad \cdot \\ \qquad \cdot \\ Z_m \rightarrow W_m \end{array} \right\} \text{Morphophonemics}$$

To produce a sentence from such a grammar we construct an extended derivation beginning with *Sentence*. Running through the rules of F we construct a terminal string that will be a sequence of morphemes, though not necessarily in the correct order. We then run through the sequence of transformations $T_1, \ldots T_j$, applying each obligatory one and perhaps certain optional ones. These transformations may rearrange strings or may add or delete morphemes. As a result they yield a string of words. We then run through the morphophonemic rules, thereby converting this string of words into a string of phonemes. The phrase structure segment of the grammar will include such rules as those of (13), (17), and (28). The transformational part will include such rules as (26), (29), and (34), formulated properly in the terms that must be developed in a full-scale theory of transformations. The morphophonemic part will include such rules as (19). This sketch of the process of generation of sentences must (and easily can) be generalized to allow for proper functioning of such rules as (26) which operate on a set of sentences, and to allow transformations to reapply to transforms so that more and more complex sentences can be produced.

When we apply only obligatory transformations in the generation of a given sentence, we call the resulting sentence a kernel sentence. Further investigation would show that in the phrase structure and morphophonemic parts of the grammar we can also extract a skeleton of obligatory rules that *must* be applied whenever we reach them in the process of generating a sentence. In the last few paragraphs of section 4* we pointed out that the phrase structure rules lead to a conception of linguistic structure and "level of representation" that is fundamentally different from that provided by the morphophonemic rules. On each of the lower levels corresponding to the lower third of the grammar an utterance is, in general, represented by a single sequence of elements. But phrase structure cannot be broken down into sublevels: on the level of phrase structure an utterance is represented by a set of strings that cannot be ordered into higher or lower levels. This set of representing strings is equivalent to a diagram of the form (15). On the transformational level, an utterance is represented even more abstractedly in terms of a sequence of transformations by which it is derived, ultimately from kernel sentences (more correctly, from the strings which underlie kernel sentences). There is a very natural general definition of "linguistic level" that includes all of these cases,[10] and as we shall see later, there is good reason to consider each of these structures to be a linguistic level.

When transformational analysis is properly formulated we find that it is essentially more powerful than description in terms of phrase structure, just as the latter is essentially more powerful than description in terms of finite state Markov processes that generate sentences from left to right. In particular, such languages as (10iii)† which lie beyond the bounds of phrase structure description with context-free rules can be derived transformationally.[11] It is important to observe that the grammar is materially simplified when we add a transformational level, since it is now necessary to provide phrase structure directly only for kernel sentences — the terminal strings of the [Σ, F] grammar are just those which underlie kernel sentences. We choose the kernel sentences in such a way that the terminal strings underlying the kernel are easily derived by means of a [Σ, F] description, while all other sentences can be derived from these terminal strings by simply statable transformations. We have seen, and shall see again below, several examples of simplifications resulting from transformational analysis. Full-scale syntactic investigation of English provides a great many more cases.

[*Not included in this selection–ed.]

[†Not included in this selection: see Ch. 3, p. 21–ed.]

[10]Cf. *The logical structure of linguistic theory* and *Transformational Analysis*.

[11]Let G be a [Σ, F] grammar with the initial string *Sentence* and with the set of all finite strings of *a*'s and *b*'s as its terminal output. There is such a grammar. Let G' be the grammar which contains G as its phrase structure part, supplemented by the transformation T that operates on any string K which is a *Sentence*, converting it into K + K. Then the output of G' is (10iii).

One further point about grammars of the form (35) deserves mention, since it has apparently led to some misunderstanding. We have described these grammars as devices for generating sentences. This formulation has occasionally led to the idea that there is a certain asymmetry in grammatical theory in the sense that grammar is taking the point of view of the speaker rather than the hearer; that it is concerned with the process of producing utterances rather than the "inverse" process of analyzing and reconstructing the structure of given utterances. Actually, grammars of the form that we have been discussing are quite neutral as between speaker and hearer, between synthesis and analysis of utterances. A grammar does not tell us how to synthesize a specific utterance; it does not tell us how to analyze a particular given utterance. In fact, these two tasks which the speaker and hearer must perform are essentially the same, and are both outside the scope of grammars of the form (35). Each such grammar is simply a description of a certain set of utterances, namely, those which it generates. From this grammar we can reconstruct the formal relations that hold among these utterances in terms of the notions of phrase structure, transformational structure, etc. Perhaps the issue can be clarified by an analogy to a part of chemical theory concerned with the structurally possible compounds. This theory might be said to generate all physically possible compounds just as a grammar generates all grammatically "possible" utterances. It would serve as a theoretical basis for techniques of qualitative analysis and synthesis of specific compounds, just as one might rely on a grammar in the investigation of such special problems as analysis and synthesis of particular utterances.

On the Bases of Phonology

MORRIS HALLE

I. Our central concern in this section is the framework to be used for characterizing speech in a linguistic description. It is required of such a framework that
it not only make it possible to represent the observed data with a sufficient degree
of accuracy, but also that this representation lead to reasonable, fruitful, insightful, and simple descriptions of the relevant facts. As an illustration consider the
following example.

It is an easily observed fact that speakers of English can produce plural
forms of nouns regardless of whether or not they have ever heard the noun before. This bit of linguistic behavior is usually described by saying that in forming
the regular plural [iz] is added if the noun ends in [s, z, š, ž, č, ǰ] (e.g., *busses,
causes, bushes, garages, beaches, badges*); [s] is added if the noun ends in [p, t,
k, θ, f] (e.g., *caps, cats, cakes, fourths, cuffs*); and [z] is added in all other cases.

Underlying this rule is the assumption that the speech signal is a linear sequence of discrete entities variously termed phonemes, sounds, segments, allophones, and so on. It is this assumption which makes it possible to give the
concise account quoted above. Without making use of the phoneme these facts
can be expressed only with the greatest laboriousness as one can easily convince
oneself by trying to give the rule in terms of syllables, words, or such clear
acoustical properties as periodicity, formant behavior, noise spectrum, and the
like.

The layman may regard as somewhat paradoxical our terming as an assumption the proposition that speech is a linear sequence of sounds. It does not seem
to be widely known that when one examines an actual utterance in its purely
physical manifestation as an acoustical event, one does not find in it obvious
markers which would allow one to segment the signal into entities standing in a
one-to-one relationship with the phonemes that, the linguist would say, compose
the utterance.[1]

The inability of instrumental phoneticians to propose a workable segmentation procedure has, however, not resulted in a wholesale abandonment of the
phoneme concept. Only a few easily frightened souls have been ready to do

(from *The Structure of Language*, eds. J. A. Foder and J. J. Katz, Englewood Cliffs, N.J.:
Prentice-Hall, 1964, pp. 324–33. This is a revised version of M. Halle, "Questions of Linguistics," published in the supplement to *Il Nuovo Cimento*, 13, Series X (1958), 494–517.)

[1]For discussion of some of the evidence, see P. Ladefoged's contribution to the Teddington
Symposium, *The Mechanization of Thought Processes*, National Physical Laboratories, Symposium
#10 (London, 1959). Analogous observations have been made also with regard to other physiological
motor aspects of speech; cf. the report by Menzerath on his x-ray moving pictures of speech at the
Fourth International Congress of Linguists (Copenhagen, 1938).

without the phoneme. The majority has apparently felt that absence of a simple segmentation procedure does not warrant abandoning the discrete picture of speech. The most important justification that could perhaps be offered for this stand is that almost every insight gained by modern linguistics from Grimm's Law to Jakobson's distinctive features depend crucially on the assumption that speech is a sequence of discrete entities. In view of this fact many linguists have been willing to postulate the existence of discrete entities in speech even while accepting as true the assertion of instrumental phoneticians that there are no procedures for isolating these entities. There are numerous precedents in science for such a position. For instance, Helmholtz postulated that electric current is a flow of discrete particles without having isolated or even having much hope of isolating one of these particles. The status of the phoneme in linguistics is, therefore, analogous to that of electrons in physics, and since we do not regard the latter as fictional, there is little reason for applying this term to phonemes. They are every bit as real as any other theoretical entity in science. It now appears, moreover, that the insurmountable difficulties encountered in the attempt to state a procedure for segmenting the speech signal are no bar to constructing a device which will transform (continuous) speech into sequences of discrete entities.[2]

In addition to viewing utterances as composed of phonemes, the phonemes themselves shall be regarded here as simultaneous actualizations of a set of attributes. This view can be traced back almost to the very beginnings of abstract concern with language since rudimentary schemes for classifying speech sounds are implicit already in the earliest alphabets. This is hardly surprising, for it is all but self-evident that speech sounds form various intersecting classes. Thus, for instance, the final sounds in the words *ram, ran, rang* share the property of nasality; i.e., the property of being produced with a lowered velum, which allows air to flow through the nose. In a similar fashion, the sound [m] shares with the sounds [p] and [b] the property of being produced with a closure at the lips, or, as phoneticians would say, of having a bilabial *point of articulation*.

The proposed frameworks differ, of course, from one another, and up to the present, phoneticians have not agreed on any single framework that is to be used in all linguistic descriptions. In the present study I shall utilize the *distinctive feature framework* that is due primarily to R. Jakobson. Since the distinctive features have been described in detail elsewhere, I shall present here only the articulatory correlates of the most important features and comment briefly on some of them.[3]

---

[2]For a discussion of these procedures see D. MacKay, "Mindlike Behaviours of Artefacts," *Brit. J. for the Phil. of Sci.*, 2 (1959), 105–21, and M. Halle and K. N. Stevens, "Speech Recognition: A Model and a Program for Research."

[3]The fact that in the following list, reference is made only to the articulatory properties of speech and nothing is said about the acoustical properties, is not to be taken as an indication that the latter are somehow less important. The only reason for concentrating here exclusively on the former is that these are more readily observed without instruments. If reference were to be made to the acoustical properties of speech it would be necessary to report on experimental findings of fair complexity which would expand this paper beyond its allowed limits. For a further discussion see R. Jakobson, C. G. M. Fant, M. Halle, *Preliminaries to Speech Analysis* (Cambridge, Mass.: MIT Press, 1963).

Articulatory Correlates of the Distinctive Features (Partial List)

In the description below four degrees of narrowing in the vocal tract will be distinguished.

The most extreme degree of narrowing, termed *contact*, is present when two opposite parts of the vocal tract touch. Stop consonants such as [p], [d], or [k] are articulated with *contact* at different points in the vocal tract.

A less extreme degree of narrowing, termed *occlusion*, is one capable of producing turbulence. *Occlusions* are characteristically involved in the production of fricatives such as [v], [s], or [š].

The next degree of narrowing, termed *obstruction*, is exemplified in the articulation of glides such as [w] or [j].

The fourth degree of narrowing, termed *constriction*, is that manifest in the articulation of diffuse ("high") vowels such as [i] or [u].

Vocalic-Nonvocalic: vocalic sounds are produced with a periodic excitation and with an open oral cavity, i.e., one in which the most extreme degree of narrowing is a *constriction*; nonvocalic sounds are produced with an oral cavity narrowed at least to the degree of an *obstruction* or with an excitation that is not periodic.

Consonantal-Nonconsonantal: consonantal sounds are produced with *occlusion* or *contact* in the central path through the oral cavity; nonconsonantal sounds are produced with lesser degrees of narrowing in the central path of the oral cavity.

Grave-Nongrave: grave sounds are articulated with a primary narrowing located at the periphery of the oral cavity (i.e., at the lips or in the velar or pharyngeal region); nongrave sounds are articulated with a primary narrowing located in the central (i.e., dental-alveolar-palatal) region of the oral cavity.

Flat-Nonflat: flat sounds are produced with a secondary narrowing at the periphery of the oral cavity; nonflat sounds are produced without such a narrowing.[4]

Diffuse-Nondiffuse: diffuse sounds are produced with a narrowing which in degree equals or exceeds that of a constriction and is located in the front part of the vocal tract; nondiffuse sounds are articulated with narrowings which are either of a lesser degree or are located in the back part of the vocal tract. The dividing line between *front* and *back* is further retracted for vowels than for other sounds: for the vowels, *front* includes almost the entire oral cavity, while for other sounds, the dividing line between *front* and *back* runs between the alveolar and palatal regions.

Compact-Noncompact: this feature is restricted to vowels. Compact vowels are produced with a forward flanged oral cavity which contains no *con-*

---

[4]Sounds produced with a single narrowing which is located at the periphery of the oral cavity may be classed either as flat or nonflat; they are, of course, grave. Sounds articulated with two narrowings, of which one is central and the other peripheral, are acute and flat; whereas sounds articulated with two narrowings both of which are peripheral are grave and flat.

strictions or narrowings of higher degree; noncompact vowels are produced with an oral cavity that is not forward flanged.

Strident-Nonstrident: this feature is restricted to consonantal sounds. Strident sounds are produced by directing the air stream at right angles across a sharp-edged obstacle or parallel over a rough surface, thereby producing considerable noisiness which is the major acoustical correlate of stridency. Nonstrident sounds are produced with configurations in which one or several of the factors mentioned are missing.

Voiced-Voiceless: voiced sounds are produced by vibrating the vocal cords; voiceless sounds are produced without vocal vibration.

Nasal-Nonnasal: nasal sounds are produced by lowering the velum, thereby allowing air to pass through the nasal pharynx and nose; nonnasal sounds are produced with a raised velum which effectively shuts off the nasal pharynx and nose from the rest of the vocal tract.

Continuant-Interrupted: continuant sounds are produced with a vocal tract in which the passage from the glottis to the lips contains no narrowing in excess of an *occlusion*; interrupted sounds are produced with a vocal tract in which the passage from the glottis to the lips is effectively closed by *contact*.

The first two features on the above list produce a quadripartite division of the sounds of speech into 1. vowels, which are vocalic and nonconsonantal; 2. liquids, [r], [l], which are vocalic and consonantal; 3. consonants, which are nonvocalic and consonantal; and 4. glides [h], [w], [j], which are nonvocalic and nonconsonantal. This division differs from the traditional one — into vowels and nonvowels (consonants).

A further difference between most standard systems and the distinctive feature system lies in the treatment of two major classes of segments, the vowels and the consonants. In most standard systems these two classes are described in terms of features which are totally different: consonants are described in terms of "points of articulation," whereas vowels are described in terms of the so-called "vowel triangle." In the distinctive feature system, on the other hand, these two classes are handled by the same features, *diffuse-nondiffuse*, and *grave-acute*.[5]

The manner in which individual speech sounds are characterized in terms of distinctive features is illustrated in Table 1. As can be seen there, [s] is characterized as nonvocalic, consonantal, nongrave, diffuse, strident, nonnasal, continuant, voiceless; or [m] is characterized as nonvocalic, consonantal, grave, diffuse, nonstrident, nasal, noncontinuant, voiced. The alphabetic symbols [s] and [m], by which we conventionally designate these sounds are, therefore, nothing but abbreviations standing for the feature complexes just mentioned. It is as feature complexes, rather than as indivisible entities, that speech sounds will be regarded hereinafter.

[5]Over 2,000 years ago, Hindu phoneticians had the idea of treating vowels and consonants together. Their solution differs from the one proposed here in that it classified vowels as well as consonants in terms of their points of articulation.

Table 1
Distinctive Feature Representation
of the Consonants of English

	p	b	m	f	v	k	g	t	d	θ	ð	n	s	z	č	ǯ	š	ž
VOCALIC	−	−	−	−	−	−	−	−	−	−	−	−	−	−	−	−	−	−
CONSONANTAL	+	+	+	+	+	+	+	+	+	+	+	+	+	+	+	+	+	+
GRAVE	+	+	+	+	+	+	+	−	−	−	−	−	−	−	−	−	−	−
DIFFUSE	+	+	+	+	+	−	−	+	+	+	+	+	+	+	−	−	−	−
STRIDENT	−	−	−	+	+	−	−	−	−	−	−	−	+	+	+	+	+	+
NASAL	−	−	+	−	−	−	−	−	−	−	−	+	−	−	−	−	−	−
CONTINUANT	−	−	−	+	+	−	−	−	−	+	+	−	+	+	−	−	+	+
VOICED	−	+	+	−	+	−	+	−	+	−	+	+	−	+	−	+	−	+

It is obvious that we can use the features to refer conveniently to classes of speech sounds. Thus, for instance, all sounds represented in Table 1 belong to the class of consonants, and as such they share the features *nonvocalic* and *consonantal*. We note moreover that the consonants [s, z, č, ǯ, š, ž] are the only ones that share the features *nongrave* and *strident*; or [p, b, f, v, m] alone share the features *grave* and *diffuse*. On the other hand, [m] and [s] share no features which would distinguish them from all other consonants. If we wanted to designate the class containing the sounds [m] and [s] in distinctive feature terminology, we should have to give a long, cumbersome list of features. We shall say that a set of speech sounds forms a *natural class* if fewer features are required to designate the class than to designate any individual sound in the class. Hence, the first three sets of sounds cited above form natural classes, whereas the set containing [m] and [s] is not a natural class.

Jakobson has shown that in describing the most varied linguistic facts we commonly encounter sets of sounds which form natural classes in the distinctive feature framework and that only rarely does one meet sets of sounds which require long, cumbersome lists of distinctive features for their characterization. As a case in point consider again the formation of English noun plurals. As was noted above, [iz] is added if and only if the noun ends in [s, z, š, ž, č, ǯ]. But as we have already seen it is precisely this class of consonants that is exhaustively characterized by the features *nongrave* and *strident*. Similarly, the nouns to which the suffix [s] is added end in consonants all of which are characterized by the feature *unvoiced*. These coincidences are important, for the distinctive features are evidently not postulated with the express purpose of affording a convenient description of the rules for forming the English plural.

The total number of different distinctive features is quite small; there seems to be about fifteen. These 15 attributes are sufficient to characterize all segments in all languages. Since we cannot have knowledge of all languages — e.g., of languages which will be spoken in the future — the preceding assertion must be understood as a statement about the nature of human language in general. It asserts in effect that human languages are phonetically much alike, that they do *not* "differ from one another without limit and in unpredictable ways." Like all generalizations this statement can be falsified by valid counter-examples. It can, however, not be proven true with the same conclusiveness. The best that can be done is to show that the available evidence makes it very likely that the statement is true. Most important in this connection is the fact that all investigations in which large numbers of languages have been examined — from E. Siever's *Grundzüge der Phonetik* (1876) to Trubetzkoy's *Grundzüge der Phonologie* (1939) — have operated with an extremely restricted set of attributes. If this can be done with about a hundred languages from all parts of the globe, there appears good reason to believe that a not greatly enlarged catalogue of attributes will be capable of handling the remaining languages as well.

If it is true that a small set of attributes suffices to describe the phonetic properties of all languages of the world, then it would appear quite likely that these attributes are connected with something fairly basic in man's constitution, something which is quite independent of his cultural background. Psychologists might, therefore, find it rewarding to investigate the phonetic attributes, for it is not inconceivable that these attributes will prove to be productive parameters for describing man's responses to auditory stimuli in general. It must, however, be noted that for purposes of linguistics, the lack of psychological work in this area is not fatal. For the linguist it suffices if the attributes selected yield reasonable, elegant, and insightful descriptions of all relevant linguistic data. And this in fact they accomplish.

II.   It has been noted that in linguistic descriptions utterances are represented as sequences of discrete segments, which themselves are characterized by means of distinctive features. Although in many instances there is a one-to-one relationship between the segments and specific stretches of the acoustical signal, there are many instances where this relationship is anything but simple. The part of linguistics that is concerned with the relationship between segment (phoneme) and sound is called *phonology*.

A complete description of a language must include a list of all existing morphemes of the languages, for without such a list the grammar would fail to distinguish a normal English sentence such as "it was summer," from the Jabberwocky "'twas brilling." Our purpose in preparing a scientific description of a language is, however, not achieved if we give only an inventory of all existing morphemes; we must also describe the structural principles that underlie all existing forms. Just as syntax must be more than an inventory of all observed sentences of a language, so phonology must be more than a list of its morphemes.

In order to generate a specific sentence it is obviously necessary to supply the grammar with instructions for selecting from the list of morphemes the particular morphemes appearing in the sentence. Instead of using an arbitrary numerical code which tells us nothing about the phonetic structure of the morphemes, it is possible — and also more consonant with the aims of a linguistic description — to utilize for this purpose the distinctive feature representation of the morphemes directly. In other words, instead of instructing the grammar to select item (#7354), we instruct the grammar to select the morpheme which in its first segment has the features *nonvocalic, consonantal, diffuse, grave, voiced,* and so on; in its second segment, the features *vocalic, nonconsonantal, diffuse, acute,* and the like; in its third segment, the features *vocalic, consonantal,* and so forth. Instructions of this type need not contain information about all features but only about features or feature combinations which serve to distinguish one morpheme from another. This is a very important fact since in every language only certain features or feature combinations can serve to distinguish morphemes from one another. We call these features and feature combinations *phonemic,* and we say that in the input instructions only phonemic features or feature combinations must occur.[6]

Languages differ also in the way they handle nonphonemic features or feature combinations. For some of the nonphonemic features there are definite rules; for others the decision is left up to the speaker who can do as he likes. For example, the feature of aspiration is nonphonemic in English; its occurrence is subject to the following conditions:

All segments other than the voiceless stops [k], [p], [t] are unaspirated.

The voiceless stops are never aspirated after [s].

Except after [s], voiceless stops are always aspirated before an accented vowel.

In all other positions, aspiration of voiceless stops is optional.

A complete grammar must obviously contain a statement of such facts, for they are of crucial importance to one who would speak the language correctly.

In addition to features which, like *aspiration* in English, are never phonemic, there are features in every language that *are* phonemic, but only in those segments where they occur in conjunction with certain other features; for example, the feature of voicing in English is phonemic only in the nonnasal consonants — all other segments except [h] are normally voiced, while [h] is voiceless.

So far we have dealt only with features which are nonphonemic regardless of neighboring segments. There are also cases where features are nonphonemic because they occur in the vicinity of certain other segments. As an example we might take the segment sequences at the beginning of English words. It will be recalled here that the features *vocalic-nonvocalic* and *consonantal-nonconsonantal* distinguish four classes of segments: vowels, symbolized here by V, that are vocalic and nonconsonantal; consonants, symbolized by C, that are nonvocalic and consonantal; liquids [r], [l], symbolized by L, that are vocalic and consonantal; the glide [h], symbolized by H, that is nonvocalic

---

[6]The requirement to represent morphemes in the dictionary by phonemic features only is a direct consequence of the simplicity criterion.

and nonconsonantal.[7] We shall be concerned solely with restrictions on these four classes; all further restrictions within the classes are disregarded here.

English morphemes can begin only with V, CV, LV, HV, CCV, CLV, CCLV: *odd, do, rue, who, stew, clew, screw*. A number of sequences are not admitted initially, e.g. LCV, LLV. These constraints are reflected in the following three rules which are part of the grammar of English:

Rule 1:   If a morpheme begins with a consonant followed by a nonvocalic segment, the latter is also consonantal.

Rule 2:   If a morpheme begins with a sequence of two consonants, the third segment in the sequence is vocalic.

Rule 3:   If between the beginning of a morpheme and a liquid or a glide no vowel intervenes, the segment following the liquid or the glide is a vowel.

These rules enable us to specify uniquely a number of features in certain segment sequences:

vocalic	−	−		
consonantal	+		+	

is converted by rules 1, 2, and 3

into

vocalic	−	−	+	+
consonantal	+	+	+	−

which stands for a sequence CCLV, e.g., *straw*.

The above rules must be applied in the given order. If no order is imposed, they will have to be given in a much more complex form. An interesting illustration of the effects of ordering on the complexity of the rules is provided by the Finnish vowel system, which shall now be examined. Finnish has eight vowel sounds which can be characterized by means of the following distinctive feature matrix.

	[æ]	[a]	[e]	[ö]	[o]	[i]	[ü]	[u]
flat	−	−	−	+	+	−	+	+
compact	+	+	−	−	−	−	−	−
diffuse	−	−	−	−	−	+	+	+
grave	−	+	−	−	+	−	−	+

This matrix is clearly redundant, since it utilizes four binary features to characterize eight entities. The redundant features have been omitted in the following table.

[7]We consider the semivowels [j] as in *you* and [w] as in *woo*, to be positional variants of the lax vowels [i], [u], respectively; cf. N. Chomsky and M. Halle, *The Sound Pattern of English* (N.Y.: Harper & Row, 1968).

	[æ]	[a]	[e]	[ö]	[o]	[i]	[ü]	[u]
flat	−	−	−	+	+	−	+	+
compact	+	+	−			−		
diffuse			−	−	−	+	+	+
grave	−	+		−	+		−	+

The omitted nonphonemic features are supplied by the following rules:

Rule 4: Flat vowels are noncompact.
Rule 5: Compact vowels are nondiffuse.
Rule 6: Noncompact nonflat vowels are nongrave.

The treatment just proposed has an interesting further consequence. In Finnish there is a restriction on what vowels can occur in a given word (vowel harmony). The Finnish word can contain a selection either from the set [i, e, ü, ö, æ] or from the set [i, e, u, o, a]. If [e, i] are temporarily set aside, one could propose that Finnish is subject to

Rule 7: In a word all vowels are either grave or nongrave, depending on the nature of the root morpheme.

If [e, i] are included, Rule 7 leads to incorrect results, since in words with *grave* root morphemes, [e] and [i] would be turned by Rule 7 into grave vowels, whereas in fact they remain nongrave. This incorrect result is immediately avoided if we let Rule 6 apply after, rather than before Rule 7, for Rule 6 makes all nonflat noncompact vowels nongrave and Rule 7 does not affect either flatness or compactness of any vowel.

III.   In the preceding, the distinctive features have been utilized for two separate purposes. On the one hand, they have been used to characterize different aspects of vocal tract behavior, such as the location of the different narrowings in the vocal tract, the presence or absence of vocal cord vibration, lowering or raising of velum, and so forth. On the other hand, the features have functioned as abstract markers for the designation of individual morphemes. It is necessary at this point to give an account of how this dual function of the features is built into the theory.

As already noted the rules that constitute the phonological component of a grammar relate a matrix consisting of abstract markers — the phonemic representation — to a matrix where each marker represents a particular aspect of vocal tract behavior. The latter matrix is our counterpart of the conventional phonetic transcription. In the phonemic representation the different features are allowed to assume only two values, plus or minus. In this representation, however, no phonetic content is associated directly with the features which function here as abstract differential markers.

The rules of the phonological component modify — at times quite radically — the matrices of the phonological representation: the rules supply values to nonphonemic features, they change the values of certain features, and they assign a phonetic interpretation to the individual rows of the matrix. The phonetic interpretation assigned to the rows of the matrix is uniform for all languages; i.e., some row in the matrix will be associated with the feature *vocalic-nonvocalic*, another with the feature *consonantal-nonconsonantal*, and so on. This fact explains our practice of designating the rows in the phonemic matrices which represent abstract differential markers, by names of the different phonetic features. When we designate a given row in the phonemic matrix by the name of a particular phonetic feature, we imply that the grammar will ultimately associate this row with the phonetic feature in question.

The statement that the assignment of phonetic interpretations to phonemic matrices is uniform for all languages reflects the fact that the articulatory apparatus of man is the same everywhere, that men everywhere are capable of controlling the same few aspects of their vocal tract behavior. The phonetic features represent, therefore, the capacities of man to produce speech sounds and constitute, in this sense, the universal phonetic framework of language. Since not all phonetic features are binary, the phonological component will include rules replacing some of the pluses and minuses in the matrices by integers representing the different degrees of intensity which the feature in question manifests in the utterance. Thus, for instance, the fact that the English [ʌ] as in *pup* is less grave ("back") than English [u] as in *poop* will be embodied in a phonological rule replacing the plus for the feature gravity by a higher integer in the vowel in *poop* than in the vowel in *pup*.

In the light of the above, the extensive discussion concerning the claim that the distinctive features are binary appears to have been due primarily to an identification of abstract phonemic markers with the phonetic features with which they are associated by the rules of the grammar. Once a distinction is made between abstract phonemic markers and phonetic features, there is little ground for disagreement, for the fact that there are many more than two phonetically distinct degrees of gravity does not invalidate the claim that in the abstract phonemic representation of morphemes there are only binary features.

Aspects of the Theory of Syntax

NOAM CHOMSKY

GENERATIVE GRAMMARS AS THEORIES OF LINGUISTIC COMPETENCE

This study will touch on a variety of topics in syntactic theory and English syntax, a few in some detail, several quite superficially, and none exhaustively. It will be concerned with the syntactic component of a generative grammar, that is, with the rules that specify the well-formed strings of minimal syntactically functioning units (*formatives*) and assign structural information of various kinds both to these strings and to strings that deviate from well-formedness in certain respects.

The general framework within which this investigation will proceed has been presented in many places, and some familiarity with the theoretical and descriptive studies listed in the bibliography is presupposed. In this chapter, I shall survey briefly some of the main background assumptions, making no serious attempt here to justify them but only to sketch them clearly.

Linguistic theory is concerned primarily with an ideal speaker-listener, in a completely homogeneous speech-community, who knows its language perfectly and is unaffected by such grammatically irrelevant conditions as memory limitations, distractions, shifts of attention and interest, and errors (random or characteristic) in applying his knowledge of the language in actual performance. This seems to me to have been the position of the founders of modern general linguistics, and no cogent reason for modifying it has been offered. To study actual linguistic performance, we must consider the interaction of a variety of factors, of which the underlying competence of the speaker-hearer is only one. In this respect, study of language is no different from empirical investigation of other complex phenomena.

We thus make a fundamental distinction between *competence* (the speaker-hearer's knowledge of his language) and *performance* (the actual use of language in concrete situations). Only under the idealization set forth in the preceding paragraph is performance a direct reflection of competence. In actual fact, it obviously could not directly reflect competence. A record of natural speech will show numerous false starts, deviations from rules, changes of plan in midcourse, and so on. The problem for the linguist, as well as for the child learning

(from Noam Chomsky, *Aspects of the Theory of Syntax*, Cambridge, Mass.: MIT Press, 1965, pp. 3–9, 15–18, 27–30, 63–74.)

he language, is to determine from the data of performance the underlying system of rules that has been mastered by the speaker-hearer and that he puts to use in actual performance. Hence, in the technical sense, linguistic theory is mentalistic, since it is concerned with discovering a mental reality underlying actual behavior.[1] Observed use of language or hypothesized dispositions to respond, habits, and so on, may provide evidence as to the nature of this mental reality, but surely cannot constitute the actual subject matter of linguistics, if this is to be a serious discipline. The distinction I am noting here is related to the *langue-parole* distinction of Saussure; but it is necessary to reject his concept of *langue* as merely a systematic inventory of items and to return rather to the Humboldtian conception of underlying competence as a system of generative processes. For discussion, see Chomsky (1964).

A grammar of a language purports to be a description of the ideal speaker-hearer's intrinsic competence. If the grammar is, furthermore, perfectly

[Notes have been renumbered to match the selections chosen for this text.]

[1]To accept traditional mentalism, in this way, is not to accept Bloomfield's dichotomy of "mentalism" versus "mechanism." Mentalistic linguistics is simply theoretical linguistics that uses performance as data (along with other data, for example, the data provided by introspection) for the determination of competence, the latter being taken as the primary object of its investigation. The mentalist, in this traditional sense, need make no assumptions about the possible physiological basis for the mental reality that he studies. In particular, he need not deny that there is such a basis. One would guess, rather, that it is the mentalistic studies that will ultimately be of greatest value for the investigation of neurophysiological mechanisms, since they alone are concerned with determining abstractly the properties that such mechanisms must exhibit and the functions they must perform.

In fact, the issue of mentalism versus antimentalism in linguistics apparently has to do only with goals and interests, and not with questions of truth or falsity, sense or nonsense. At least three issues are involved in this rather idle controversy: a) dualism — are the rules that underlie performance represented in a nonmaterial medium? b) behaviorism — do the data of performance exhaust the domain of interest to the linguist, or is he also concerned with other facts, in particular those pertaining to the deeper systems that underlie behavior? c) introspectionism — should one make use of introspective data in the attempt to ascertain the properties of these underlying systems? It is the dualistic position against which Bloomfield irrelevantly inveighed. The behaviorist position is not an arguable matter. It is simply an expression of lack of interest in theory and explanation. This is clear, for example, in Twaddell's critique (1935) of Sapir's mentalistic phonology, which used informant responses and comments as evidence bearing on the psychological reality of some abstract system of phonological elements. For Twaddell, the enterprise has no point because all that interests him is the behavior itself, "which is already available for the student of language, though in less concentrated form." Characteristically, this lack of interest in linguistic theory expresses itself in the proposal to limit the term "theory" to "summary of data" (as in Twaddell's paper, or, to take a more recent example, in Dixon, 1963, although the discussion of "theories" in the latter is sufficiently vague as to allow other interpretations of what he may have in mind). Perhaps this loss of interest in theory, in the usual sense, was fostered by certain ideas (e.g., strict operationalism or strong verificationism) that were considered briefly in positivist philosophy of science, but rejected forthwith, in the early nineteen-thirties. In any event, question (b) poses no substantive issue. Question (c) arises only if one rejects the behaviorist limitations of (b). To maintain, on grounds of methodological purity, that introspective judgments of the informant (often, the linguist himself) should be disregarded is, for the present, to condemn the study of language to utter sterility. It is difficult to imagine what possible reason might be given for this. We return to this matter later. For further discussion, see Katz (1964c).

explicit — in other words, if it does not rely on the intelligence of the understanding reader but rather provides an explicit analysis of his contribution — we may (somewhat redundantly) call it a *generative grammar*.

A fully adequate grammar must assign to each of an infinite range of sentences a structural description indicating how this sentence is understood by the ideal speaker-hearer. This is the traditional problem of descriptive linguistics, and traditional grammars give a wealth of information concerning structural descriptions of sentences. However, valuable as they obviously are, traditional grammars are deficient in that they leave unexpressed many of the basic regularities of the language with which they are concerned. This fact is particularly clear on the level of syntax, where no traditional or structuralist grammar goes beyond classification of particular examples to the stage of formulation of generative rules on any significant scale. An analysis of the best existing grammars will quickly reveal that this is a defect of principle, not just a matter of empirical detail or logical preciseness. Nevertheless, it seems obvious that the attempt to explore this largely uncharted territory can most profitably begin with a study of the kind of structural information presented by traditional grammars and the kind of linguistic processes that have been exhibited, however informally, in these grammars.[2]

The limitations of traditional and structuralist grammars should be clearly appreciated. Although such grammars may contain full and explicit lists of exceptions and irregularities, they provide only examples and hints concerning the regular and productive syntactic processes. Traditional linguistic theory was not unaware of this fact. For example, James Beattie (1788) remarks that

> Languages, therefore, resemble men in this respect, that, though each has peculiarities, whereby it is distinguished from every other, yet all have certain qualities in common. The peculiarities of individual tongues are explained in their respective grammars and dictionaries. Those things, that all languages have in common, or that are necessary to every language, are treated of in a science, which some have called *Universal* or *Philosophical* grammar.

[2] This has been denied recently by several European linguists (e.g., Dixon, 1963; Uhlenbeck, 1963, 1964). They offer no reasons for their skepticism concerning traditional grammar, however. Whatever evidence is available today seems to me to show that by and large the traditional views are basically correct, so far as they go, and that the suggested innovations are totally unjustifiable. For example, consider Uhlenbeck's proposal that the constituent analysis of "the man saw the boy" is [*the man saw*] [*the boy*], a proposal which presumably also implies that in the sentences [*the man put*] [*it into the box*], [*the man aimed*] [*it at John*], [*the man persuaded*] [*Bill that it was unlikely*], etc., the constituents are as indicated. There are many considerations relevant to the determination of constituent structure, to my knowledge, they support the traditional analysis without exception against this proposal, for which the only argument offered is that it is the result of a "pure linguistic analysis." Cf. Uhlenbeck (1964), and the discussion there. As to Dixon's objections to traditional grammars, since he offers neither any alternative nor any argument (beyond the correct but irrelevant observation that they have been "long condemned by professional linguists"), there is nothing further to discuss, in this case.

Somewhat earlier, Du Marsais defines universal and particular grammar in the following way (1729; quoted in Sahlin, 1928, pp. 29–30):

Il y a dans la grammaire des observations qui conviènnent à toutes les langues; ces observations forment ce qu'on appelle la grammaire générale: telles sont les remarques que l'on a faites sur les sons articulés, sur les lettres qui sont les signes de ces sons; sur la nature des mots, et sur les différentes manières dont ils doivent être ou arrangés ou terminés pour faire un sens. Outre ces observations générale, il y en a qui ne sont propres qu'à une langue particulière; et c'est ce qui forme les grammaires particulières de chaque langue.

Within traditional linguistic theory, furthermore, it was clearly understood that one of the qualities that all languages have in common is their "creative" aspect. Thus an essential property of language is that it provides the means for expressing indefinitely many thoughts and for reacting appropriately in an indefinite range of new situations (for references, cf. Chomsky, 1964). The grammar of a particular language, then, is to be supplemented by a universal grammar that accommodates the creative aspect of language use and expresses the deep-seated regularities which, being universal, are omitted from the grammar itself. Therefore it is quite proper for a grammar to discuss only exceptions and irregularities in any detail. It is only when supplemented by a universal grammar that the grammar of a language provides a full account of the speaker-hearer's competence.

Modern linguistics, however, has not explicitly recognized the necessity for supplementing a "particular grammar" of a language by a universal grammar if it is to achieve descriptive adequacy. It has, in fact, characteristically rejected the study of universal grammar as misguided; and, as noted before, it has not attempted to deal with the creative aspect of language use. It thus suggests no way to overcome the fundamental descriptive inadequacy of structuralist grammars.

Another reason for the failure of traditional grammars, particular or universal, to attempt a precise statement of regular processes of sentence formation and sentence interpretation lay in the widely held belief that there is a "natural order of thoughts" that is mirrored by the order of words. Hence, the rules of sentence formation do not really belong to grammar but to some other subject in which the "order of thoughts" is studied. Thus in the *Grammaire générale et raisonnée* (Lancelot *et al.*, 1660) it is asserted that, aside from figurative speech, the sequence of words follows an "ordre naturel," which conforms "a l'expression naturelle de nos pensées." Consequently, few grammatical rules need be formulated beyond the rules of ellipsis, inversion, and so on, which determine the figurative use of language. The same view appears in many forms and variants. To mention just one additional example, in an interesting essay devoted largely to the question of how the simultaneous and sequential array of ideas is reflected in the order of words, Diderot concludes that French is unique among languages in the degree to which the order of words corresponds to the natural order of thoughts and ideas (Diderot, 1751). Thus "quel que soit l'ordre des termes dans une langue ancienne ou moderne, l'esprit de l'ecrivain a suivi l'ordre didactique de la syntaxe française" (p. 390); "Nous disons les choses en français, comme l'esprit est force de les considerer en quelque langue qu'on ecrive" (p. 371). With admirable consistency he goes on to conclude that "notre langue pédestre a sur les autres l'avantage de l'utile sur l'agreable" (p. 372); thus French is appropriate for the sciences, whereas Greek, Latin, Italian, and English "sont plus avantageuses pour les lettres." Moreover,

> le bons sens choisirait la langue française; mais . . . l'imagination et les passions donneront la préférence aux langues anciennes et à celles de nos voisins . . . il faut parler français dans la société et dans les écoles de philosophie; et grec, latin, anglais, dans les chaires et sur les theâtres; . . . notre langue sera celle de la vérité, si jamais elle revient sur la terre; et . . . la grecque, la latine et les autres seront les langues de la fable et du mensonge. Le français est fait pour instruire, éclairer et convaincre; le grec, le latin, l'italien, l'anglais, pour persuader, émouver et tromper: parlez grec, latin, italien au peuple; mais parlez français au sage. (pp. 371–372)

In any event, insofar as the order of words is determined by factors independent of language, it is not necessary to describe it in a particular or universal grammar, and we therefore have principled grounds for excluding an explicit formulation of syntactic processes from grammar. It is worth noting that this naïve view of language structure persists to modern times in various forms, for example, in Saussure's image of a sequence of expressions corresponding to an amorphous sequence of concepts or in the common characterization of language use as merely a matter of use of words and phrases (for example, Ryle, 1953).

But the fundamental reason for this inadequacy of traditional grammars is a more technical one. Although it was well understood that linguistic processes are in some sense "creative," the technical devices for expressing a system of recursive processes were simply not available until much more recently. In fact, a real understanding of how a language can (in Humboldt's words) "make infinite use of finite means" has developed only within the last thirty years, in the course of studies in the foundation of mathematics. Now that these insights are readily available it is possible to return to the problems that were raised, but not solved, in traditional linguistic theory, and to attempt an explicit formulation of the "creative" processes of language. There is, in short, no longer a technical barrier to the full-scale study of generative grammars.

Returning to the main theme, by a generative grammar I mean simply a system of rules that in some explicit and well-defined way assigns structural descriptions to sentences. Obviously, every speaker of a language has mastered and internalized a generative grammar that expresses his knowledge of his language. This is not to say that he is aware of the rules of the grammar or even that he can become aware of them, or that his statements about his intuitive knowledge of the language are necessarily accurate. Any interesting generative grammar will be dealing for the most part, with mental processes that are far beyond the level of actual or even potential consciousness; furthermore, it is quite apparent that a speaker's reports and viewpoints about his behavior and his competence may be in error. Thus a generative grammar attempts to specify what the speaker actually knows, not what he may report about his knowledge. Similarly, a theory of visual perception would attempt to account for what a person actually sees and the mechanisms that determine this rather than his statements about what he sees and why, though these statements may provide useful, in fact, compelling evidence for such a theory.

To avoid what has been a continuing misunderstanding, it is perhaps worth while to reiterate that a generative grammar is not a model for a speaker or a hearer. It attempts to characterize in the most neutral possible terms the knowledge of the language that provides the basis for actual use of language by a speaker-hearer. When we speak of a grammar as generating a sentence with a certain structural description, we mean simply that the grammar assigns this structural description to the sentence. When we say that a sentence has a certain derivation with respect to a particular generative grammar, we say nothing about how the speaker or hearer might proceed, in some practical or efficient way, to construct such a derivation. These questions belong to the theory of language use — the theory of performance. No doubt, a reasonable model of language use will incorporate, as a basic component, the generative grammar that expresses the speaker-hearer's knowledge of the language; but this generative grammar does not, in itself, prescribe the character or functioning of a perceptual model or a model of speech production. For various attempts to clarify this point, see Chomsky (1957), Gleason (1961), Miller and Chomsky (1963), and many other publications.

Confusion over this matter has been sufficiently persistent to suggest that a terminological change might be in order. Nevertheless, I think that the term "generative grammar" is completely appropriate, and have therefore continued to use it. The term "generate" is familiar in the sense intended here in logic, particularly in Post's theory of combinatorial systems. Furthermore, "generate" seems to be the most appropriate translation for Humboldt's term *erzeugen*, which he frequently uses, it seems, in essentially the sense here intended. Since this use of the term "generate" is well established both in logic and in the tradition of linguistic theory, I can see no reason for a revision of terminology.

THE ORGANIZATION OF A GENERATIVE GRAMMAR

Returning now to the question of competence and the generative grammars that purport to describe it, we stress again that knowledge of a language involves the implicit ability to understand indefinitely many sentences.[3] Hence, a generative grammar must be a system of rules that can iterate to generate an indefinitely large number of structures. This system of rules can be analyzed into the three major components of a generative grammar: the syntactic, phonological, and semantic components.[4]

The syntactic component specifies an infinite set of abstract formal objects, each of which incorporates all information relevant to a single interpretation of a particular sentence.[5] Since I shall be concerned here only with the syntactic component, I shall use the term "sentence" to refer to strings of formatives rather than to strings of phones. It will be recalled that a string of formatives specifies a string of phones uniquely (up to free variation) but not conversely.

The phonological component of a grammar determines the phonetic form of a sentence generated by the syntactic rules. That is, it relates a structure generated by the syntactic component to a phonetically represented signal. The semantic component determines the semantic interpretation of a sentence. That is, it relates a structure generated by the syntactic component to a certain semantic representation. Both the phonological and semantic components are therefore purely interpretive. Each utilizes information provided by the syntactic component concerning formatives, their inherent properties, and their interrelations in a given sentence. Consequently, the syntactic component of a grammar must specify, for each sentence, a *deep structure* that determines its semantic interpretation and a *surface structure* that determines its phonetic interpretation. The first of these is interpreted by the semantic component; the second, by the phonological component.[6]

It might be supposed that surface structure and deep structure will always be identical. In fact, one might briefly characterize the syntactic theories that have

---

[3]It is astonishing to find that even this truism has recently been challenged. See Dixon (1963). However, it seems that when Dixon denies that a language has infinitely many sentences, he is using the term "infinite" in some special and rather obscure sense. Thus on the same page (p. 83) on which he objects to the assertion "that there are an infinite number of sentences in a language" he states that "we are clearly unable to say that there is any definite number, N, such that no sentence contains more than N clauses" (that is, he states that the language is infinite). Either this is a blatant self-contradiction, or else he has some new sense of the word "infinite" in mind. For further discussion of his remarks in this connection, see Chomsky (1968).

[4]Aside from terminology, I follow here the exposition in Katz and Postal (1964). In particular, I shall assume throughout that the semantic component is essentially as they describe it and that the phonological component is essentially as described in Chomsky, Halle, and Lukoff (1956); Halle (1959a, 1959b, 1962a); Chomsky (1962b); Chomsky and Miller (1963); Halle and Chomsky (1960; 1968).

[5]I assume throughout that the syntactic component contains a lexicon, and that each lexical item is specified in the lexicon in terms of its intrinsic semantic features, whatever these may be.

[6]In place of the terms "deep structure" and "surface structure," one might use the corresponding Humboldtian notions "inner form" of a sentence and "outer form" of a sentence. However, though it seems to me that "deep structure" and "surface structure," in the sense in which these terms will be used here, do correspond quite closely to Humboldtian "inner form" and "outer form," respectively (as used of a sentence), I have adopted the more neutral terminology to avoid the question, here, of textual interpretation. The terms "depth grammar" and "surface grammar" are familiar in modern philosophy in something roughly like the sense here intended (cf. Wittgenstein's

arisen in modern structural (taxonomic) linguistics as based on the assumption that deep and surface structures are actually the same (cf. Postal, 1964a, Chomsky, 1964). The central idea of transformational grammar is that they are, in general, distinct and that the surface structure is determined by repeated application of certain formal operations called "grammatical transformations" to objects of a more elementary sort. If this is true (as I assume, henceforth), then the

---

distinction of "*Tiefengrammatik*" and "*Oberflächengrammatik*", 1953, p. 168); Hockett uses similar terminology in his discussion of the inadequacy of taxonomic linguistics (Hockett, 1958, Chapter 29). Postal has used the terms "underlying structure" and "superficial structure" (Postal, 1964b) for the same notions.

The distinction between deep and surface structure, in the sense in which these terms are used here, is drawn quite clearly in the Port-Royal *Grammar* (Lancelot *et. al*., 1660). See Chomsky (1964, pp. 15–16; 1968) for some discussion and references. In philosophical discussion, it is often introduced in an attempt to show how certain philosophical positions arise from false grammatical analogies, the surface structure of certain expressions being mistakenly considered to be semantically interpretable by means appropriate only to other, superficially similar sentences. Thus Thomas Reid (1785) holds a common source of philosophical error to lie in the fact that

> in all languages, there are phrases which have a distinct meaning; while at the same time, there may be something in the structure of them that disagrees with the analogy of grammar or with the principles of philosophy. . . . Thus, we speak of feeling pain as if pain was something distinct from the feeling of it. We speak of pain coming and going, and removing from one place to another. Such phrases are meant by those who use them in a sense that is neither obscure nor false. But the philosopher puts them into his alembic, reduces them to their first principles, draws out of them a sense that was never meant, and so imagines that he has discovered an error of the vulgar [pp. 167–168].

More generally, he criticizes the theory of ideas as based on a deviation from the "popular meaning," in which "to have an idea of anything signifies nothing more than to think of it" (p. 105). But philosophers take an idea to be "the object that the mind contemplates" (p. 105); to have an idea, then, is to possess in the mind such an image, picture, or representation as the immediate object of thought. It follows that there are two objects of thought: the idea, which is in the mind, and the thing represented by it. From this conclusion follow the absurdities, as Reid regards them, of the traditional theory of ideas. One of the sources of these absurdities is the failure of the philosopher to attend "to the distinction between the operations of the mind and the objects of these operations . . . although this distinction be familiar to the vulgar, and found in the structure of all languages" (p. 110). Notice that these two senses of "having an idea" are distinguished by Descartes in the Preface to the *Meditations* (1641, p. 138). Reid's linguistic observation is made considerably earlier by DuMarsias, in a work published posthumously in 1769, in the following passage (pp. 179–180):

> Ainsi, comme nous avons dit *j'ai un livre*, *j'ai un diamant*, *j'ai une montre*, nous disons par imitation, *j'ai la fièvre*, *j'ai envie*, *j'ai peur*, *j'ai un doute*, *j'ai pitié*, *j'ai une idée*, etc. Mais *livre*, *diamant*, *montre* sont autant de noms d'objects réels qui existent independamment de notre manière de penser; au lieu que *santé*, *fièvre*, *peur*, *doute*, *envie*, ne sont que des termes métaphysiques qui ne designent que des manières d'êtres considerés par des points de vue particuliers de l'esprit.
>
> Dans cet example, *j'ai une montre*, *j'ai* est une expression qui doit être prise dans le sens propre: mais dans *j'ai une idée*, *j'ai* n'est dit que par une imitation. C'est une expression empruntée. *J'ai une idée*, c'est-à-dire, *je pense*, *je conçois de telle ou telle manière*. *J'ai envie*, c'est-à-dire, *je desire*; *j'ai la volonté*, c'est-à-dire, *je veux*, etc.
>
> Ainsi, *idée*, *concept*, *imagination*, ne marquent point d'objets réels, et encore moins des êtres sensibles que l'on puisse unir l'un avec l'autre.

In more recent years, it has been widely held that the aims of philosophy should, in fact, be strictly limited to "the detection of the sources in linguistic idioms of recurrent misconstructions and absurd theories" (Ryle, 1931).

syntactic component must generate deep and surface structures, for each sentence, and must interrelate them. This idea has been clarified substantially in recent work, in ways that will be described later. In Chapter 3,* I shall present a specific and, in part, new proposal as to precisely how it should be formulated. For the moment, it is sufficient to observe that although the Immediate Constituent analysis (labeled bracketing) of an actual string of formatives may be adequate as an account of surface structure, it is certainly not adequate as an account of deep structure. My concern in this book is primarily with deep structure and, in particular, with the elementary objects of which deep structure is constituted.

To clarify exposition, I shall use the following terminology with occasional revisions as the discussion proceeds.

The *base* of the syntactic component is a system of rules that generate a highly restricted (perhaps finite) set of *basic strings*, each with an associated structural description called a *base Phrase-marker*. These base Phrase-markers are the elementary units of which deep structures are constituted. I shall assume that no ambiguity is introduced by rules of the base. This assumption seems to me correct, but has no important consequences for what follows here, though it simplifies exposition. Underlying each sentence of the language there is a sequence of base Phrase-markers, each generated by the base of the syntactic component. I shall refer to this sequence as the *basis* of the sentence that it underlies.

In addition to its base, the syntactic component of a generative grammar contains a *transformational* subcomponent. This is concerned with generating a sentence, with its surface structure, from its basis. Some familiarity with the operation and effects of transformational rules is henceforth presupposed.

Since the base generates only a restricted set of base Phrase-markers, most sentences will have a sequence of such objects as an underlying basis. Among the sentences with a single base Phrase-marker as basis, we can delimit a proper subset called "kernel sentences." These are sentences of a particularly simple sort that involve a minimum of transformational apparatus in their generation. The notion "kernel sentence" has, I think, an important intuitive significance, but since kernel sentences play no distinctive role in generation or interpretation of sentences, I shall say nothing more about them here. One must be careful not to confuse kernel sentences with the basic strings that underlie them. The basic strings and base Phrase-markers do, it seems, play a distinctive and crucial role in language use.

Since transformations will not be considered here in detail, no careful distinction will be made, in the case of a sentence with a single element in its basis, between the basic string underlying this sentence and the sentence itself. In other words, at many points in the exposition, I shall make the tacit simplifying (and contrary-to-fact) assumption that the underlying basic string is the sentence, in this case, and that the base Phrase-marker is the surface structure as well as the

[*Not included in this selection – ed.]

deep structure. I shall try to select examples in such a way as to minimize possible confusion, but the simplifying assumption should be borne in mind throughout.

FORMAL AND SUBSTANTIVE UNIVERSALS

A theory of linguistic structure that aims for explanatory adequacy incorporates an account of linguistic universals, and it attributes tacit knowledge of these universals to the child. It proposes, then, that the child approaches the data with the presumption that they are drawn from a language of a certain antecedently well-defined type, his problem being to determine which of the (humanly) possible languages is that of the community in which he is placed. Language learning would be impossible unless this were the case. The important question is: What are the initial assumptions concerning the nature of language that the child brings to language learning, and how detailed and specific is the innate schema (the general definition of "grammar") that gradually becomes more explicit and differentiated as the child learns the language? For the present we cannot come at all close to making a hypothesis about innate schemata that is rich, detailed, and specific enough to account for the fact of language acquisition. Consequently, the main task of linguistic theory must be to develop an account of linguistic universals that, on the one hand, will not be falsified by the actual diversity of languages and, on the other, will be sufficiently rich and explicit to account for the rapidity and uniformity of language learning, and the remarkable complexity and range of the generative grammars that are the product of language learning.

The study of linguistic universals is the study of the properties of any generative grammar for a natural language. Particular assumptions about linguistic universals may pertain to either the syntactic, semantic, or phonological component, or to interrelations among the three components.

It is useful to classify linguistic universals as *formal* or *substantive*. A theory of substantive universals claims that items of a particular kind in any language must be drawn from a fixed class of items. For example, Jakobson's theory of distinctive features can be interpreted as making an assertion about substantive universals with respect to the phonological component of a generative grammar. It asserts that each output of this component consists of elements that are characterized in terms of some small number of fixed, universal, phonetic features (perhaps on the order of fifteen or twenty), each of which has a substantive acoustic-articulatory characterization independent of any particular language. Traditional universal grammar was also a theory of substantive universals, in this sense. It not only put forth interesting views as to the nature of universal phonetics, but also advanced the position that certain fixed syntactic categories (Noun, Verb, etc.) can be found in the syntactic representations of the sentences of any language, and that these provide the general underlying syntactic structure of each language. A theory of substantive semantic universals might hold for example, that certain designative functions must be carried out in a specified way in each language. Thus it might assert that each language will contain terms that designate persons or lexical items referring to certain specific kinds of objects, feelings, behavior, and so on.

It is also possible, however, to search for universal properties of a more abstract sort. Consider a claim that the grammar of every language meets certain specified formal conditions. The truth of this hypothesis would not in itself imply that any particular rule must appear in all or even in any two grammars. The property of having a grammar meeting a certain abstract condition might be called a *formal* linguistic universal, if shown to be a general property of natural languages. Recent attempts to specify the abstract conditions that a generative grammar must meet have produced a variety of proposals concerning formal universals, in this sense. For example, consider the proposal that the syntactic component of a grammar must contain transformational rules (these being operations of a highly special kind) mapping semantically interpreted deep structures into phonetically interpreted surface structures, or the proposal that the phonological component of a grammar consists of a sequence of rules, a subset of which may apply cyclically to successively more dominant constituents of the surface structure (a transformational cycle, in the sense of much recent work on phonology). Such proposals make claims of a quite different sort from the claim that certain substantive phonetic elements are available for phonetic representation in all languages, or that certain specific categories must be central to the syntax of all languages, or that certain semantic features or categories provide a universal framework for semantic description. Substantive universals such as these concern the vocabulary for the description of language; formal universals involve rather the character of the rules that appear in grammars and the ways in which they can be interconnected.

On the semantic level, too, it is possible to search for what might be called formal universals, in essentially the sense just described. Consider, for example, the assumption that proper names, in any language, must designate objects meeting a condition of spatiotemporal contiguity,[7] and that the same is true of other terms designating objects; or the condition that the color words of any language

---

[7]For example, Russell (1940, p. 33: "from a logical point of view, a proper name may be assigned to any continuous portion of space-time"), if we interpret his notion of "logically proper name" as embodying an empirical hypothesis. Interpreted in this way, Russell is stating what is, no doubt, a psychological truth. Interpreted otherwise, he is giving an unmotivated definition of "proper name." There is no logical necessity for names or other "object words" to meet any condition of spatiotemporal contiguity or to have other Gestalt qualities, and it is a nontrivial fact that they apparently do, insofar as the designated objects are of the type that can actually be perceived (for example, it is not true of "United States" — similarly, it need not be true of somewhat more abstract and functionally defined notions such as "barrier"). Thus there are no logical grounds for the apparent nonexistence in natural languages of words such as "LIMB," similar to "limb" except that it designates the single object consisting of a dog's four legs, so that "its LIMB is brown" (like "its head is brown") would mean that the object consisting of the four legs is brown. Similarly, there is no a priori reason why a natural language could not contain a word "HERD", like the collective "herd" except that it denotes a single scattered object with cows as parts, so that "a cow lost a leg" implies "the HERD lost a leg," etc.

must subdivide the color spectrum into continuous segments; or the condition that artifacts are defined in terms of certain human goals, needs, and functions instead of solely in terms of physical qualities.[8] Formal constraints of this sort on a system of concepts may severely limit the choice (by the child, or the linguist) of a descriptive grammar, given primary linguistic data.

The existence of deep-seated formal universals, in the sense suggested by such examples as these, implies that all languages are cut to the same pattern, but does not imply that there is any point by point correspondence between particular languages. It does not, for example, imply that there must be some reasonable procedure for translating between languages.[9]

In general, there is no doubt that a theory of language, regarded as a hypothesis about the innate "language-forming capacity" of humans, should concern itself with both substantive and formal universals. But whereas substantive universals have been the traditional concern of general linguistic theory, investigations of the abstract conditions that must be satisfied by any generative grammar have been undertaken only quite recently. They seem to offer extremely rich and varied possibilities for study in all aspects of grammar.

THE SCOPE OF THE BASE

We now return to the problem of refining and elaborating the sketch of how a generative grammar is organized. Putting off to the next chapter any question as to the adequacy of earlier accounts of grammatical transformations, we shall consider here only the formal properties of the base of the syntactic component. We are therefore concerned primarily with extremely simple sentences.

The investigation of generative grammar can profitably begin with a careful analysis of the kind of information presented in traditional grammars. Adopting this as a heuristic procedure, let us consider what a traditional grammar has to say about a simple English sentence such as the following:

1. Sincerity may frighten the boy.

Concerning this sentence, a traditional grammar might provide information of the following sort:
2. i. the string (1) is a Sentence (S): *frighten the boy* is a Verb Phrase (VP) consisting of the Verb (V) *frighten* and the Noun Phrase (NP) *the boy*;

---

[8]Thus for Aristotle (*De Anima*, 403b), the "essence of a house is assigned in such a formula as 'a shelter against destruction by wind, rain, and heat,'" though "the physicist would describe it as 'stones, bricks, and timbers.'" For interesting comments on such definitions, see Foot (1961), Katz (1964d).

[9]By a "reasonable procedure" I mean one that does not involve extralinguistic information — that is, one that does not incorporate an "encyclopedia." See Bar-Hillel (1960) for discussion. The possibility of a reasonable procedure for translation between arbitrary languages depends on the sufficiency of substantive universals. In fact, although there is much reason to believe that languages are to a significant extent cast in the same mold, there is little reason to suppose that reasonable procedures of translation are in general possible.

sincerity is also an NP; the NP *the boy* consists of the Determiner (Det) *the*, followed by a Noun (N); the NP *sincerity* consists of just an N; *the* is, furthermore, an Article (Art); *may* is a Verbal Auxiliary (Aux) and, furthermore, a Modal (M).

ii. the NP *sincerity* functions as the Subject of the sentence (1), whereas the VP *frighten the boy* functions as the Predicate of this sentence; the NP *the boy* functions as the Object of the VP, and the V *frighten* as its Main Verb; the grammatical relation Subject-Verb holds of the pair (*sincerity*, *frighten*) and the grammatical relation Verb-Object holds of the pair (*frighten, the boy*).[10]

iii. the N *boy* is a Count Noun (as distinct from the Mass Noun *butter* and the Abstract Noun *sincerity*) and a Common Noun (as distinct from the Proper Noun *John* and the Pronoun *it*); it is, furthermore, an Animate Noun (as distinct from *book*) and a Human Noun (as distinct from *bee*);*frighten* is a Transitive Verb (as distinct from *occur*), and one that does not freely permit Object deletion (as distinct from *read, eat*); it takes Progressive Aspect freely (as distinct from *know, own*); it allows Abstract Subjects (as distinct from *eat, admire*) and Human Objects (as distinct from *read, wear*).

It seems to me that the information presented in (2) is, without question, substantially correct and is essential to any account of how the language is used or acquired. The main topic I should like to consider is how information of this sort can be formally presented in a structural description, and how such structural descriptions can be generated by a system of explicit rules. The next two subsections (2.1, 2.2) discuss these questions in connection with (2i), (2ii), and (2iii), respectively.

ASPECTS OF DEEP STRUCTURE

2.1. Categorization

The remarks given in (2i) concern the subdivision of the string (1) into continuous substrings, each of which is assigned to a certain category. Information of this sort can be represented by a labeled bracketing of (1), or, equivalently, by a tree-diagram such as (3). The interpretation of such a diagram is transparent and has been discussed frequently elsewhere. If one assumes now that (1) is a basic string, the structure represented as (3) can be taken as a first approximation to its (base) Phrase-marker.

A grammar that generates simple Phrase-markers sucn as (3) may be based on a vocabulary of symbols that includes both *formatives* (*the, boy*, etc.) and

[10]In detail, there is some room for discussion about both terminology and substance throughout (2), and, particularly in the case of (2ii), alternative conventions and decisions have been applied. However, I think that the central facts are clear enough, and there has, in fact, been overwhelming accord about most of them. For present purposes, I shall raise no further question (except of detail) about the adequacy of these observations, taking them simply as facts to be accounted for by a grammatical theory.

3.

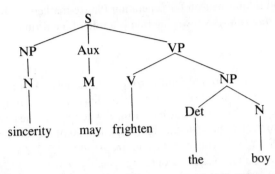

category symbols (S, NP, V, etc.). The formatives, furthermore, can be subdivided into *lexical* items (*sincerity, boy*) and *grammatical* items (Perfect, Possessive, etc.; except possibly for *the*, none of these are represented in the simplified example given.)

A question arises at once as to the choice of symbols in Phrase-markers. That is, we must ask whether the formatives and category symbols used in Phrase-markers have some language-independent characterization, or whether they are just convenient mnemonic tags, specific to a particular grammar.

In the case of the lexical formatives, the theory of phonetic distinctive features taken together with the full set of conditions on phonological representation does, in fact, give a language-independent significance to the choice of symbols, though it is by no means a trivial problem to establish this fact (or to select the proper universal set of substantive phonetic features). I shall assume, henceforth, that an appropriate phonological theory of this sort is established and that, consequently, the lexical formatives are selected in a well-defined way from a fixed universal set.

The question of substantive representation in the case of the grammatical formatives and the category symbols is, in effect the traditional question of universal grammar. I shall assume that these elements too are selected from a fixed, universal vocabulary, although this assumption will actually have no significant effect on any of the descriptive material to be presented. There is no reason to doubt the importance or reasonableness of the study of this question. It is generally held to involve extrasyntactic considerations of a sort that are at present only dimly perceived. This may very well be true. However, I shall later suggest several general definitions that appear to be correct for English and for other cases with which I am acquainted.[11]

---

[11]A theory of language must state the principles interrelating its theoretical terms (e.g., "phoneme," "morpheme," "transformation," "noun Phrase," "Subject") and ultimately must relate this system of concepts to potential empirical phenomena (to primary linguistic data). For reasons discussed in Chomsky (1957) and elsewhere, it seems to me that all significant structural notions will have to be characterized in terms of the previously defined notion "generative grammar" (whereas structural linguistics has assumed, in general, that the notion "grammar" must be developed and explained in terms of previously defined notions such as "phoneme," and "morpheme"). That is, I am assuming that the basic notion to be defined as "G is a most highly valued

The natural mechanism for generating Phrase-markers such as (3) is a system of *rewriting rules*. A rewriting rule is a rule of the form

4. $A \rightarrow Z/X \underline{\hspace{1cm}} Y$

where X and Y are (possibly null) strings of symbols. A is a single category symbol, and Z is a nonnull string of symbols. This rule is interpreted as asserting that the category A is realized as the string Z when it is in the environment consisting of X to the left and Y to the right. Application of the rewriting rule (4) to a string . . .XAY. . . converts this to the string . . .XZY. . . . Given a grammar, we say that a sequence of strings is a *W-derivation of V* if W is the first and V the last string in the sequence, and each string of the sequence is derived from the one preceding it by application of one of the rewriting rules (with an ordering condition to be added later). Where V is a string of formatives, we say that a W-derivation of V is *terminated*. We call V a *terminal string* if there is an #S# derivation of #V#, where S is the designated *initial symbol* of the grammar (representing the category "Sentence"), and # is the *boundary symbol* (regarded as a grammatical formative). Thus we construct a derivation of a *terminal string* by successively applying the rewriting rules of the grammar, beginning with the string #S#, until the final string of the derivation consists only of formatives and therefore no further rewriting is possible. If several other conditions are imposed on the system of rewriting rules,[12] it is easy to provide a simple method for as-

---

grammar of the language of which primary linguistic data D constitutes a sample" where D is represented in terms of primitive notions of the theory; the phonemes, morphemes, transformations, etc., of the language are, then, the elements that play a specified role in the derivations and representations determined by G. If so, partial generative grammars will provide the only empirical data critical for evaluating a theory of the form of language. For the present, then, such evidence must be drawn from grammatical descriptions of relatively few languages. This is not particularly disturbing. What is important is that such assumptions be supported by available evidence and formulated with enough clarity so that new or improved generative grammars will have bearing on their correctness, as the depth and range of linguistic study increases. We must, in short, accept Humboldt's conclusion, expressed in a letter of 1822 to Schlegel (Leitzmann, 1908, p. 84): "dass jede grammatische Discussion nur dann wahrhaften wissenschaftlichen Gewinn bringt, wenn sie so durchgeführt wird, als läge in ihr allein der ganze Zweck, und wenn man jede, noch so rohe Sprache selbst, gerade mit derselben Sorgfalt behandelt als Griechisch und Lateinisch."

Study of a wide range of languages is only one of the ways to evaluate the hypothesis that some formal condition is a linguistic universal. Paradoxical as this may seem at first glance, considerations internal to a single language may provide significant support for the conclusion that some formal property should be attributed not to the theory of the particular language in question (its grammar) but rather to the general linguistic theory on which the particular grammar is based. Study of descriptive or explanatory adequacy may lead to such a conclusion; furthermore, the difficulty or impossibility of formulating certain conditions within the framework of an otherwise well-supported theory of grammar provides some evidence that these are, in reality, general conditions on the applicability of grammatical rules rather than aspects of the particular language, to be expressed within the system of grammatical rules itself. Several cases of this sort will be mentioned later.

In general, it should be expected that only descriptions concerned with deep structure will have serious import for proposals concerning linguistic universals. Since descriptions of this sort are few, any such proposals are hazardous, but are clearly no less interesting or important for being hazardous.

[12]A weak though sufficient condition is given in Chomsky (1955, Chapter 6). A stronger but rather well-motivated condition is proposed by Postal (1964a). Some aspects of this question are discussed in Chomsky and Miller (1963, sec. 4); Chomsky (1963, sec. 3).

signing a unique and appropriate Phrase-marker to a terminal string, given its derivation. Thus a system of rewriting rules, appropriately constrained, can serve as a part of a generative grammar.

An *unordered* set of rewriting rules, applied in the manner described loosely here (and precisely elsewhere), is called a *constituent structure grammar* (or *phrase structure grammar*). The grammar is, furthermore, called *context-free* (or *simple*) if in each rule of the form (4), X and Y are null, so that the rules apply independently of context. As noted earlier, the formal properties of constituent structure grammars have been studied fairly intensively during the past few years; and it has also been shown that almost all of the non-transformational syntactic theories that have been developed within modern linguistics, pure or applied, fall within this framework. In fact, such a system is apparently what is implicit in modern taxonomic ("structuralist") grammars, if these are reformulated as explicit systems for presenting grammatical information. The inadequacy of such systems as grammars for natural languages seems to me to have been established beyond any reasonable doubt,[13] and I shall not discuss the issue here.

[13]For some discussion, see the references cited on p. 16, and many others. These demonstrations of the inadequacies of phrase structure grammar have not been challenged, although some confusions have been introduced by terminological equivocations. The most extreme example of this can be found in Harman (1963), where many of the standard arguments against phrase structure grammar are repeated, with approval, in an article with the subtitle "a defense of phrase structure." This curious situation results simply from the author's redefinition of the term "phrase structure" to refer to a system far richer than that to which the term "phrase structure grammar" has been universally applied in the rather ample literature on this subject (in particular, to a system in which in place of symbols, in the sense of phrase structure grammar, we have pairs (a, ∅), where a is a category symbol and ∅ is a set of indices used to code transformations, contextual restrictions, etc.). That is, Harman in effect restates the arguments against phrase structure grammar as arguments against limiting the term "phrase structure grammar" to the particular systems that have previously been defined as "phrase structure grammar." This terminological proposal does not touch on the substantive issue as to the adequacy of the taxonomic theory of grammar for which phrase structure grammar (in the usual sense) is a model. The essential adequacy of phrase structure grammar as a model for taxonomic grammatical theory (with the possible but irrelevant exception of problems involving discontinuous constituents — see Chomsky, 1957, Postal, 1964a) is demonstrated quite convincingly by Postal, and is not challenged by Harman, or anyone else, to my knowledge. The only issue that Harman raises, in this connection, is whether the term "phrase structure grammar" should be restricted to taxonomic models or whether the term should be used in some far richer sense as well, and this terminological question is of no conceivable importance. The terminological equivocation has only the effect of suggesting to the casual reader, quite erroneously, that there is some issue about the linguistic adequacy of the theory of phrase structure grammar (in the usual sense).

A further source of possible confusion, in connection with this paper, is that there is a way of interpreting the grammar presented there as a phrase structure grammar, namely by regarding each complex element (a, ∅) as a single, unanalyzable category symbol. Under this interpretation, what we have here is a new proposal as to the proper evaluation procedure for a phrase structure grammar, a proposal which is immediately refuted by the fact that under this interpretation, the structural description provided by the Phrase-marker of the now highest-valued grammar is invariably incorrect. For example, in *John saw Bill, did Tom see you?*, the three elements *John, Bill, Tom* would belong to three distinct and entirely unrelated categories, and would have no categorial assignment in common. Thus we have the following alternatives: we may interpret the paper as proposing a new evaluation measure for phrase structure grammars, in which case it is immediately refuted on grounds of descriptive inadequacy; or we may interpret it as proposing that the term "phrase structure grammar" be used in some entirely new sense, in which case it has no bearing on the issue of the adequacy of phrase structure grammar. For some further discussion see Chomsky (in press), where this and other criticisms of transformational grammar, some real, some only apparent, are taken up.

It seems clear that certain kinds of grammatical information are presented in the most natural way by a system of rewriting rules, and we may therefore conclude that rewriting rules constitute part of the base of the syntactic component. Furthermore, we shall assume that these rules are arranged in a linear sequence, and shall define a *sequential derivation* as a derivation formed by a series of rule applications that preserves this ordering. Thus, suppose that the grammar consists of the sequence of rules $R_1, \ldots, R_n$ and that the sequence $\#S\#, \#X_1\#, \ldots, \#X_m\#$ is a derivation of the terminal string X_m. For this to be a sequential derivation, it must be the case that if rule R_i was used to form line $\#X_j\#$ from the line that precedes it, then no rule R_k (for $k > i$) can have been used to form a line $\#X_l\#$ (for $1 < j$) from $\#X_{l-1}\#$. We stipulate now that only sequential derivations are generated by the sequence of rules constituting this part of the base.[14]

To provide a Phrase-marker such as (3), the base component might contain the following sequence of rewriting rules:

5. I. $S \rightarrow NP$ ⌒ Aux ⌒ VP
        $VP \rightarrow V$ ⌒ NP
        $NP \rightarrow Det$ ⌒ N
        $NP \rightarrow N$
        $Det \rightarrow the$
        $Aux \rightarrow M$
    II. $M \rightarrow may$
        $N \rightarrow sincerity$
        $N \rightarrow boy$
        $V \rightarrow frighten$

Notice that the rules (5), although they do suffice to generate (3), will also generate such deviant strings as *boy may frighten the sincerity*.

There is a natural distinction in (5) between rules that introduce lexical formatives (class II) and the others. In fact, we shall see in 2.3* that it is necessary to distinguish these sets and to assign the lexical rules to a distinct subpart of the base of the syntactic component.

2.2. Functional notions

Turning now to (2ii), we can immediately see that the notions in question have an entirely different status. The notion "Subject," as distinct from the notion

[*Not included in this selection—ed.]

[14]This assumption is made explicitly in Chomsky (1955), in the discussion of the base of a transformational grammar (Chapter 7), and, to my knowledge, in all subsequent empirical studies of transformational grammar. An analogous assumption with respect to transformational rules is made in Matthews (1964, Appendix A, sec. 2). Formal properties of *sequential grammars* have been studied by Ginsburg and Rice (1962) and Shamir (1961), these being context-free grammars where the sequential property is, furthermore, intrinsic, rather than extrinsic, as presupposed here (for the context-sensitive case, at least).

"NP," designates a *grammatical function* rather than a *grammatical category*. It is, in other words, an inherently relational notion. We say, in traditional terms, that in (1) *sincerity* is an NP (not that it is the NP of the sentence) and that it is (functions as) the *Subject-of* the sentence (not that it is a Subject). Functional notions like "Subject," "Predicate" are to be sharply distinguished from categorial notions such as "Noun Phrase," "Verb," a distinction that is not to be obscured by the occasional use of the same term for notions of both kinds. Thus it would merely confuse the issue to attempt to represent the information presented in (2ii) formally by extending the Phrase-marker (3) to (6), adding the necessary rewriting rules to (5 I). This approach is mistaken in two ways. For one thing, it confuses categorial and functional notions by assigning categorial status to both, and thus fails to express the relational character of the functional notions. For another, it fails to observe that both (6) and the grammar on which it is based are redundant,

6.

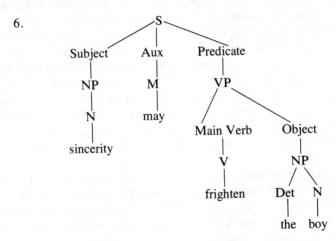

since the notions Subject, Predicate, Main-Verb, and Object, being relational, are already represented in the Phrase-marker (3), and no new rewriting rules are required to introduce them. It is necessary only to make explicit the relational character of these notions by defining "Subject-of," for English, as the relation holding between the NP of a sentence of the form NP⌒Aux⌒VP and the whole sentence,[15] "Object-of" as the relation between the NP of a VP of the form V⌒NP and the whole VP, etc. More generally, we can regard any rewriting rule as defining a set of grammatical functions, in this way, only some of which (namely, those that involve the "higher-level," more abstract grammatical categories) have been provided, traditionally, with explicit names.

[15] As noted earlier, there are rather different conventions, and some substantive disagreements about the usage of these terms. Thus if we were to change the rules of (5), and, correspondingly, the Phrase-marker (3), to provide a binary analysis of the major category S into *sincerity* (NP) and *may frighten the boy* (VP), then the latter would be the Predicate-of the sentence in the sense defined in (11).

The fundamental error of regarding functional notions as categorial is somewhat masked in such examples as (6), in which there is only a single Subject, a single Object, and a single Main-Verb. In this case, the relational information can be supplied, intuitively, by the reader. But consider such sentences as (7), in which many grammatical functions are realized, several by the same phrase:

7. a. John was persuaded by Bill to leave.
   b. John was persuaded by Bill to be examined.
   c. What disturbed John was being regarded as incompetent.

In (7a), *John* is simultaneously Object-of *persuade* (*to leave*) and Subject-of *leave*; in (7b), *John* is simultaneously Object-of *persuade* (*to be examined*) and Object-of *examine*; in (7c), *John* is simultaneously Object-of *disturb*, Object-of *regard* (*as incompetent*), and Subject-of the predication *as incompetent*. In both (7a) and (7b), *Bill* is the ("logical") Subject-of the Sentence, rather than *John*, which is the so-called "grammatical" Subject-of the Sentence, that is, the Subject with respect to the surface structure. In such cases as these, the impossibility of a categorial interpretation of functional notions becomes at once apparent; correspondingly, the deep structure in which the significant grammatical functions are represented will be very different from the surface structure. Examples of this sort, of course, provide the primary motivation and empirical justification for the theory of transformational grammar. That is, each sentence of (7) will have a basis consisting of a sequence of base Phrase-markers, each of which represents some of the semantically relevant information concerning grammatical function.

Returning now to the main question, let us consider the problem of presenting information about grammatical function in an explicit and adequate way, restricting ourselves now to base Phrase-markers. To develop a uniform approach to this question, we may proceed as follows. Suppose that we have a sequence of rewriting rules, such as (5), including in particular the rule

8. A → X

Associated with this rule is each grammatical function

9. [B, A]

where B is a category and X = YBZ, for some Y, Z (possibly null).[16] Given a Phrase-marker of the terminal string W, we say that the substring U of W bears the grammatical relation [B, A] to the substring V of W if V is dominated by a node labeled A which directly dominates YBZ, and U is dominated by this oc-

---

[16]Let us assume, furthermore, that Y, Z are unique, in this case — in other words, that there is only one occurrence of B in X. The definition can be generalized to accommodate the case where this condition is violated, but it seems to me reasonable to impose this condition of uniqueness on the system of base rules.

currence of B.[17] Thus the Phrase-marker in question contains the subconfiguration (10).

10.

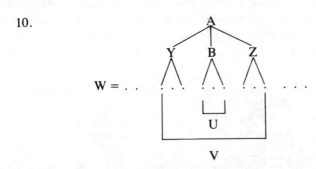

$$W = \ldots$$

In particular, given the Phrase-marker (3) generated by the rules (5), we should have the result that *sincerity* bears the relation [NP, S] to *sincerity may frighten the boy*, *frighten the boy* bears the relation [VP, S] to *sincerity may frighten the boy*, *the boy* bears the relation [NP, VP] to *frighten the boy*, and *frighten* bears the relation [V, VP] to *frighten the boy*.

Suppose further that we propose the following general definitions:

(11)   i.   Subject-of: [NP, S]
          ii.   Predicate-of: [VP, S]
         iii.   Direct-Object-of: [NP, VP]
         iv.   Main-Verb-of: [V, VP]

In this case, we can now say that with respect to the Phrase-marker (3) generated by the rules (5), *sincerity* is the Subject-of the sentence *sincerity may frighten the boy* and *frighten the boy* is its Predicate; and *the boy* is the Direct-Object-of the Verb Phrase *frighten the boy* and *frighten* is its Main Verb. With these definitions, the information presented in the redundant representation (6) is derivable directly from (3), that is, from the grammar (5) itself. These definitions must be thought of as belonging to general linguistic theory; in other words, they form part of the general procedure for assigning a full structural description to a sentence, given a grammar.

In such examples as (7), the grammatical functions will also be given directly by the system of rewriting rules that generate the base Phrase-markers that underlie these sentences, though these grammatical functions are not represented in the configurations of the surface structures in these cases. For example (details

---

[17]Notice that accurate definitions require a precise specification of the notions "occurrence," "dominate," etc. This raises no difficulty of principle, and throughout the informal discussion here I shall simply avoid these questions. Precise definitions for most of the notions that will be used here, taking occurrences into account, may be found in Chomsky (1955).

aside), the basis for (7a) will contain base Phrase-markers for the strings *Bill persuaded John Sentence, John left*, and these base Phrase-markers present the semantically relevant functional information exactly as in the case of (3).

Notice that the same grammatical function may be defined by several different rewriting rules of the base. Thus suppose that a grammar were to contain the rewriting rules

12.
     i.   S → Adverbial NP   (Naturally, John will leave)
            Aux VP
     ii.   S → NP Aux VP   (John will leave)
     iii.   VP → V NP   (examine Bill)
     iv.   VP → V   (leave)
     v.   VP → V NP Sentence   (persuade Bill that John
                                         left)
     vi.   VP → Copula Predicate   (be President)
     vii.   Predicate → N   (President)

then Subject-of is defined by both (i) and (ii), so that *John* is Subject-of-the sentences accompanying both (i) and (ii); Object-of is defined by both (iii) and (v), so that *Bill* is the Object-of the Verb Phrases given as examples to both (iii) and (v); Main-Verb-of is defined by (iii), (iv), and (v), so that *examine, leave, persuade* are the Main-Verbs of the accompanying examples. But notice that "president" is not the Object-of *John is President*, if the rules are as in (12).

Notice that the general significance of the definitions (11) depends on the assumption that the symbols S, NP, VP, N, and V have been characterized as grammatical universals. We shall return to this question later. Quite apart from this, it is likely that these definitions are too restricted to serve as general explications for the traditionally designated grammatical functions in that they assume too narrow a substantive specification of the form of grammar. They can be generalized in various ways, but I do not, at the moment, see any strong empirical motivation for one or another specific extension or refinement. In any event, these questions aside, it is clear that information concerning grammatical functions of the sort exemplified in (2ii) can be extracted directly from the rewriting rules of the base, without any necessity for *ad hoc* extensions and elaborations of these rules to provide specific mention of grammatical function. Such extensions, aside from their redundancy, have the defect of failing to express properly the relational character of the functional notions and are thus useless in all but the simplest cases.

However, we have not yet exhausted the information presented in (2ii). Thus it is still necessary to define grammatical relations of the sort that hold between *sincerity* and *frighten* (Subject-Verb) and between *frighten* and *the boy* (Verb-Object) in (1). Such relations can be defined derivatively in terms of the functional notions suggested earlier. Thus Subject-Verb can be defined as the relation between the Subject-of a Sentence and Main-Verb-of the Predicate-of the Sentence, where Subject-of, Main-Verb-of, and Predicate-of are the notions of (11); and Verb-Object can be defined as the relation between the Main-Verb-of and the Direct-Object-of a VP. However, there is still something missing in this account. Thus we have no basis, as yet, for distinguishing the legitimate and traditionally recognized grammatical relation Subject-Verb, as just defined, from the irrelevant pseudorelation Subject-Object, which is definable just as easily in the same terms. Traditional grammar seems to define such relations where there are selectional restrictions governing the paired categories. Thus the choice of Main-Verb is determined by the choice of Subject and Object, though Subject and Object are in general chosen independently of one another and, correspondingly, have no grammatical relation of the sort in question holding between them. I shall defer the discussion of selectional relations, but in any event, it is fairly clear that nothing essentially new is involved here beyond the rules that generate strings and Phrase-markers.

In summary, then, it seems unnecessary to extend the system of rewriting rules in order to accommodate information of the sort presented in (2ii). With appropriate general definitions of the relational notions involved, this information can be extracted directly from Phrase-markers that are generated by simple rewriting rules such as (5) and (12). This information is already contained, implicitly, in the system of elementary rewriting rules. Representations such as (6) and new or elaborated rewriting rules to generate them are unnecessary, as well as misleading and inappropriate.

Finally, I should like to call attention, once again, to the fact that various modifications and extensions of these functional notions are possible, and that it is important to find empirical motivation for such improvements. For example, the characterization might be sharpened somewhat in terms of several notions that will be useful later on. Suppose again that we have a base grammar consisting of a sequence of rewriting rules, and that (as in 5) we have distinguished lexical rules (such as 5 II), which introduce lexical formatives, from the others. We shall see later that this distinction is formally quite clearly marked. A category that appears on the left in a lexical rule we shall call a *lexical category*; a lexical category or a category that dominates a string . . .X. . ., where X is a lexical category, we shall call a *major category*. Thus in the grammar (5), the categories N, V, and M are lexical categories,[18] and all categories except Det

---

[18]One might question whether M should be regarded as a lexical category, or whether, alternatively, the rules M → *may, can,* . . . should not be included in the set (5 I). The significance of this distinction will be discussed later. This is by no means merely a terminological issue. Thus, for example, we might hope to establish general conventions involving the distinction between lexical and nonlexical categories. To illustrate the range of possibilities that may be relevant, I mention just two considerations. The general rule for conjunction seems to be roughly this: if XZY and XZ'Y are two strings such that for some category A, Z is an A and Z' is an A, then we may form the string X⌢Z and Z'⌢Y, where Z and Z' is an A (see Chomsky 1957, sec. 5.2, and for a much more far-reaching study, Gleitman, 1961). But, clearly, A must be a category of a special type; in fact, we

(and possibly M and Aux — see note 18) are major categories. It would, then, be in accord with traditional usage to limit the functional notions to major categories.

---

come much closer to characterizing the actual range of possibilities if we limit A to major categories. By this criterion, M should be a lexical category.

Second, consider the phonological rules that assign stress in English by a transformational cycle (see Chomsky, Halle, and Lukoff, 1956; Halle and Chomsky, 1960, 1968; Chomsky and Miller, 1963). These rules assign stress in a fixed way in strings belonging to certain categories. By and large, the categories in question seem to be the major categories, in the sense just described. In particular, elements of nonlexical formative categories (e.g., Articles) are unstressed. By this criterion, one might want M to be a nonlexical category, though even here the situation is unclear; cf. the well-known contrast of *mây - mây*, as in *John mây try* (it is permitted) and *John mây try* (it is possible).

Language and the Mind

NOAM CHOMSKY

How does the mind work? To answer this question we must look at some of the work performed by the mind. One of its main functions is the acquisition of knowledge. The two major factors in acquisition of knowledge, perception and learning, have been the subject of study and speculation for centuries. It would not, I think, be misleading to characterize the major positions that have developed as outgrowths of classical rationalism and empiricism. The rationalist theories are marked by the importance they assign to *intrinsic* structures in mental operations — to central processes and organizing principles in perception, and to innate ideas and principles in learning. The empiricist approach, in contrast, has stressed the role of experience and control by environmental factors.

The classical empiricist view is that sensory images are transmitted to the brain as impressions. They remain as ideas that will be associated in various ways, depending on the fortuitous character of experience. In this view a language is merely a collection of words, phrases, and sentences, a habit system, acquired accidentally and extrinsically. In the formulation of Willard Quine, knowledge of a language (and, in fact, knowledge in general) can be represented as ''a fabric of sentences variously associated to one another and to nonverbal stimuli by the mechanism of conditioned response.'' Acquisition of knowledge is only a matter of the gradual construction of this fabric. When sensory experience is interpreted, the already established network may be activated in some fashion. In its essentials, this view has been predominant in modern behavioral science, and it has been accepted with little question by many philosophers as well.

The classical rationalist view is quite different. In this view the mind contains a system of ''common notions'' that enable it to interpret the scattered and incoherent data of sense in terms of objects and their relations, cause and effect, whole and part, symmetry, gestalt properties, functions, and so on. Sensation, providing only fleeting and meaningless images, is degenerate and particular. Knowledge, much of it beyond immediate awareness, is rich in structure, involves universals, and is highly organized. The innate general principles that underlie and organize this knowledge, according to Leibniz, ''enter into our thoughts, of which they form the soul and the connection . . . although we do not at all think of them.''

This ''active'' rationalist view of the acquisition of knowledge persisted through the romantic period in its essentials. With respect to language, it

(from *Psychology Today* (1968), pp. 48–68.)

achieves its most illuminating expression in the profound investigations of Wilhelm von Humboldt. His theory of speech perception supposes a generative system of rules that underlies speech production as well as its interpretation. The system is generative in that it makes infinite use of finite means. He regards a language as a structure of forms and concepts based on a system of rules that determine their interrelations, arrangement, and organization. But these finite materials can be combined to make a never-ending product.

In the rationalist and romantic tradition of linguistic theory, the normal use of language is regarded as characteristically innovative. We construct sentences that are entirely new to us. There is no substantive notion of "analogy" or "generalization" that accounts for this creative aspect of language use. It is equally erroneous to describe language as a "habit structure" or as a network of associated responses. The innovative element in normal use of language quickly exceeds the bounds of such marginal principles as analogy or generalization (under any substantive interpretation of these notions). It is important to emphasize this fact because the insight has been lost under the impact of the behaviorist assumptions that have dominated speculation and research in the twentieth century.

In Humboldt's view, acquisition of language is largely a matter of maturation of an innate language capacity. The maturation is guided by internal factors, by an innate "form of language" that is sharpened, differentiated, and given its specific realization through experience. Language is thus a kind of latent structure in the human mind, developed and fixed by exposure to specific linguistic experience. Humboldt believes that all languages will be found to be very similar in their grammatical form, similar not on the surface but in their deeper inner structures. The innate organizing principles severely limit the class of possible languages, and these principles determine the properties of the language that is learned in the normal way.

The active and passive views of perception and learning have elaborated with varying degrees of clarity since the seventeenth century. These views can be confronted with empirical evidence in a variety of ways. Some recent work in psychology and neurophysiology is highly suggestive in this regard. There is evidence for the existence of central processes in perception, specifically for control over the functioning of sensory neurons by the brain-stem reticular system. Behavioral counterparts of this central control have been under investigation for several years. Furthermore, there is evidence for innate organization of the perceptual system of a highly specific sort at every level of biological organization. Studies of the visual system of the frog, the discovery of specialized cells responding to angle and motion in the lower cortical centers of cats and rabbits, and the somewhat comparable investigations of the auditory system of frogs — all are relevant to the classical questions of intrinsic structure mentioned earlier. These studies suggest that there are highly organized, innately determined perceptual systems that are adapted closely to the animal's "life space" and that provide the basis for what we might call "acquisition of knowledge." Also relevant are certain behavioral studies of human infants, for example those showing the preference for faces over other complex stimuli.

These and other studies make it reasonable to inquire into the possibility that complex intellectual structures are determined narrowly by innate mental organization. What is perceived may be determined by mental processes of considerable depth. As far as language learning is concerned, it seems to me that a rather convincing argument can be made for the view that certain principles intrinsic to the mind provide invariant structures that are a precondition for linguistic experience. In the course of this article I would like to sketch some of the ways such conclusions might be clarified and firmly established.

There are several ways linguistic evidence can be used to reveal properties of human perception and learning. In this section we consider one research strategy that might take us nearer to this goal.

Let us say that in interpreting a certain physical stimulus a person constructs a "percept." This percept represents some of his conclusions (in general, unconscious) about the stimulus. To the extent that we can characterize such percepts, we can go on to investigate the mechanisms that relate stimulus and percept. Imagine a model of perception that takes stimuli as inputs and arrives at percepts as "outputs." The model might contain a system of beliefs, strategies for interpreting stimuli, and other factors, such as the organization of memory. We would then have a perceptual model that might be represented graphically:

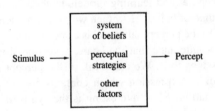

MODEL FOR PERCEPTION. Each physical stimulus, after interpretation by the mental processes, will result in a percept.

Consider next the system of beliefs that is a component of the perceptual model. How was this acquired? To study this problem, we must investigate a second model, which takes certain data as input and gives as "output" (again, internally represented) the system of beliefs operating in the perceptual model. This second model, a model of learning, would have its own intrinsic structure, as did the first. This structure might consist of conditions on the nature of the system of beliefs that can be acquired, of innate inductive strategies, and again, of other factors such as the organization of memory.

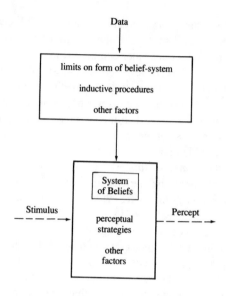

MODEL FOR LEARNING. One's system of beliefs, a part of the perception model, is acquired from data as shown above.

Under further conditions, which are interesting but not relevant here, we can take these perceptual and learning models as theories of the acquisition of knowledge, rather than of belief. How then would the models apply to language? The input stimulus to the perceptual model is a speech signal, and the percept is a representation of the utterance that the hearer takes the signal to be and of the interpretation he assigns to it. We can think of the percept as the structural description of a linguistic expression which contains certain phonetic, semantic, and syntactic information. Most interesting is the syntactic information, which best can be discussed by examining a few typical cases. The three sentences in the example seem to be the same syntactic structure.

Each contains the subject I, and the predicate of each consists of a verb (*told, expected, persuaded*), a noun phrase (*John*), and an embedded predicate phrase (*to leave*). This similarity is only superficial, however — a similarity in what we may call the "surface structure" of these sentences, which differ in important ways when we consider them with somewhat greater care.

The differences can be seen when the sentences are paraphrased or subjected to certain grammatical operations, such as the conversion from active to passive forms. For example, in normal conversation the sentence "I told John to leave" can be roughly paraphrased as "What I told John was to leave." But the other two sentences cannot be paraphrased as "What I persuaded John was to leave" or "What I expected John was to leave." Sentence 2 can be paraphrased as: "It was expected by me that John would leave." But the other two sentences cannot undergo a corresponding formal operation, yielding: "It was persuaded by me that John would leave" or "It was told by me that John should leave."

Sentences 2 and 3 differ more subtly. In Sentence 3 *John* is the direct object of *persuade*, but in Sentence 2 *John* is not the direct object of *expect*. We can show this by using these verbs in slightly more complex sentences: "I persuaded the doctor to examine John" and "I expected the doctor to examine John." If we replace the embedded proposition *the doctor to examine John* with its passive form *John to be examined by the doctor*, the change to the passive does not, in itself, change the meaning. We can accept as paraphrases "I expected the doctor to examine John" and "I expected John to be examined by the doctor." But we cannot accept as paraphrases "I persuaded the doctor to examine John" and "I persuaded John to be examined by the doctor."

The parts of these sentences differ in their grammatical functions. In "I persuaded John to leave" John is both the object of *persuade* and the subject of *leave*. These facts must be represented in the percept since they are known, intuitively, to the hearer of the speech signal. No special training or instruction is necessary to enable the native speaker to understand these examples, to know which are "wrong" and which "right," although they may all be quite new to him. They are interpreted by the native speaker instantaneously and uniformly, in accordance with structural principles that are known tacitly, intuitively, and unconsciously.

These examples illustrate two significant points. First, the surface structure of a sentence, its organization into various phrases, may not reveal or im-

(1) I told John to leave
(2) I expected John to leave
(3) I persuaded John to leave

First Paraphrase:

(1a) What I told John was to leave (ACCEPTABLE)
(2a) What I expected John was to leave (UNACCEPTABLE)
(3a) What I persuaded John was to leave (UNACCEPTABLE)

Second Paraphrase:

(1b) It was told by me that John would leave (UNACCEPTABLE)
(2b) It was expected by me that John would leave (ACCEPTABLE)
(3b) It was persuaded by me that John would leave (UNACCEPTABLE)

(4) I expected the doctor to examine John
(5) I persuaded the doctor to examine John

Passive replacement as paraphrase:

(4a) I expected John to be examined by the doctor (MEANING RETAINED)
(5a) I persuaded John to be examined by the doctor (MEANING CHANGED)

SUPERFICIAL SIMILARITY. When the sentences above are paraphrased or are converted from active to passive forms, differences in their deep structure appear.

mediately reflect its deep syntactic structure. The deep structure is not represented directly in the form of the speech signal; it is abstract. Second, the rules that determine deep and surface structure and their interrelation in particular cases must themselves be highly abstract. They are surely remote from consciousness, and in all likelihood they cannot be brought to consciousness.

A study of such examples, examples characteristic of all human languages that have been carefully studied, constitutes the first stage of the linguistic investigation outlined above, namely the study of the percept. The percept contains phonetic and semantic information related through the medium of syntactic structure. There are two aspects to this syntactic structure. It consists of a surface directly related to the phonetic form, and a deep structure that underlies the semantic interpretation. The deep structure is represented in the mind and rarely is indicated directly in the physical signal.

A language, then, involves a set of semantic-phonetic percepts, of sound-meaning correlations, the correlations being determined by the kind of intervening syntactic structure just illustrated. The English language correlates sound and meaning in one way, Japanese in another, and so on. But the general properties of percepts, their forms and mechanisms, are remarkably similar for all languages that have been carefully studied.

Returning to our models of perception and learning, we can now take up the problem of formulating the system of beliefs that is a central component in perceptual processes. In the case of language, the "system of beliefs" would now be called the "generative grammar," the system of rules that specifies the sound-meaning correlation and generates the class of structural descriptions (percepts) that constitute the language in question. The generative grammar, then, represents the speaker-hearer's knowledge of his language. We can use the term *grammar of a language* ambiguously, as referring not only to the speaker's internalized, subconscious knowledge but to the professional linguist's representation of this internalized and intuitive system of rules as well.

How is this generative grammar acquired? Or, using our learning model, what is the internal structure of the device that could develop a generative grammar?

We can think of every normal human's internalized grammar as, in effect, a theory of his language. This theory provides a sound-meaning correlation for an infinite number of sentences. It provides an infinite set of structural descriptions; each contains a surface structure that determines phonetic form and a deep structure that determines semantic content.

In formal terms, then, we can describe the child's acquisition of language as a kind of theory construction. The child discovers the theory of his language with only small amounts of data from that language. Not only does his "theory of the language" have an enormous predictive scope, but it also enables the child to reject a great deal of the very data on which the theory has been constructed. Normal speech consists, in large part, of fragments, false starts, blends, and other distortions of the underlying idealized forms. Nevertheless, as is evident from a study of the mature use of language, what the child learns is the underlying ideal theory. This is a remarkable fact. We must also bear in mind that the child constructs this ideal theory without explicit instruction, that he acquires this knowledge at a time when he is not capable of complex intellectual achievements in many other domains, and that this achievement is relatively independent of intelligence or the particular course of experience. These are facts that a theory of learning must face.

A scientist who approaches phenomena of this sort without prejudice or dogma would conclude that the acquired knowledge must be determined in a rather specific way by intrinsic properties of mental organization. He would then set himself the task of discovering the innate ideas and principles that make such acquisition of knowledge possible.

It is unimaginable that a highly specific, abstract, and tightly organized language comes by accident into the mind of every four-year-old child. If there were not an innate restriction on the form of grammar, then the child could employ innumerable theories to account for his linguistic experience, and no one system, or even small class of systems, would be found exclusively acceptable or even preferable. The child could not possibly acquire knowledge of a language. This restriction on the form of grammar is a precondition for linguistic experience, and it is surely the critical factor in determining the course and result of language learning. The child cannot know at birth which language he is going to learn. But he must "know" that its grammar must be of a predetermined form that excludes many imaginable languages.

The child's task is to select the appropriate hypothesis from this restricted class. Having selected it, he can confirm his choice with the evidence further available to him. But neither the evidence nor any process of induction (in any well-defined sense) could in themselves have led to this choice. Once the hypothesis is sufficiently well confirmed, the child knows the language defined by this hypothesis; consequently, his knowledge extends vastly beyond his linguistic experience, and he can reject much of this experience as imperfect, as resulting from the interaction of many factors, only one of which is the ideal grammar that determines a sound-meaning connection for an infinite class of linguistic expressions. Along such lines as these one might outline a theory to explain the acquisition of language.

As has been pointed out, both the form and meaning of a sentence are determined by syntactic structures that are not represented directly in the signal and that are related to the signal only at a distance, through a long sequence of interpretive rules. This property of abstractness in grammatical structure is of primary importance, and it is on this property that our inferences about mental processes are based. Let us examine this abstractness a little more closely.

Not many years ago, the process of sentence interpretation might have been described approximately along the following lines. A speech signal is received and segmented into successive units (overlapping at the borders). These units are analyzed in terms of their invariant phonetic properties and assigned to "phonemes." The sequence of phonemes, so constructed, is then segmented into minimal grammatically functioning units (morphemes and words). These are again categorized. Successive operations of segmentation and classification will lead to what I have called "surface structure" — an analysis of a sentence into phrases, which can be represented as a proper bracketing of the sentence, with the bracket units assigned to various categories. Each segment — phonetic, syntactic, or semantic — would be identified in terms of certain invariant properties. This would be an exhaustive analysis of the structure of the sentence.

With such a conception of language structure, it made good sense to look forward hopefully to certain engineering applications of linguistics — for example, to voice-operated typewriters capable of segmenting an expression into its successive phonetic units and identifying these, so that speech could be converted to some form of phonetic writing in a mechanical way; to mechanical analysis of sentence structure by fairly straightforward and well-understood computational techniques; and perhaps even beyond to such projects as machine translation. But these hopes have by now been largely abandoned with the realization that this conception of grammatical structure is inadequate at every level, semantic, phonetic, and syntactic. Most important, at the level of syntactic organization, the surface structure indicates semantically significant relations only in extremely simple cases. In general, the deeper aspects of syntactic organization are representable by labeled bracketing, but of a very different sort from that seen in surface structure.

There is evidence of various sorts, both from phonetics and from experimental psychology, that labeled bracketing is an adequate representation of surface structure. It would go beyond the bounds of this paper to survey the phonetic evidence. A good deal of it is presented in *The Sound Pattern of English* (1968), by Morris Halle and myself. Similarly, very interesting experimental work by Jerry Fodor and his colleagues based on earlier observations by D. E. Broadbent and Peter Ladefoged, has shown that the disruption of a speech signal (for example, by a superimposed click) tends to be perceived at the boundaries of phrases rather than at the point where the disruption actually occurred, and that in many cases the bracketing of surface structure can be read directly from the data on perceptual displacement. I think the evidence is rather good that labeled bracketing serves to represent the surface structure that is related to the perceived form of physical signals.

Deep structures are related to surface structures by a sequence of certain formal operations, operations now generally called "grammatical transformations." At the levels of sound, meaning, and syntax, the significant structural features of sentences are highly abstract. For this reason they cannot be recovered by elementary data-processing techniques. This fact lies behind the search for central processes in speech perception and the search for intrinsic, innate structure as the basis for language learning.

How can we represent deep structure? To answer this question we must

consider the grammatical transformations that link surface structure to the underlying deep structure that is not always apparent.

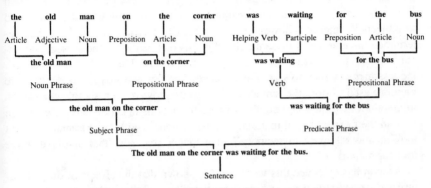

SURFACE STRUCTURE ANALYSIS. A type of sentence analysis now abandoned as inadequate
at every level is this labeled bracketing which analyzes the sentence by successive division into
larger units with each unit assigned to its own category.

Consider, for example, the operations of passivization and interrogation. In
the sentences 1) John was examined by the doctor, and 2) did the doctor examine
John, both have a deep structure similar to the paraphrase of Sentence 1, 3) the
doctor examined John. The same network of grammatical relations determines
the semantic interpretation in each case. Thus two of the grammatical transformations of English must be the operations of passivization and interrogation that
form such surface structures as Sentences 1 and 2 from a deeper structure which
in its essentials also underlies Sentence 3. Since the transformations ultimately
produce surface structures, they must produce labeled bracketings. But notice
that these operations can apply in sequence: we can form the passive question
"was John examined by the doctor" by passivization followed by interrogation.
Since the result of passivization is a labeled bracketing, it follows that the interrogative transformation operates on a labeled bracketing and forms a new labeled
bracketing. Thus a transformation such as interrogation maps a labeled bracketing into a labeled bracketing.

By similar argument, we can show that all grammatical transformations are
structure-dependent mappings of this sort and that the deep structures which underlie all sentences must themselves be labeled bracketings. Of course, the
labeled bracketing that constitutes deep structure will in general be quite different
from that representing the surface structure of a sentence. Our argument is
somewhat oversimplified, but it is roughly correct. When made precise and fully
accurate it strongly supports the view that deep structures, like surface structures,
are formally to be taken as labeled bracketings, and that grammatical transformations are mappings of such structures onto other similar structures.

Recent studies have sought to explore the ways in which grammatical structure of the sort just described enters into mental operations. Much of this work

has been based on a proposal formulated by George Miller as a first approximation, namely, that the amount of memory used to store a sentence should reflect the number of transformations used in deriving it. For example, H. B. Savin and E. Perchonock investigated this assumption in the following way: they presented to subjects a sentence followed by a sequence of unrelated words. They then determined the number of these unrelated words recalled when the subject attempted to repeat the sentence and the sequence of words. The more words recalled, the less memory used to store the sentence. The fewer words recalled, the more memory used to store the sentence. The results showed a remarkable correlation of amount of memory and number of transformations in certain simple cases. In fact, in their experimental material, shorter sentences with more transformations took up more "space in memory" than longer sentences that involved fewer transformations.

Savin has extended this work and has shown that the effects of deep structure and surface structure can be differentiated by a similar technique. He considered paired sentences with approximately the same deep structure but with one of the pair being more complex in surface structure. He showed that, under the experimental conditions just described, the paired sentences were indistinguishable. But if the sequence of unrelated words precedes, rather than follows, the sentence being tested, then the more complex (in surface structure) of the pair is more difficult to repeat correctly than the simpler member. Savin's very plausible inference is that sentences are coded in memory in terms of deep structure. When the unrelated words precede the test sentence, these words use up a certain amount of short-term memory, and the sentence that is more complex in surface structure cannot be analyzed with the amount of memory remaining. But if the test sentence precedes the unrelated words, it is, once understood, stored in terms of deep structure, which is about the same in both cases. Therefore, the same amount of memory remains, in the paired cases, for recall of the following words. This is a beautiful example of the way creative experimental studies can interweave with theoretical work in the study of language and of mental processes.

In speaking of mental processes we have returned to our original problem. We can now see why it is reasonable to maintain that the linguistic evidence supports an "active" theory of acquisition of knowledge. The study of sentences and of speech perception, it seems to me, leads to a perceptual theory of a classical rationalist sort. Representative of this school, among others, were the seventeenth-century Cambridge Platonists, who developed the idea that our perception is guided by notions that originate from the mind and that provide the framework for the interpretation of sensory stimuli. It is not sufficient to suggest that this framework is a store of "neural models" or "schemata" which are in some manner applied to perception (as is postulated in some current theories of perception). We must go well beyond this assumption and return to the view of Wilhelm von Humboldt, who attributed to the mind a system of rules that generates such models and schemata under the stimulation of the senses. The system of rules itself determines the content of the percept that is formed.

We can offer more than this vague and metaphoric account. A generative grammar and an associated theory of speech perception provide a concrete example of the rules that operate and of the mental objects that they construct and manipulate. Physiology cannot yet explain the physical mechanisms that affect these abstract functions. But neither physiology nor psychology provides evidence that calls this account into question or that suggests an alternative. As mentioned earlier, the most exciting current work in the physiology of perception shows that even the peripheral systems analyze stimuli into the complex properties of objects, and that central processes may significantly affect the information transmitted by the receptor organs.

The study of language, it seems to me, offers strong empirical evidence that empiricist theories of learning are quite inadequate. Serious efforts have been made in recent years to develop principles of induction, generalization, and data analysis that would account for knowledge of a language. These efforts have been a total failure. The methods and principles fail not for any superficial reason such as lack of time or data. They fail because they are intrinsically incapable of giving rise to the system of rules that underlies the normal use of language. What evidence is now available supports the view that all human languages share deep-seated properties of organization and structure. These properties — these linguistic universals — can be plausibly assumed to be an innate mental endowment rather than the result of learning. If this is true, then the study of language sheds light on certain long-standing issues in the theory of knowledge. Once again, I see little reason to doubt that what is true of language is true of other forms of human knowledge as well.

There is one further question that might be raised at this point. How does the human mind come to have the innate properties that underlie acquisition of knowledge? Here linguistic evidence obviously provides no information at all. The processes by which the human mind has achieved its present state of complexity and its particular form of innate organization are a complete mystery, as much of a mystery as the analogous questions that can be asked about the processes leading to the physical and mental organization of any other complex organism. It is perfectly safe to attribute this to evolution, so long as we bear in mind that there is no substance to this assertion — it amounts to nothing more than the belief that there is surely some naturalistic explanation for these phenomena.

There are, however, important aspects of the problem of language and mind that can be studied sensibly within the limitations of present understanding and technique. I think that, for the moment, the most productive investigations are those dealing with the nature of particular grammars and with the universal conditions met by all human languages. I have tried to suggest how one can move, in successive steps of increasing abstractness, from the study of percepts to the study of grammar and perceptual mechanisms, and from the study of grammar to the study of universal grammar and the mechanisms of learning.

In this area of convergence of linguistics, psychology, and philosophy, we can look forward to much exciting work in coming years.

Toward a Modern Theory of Case

CHARLES J. FILLMORE

I. In Chapter 2 of his book *Aspects of the Theory of Syntax*,[1] Chomsky points out the essentially *relational* nature of such grammatical concepts as subject (of a sentence) and object (of a verb, or of a predicate phrase) as opposed to the *categorial* nature of such notions as verb or noun phrase. The important distinction is there drawn between grammatical relations or grammatical functions, on the one hand, and grammatical categories on the other hand.

The distinction can be captured in formal grammars, according to Chomsky, by introducing category symbols as constituent labels in the phrase structure rules of the base component, and by defining the grammatical relations as in fact relations among category symbols within the underlying phrase-markers provided by the base. Thus sentence, noun phrase, and verb phrase, for example, are provided as category symbols by the base, while the notion subject is defined as a relation between a noun phrase and an immediately dominating sentence, the term object as a relation between a noun phrase and an immediately dominating verb phrase.

My purpose in this essay is to question the deep-structure validity of the notions subject and object, and also to raise doubts about the adequacy of Chomsky's proposals for formally reconstructing the distinction between grammatical categories and grammatical functions. My inquiry will lead to a proposal which renders unnecessary the distinction in English grammar between noun phrase and preposition phrase, and to the suggestion that something very much like grammatical *case* plays a role in the groundwork of grammars that is much less superficial than is usually recognized.

I begin my argument by asking, concerning such expressions as *in the room, toward the moon, on the next day, in a careless way, with a sharp knife*, and *by my brother*, how it is possible in grammars of the type illustrated in *Aspects* to reveal both the categorial information that all of these expressions are preposition phrases and the functional information that they are adverbials of location, direction, time, manner, instrument, and agent respectively. Instead of having a category label *Time*, it ought to be possible — if Chomsky's proposal is adequate — to recognize that a preposition phrase whose head is a Time noun has the syntactic function *Time Adverbial* within the constituent which immediately contains it.

(from *Modern Studies in English*, eds. D. A. Reibel and S. A. Schane, Englewood Cliffs, N.J.: Prentice-Hall, 1969, pp. 361–75. Reprinted with permission of Prentice-Hall and the Project on Linguistic Atlas, The Ohio State University Research Foundations.)

[1]Noam Chomsky, *Aspects of the Theory of Syntax* (Cambridge, Mass.: MIT Press, 1965), especially pp. 63–74.

It seems impossible to provide both types of information in a natural way for the reason that there may be several adverbial expressions in a simple sentence, there are ordering restrictions among these, and if they all start out with the same category, Preposition Phrase, there is no known device by which the further expansion of this category can be constrained according to the permitted order of adverbial types in a single sentence.

Most of the sample phrase structure rules for English that I have seen recently have introduced categorially such terms as *Manner, Frequency, Extent, Location, Direction*, etc. In these grammars, for the constituents mentioned, either the strictly categorial information is lost, or else it is rescued by having nonbranching rules which rewrite each of these adverbial-type categories as *Preposition Phrase*. In any case the formal distinction between relations and categories is lost, and the constraints on the further expansion of these preposition phrases that depend on the types of adverbials they manifest need to be provided, as suggested above, in ways that have not yet been made clear.[2]

Other grammars that I have seen contain rules allowing more than one preposition phrase in the expansion of a single category. In the abbreviated form of these rules, each of these preposition phrases is independently optional. Difficulties in establishing the constraints on expanding these categories just in case more than one was chosen remain as before, and two new technical difficulties arise. If there are two independently optional preposition phrases in the expansion of *Verb Phrase*, then we get the same result by skipping the first and choosing the second as we do by choosing the first and skipping the second. The first technical difficulty, then, is that different choices in the base do not correspond to differences in the structure of sentences.[3] The second is that now the syntactic relation *preposition-phrase-under-verb-phrase* is not unique in a verb phrase just in case more than one preposition phrase has been chosen.

The obvious alternative within the present conception of grammar is to introduce new structure in such a way that whenever a sentence contains more than one preposition phrase, they are all under immediate domination of categories of different types. If the number of distinct types of preposition phrases is large, this

---

[2]The problem on such restricted expansion has not been ignored. Chomsky has proposed (ibid., p. 215) that "there is some reason to suspect that it might be appropriate to intersperse certain local transformations among the rewriting rules of the base. Thus adverbial phrases consisting of Preposition-Determiner-Noun are in general restricted as to the choice of these elements, and these restrictions could be stated by local transformations to the effect that *Preposition* and *Noun* can be rewritten in certain restricted ways when dominated by such category symbols as *Place Adverbial* and *Time Adverbial*. In fact, one might consider a new extension of the theory of context-free grammar, permitting rules that restrict rewriting by local transformations (i.e., in terms of the dominating category symbol), alongside of the fairly widely studied extension of context-free grammar to context-sensitive grammars that permit rules that restrict rewriting in terms of contiguous symbols." The proposal given below amounts to incorporating Chomsky's suggestions in the form of a convention on the rules which assign complex symbols to prepositions and nouns.

[3]This problem vanishes if parentheses in phrase structure rules are understood as having purely abbreviatory functions.

solution differs from providing separate category labels for each adverbial only by greatly increasing the constituent-structure complexity of sentences.

With these difficulties understood, I should next like to ask whether two of the grammatical functions which Chomsky accepts — namely subject and object — are in fact linguistically significant notions on the deep structure level. The deep structure relevance of syntactic functions is with respect to the projection rules of the semantic theory. The semantic component recognizes semantic features associated with lexical elements in a string and projects from them the meaning of the string in ways appropriate to the syntactic relations which hold among these elements. It is my opinion that the traditional subject and object are not to be found among the syntactic functions to which semantic rules must be sensitive.

Consider uses of the verb *open*. It seems to me that in sentences (1) and (2)

1. The door will open.
2. The janitor will open the door.

there is a semantically relevant relation between *the door* and *open* that is the same in the two sentences, in spite of the fact that *the door* is the subject of the so-called intransitive verb and the object of the so-called transitive verb. It seems to me, too, that in sentences (3) and (4)

3. The janitor will open the door with this key.
4. This key will open the door.

the common semantically relevant relation is that between *this key* and *open* in both of the sentences, in spite of the fact that *this key* superficially is the subject of one of the sentences, the object of a preposition in the other.

In naming the functions of the nominals in these sentences, that of *the janitor* we might call *Agentive*; and that of *this key*, *Instrumental*. The remaining function to find a name for is that of the subject of an intransitive verb and the object of a transitive verb: a term we might use for this function is *Objective*.[4] None of these functions, as we have seen, can be identified with either subject or object.

If we allow ourselves to use these terms *Objective*, *Instrumental*, and *Agentive*, we might describe the syntax of the verb *open* as follows: it requires an Objective, and tolerates an Instrumental and/or an Agentive. If only the Objective occurs, the Objective noun is automatically the subject. If an Instrumental

[4]The term *Objective* should not be confused with the surface syntactic relation *object* nor with the surface case *accusative*. It would be possible to borrow the term *nominative* from the grammatical tradition of studies of the so-called "ergative" languages (e.g. the northern Caucasian languages), but it is my belief that the choice of this term may well have been responsible for the common assumption that the "ergative" languages are languages in which transitive sentences are obligatorily passive.

also occurs, either the Objective or the Instrumental noun may be the subject, as seen in sentences (5) and (6).

5. This key will open the door.
6. The door will open with this key.

If an Agentive occurs, an Instrumental noun cannot be the subject, but, if it occurs, it must appear in a preposition phrase after the Objective, as in (7).

7. The janitor will open the door with this key.

The Objective noun can be made subject even if the sentence contains Instrumental and Agentive elements, just in case the verb is capable of assuming its passive form. The Instrumental and Agentive expressions, in this case, contain their appropriate prepositions, as in (8) and (9).

8. The door will be opened with this key.
9. The door will be opened by the janitor.

In the case of two syntactic functions — Instrumental and Agentive — the noun phrase is preceded by a preposition just in case it has not been made the subject of the sentence. When we add to our consideration the many cases where object nouns are also marked by prepositions as in such sentences as (10) and (11)

10. She objects to me.
11. She depends on me.

and when, further, we see that even in cases like *open*, the Objective has a preposition associated with it in certain nominalizations, as in (12)

12. The opening of the door by the janitor with this key

we see that an analysis of syntactic functions in English requires a general account of the role of prepositions in our language.

The verb *open*, fortunately, is not unique in governing syntactic relations that are not identifiable with subjects and objects. Other verbs that behave in similar ways are *advance, bend, bounce, break, burn up, burst, circulate, close, connect, continue, crumple, dash, decrease, develop, drop, end, enter (contest), expand, hang, hide, hurt, improve, increase, jerk, keep away, keep out, move, pour, repeat, retreat, rotate, run, rush, shake, shift, shine, shrink, sink, slide, spill, spread, stand, start, starve, stir, stretch, turn, twist, wake up, wind, withdraw*. My interpretation of these words is that they have a certain amount of freedom with respect to the syntactic environments into which they can be inserted — a freedom which I assume can be stated very simply. The alternative is to regard these verbs as having each two or three meanings corresponding to their intransitive use or their capability of taking subjects whose relation to the verb can be construed instrumentally in one meaning, agentively in another.[5]

II. I recognize, therefore, various categorially introduced noun phrase types — suggestive, it seems to me, of the traditional notion of "cases" — each, in English, beginning with a preposition. The syntactic relationship of each of these types to the main verb of the sentence is defined with reference to the category under which it is introduced, having no direct connection with whatever eventual status it may have as subject or object. The following assumptions are meant to develop the scheme I have in mind by means of a series of specific assumptions.

2.1. The first of these assumptions is that the major constituents of a sentence (S) are Modality (Mod), Auxiliary (Aux), and Proposition (Prop). The first phrase structure rule is (13).

13. S → Mod - Aux - Prop

I use *Proposition* rather than *Predicate* because it includes what will end up to be the subject of the sentence. Notice that the Auxiliary is in immediate constituent relationship with the entire Proposition, not a subconstituent of the Proposition. I assume this structure assignment to be semantically justified.

2.2. The constituent Modality contains interrogative and negative elements, sentence adverbials, time adverbials, and various other adverbial elements that are understood as modalities on the sentence as a whole rather than subconstituents of the constituent containing the main verb. I have no strong convictions that these various elements actually comprise a single constituent, but for the time being we may assume that they do. For the purpose of the present discussion I shall also assume that this modality element is optional, and that it is not involved in any of the observations that I shall be dealing with here.[6]

In the rest of the present discussion, however, I shall omit mention of the Modality constituent, acting as if the first rule rewrites *Sentence* as *Auxiliary + Proposition*.

2.3. The category Proposition includes the verb and all those nominal elements which are relevant to the sub-classification of verbs. The rules for rewriting Proposition take it into an obligatory verb followed by the somewhat in-

---

[5]Edward S. Klima has pointed out to me that the instrumental versus agentive role of the possible subjects of *open* has syntactic as well as semantic importance, as can be seen in the unacceptability of the conjunction seen in (i):

i. The janitor and the key will open the door.

Two agentive subjects may be conjoined, two instrumental subjects may be conjoined, but not one of each.

[6]For various reasons, I am convinced that instead of treating *Negative* as an optional subconstituent of the optional constituent Modality, it is better to introduce, as an obligatory subconstituent of the obligatory constituent Modality, a disjunction of the elements *Negative* and *Affirmative*. This choice appears to be necessary because of various semantic rules whose effect is to reverse the negativity value of a sentence — changing affirmatives to negatives and negatives to affirmatives.

dependently optional elements Objective (Obj), Dative (Dat), Locative (Loc), Comitative (Com), Instrumental (Ins), and Agentive (Ag).[7]

Roughly speaking, all adverbial elements capable of becoming subjects or objects are introduced in the expansion of Proposition; all others — Time, Benefactive, Frequentative, etc. — are modality elements. The concepts involved are presumed to be among the substantive universals specified by the grammatical theory.

2.4. All of the nonverb constituents of propositions are Noun Phrase (NP). The relevant rule takes each of the terms I have mentioned and rewrites it as noun phrase:

14.
$$\left\{ \begin{array}{l} \text{Obj} \\ \text{Dat} \\ \text{Loc} \\ \ldots \end{array} \right\} \rightarrow \text{NP}$$

The syntactic functions appropriate to noun phrases, in other words, are identified categorially. The elements which dominate NP are distinct from what we might wish to call the true grammatical categories in that their further expansion is unary and many-to-one. What this suggests is that the form of grammars which I am proposing is at bottom one in which the underlying structures of sentences are representable as rooted trees with labeled nodes and labeled branches. This could be equivalent to a phrase structure grammar in which, beginning from S, all even-numbered branchings are unary.

[7]The variety of expansions of the proposition displays the range of kernel sentence types in the language. Some possible expansions of *Prop* are these (linked parentheses indicate that at least one of two adjacent terms must be chosen):

Prop → V Obj (Dat|Ag)
Prop → V Obj Loc (Dat|Ag)
Prop → V Obj (Ins|Ag)
Prop → V Obj Com
Prop → V S (Dat (Ag))
Prop → V S Obj (Ag)

Sentences illustrating various choices in the expansion of *Prop* are given below:

i. John has a car.	V͡Obj͡Dat
ii. I gave John a car.	V͡Obj͡Dat͡Ag
iii. I bought a car.	V͡Obj͡Ag
iv. A coat is in the closet.	V͡Obj͡Loc
v. John has a coat in the closet.	V͡Obj͡Loc͡Dat
vi. John put a coat in the closet.	V͡Obj͡Loc͡Ag
vii. The door opened.	V͡Obj
viii. The key opened the door.	V͡Obj͡Ins
ix. The janitor opened the door.	V͡Obj͡Ag
x. The janitor opened the door with the key.	V͡Obj͡Ins͡Ag
xi. John is with his brother.	V͡Obj͡Com
xii. John turned out to be a liar.	V͡S
xiii. John thinks that he is too old.	V͡S͡Dat
xiv. I persuaded John that he was too old.	V͡S͡Dat͡Ag
xv. I forced John to go.	V͡S͡Obj͡Ag

Borrowing from Tesnière,[8] I shall use the term *actant* for these elements within propositions which unarily dominate noun phrases.

2.5.   Another important assumption is that every noun phrase begins with a preposition.

15. NP → P (Det) (S) N

Thus we see that the distinction between noun phrase and preposition phrase is no longer necessary. This is all to the good, of course, since *preposition phrase* has always been a terminological nuisance. We would really like all constituents labeled X-Phrase to be constituents having X's as their heads.

2.6.   The lexical categories Preposition (P) and Noun (N) take by convention the name of the actant dominating their noun phrase as one of the features making up the complex symbols associated with each of these categories. For Agentives, for example, the convention will fill in the feature [+ Agentive] as shown in (16).

16.

$$
\begin{array}{ccc}
& Ag & \\
& | & \\
& NP & \\
P \quad & Det \quad & N
\end{array}
\quad\Longrightarrow\quad
\begin{array}{ccc}
& Ag & \\
& | & \\
& NP & \\
\begin{bmatrix} +P \\ +Ag \end{bmatrix} \quad & Det & \begin{bmatrix} +N \\ +Ag \end{bmatrix}
\end{array}
$$

2.7.   The selectional restrictions associated with lexical categories serving given syntactic functions will be provided by appropriate subcategorization. We may wish to guarantee, for instance, that agent nouns are animate, a decision expressed by rule (17).

17.

$$
\begin{bmatrix} +N \\ +Ag \end{bmatrix} \rightarrow [+\text{Anim}]
$$

The feature [+ Animate] may be required for Benefactives and, under certain environmental conditions, for Datives as well.

2.8.   Some prepositions may be filled in by optional choices from the lexicon. In Locative phrases, though in some cases the preposition may be automati-

---

[8]Lucien Tesnière, *Eléments de syntaxe structurale* (Klincksieck, Paris, 1959), especially pp. 105–115.

cally determined, generally the choice is optional: *over, under, in, on, beside*, etc. These are the prepositions that bring with them semantic information.

2.9.   Other prepositions are determined by inherent syntactic features of specific governing verbs. Thus *blame* requires the Objective preposition to be *for*, the Dative preposition to be *on*.

2.10.   The remaining prepositions are filled in by rules which make use of information about the actants. Thus, the Objective preposition is *of* if it is the only actant in the proposition or if the proposition contains an Instrumental or an Agentive; otherwise it is *with*. The Instrumental preposition is *with* just in case the Agentive co-occurs; otherwise it is *by*.

2.11.   The subject of a sentence is selected, in accordance with certain rules, from among the propositional actants. A transformation places the noun phrase selected to serve as subject to the left of the auxiliary. In Objective-Agentive sentences, unless the auxiliary contains the passive marker, the Agentive becomes the subject, as in (18).[9]

18.

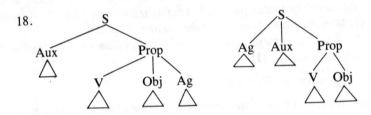

Notice that the proposition that has had one of its actants moved to the subject position is what is traditionally called the predicate.

2.12.   All prepositions are deleted in subject position. (19) shows that after the Objective *of the dog* becomes the subject of the verb *die*, it loses its preposition.

19.

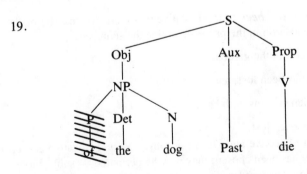

[9]The triangles represent the subtrees dominated by the categories under which they are drawn.

2.13.   A later rule — a rule to which many verbs and certain actants are exceptions — deletes prepositions after verbs:

20.

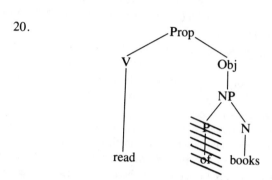

2.14.   Various grammatical processes affect the conditions under which the preposition-deletion rule operates. In nominalizations the Objective preposition stays, as in *the death of the dog* or *the reading of books*.

2.15.   In some contexts, the choice of subject offers certain options. We have seen already that in (21)

21.   will open of the door with this key

either the Objective or the Instrumental can be made subject, giving us either (22) or (23).

22.   The door will open with this key.
23.   This key will open the door.

In the sentence whose underlying form is (24)

24.   Pres   swarm with bees in the garden

either the Objective *with bees* or the Locative *in the garden* may be made subject, losing its preposition in the process. Notice the sentences

25.   Bees swarm in the garden.

where initial *with* has been lost, and

26.   The garden swarms with bees.

where initial *in* has been lost.

2.16.   When Objective and Dative or Objective and Locative are left behind after a subject has been chosen, they may be permuted — subject to certain constraints involving the identification of pronouns. Examples where preposition deletion does not take place are (27) and (28).

27. Talk about this to Dr. Smith.
28. Talk to Dr. Smith about this.

Examples with loss of the postverbal preposition are (29)

29. Blame the accident on John.

where *for* was deleted, and (30)

30. Blame John for the accident.

where *on* was deleted. James Heringer of Ohio State University and J. Bruce Fraser of the MITRE Corporation have given me many more examples like this one.[10]

2.17. In some cases the transformation which provides the subject of a sentence must be thought of as *copying* the selected actant in front of the auxiliary. In Objective-Locative sentences in which the verb is *be*, one subject-selection possibility is the Objective. Thus from (31)

31. Pres   be with some books on the shelf.

with some books can be made subject giving us, after the *with* drops out, (32).

32. Some books are on the shelf.

Alternatively, however, the Locative actant may be *copied* in the subject position, giving us (33).

33. on the shelf are with some books on the shelf

If the left copy of the Locative actant is replaced by its pro-form, we end up with (34).

---

[10]Fraser speaks of these verbs as having alternate meanings. *Spray*, according to Fraser, has one meaning in (i)

    i. Spray the wall with paint.

another in (ii).

    ii. Spray paint on the wall.

I would say merely that the nonagentive actants associated with *spray* are, in these sentences, *with paint* and *on the wall*. They may occur in either order, but whichever one comes first loses its preposition. Other examples from Fraser are (iii) to (x):

    iii. Stuff cotton into the sack.
    iv. Stuff the sack with cotton.
    v. Plant the garden with roses.
    vi. Plant roses in the garden.
    vii. Stack the table with dishes.
    viii. Stack dishes onto the table.
    ix. Make a chair out of wood.
    x. Make wood into a chair.

34. There are some books on the shelf.[11]

2.18. The verb *have* is here interpreted as a variant of the verb *be* in front of the Objective after a noun phrase. Whenever a Locative or a Comitative is made the subject of a proposition whose verb is *be*, this is done by subject copying. Unless, as in the existential sentences, the left copy is changed to *there*, the nominal part of the right copy will be pronominalized. (Possibly what this means is that the repeated noun gets deleted and the features that at this stage have been assigned to the determiner serve now to select a pronoun.)

The Locative copying can be seen in (35):

35.

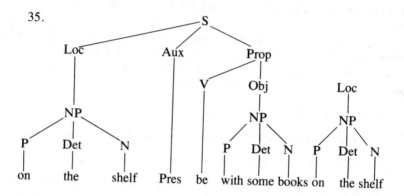

From (35) we get, at a certain stage, something like (36).

36. *on the shelf is with some books on the shelf

[11]I would expect that the expletive *it* can be handled in an analogous way. Nominalized sentences are copied in the subject position, giving us something like (i).

    i. that he is a liar is true that he is a liar

Now, either the right copy can be deleted or the left copy can be replaced by *it*, resulting in (ii) or (iii), respectively.

    ii. That he is a liar is true.
    iii. It is true that he is a liar.

It is likely that the *copying* method of providing subjects should be generalized to all cases, with, simply, the right copy getting deleted in a majority of cases. Where the expected deletion of the right copy is not effected, we get such somewhat deviant sentences as (iv) and (v), borrowed from Jespersen,

    iv. He is a great scoundrel, that husband of hers.
    v. It is perfectly wonderful the way in which he
        remembers things.

because where the right copy didn't get deleted, the left copy got pronominalized. This seems, too, to be a way of handling cases where a preposition gets left behind in passive sentences. The deletion of the right copy is sometimes only partial, leaving the preposition behind, as in

    vi. Mary can be depended on.

The sentence-initial preposition is deleted, the repeated phrase *the shelf* is replaced by *it*, *with* is deleted, and *be*, after noun phrase and before an Objective, gets changed to *have*.[12] The resulting sentence is (37)

37. The shelf has some books on it.

which, thus, I regard as a simplex.

Analogous phenomena are observed in Objective-Comitative sentences. There too we find *have* only when the Objective is not the subject. In sentence (38)

38. The children are with Mary.

the Objective is the subject, *be* remains unchanged, and the Comitative preposition stays. If the Comitative is made subject, it is done so by copying, the right copy eventually undergoing pronominalization. Here *be* is followed by an Objective, so it becomes *have*, and in the Objective case the preposition is deleted. Whereas before we had (38) with *are*, we now have (39) with *has*.

39. Mary has the children with her.

In Objective-Dative sentences, at least for those cases where the Dative noun is animate, the Dative becomes subject by transposition rather than by copying. (Alternatively we can say that in this case the right copy is always deleted).

With Objective-Dative sentences it appears that the choice of subject is determined by the verb. The verb *belong*, for example, requires the Objective to be subject, as in (40)

40. The typewriter belongs to Terry.

while the verb *be* requires the Dative as subject, as in (41).

41. Terry has the typewriter.

2.19. Verbs in the lexicon will be classified according to the propositional environments into which they may be inserted. Using brute force methods for the time being I allow options in the statement of these environments. Thus a verb like *wake up* would have the feature (42)

42. [+ _____ Obj (Inst) (Ag)]

while a verb like *kill* would have the feature (43)

[12]In my present view of the design of a grammar I hold that the lexicon may be divided into two sections, a major-category lexicon which inserts semantically relevant lexical items into underlying phrase-markers, and a minor-category lexicon which inserts "function words" into surface phrase-markers. If *be* and *have* are regarded as words in the minor-category lexicon, it will not be necessary to speak, as I have here, of "changing *be* to *have*." The structural conditions for inserting *be* and *have* will simply be different.

43. [+ _____ Obj (Inst)(Ag)]

where the linked parentheses indicate that at least one of two adjacent terms must be chosen.

For *wake up* we have sentences like (44) with Objective only; (45) with Agentive; (46) with Instrumental; and (47) with both Agentive and Instrumental in addition to the Objective.

44. I woke up.
45. My daughter woke me up.
46. An explosion woke me up.
47. My daughter woke me up with an explosion.

For *kill*, on the other hand, we have (48)–(50) but not (51).

48. Fire killed the rats.
49. Mother killed the rats.
50. Mother killed the rats with fire.
51. *The rats killed.

2.20.   Notions of synonymy can now be separated from notions of syntactic distribution. The verbs *kill* and *die*, for instance, may be given the same semantic characterizations. The relation between the verb and the Objective is the same for both words, the difference between the verbs being of a syntactic nature, in that *kill* requires a co-occurring Agent or Instrument, *die* does not allow an Agent to be directly expressed as part of the same proposition. In this respect, the essential difference between the proposals presented in this paper and those of Lakoff[13] appears to be that Lakoff seeks for "synonymous" words identity of semantic reading and what he calls the *lexical base*, but not identity in *lexical extension*; I seek only identity of semantic reading. In other words, I do not expect to find in formal grammars support for the distributional definition of meaning.

III.   I believe that certain advantages derive from incorporating into a transformational grammar the proposals that have just been sketched, in addition to the possibly unimportant one that sentences do not turn out to need quite so much branching structure as they do in grammars that need to recognize syntactic relations in terms of immediate-domination relation between categories.

3.1.   One of the specific advantages of my interpretation of *have* is in the simplification this analysis allows to the relative clause reduction rule.

I have said that the Objective preposition in sentences with Datives, Locatives, or Comitatives but without Instrumentals and Agentives is *with*. The prep-

[13]See George Lakoff, *On the Nature of Syntactic Irregularity* (Ph.D. dissertation, Indiana University), *Mathematical Linguistics and Automatic Translation*, Harvard Computation Laboratory, Report No. NSF-16, 1965.

osition appears in this form in a sentence like (26), but it disappears after *be* under those conditions which ordinarily change *be* to *have*, as in (52).

52. The garden has bees in it.

In older versions of the grammar of English, one relative clause reduction rule was needed for relative-clause-plus-*be*, changing (53) into (54)

53. the boy who is in the next room
54. the boy in the next room

and another rule was needed for relative-pronoun-plus-*have*, changing (55) into (56).

55. the boy who has the red hat
56. the boy with the red hat

The first of these rules deleted the identified element, the second replaced the identified element by *with*.

If it is true, however, that *have*, abstractly, is *be* before Objectives, then a single rule will now cover both of these cases. From (53) we get (54) and from (57) we get (56).

57. the boy who is with the red hat

We need to require only that the relative-clause reduction rule precede the rules for creating *have* and deleting *with* after *be*.[14]

3.2. Notions like that of the "understood agent" can be clarified within this scheme. There is a distinction, in other words, between not choosing an Agent on the one hand, and choosing an Agent and subsequently deleting it on the other hand. The distinction is revealed in the choice of preposition.

The verb *kill*, I have said, must take either Instrumental or Agentive and may take both. The Instrumental preposition is *by* if there is no Agentive present, otherwise it is *with*. The Agentive — as in the case of passive sentences — may be a dummy.

Suppose that we construct passive sentences with *kill* where the Objective is *the rats* and the Instrumental is *fire*. In one case we will omit an Agentive, in the other case the Agentive will be chosen but it will be a dummy. Where the Agentive is present in the deep structure, the Instrumental preposition is *with*; where there is no Agentive, the Instrumental preposition is *by*. Since the Agentive is a dummy, it gets deleted.

The resulting sentences are (58) and (59).

58. The rats were killed by fire.
59. The rats were killed with fire.

[14]But see footnote 12.

If my analysis is correct, there is an "understood agent" in the sentence with *with*.

Incidentally, the earlier examples with *open* were a little misleading. I implied that in a sentence like (60)

60. The door was opened with this key.

the underlying representation of the sentence contained only the actants Objective and Instrumental. If the above observations on *with* and *by* are true, however, the sentence should actually be understood as having an implied human agent, and it should be distinct in this respect from a sentence like (61); and I believe it is.

61. The door was opened by the wind.

3.3.   More general advantages associated with these proposals relate to the interpretation of historical changes and cross-language differences in lexical structure.

3.3.1.   Certain historical changes in language may turn out to be purely syntactic, and, in fact, may pertain exclusively to the status of particular lexical items as exceptions to given transformations, in the sense of Lakoff. Thus the English verb *like* did not change in its meaning or in its selection for Objective-Dative sentences, but only in its status as an exception to the rule that fronted actants are neutralized to the so-called nominative form.

3.3.2.   Lexical differences across languages may not be as great as we might otherwise have thought. It would ordinarily be said that English *kill* and Japanese *korosu* have different "meanings" because the Japanese verb requires an animate subject while English allows us to say that *fire killed him, a falling stone killed him*, and the like. Once we see that even in English both *kill* and *die* have the same underlying semantic representation, the difference between the two situations appears to be rather superficial. Both languages have words with the same meaning which can co-occur with Objective and Instrumental. English has two such verbs, one of which allows the Instrumental phrase to become the subject. The difference is no deeper than that.

4.   There are, as the reader may have guessed, a great many extremely serious problems which continue to be completely mysterious. Does this system provide the constituent structure needed for co-ordinate conjunction? How are predicate-adjective or predicate-noun sentences to be dealt with in this scheme? Do manner adverbials belong inside the proposition or are they part of the modality? How is the relation sometimes found between manner adverbials and the "subject" of the sentence to be expressed in this system? What about the generalizations on noun phrase interchange? Many of these problems, fortunately, are no *less* serious in subject-object grammars.

I could summarize my remarks by saying that I regard each simple sentence in a language as made up of a verb and a collection of nouns in various "cases" in the deep structure sense. In the surface structure, case distinctions are sometimes preserved, sometimes not - depending on the language, depending on the noun, or depending on idiosyncratic properties of certain governing words. Belief in the superficiality of grammatical case rises from consideration of the "nominative," which really constitutes a case neutralization that affects noun phrases that have been made the subject of a sentence, and of the "genitive," which represents another kind of neutralization of case distinctions, one which occurs in noun phrase modifiers derived from sentences, as illustrated by the reduction to the so-called "genitive" of both Agentive and Objective in such expressions as *the shooting of the hunters*.

Irregularity in Syntax

GEORGE LAKOFF

ADJECTIVES AND VERBS

We will try to present a case for the plausibility of the assertion that adjectives and verbs, are members of a single lexical category (which we will call **VERB**) and that they differ only by a single syntactic feature (which we will call AD-JECTIVAL).

Of the arguments given below, 1, 4, 5, 7, and 9 were worked out by Paul Postal and by the author, working independently. Arguments 2, 6, and 8 are due solely to Postal; 3 was pointed out by Lester Rice.

1. Grammatical Relations

There are a great many pairs of sentences — in which one contains a verb where the other contains an adjective — that are understood in the same way. For example,

1. a. I regret that.   (A-1)
   b. I am sorry about that.
2. a. I like jazz.
   b. I am fond of jazz.
3. a. I forgot that fact.
   b. I was oblivious of that fact.
4. a. I know about that.
   b. I am cognizant of that.
   b. I am aware of that.

There are other pairs of the same sort, where the adjective and verb seem to be the same lexical item.

1. a. I desire that.   (A-2)
   b. I am desirous of that.
2. a. John hopes that peace will come soon.
   b. John is hopeful that peace will come soon.
3. a. I fear that the Dodgers will win.
   b. I am fearful that the Dodgers will win.

(from George Lakoff, *Irregularity in Syntax*, N.Y.: Holt, 1970, pp. 115–33.)

4. a. John considers Mary's feelings.
   b. John is considerate of Mary's feelings.
5. a. That will please John.
   b. That will be pleasing to John.
6. a. That excites me.
   b. That is exciting to me.
7. a. Our actions in the Dominican Republic appall me.
   b. Our actions in the Dominican Republic are appalling to me.
8. a. Massachusetts politics amuses me.
   b. Massachusetts politics is amusing to me.
9. a. Cigarettes harm people.
   b. Cigarettes are harmful to people.
10. a. The President's decision surprised me.
    b. The President's decision was surprising to me.

In most of the above cases, the *a* and *b* sentences differ only in that the *b* sentences contain *be* + adjective + preposition where the *a* sentences contain a verb. These differences are quite superficial. The auxiliary verb, *be*, serves only to carry the tense marker before adjectives, in just the same way as *do* carries the tense marker before verbs in negative and question sentences. Although no preposition appears after the verb in the surface structure of the *a* sentences, there is good reason to believe that the preposition is there on some level of analysis, since prepositions do show up when verbs are nominalized. Thus we get:

a. My fear *of* rain . . .⟷I fear rain.　　　　　　　　　　　(A-3)
b. My liking *for* jazz . . .⟷I like jazz.
c. John's desire *for* Mary . . .⟷John desires Mary.
d. John's consideration *of* Mary's feelings . . .
　 ⟷John considers Mary's feelings.

It appears that there is a late rule in English which drops prepositions after verbs that have not been nominalized. It is a moot question whether such prepositions appear in the deep structures of the above sentences or whether they are introduced by "spelling rules" which insert them before the object noun phrase as a kind of case marking. I will assume that the latter is the case, though this assumption will not matter in any of the following arguments. Similarly, it is not clear at present whether tense markings should be introduced as part of an auxiliary constituent or as features of verbs and adjectives, which are later inserted before the adjective or verb by spelling rules. I will assume the latter, though again the arguments to follow will be independent of this assumption.

It seems highly significant that the *a* and *b* sentences of (A-1) and (A-2) are understood in the same way and this fact seems to be a consequence of the presence of the same grammatical relationships in each pair of sentences. For example, in the sentences *I like John* and *I am fond of John, fond* seems to bear the same relation to *John* as *like* bears to *John*. And *John* seems to bear the same relation to *like* as it does to *fond*. But, in order for *like* and *fond* to be involved in the same grammatical relations, they would have to be members of the same lexical category.

Of course, just because the *a* and *b* sentences of (A-1) and (A-2) are synonymous and seem to be understood in the same way, it does not necessarily follow that the same grammatical relations hold in each pair of sentences. It might very well be the case that the semantic component of a grammar of English might have projection rules that interpret two different sets of grammatical relations as though they were identical. Thus, it might be the case that the projection rules of English interpret the following two structures in exactly the same way:

a.

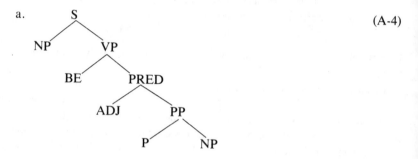

(A-4)

b.

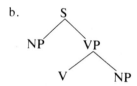

Though we do not rule this alternative out as a possibility, we would argue that the semantic component would be simpler if it had to contain only projection rules to interpret one of these structures. Still, such a simplification in the semantic component could be offset if our assumption were to hopelessly complicate the syntactic component of a grammar of English. As we will try to show below, this does not seem to be the case. We will argue that, just as we do not lose anything semantically by making this assumption, so we do not lose anything syntactically either. On the contrary, it seems that this assumption points the way to greater syntactic generalization.

We ought to present some examples of the kinds of grammatical analyses that we have in mind. We would represent the derivations of *I like John* and *I am fond of John* as in (A-5). Note that the deep structures of these sentences a.(i) and b.(i) are nearly identical.

a.(i) Deep Structure   (A-5)

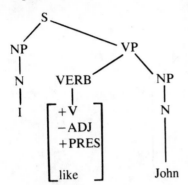

(ii) Prep-Spelling

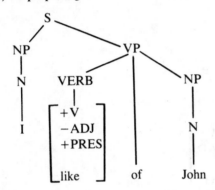

(Note, if nominalization occurred at this point in the derivation, we would get *my liking of John*.)

(iii) Prep-Deletion

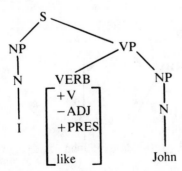

b.(i) Deep Structure

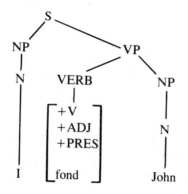

(ii) Tense-Spelling

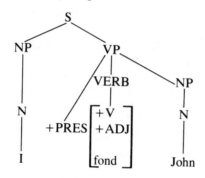

(iii) Prep-Spelling

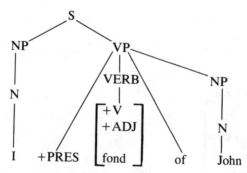

(iv) Be-Addition

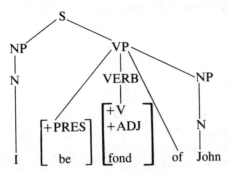

2. Selectional Restrictions

Perhaps the most striking syntactic similarity between adjectives and verbs is the fact that they take almost all of the same contextual restrictions. Taking into account, as we did in the preceding section, that the presence of *be* in front of adjectives and prepositions after them is a superficial phenomenon, we can speak of transitive adjectives, just as we can speak of transitive verbs, as having the feature [+___NP]. All of the adjectives in (A-1) and (A-2) are examples. Similarly, we can speak of intransitive adjectives, just as we can speak of intransitive verbs. For example,

    a. John is alive.   (A-6)
    b. John walks.

Both have the feature [+___#].

    Moreover, adjectives and verbs can take the same kinds of subjects and objects.

    a. Animate subject: (A-7)
        I know that fact.
        I am aware of that fact.
        *The rock knows that fact.
        *The rock is aware of that fact.
    b. Physical object subject:
        The box weighs a lot.
        The box is very heavy.
        *Sincerity weighs a lot.
        *Sincerity is very heavy.
    c. Abstract subject:
        His running away meant that we would have to leave.
        His running away was equivalent to treason.

   *The rock meant that we would have to leave.
   *The rock was equivalent to treason.
   d. Animate objects:
   Bill hurt John.
   Bill was brutal to John.
   *Bill hurt the rock.
   *Bill was brutal to the rock.
   e. Abstract objects:
   Bill understood the idea.
   Bill was receptive to the idea.
   *Bill understood the rock.
   *Bill was receptive to the rock.

Adjectives and verbs also take many of the same types of adverbials.

   a. Time adverbials: (A-8)
   They were noisy all night.
   They caroused all night.
   They were noisy till 4 A.M.
   They caroused till 4 A.M.
   They were being noisy at midnight.
   They were carousing at midnight.
   They are often noisy.
   They often carouse.
   b. Locative adverbials:
   They were being noisy in the living room.
   They were carousing in the living room.
   c. Manner adverbials:
   They were being noisy deliberately.
   They were screaming deliberately.

3. Stative and Nonstative Verbs and Adjectives

Both adjectives and verbs can be subcategorized with respect to the feature
STATIVE (or NONACTIVITY) and as a result, both can undergo, or fail to
undergo, rules conditioned by that feature.

   a. Imperative: (A-9)
   Look at the picture.
   *Know that Bill went there.
   Don't be noisy.
   *Don't be tall.
   b. Do-something:
   What I'm doing is looking at the picture.
   *What I'm doing is knowing that Bill went there.

What I'm doing is being noisy.
*What I'm doing is being tall.
c. Progressive:
I'm looking at the picture.
*I'm knowing that Bill went there.
I'm being noisy.
*I'm being tall.

The subcategorization of these verbs and adjectives with respect to the feature STATIVE is the following:

	look at	know	noisy	tall
STATIVE	−	+	−	+

Note that if we do not assume that verbs and adjectives belong to the same major category, the rules that yield a, b, and c above will all have to refer to both verbs and adjectives in the same place in the structural description of each rule. That is, one term of the SD in each rule will be: $\left\{ \begin{array}{c} \text{verb} \\ \text{adjective} \end{array} \right\}$. For three rules to have the same disjunction of different major categories in their structural descriptions would be somewhat coincidental. As we shall see below, there are more than three such rules. Indeed, there are so many more that we can effectively rule out coincidence.

4. The Adjective Shift

There are two rules in English which are necessary to derive the common adjectival construction that appears in *the tall man* from relative clauses like *the man who is tall*. The first rule, call it WH-DEL, deletes the sequence WH + PRONOUN + BE when preceded by a noun and followed by either an adjective or a verb $\left\{ \begin{array}{c} \text{adjective} \\ \text{verb} \end{array} \right\}$. WH-DEL will convert *the man who is tall* into *the man tall*, *the child who is sleeping soundly* into *the child sleeping soundly*, and *the man who is in the yard* into *the man in the yard*. Following WH-DEL, there is an obligatory rule which converts *the man tall* into *the tall man*. Call this ADJ-SHIFT. ADJ-SHIFT permutes a noun with a following adjective or verb $\left\{ \begin{array}{c} \text{adjective} \\ \text{verb} \end{array} \right\}$ when both are dominated by a noun phrase which immediately dominates the noun.

The following derivations result from applying WH-DEL and ADJ-SHIFT in that order.

The man who was murdered ⟹ the murdered man   (A-10)
The man who is dead ⟹ the dead man
The child who is sleeping ⟹ the sleeping child

The child who is quiet $\Longrightarrow$ the quiet child
The dog that is barking $\Longrightarrow$ the barking dog
The dog that is noisy $\Longrightarrow$ the noisy dog

Thus, we have examples of two more rules that apply to $\begin{Bmatrix} \text{adjective} \\ \text{verb} \end{Bmatrix}$

Note, by the way, that **ADJ-SHIFT** as we have described it is not adequately formulated. The rule that we gave will not account for the following derivations:

The child who is soundly sleeping $\Longrightarrow$ the soundly sleeping child   (A-11)

The boy who is occasionally obnoxious $\Longrightarrow$ the occasionally obnoxious boy

Our first guess as to how these may be derived might be that instead of permuting $\begin{Bmatrix} \text{adjective} \\ \text{verb} \end{Bmatrix}$ in **ADJ-SHIFT**, we should permute the entire verb phrase. If this is so, it would nullify our argument that $\begin{Bmatrix} \text{adjective} \\ \text{verb} \end{Bmatrix}$ must appear in the structural description of **ADJ-SHIFT**. However, if we adopt this suggestion, we cannot account for the nonoccurrence of the following derivations:

The child who is sleeping soundly $\not\Longrightarrow$ *the sleeping soundly child   (A-12)

The boy who is obnoxious occasionally $\not\Longrightarrow$ *the obnoxious occasionally boy

To account for this phenomenon we must hypothesize that the permuted element in **ADJ-SHIFT** is a verb phrase that ends in $\begin{Bmatrix} \text{adjective} \\ \text{verb} \end{Bmatrix}$. In fact, we must modify this proposal to include the condition that the verb phrase must immediately dominate the final $\begin{Bmatrix} \text{adjective} \\ \text{verb} \end{Bmatrix}$ in order to account for the fact that we can have derivation a of (A-13) but not b or c of (A-13).

a. John is a man who is hard to please $\Longrightarrow$
    John is a hard man to please   (A-13)

b. John is a man who is able to run $\not\Longrightarrow$ *John is an able man to run

c. John is a man who is able to run $\not\Longrightarrow$ *John is an able to run man

ADJ-SHIFT would apply to a tree of the form

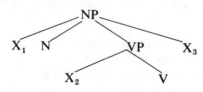

and would map such trees into trees of the form

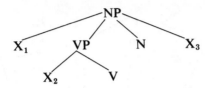

The fact that we get *a* but not *b* is due to the fact that the derived constituent structures of the two sentences are different.

a starts out in the embedded clause as

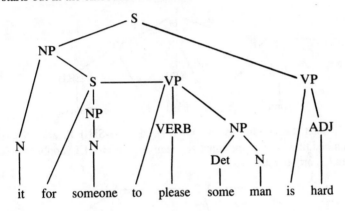

This gets transformed to:

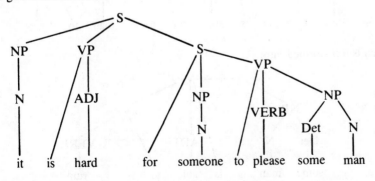

This becomes:

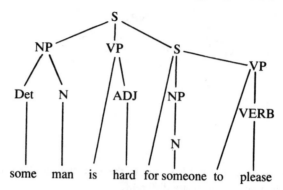

which, after the deletion of *for someone*, becomes,

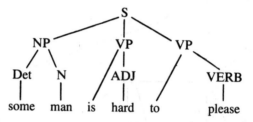

This will meet the conditions for our revised ADJ-SHIFT, after the relative clause embedding rule pronominalizes *man* and WH-DEL applies. *b*, on the other hand, starts out as:

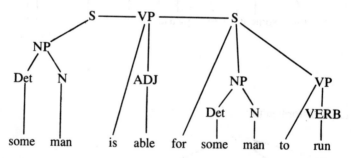

which is transformed into:

This structure will not meet the structural description of our revised ADJ-SHIFT rule, after the relative clause rule and WH-DEL apply.

5. Nominalizations

Adjectives and verbs both undergo the same factive, action, and manner nominalizations. Since the structures that result from these rules look identical, it is not certain whether there is a single rule that operates to produce these structures, or whether there is a battery of separate, but partially similar, rules. If the former is the case, then there is at least one more rule in a grammar of English that refers to $\left\{ \begin{array}{c} \text{adjective} \\ \text{verb} \end{array} \right\}$. If there is more than one such rule, then our case is that much stronger.

The following are some examples of such nominalizations:

John knows that fact $\Longrightarrow$ John's knowledge of that fact (A-14)
John is cognizant of that fact $\Longrightarrow$ John's cognizance of that fact
John yelled $\Longrightarrow$ John's yelling
John was noisy $\Longrightarrow$ John's noisiness
John distrusted Bill $\Longrightarrow$ John's distrust of Bill
John was wary of Bill $\Longrightarrow$ John's wariness of Bill

6. Subject-Object Interchange

It seems necessary to postulate a transformation that interchanges the subject and object of some adjectives and verbs, in order to account for the relationships between pairs of sentences like the following:

a. What he did amused me. (A-15)
   I was amused at what he did.
b. What he did surprised me.
   I was surprised at what he did.
c. What he had done pleased her.
   She was pleased at what he had done.
d. His explanation satisfied me.
   I was satisfied with his explanation.
e. I enjoy movies.
   Movies are enjoyable to me.

We will call this transformation FLIP. In a-d, FLIP has applied to the sentence containing the verb. In e, it has applied to the sentence containing the adjective. We know this from our intuitions about what the underlying subjects and objects are, and these intuitions are strengthened by the fact that they are mirrored in actual data, since the underlying subject-object relation is unchanged under nominalization. This is clear in the following examples.

a. My amusement at what he did   (A-16)
b. My surprise at what he did
c. Her pleasure at what he had done
d. My satisfaction with his explanation
e. My enjoyment of movies

The FLIP rule can also account for the fact that in   (A-17)

a. What he had done pleased her   (A-17)
b. She liked what he had done

she seems to bear the same relation to *like* as *her* bears to *please*. We can describe this fact easily if we assume that either *a* or *b* has undergone FLIP.

From the nominalization of *b*,

Her liking of what he had done   (A-18)

it is clear that *a*, not *b*, has undergone FLIP.

FLIP is then another rule of English which applies to either adjectives or verbs and which must refer to $\left\{ \begin{array}{c} \text{adjective} \\ \text{verb} \end{array} \right\}$ in its structural description.

7.   Object Deletion

Object deletion is a common phenomenon in English. There is a rule which deletes indefinite direct object pronouns optionally after certain verbs. For example,

a. John is eating something $\Longrightarrow$ John is eating   (A-19)
b. John is drinking something $\Longrightarrow$ John is drinking

There is also a rule that optionally deletes a preposition and an indefinite pronoun after certain adjectives. For instance,

a. The movie was enjoyable to
   someone $\Longrightarrow$ The movie was enjoyable   (A-20)
b. The results are suggestive of
   something $\Longrightarrow$ The results are suggestive
c. The movie was objectionable
   to someone $\Longrightarrow$ The movie was objectionable

Considering that the occurrence of a preposition after an adjective is a superficial feature of English [see (A-1)], then the indefinite pronouns deleted in (A-20) are actually in direct object position, and the rule that deletes them is actually the same as the rule that deletes such pronouns in (A-19). Here is another rule that applies both in the case of adjectives and verbs.

8. Agent Nominals

Both adjectives and verbs may be transformed into agent nouns. For example,

(A-21)

a. She is beautiful.
   She is a beauty.
b. He is idiotic.
   He is an idiot.
c. John is foolish.
   John is a fool.
d. John cooks.
   John is a cook.
e. John kills men.
   John is a killer of men.
f. John destroys houses.
   John is a destroyer of houses.

(I assume that the adjective endings -*ful*, -*ic*, -*ish*, are added by late spelling rules onto adjectives that have not been transformed into nouns.)

Note that adverbs that modify verbs and adjectives are transformed into adjectives when the agent rule applies. For instance,

(A-22)

a. She is really beautiful.
   She is a real beauty.
b. He is utterly idiotic.
   He is an utter idiot.
c. John is completely foolish.
   John is a complete fool.
d. John cooks well.
   John is a good cook.
e. John kills men mercilessly.
   John is a merciless killer of men.
f. John destroys houses professionally.
   John is a professional destroyer of houses.

Thus, AGENT is another rule that applies to both adjectives and verbs.

9. Complements

Both adjectives and verbs seem to be able to take the same variety of subject, object, and predicate complements, and the same complement rules seem to apply regardless of whether an adjective or verb is present. A detailed justification of this assertion is impossible here, and though none has yet appeared in the literature, P. S. Rosenbaum [1967, Chapter 6] discusses some of the similarities between adjectives and verbal complements.

Instead, I will try to make a case for the plausibility of the assertion by presenting some examples of sentences with verb and adjective complements that seem to have the same underlying structure and seem to have undergone the same rules.

    a. John wants to go.   (A-23)
       John is eager to go.
    b. John knew that Bill had done it.
       John was aware that Bill had done it.
    c. John feared that Bill would come.
       John was afraid that Bill would come.
    d. John can hit a ball 400 feet.
       John is able to hit a ball 400 feet.
    e. John hesitated to do that.
       John was reluctant to do that.
    f. It happened that John left.
       It is likely that John will leave.
    g. John happened to leave.
       John is likely to leave.

A more complicated example is the following:

    a. I need to know that.   (A-24)
    b. It is necessary for me to know that.

Sentence *a* is straightforward.

a. i.

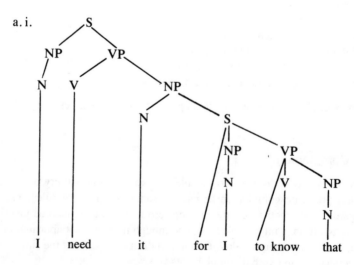

Deletion of embedded subject under identity: (ID-NP-DEL).

ii.

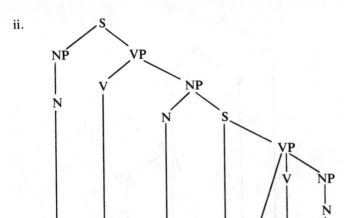

IT-DELETION

iii.

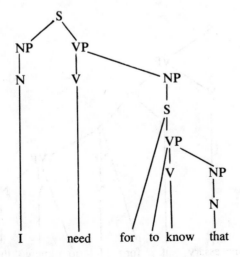

FOR-DELETION

iv.

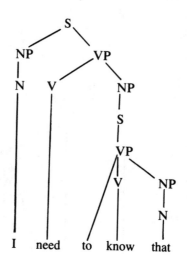

b.i.

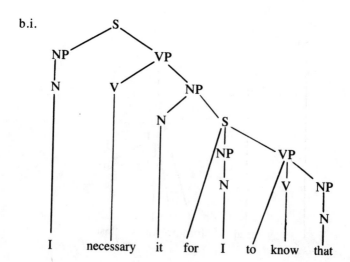

ID-NP-DEL

ii.

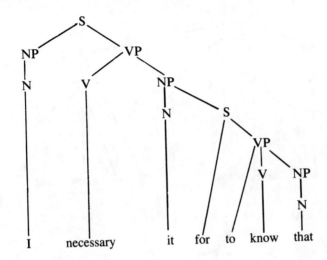

FLIP

iii.

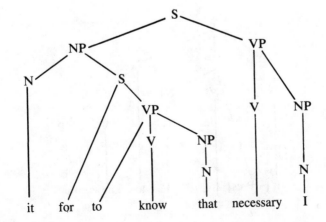

EXTRAPOSITION

iv.

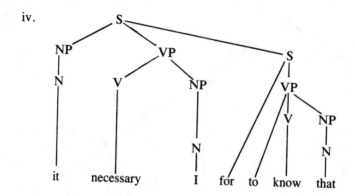

FOR-DELETION

v.

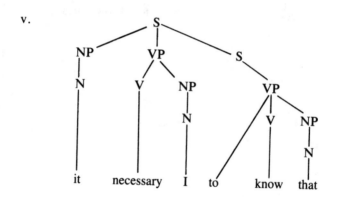

TENSE-SPELLING

vi.

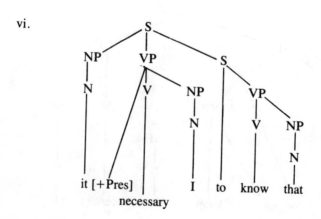

PREP-SPELLING

vii.

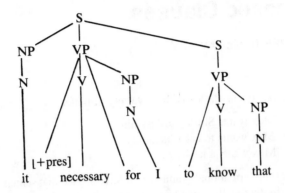

BE ADDITION

viii.

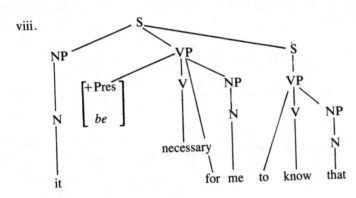

Conclusion:

We have seen that there are at least ten very general rules of English in which adjectives and verbs are treated identically. This hardly seems accidental. If it were, we would expect to find just as many transformational rules in which verbs and nouns were treated identically — or in which nouns and adjectives were treated identically. This is not the case.

These considerations are mirrored by considerations of generality. If we postulate a single category, **VERB**, we will save one symbol for each occurrence of $\begin{Bmatrix} \text{adjective} \\ \text{verb} \end{Bmatrix}$ in the transformatial nal rules of English, and so achieve some greater generality. Thus, our assert on not only simplifies the semantic component somewhat, but also does the same for the syntactic component.

On Identifying the Remains of Deceased Clauses

JAMES D. McCAWLEY

The verb *want* occurs followed by a variety of material:

1. a. Max wants Shirley to kiss him.
   b. Max wants to eat a banana.
   c. Max wants a lollipop.

Numerous transformational grammarians have argued that sentences of the forms (1a) and (1b) involve the same kind of underlying structure, namely one in which *want* has a sentence object, and differ only as regards whether the subject of the embedded sentence is deleted. Specifically, a rule of Equi-NP-deletion is posited, which deletes the subject of the complement of *want* if it is identical to the subject of *want*:

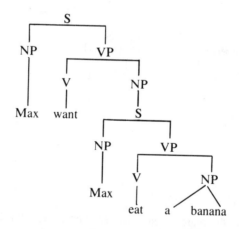

I will argue below that sentences of the form (1c) also have an underlying structure in which *want* has a sentential object, and that the surface object of *want* in (1c) is in fact the residue of an embedded clause. I will be concerned first with demonstrating that there IS an underlying embedded clause in sentences like (1c), and then with determining exactly what that clause is. There is in fact a fairly obvious analysis of (1c) in which *want* has a sentential object, namely that in which it has the same underlying structure as *Max wants to have a lollipop* and

(Reprinted from *Language Research*, Vol. 9, No. 2, December, 1973, Language Research Institute, Seoul National University, Seoul, Korea, pp. 73–83.)

undergoes not only Equi-NP-deletion but also deletion of the verb of the embedded clause, and it is in fact that analysis (or at least, something very close to it) which I will be presenting justification for.

The first argument that the surface object in sentences like (1c) is the residue of an embedded clause has to do with time adverbs. The time adverbs in

2. Bill wants your apartment $\begin{cases} \text{until June.} \\ \text{for 6 months.} \\ \text{while you're in Botswana.} \end{cases}$

do not give the time when the wanting takes place, as is especially clear when one considers sentences such as

3. Right now Bill wants your apartment until June, but tomorrow he'll probably want it until October.

in which there is another time adverb which explicitly indicates another time as the time when the wanting takes place. If an embedded clause such as *Bill have your apartment* is posited, that clause can serve as the scope of the time adverb (i.e., in (2) *until June* is not the time when Bill's wanting takes place but the time when Bill is to have your apartment if his wish is to be satisfied). Without such an embedded clause, there is nothing that the time adverbs can plausibly be taken as modifying.

Two other arguments are closely related to this one. First, positing an underlying sentence object with *want* allows a ready explanation of why clauses with *want* can have two time adverbs, as contrasted with verbs such as *paint*, for which such an analysis would be senseless and which allow only one time adverb:

4. a. A week ago Bill wanted your car yesterday.
   b. *A week ago Bill painted your car yesterday.

Secondly, the hypothesis allows one to explain which of the two time adverbs controls the tense of *want*. In simple sentences, *yesterday* allows past tense but not future tense, and *tomorrow* allows future tense but not past tense:

5. a. Yesterday I played 10 Scarlatti sonatas.
   a'. *Yesterday I'll play 10 Scarlatti sonatas.
   b. Tomorrow I'll play 10 Scarlatti sonatas.
   b'. *Tomorrow I played 10 Scarlatti sonatas.

In the following sentence,[1] the tense is determined by *yesterday*, not by *tomorrow*:

6. a. Yesterday Bill wanted your bicycle tomorrow.
   b. *Yesterday Bill will want your bicycle tomorrow.

[1]This example was brought to my attention by Masaru Kajita.

If *want* in fact has a sentence object, the only coherent interpretation of the adverbs in (6a) is that in which *yesterday* modifies the main clause and *tomorrow* the embedded clause. Each time adverb controls the tense of the clause that it modifies, and thus *yesterday* rather than *tomorrow* controls the tense of *want* in (6a). The hypothesis that (1c) arises through deletion from a structure with a sentence object thus gives one a way of predicting when *tomorrow* can co-occur with a past tense verb.

The next argument is based on facts that are more within the domain of logic than of what is usually regarded as grammar. The sentence *Max wanted a lollipop* is ambiguous between a "referential" sense which implies that there is a lollipop such that Max wanted it, and a "non-referential" sense which does not imply that. The referential sense has to do with a desire to have a specific lollipop; having that specific lollipop will satisfy Max's desire and having any other lollipop will not suffice to satisfy it. The non-referential sense has to do with a desire that will be satisfied when Max has a lollipop, regardless of the identity of the lollipop. Quine (1960:154–6), discussing examples such as *Ernest is looking for a lion,* observed that that apparently simple sentence displays the same ambiguity as does the complex sentence *Ernest is trying to find a lion* and that the logical properties of the former can be accounted for in a natural way if one analyzes it as having the same logical structure as the latter. Specifically, let us assume that logicians are correct in representing the content of a simple sentence such as *Sam kicked a dog* by factoring out a quantifier and an associated noun:

7. (Some x : x is a dog) (Sam kicked x)

which may be recast in tree form as

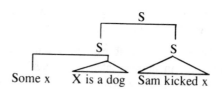

When applied to a complex sentence such as *Ernest tried to find a lion*, this factorization could take place on either the main or the subordinate clause, yielding the following two structures (8a) and (8b). (8a) is a natural way to represent the referential interpretation and (8b) the non-referential interpretation, since in each case the complement of *try* correctly matches the conditions for success of the attempt, and only (8a) implies the existence of a lion that figures in Ernest's attempt; Quine thus proposes these structures as representing the logical structure of the two senses of *Ernest is trying to find a lion* (and also of the two senses of *Ernest is looking for a lion*).

8.a.

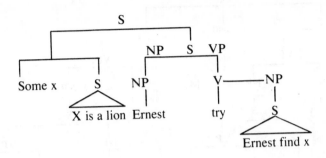

8.b.

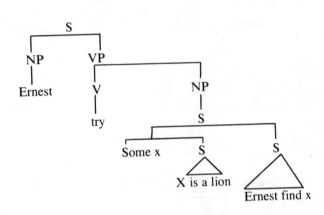

Note, however, that Quine's mode of representing the content of the non-referential interpretation is possible only if there is an embedded clause to serve as the scope of the quantifier. Thus, positing an underlying sentential object in (1c) allows one in a natural way to represent its nonreferential interpretation and correctly predicts that *Max wanted a lollipop* allows a non-referential interpretation but *Max ate a lollipop*, in which it would be absurd to posit a sentential object, does not.[2]

The last argument had to do with whether a quantifier applied to the main clause or the hypothesized subordinate clause, and the first group of arguments had to do with whether an adverb applies to the main clause or the hypothesized subordinate clause. A similar argument can be made having to do with conjoining. If *want* in fact has a sentential object in (1c), then there is nothing in principle to prevent both of the structures (9a) and (9b) from being realized as *Max wants a cup and a saucer*.

[2]It is far from clear that ALL non-referential NP's can be taken as originating in subordinate clauses. Such an analysis is particularly hard to justify in such cases as *John imagined a polar bear*, which Richard Montague indeed took as reason for rejecting Quine's account of non-referential NP's.

9.a.

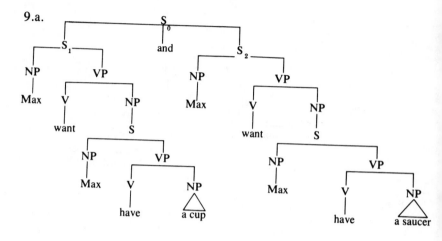

9.b.

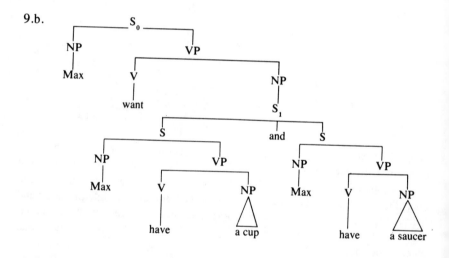

In (9a), both S_1 and S_2 would undergo Equi-NP-deletion and deletion of *have* and then S_0 would undergo conjunction reduction; in (9b), S_1 would undergo conjunction reduction, yielding *Max have a cup and a saucer*, and then S_0 would be of the appropriate form to undergo Equi-NP-deletion and deletion of *have*. *Max wants a cup and a saucer* is in fact ambiguous between a sense that fits (9a) and one that fits (9b): in the one case it refers to two independent desires one for a cup and one for a saucer, and in the other case it refers to a single desire which is satisfied by Max's having both a cup and saucer.[3] The same is true of conjunction with *or*: *Max wants a Cadillac or a Volkswagen* is ambiguous between a sense that implies that either he wants a Cadillac or he wants a Volkswagen (parallel to (9a)) and a sense that refers to a single desire which will be satisfied when he has either a Cadillac or a Volkswagen (parallel to (9b)). Not only does the hypothetical subordinate clause provide a natural way of distinguishing between these two interpretations, but it also allows one to maintain the otherwise valid generalization that constituents conjoined with *or* always arise through conjuncton reduction from conjoined sentences.[4] Unless *want* has as underlying sentence object, there is no way in which *a Cadillac or a Volkswagen* could be derived by conjunction reduction in the sense which refers to a single desire, since that sense does not mean the same as *Max wants a Cadillac or he wants a Volkswagen.*

The next argument has to do with the pronoun-antecedent relation. At first glance, the antecedent of *it* in (10a) appears to be *a horse*; however, if the antecedent were *a horse*, then replacement of *a horse* by something of a different gender or number ought to give rise to a different pronoun, though in fact it does not:

10. a. Joe wants a horse, but his mother won't allow it.
    b. Joe wants some horses, but his mother won't allow it/ *them.
    c. Joe wants a wife, but his mother won't allow it/ *her.

In addition, if the antecedent of *it* were *a horse*, then it ought to be possible to use *allow* with an object that refers to a horse; however, *allow* requires a sentential object:

11. Joe's mother won't allow $\left\{ \begin{array}{l} \text{*Dobbin} \\ \text{*that horse} \\ \text{Joe to have a horse.} \end{array} \right.$

All of these facts are explained if *want* is taken as having an underlying sentence object: the antecedent of *it* in (10) can then be taken to be the sentence *Joe have a horse*, the pronoun will be *it*, since sentences count as neuter singular, and *allow* will not require anything other than the kind of object that it usually takes.

A further fact about pronominalization also supports the analysis with a sentential object, namely that the following sentence is interpreted as having a referential object if the pronoun is *them* and a non-referential object if the pronoun is *that*.[5]

12. Bill wants a Cadillac and a Volkswagen, and his girl-friend wants them/that too.

[3]Kenny (1963:122) observes that these two senses correspond to quite different states of affairs.

[4]See McCawley (1972) for arguments in support of this claim.

[5]This argument is due to Judith N. Levi.

That can serve as the pronominal form of a sentence, but *them* cannot. *Them* would have to refer to the Cadillac and Volkswagen, which it could do only if the quantifier(s) binding *Cadillac* and *Volkswagen* has/have the whole sentence as scope, in which case *a Cadillac* and *a Volkswagen* have a referential interpretation.

I will henceforth take it as established that *want* has a sentential object in sentences like *Max wants a lollipop* and turn to the question of exactly what the deleted verb is. The question divides into a number of subsidiary questions: (i) Is there one specific verb that has been deleted, or can any of several verbs be deleted, i.e. can sentences with *want* be ambiguous as to what verb has been deleted? (ii) Is a word of English deleted, or is some semantic material deleted? This latter question has to be asked if one accepts the framework that I currently do, in which a grammar is a single system of rules that relate semantic structures to surface structures via intermediate stages. The grammar includes not only deletion rules, movement rules, and copying rules, but also rules that combine semantic units into complex units, and lexical insertion rules, which associate morphemes of the specific language to complexes of semantic material. Since there is no reason to expect that the lexical insertion rules will apply before all deletion rules (nor that they will apply after all deletion rules), it cannot be assumed from the outset either that a word of English is deleted or that semantic material is deleted.

The following sentences appear to be ambiguous as to what has been deleted:

13. a. I want more money than Sam has.
    b. Bill wants six children.
    c. Sam wants a million dollars.

These sentences allow semantically distinct paraphrases involving *have* and *get*. This is perhaps clearest in the case of (13c). Assume that Sam currently has $900,000. The sense paraphraseable as *Sam wants to have a million dollars* implies that Sam's desire will be satisfied if he increases his present wealth by $100,000; the sense paraphraseable as *Sam wants to get a million dollars* implies that Sam's desire will not be satisfied unless he gets a million dollars over and above the $900,000 that he already has. This is a real ambiguity, since the distinction between the two senses is respected by rules of grammar; for example,

14. Sam wants a million dollars, and so does Bert.

is appropriate in the case where each of them wants to have a million dollars or in the case where each of them wants to get a million dollars over and above what he presently has, but not in the case where one of them wants to have a million dollars and the other wants to get a million dollars.

The second question raises a more general question: how could you tell whether lexical material or semantic material has been deleted? I have been able to think of only one way of determining which kind of material is deleted: to look at cases where words and meanings do not match neatly (e.g. idiomatic uses of a word, or cases where a word that normally may express the meaning in question is not allowed) and see whether it is the word or the meaning that determines whether deletion may take place. For example, one could argue that the word *have* is deleted by showing that to every sentence of the form *Max wants to have X*, no matter how idiomatic the combination *have X* is, there is a sentence *Max wants X* which expresses the same meaning. Or one could argue that semantic material meaning "possess" is deleted by showing that a sentence *Max wants to V X* has an equivalent *Max wants X* if and only if "V" expresses the notion "possess" but that no one verb with that meaning was appropriate in all examples. On the basis of a not very thorough tabulation of sentences with *want*, I have concluded that in one class of sentences the English verb *have* is deleted and in another class semantic material meaning "obtain" is deleted. The following sentences illustrate idiomatic uses of *have* from which *have* has been deleted:

15. I don't want a heart attack.
    I just want a good time.
    I want a word with you.
    I want sweetbreads for dinner tonight.

Have in *have a heart attack, have a good time, have a word with X*, and *have X for dinner* does not express the notion of possession but rather a variety of meanings that do not appear to be subsumable under one semantic generalization. Not quite all sentences of the form *Max wants to have X* allow deletion of *have*; for example, corresponding to the idioms *have a ball* and *have it out with*, there are no such sentences as

16. *I want a ball.
    *I want it out with Fred.

However, such cases appear to be rare enough that one can maintain that, subject to a few exceptions, all sentences of the form *X wants to have Y* allow deletion of the word *have*, not of some corresponding semantic material. The following sentences indicate that it is not always *have* that is deleted:

17. I want $10 from you by Friday.
    Fabian wanted advice from me.
    The boss wanted some originality from his employees.
    I want $50,000 a year.

To many speakers, all of these sentences sound somewhat awkward if *have* is supplied, though there is no awkwardness with *get* or such synonyms of it as *receive* or *obtain*:

18. I want to get/?have $10 from you by Friday.
    Fabian wanted to get/?have advice from me.

> The boss wanted to get/?have some originality
> from his employees.
> I want to get/? have $50,000 a year.

While each of the *have* sentences is felt to be perfectly acceptable by quite a lot of speakers, the existence of significant numbers of speakers who find them distinctly odd is enough to show that the acceptability of sentences with *have* does not fully parallel the acceptability of sentences with a deleted verb. Moreover, what is deleted in sentences like (17) can only be characterized semantically, not lexically, since idiomatic and "non-basic" senses of *get* and *receive* cannot be deleted:

19. I want to get up at 10:00.
    I want to get elected treasurer.
    I want to receive Warsaw on my radio.
20. *I want up at 10:00.
    *I want elected treasurer.
    *I want Warsaw on my radio.

It is hardly a pleasing result that in one class of cases a word is deleted and in others semantic material is deleted; however, no other result seems to fit the facts.[6]

So far I have talked only about the verb *want*. There are many other verbs which sometimes take an infinitive object and sometimes a "simple" object, and it is generally possible to give the same kinds of arguments as in the case of *want* that the "simple" object results from deleting material from an underlying sentential object. Such verbs include *promise, offer, ask for,* and *hope for*. For example, *Fred asked Sam for a cigar or a cigarette* has the same ambiguity as does *Max wants a Cadillac or a Volkswagen*, and an embedded clause is necessary to represent the sense which implies that Fred asked that Sam either give him a cigar or give him a cigarette. However, the details of the deletion vary from verb to verb. With *promise*, Equi-NP-deletion is contingent on identity with the subject, i.e. *Max promised Shirley to wash the dishes* refers to Max's washing the dishes, not to Shirley's washing them. However, if

21. Max promised Shirley a Cadillac.

involved Equi-NP-deletion plus deletion of *have*, it ought to mean that Max promised Shirley that HE would have a Cadillac, whereas it actually means that

---

[6]It will undoubtedly be of interest to investigate how this state of affairs came about. Since *want* originally meant "lack," i.e. "not possess," English quite likely went through a stage in which *X wants Y* meant "X wants to have (= possess) Y." If that is the case, then it appears that the older deletion rule has been generalized in two ways: by being allowed to cover not only "possess" but also "come to possess" and by being allowed to cover uses of *have* which do not express its core meaning of "possess." I would be interested in finding out whether this conjectural history is correct and, if so, whether the two generalizations of the deletion are independent and whether such generalizations are attested in other languages.

he promised her that SHE would have one. Thus, either (21) involves Equi-NP-deletion that is controlled by a NP other than that which normally controls it, or it involves deletion not of *have*, but of, say, *give* plus its indirect object (i.e. it would be derived from *Max promised Shirley to give her a Cadillac*).

I will conclude this paper by pointing out that the kinds of arguments that I gave above for the existence of an underlying subordinate clause are applicable not only to the relatively innocuous cases where a subordinate clause loses its identity through an optional deletion of its verb, but also to cases that must be analyzed not in terms of deletion but in terms of the incorporation of material into the meaning of a semantically complex verb. Consider, for example, the following example, due to Masaru Kajita:

22. Yesterday Bill lent me his bicycle until tomorrow.

The same kinds of arguments as before show that *until tomorrow* modifies a subordinate clause. However, (22) cannot arise through deletion of a verb, since *lend* does not allow a sentential complement:

23. *Yesterday Bill lent me to have his bicycle until tomorrow.

The only plausible way to set up a subordinate clause for *until tomorrow* to modify is to decompose *lend* into "allow to have" (plus additional material indicating e.g. that the transfer of possession is temporary) and to take *until tomorrow* as modifying the clause "I have Bill's bicycle," which would be a constituent of the semantic structure of *Bill lent me his bicycle*. A further example of an adverb which modifies a semantic constituent of a word is found in *Max closed the door temporarily*; *temporarily* gives not the time that Max's action of closing the door took place but the time that the door was to remain closed. Only if *Max closed the door* is analyzed along the lines of *Max caused (the door be closed)*[7] is there a constituent that *temporarily* can plausibly be taken as modifying. This involves taking the adjective *closed* as semantically and syntactically more basic than the transitive verb *close*. While that may be disquieting in view of the fact that *closed* obviously divides morphologically into the verb *close* and an ending, it is a fact of life that morphological complexity does not always match syntactic and semantic complexity. Jespersen, for example, has observed that *true* is to *truth* as *beautiful* is to *beauty*, i.e. if *truth* is not only morphologically but also syntactically a derivative of *true*, then *beauty* is syntactically a derivative of *beautiful*, even though morphologically it is a constituent of *beautiful*. One final example of an adverb modifying part of the meaning of a word is due to Robert Binnick (1968):

24. The sheriff of Nottingham jailed Robin Hood for four years.

This example is ambiguous as to what *for four years* modifies. In the less likely interpretation, *for four years* modifies the main clause *The sheriff of Nottingham*

---

[7]I intend here the adjective *closed*, not the passive participle.

jailed Robin Hood, and that clause must be given an iterative interpretation: that for four years the sheriff kept repeatedly jailing Robin Hood, only to have him break out of jail. In the more likely interpretation, *for four years* gives the time that Robin Hood is to be in jail, and the verb *jail* must be decomposed into something like *cause to be in jail*, so as to provide a clause for the adverb to modify (namely *Robin Hood be in jail*).[8] Exactly the same is true if the verb *jail* is replaced by *incarcerate*: *The sheriff of Nottingham incarcerated Robin Hood for four years* has the same set of interpretations as does (24) and thus requires an underlying structure containing a clause that means "Robin Hood is in jail." The fact that the verb *jail* has a corresponding noun *jail* but the verb *incarcerate* has no corresponding noun **carcer* thus has no bearing on how these sentences are to be analyzed.

I will conclude by making explicit the message of this commercial: the same kinds of considerations which support the innocuous and relatively uncontroversial deletion of *have* in *Max wants a lollipop*, an analysis which is perfectly consistent with the theory of Chomsky's *Aspects*, in which syntax and semantics are strictly segregated, also supports analyses like those of *lend* and *incarcerate*, in which the semantic constituents of words play a significant role in syntax. It thus appears that unless one is to restrict the domain of syntax so that it does not include such things as modification relations, which have traditionally been taken without question as within the domain of syntax, one must give up any boundary between syntax and semantics.

REFERENCES

BINNICK, ROBERT I. 1968. On the nature of the "lexical item." *Papers from the Fourth Regional Meeting, Chicago Linguistic Society*, 1–13.
CHOMSKY, NOAM A. 1965. *Aspects of the Theory of Syntax*. Cambridge, Mass.: MIT Press.
KENNY, ANTHONY. 1963. *Action, Emotion, and Will*. London: Kegan Paul Routledge.
MCCAWLEY, JAMES D. 1972. A program for logic. In *Semantics of Natural Language*, eds. D. Davidson and G. Harman. Dordrecht: Reidal. pp. 498–544.
QUINE, WILLARD VAN ORMAN. 1960. *Word and Object*. Cambridge, Mass.: MIT Press.

[8]Many details will have to be added to this decomposition. Robin Hood is not merely in a jail but is confined there against his will, and for many speakers the sentence does not imply that Robin Hood spent 4 years in a jail (it does not preclude his having escaped or his having been released early for good behavior) but only that he was required to be there for four years.

Fact

PAUL KIPARSKY AND CAROL KIPARSKY

The object of this paper is to explore the interrelationship of syntax and semantics in the English complement system. Our thesis is that the choice of complement type is in large measure predictable from a number of basic semantic factors. Among these we single out for special attention *presupposition* by the speaker that the complement of the sentence expresses a true proposition. It will be shown that whether the speaker presupposes the truth of a complement contributes in several important ways to determining the syntactic form in which the complement can appear in the surface structure. A possible explanation for these observations will be suggested.

I. Two syntactic paradigms

The following two lists both contain predicates which take sentences as their subjects. For reasons that will become apparent in a moment, we term them *factive* and *nonfactive*.

Factive	Nonfactive	Factive	Nonfactive
significant	likely	counts	appears
odd	sure	makes sense	happens
tragic	possible	suffices	chances
exciting	true	amuses	turns out
relevant	false	bothers	
matters	seems		

We shall be concerned with the differences in structure between sentences constructed with factive and nonfactive predicates, e.g.

> Factive: It is significant that he has been found guilty.
> Nonfactive: It is likely that he has been found guilty.

On the surface, the two seem to be identically constructed. But as soon as we replace the *that*-clauses by other kinds of expressions, a series of systematic differences between the factive and non-factive predicates begins to appear.

1. Only factive predicates allow the noun *fact* with a sentential complement consisting of a *that*-clause or a gerund to replace the simple *that*-clause. For example,

> The fact that the dog barked during the night
> The fact of the dog's barking during the night

(Reprinted from *Progress in Linguistics*, eds. M. Bierwisch and K. Heidolph, The Hague: Mouton, 1970)

can be continued by the factive predicates *is significant, bothers me*, but not by the non-factive predicates *is likely, seems to me*.

2. Only factive predicates allow the full range of gerundial constructions, and adjectival nominalizations in *-ness*, to stand in place of the *that*-clause. For example, the expressions

His being found guilty
John's having died of cancer last week
Their suddenly insisting on very detailed reports
The whiteness of the whale

can be subjects of factive predicates such as *is tragic, makes sense, suffices*, but not of non-factive predicates such as *is sure, seems, turns out*.

3. On the other hand, there are constructions which are permissible only with non-factive predicates. One such construction is obtained by turning the initial noun phrase of the subordinate clause into the subject of the main clause, and converting the remainder of the subordinate clause into an infinitive phrase. This operation converts structures of the form

It is likely that he will accomplish even more.
It seems that there has been a snowstorm.

into structures of the form

He is likely to accomplish even more.
There seems to have been a snowstorm.

We can do this with many nonfactive predicates, although some, like *possible*, are exceptions:

It is possible that he will accomplish even more.
*He is possible to accomplish even more.

However, none of the factive predicates can ever be used so:

*He is relevant to accomplish even more.
*There is tragic to have been a snowstorm.

4. For the verbs in the factive group, extraposition[1] is optional, whereas it is obligatory for the verbs in the nonfactive group. For example, the following two sentences are optional variants:

That there are porcupines in our basement makes sense to me.
It makes sense to me that there are porcupines in our basement.

---

[1]Extraposition is a term introduced by Jespersen for the placement of a complement at the end of a sentence. For recent transformational discussion of the complexities of this rule, see Ross (1967).

But in the corresponding nonfactive case the sentence with the initial *that*-clause is ungrammatical:

*That there are porcupines in our basement seems to me.
It seems to me that there are porcupines in our basement.

In the much more complex domain of object clauses, these syntactic criteria, and many additional ones, effect a similar division into factive and nonfactive predicates. The following lists contain predicates of these two types:

Factive	*Nonfactive*	*Factive*	*Nonfactive*
regret	suppose	ignore	believe
be aware (of)	assert	make clear	conclude
grasp	allege	mind	conjecture
comprehend	assume	forget (about)	intimate
take into	claim	deplore	deem
consideration	charge	resent	fancy
take into	maintain	care (about)	figure
account			
bear in mind			

1. Only factive predicates can have as their objects the noun *fact* with a gerund or *that*-clause:

Factive: I want to make clear the fact that I don't
          intend to participate.
          You have to keep in mind the fact of his
          having proposed several alternatives.
Nonfactive: *I assert the fact that I don't intend
             to participate.
             *We may conclude the fact of his having
             proposed several alternatives.

2. Gerunds can be objects of factive predicates, but not freely of nonfactive predicates:

Factive: Everyone ignored Joan's being completely drunk.
          I regret having agreed to the proposal.
          I don't mind your saying so.
Nonfactive: *Everyone supposed Joan's being completely drunk.
             *I believe having agreed to the proposal.
             *I maintain your saying so.

The gerunds relevant here are what Lees (1960) has termed "factive nominals." They occur freely both in the present tense and in the past tense (*having*

-en). They take direct accusative objects, and all kinds of adverbs, and they occur without any identity restriction on their subject.[2] Other, non-factive, types of gerunds are subject to one or more of these restrictions. One type refers to actions or events:

> He avoided getting caught.
> *He avoided having got caught.
> *He avoided John's getting caught.

Gerunds also serve as substitutes for infinitives after prepositions:

> I plan to enter the primary.
> I plan on entering the primary.
> *I plan on having entered the primary last week.

Such gerunds are not at all restricted to factive predicates.

3. Only nonfactive predicates allow the accusative and infinitive construction:

> Nonfactive: I believe Mary to have been the one who did it.
> He fancies himself to be an expert in pottery.
> I supposed there to have been a mistake somewhere.
>
> Factive: *I resent Mary to have been the one who did it.
> *He comprehends himself to be an expert in pottery.
> *I took into consideration there to have been a mistake somewhere.

As we earlier found in the case of subject complements, the infinitive construction is excluded, for no apparent reason, even with some nonfactive predicates, e.g. *charge*. There is, furthermore, considerable variation from one speaker to another as to which predicates permit the accusative and infinitive construction, a fact which may be connected with its fairly bookish flavor. What is significant, however, is that the accusative and infinitive is not used with factive predicates.

II. Presupposition

These syntactic differences are correlated with a semantic difference. The force of the *that*-clause is not the same in the two sentences

> It is odd that it is raining. (factive)
> It is likely that it is raining. (nonfactive)

---

[2]There is, however, one limitation on subjects of factive gerunds:

*It's surprising me that he succeeded dismayed John.
*There's being a nut loose disgruntles me.

The restriction is that clauses cannot be subjects of gerunds, and the gerund formation rule precedes extraposition and *there*-insertion.

or in the two sentences

> I regret that it is raining. (factive)
> I suppose that it is raining. (nonfactive)

The first sentence in each pair (the factive sentence) carries with it the presupposition "it is raining." The speaker presupposes that the embedded clause expresses a true proposition, and makes some assertion about that proposition. All predicates which behave syntactically as factives have this semantic property, and almost none of those which behave syntactically as nonfactives have it.[3] This, we propose, is the basic difference between the two types of predicates. It is important that the following things should be clearly distinguished:

> 1. Propositions the speaker asserts, directly or indirectly, to be true
> 2. Propositions the speaker presupposes to be true.

Factivity depends on presupposition and not on assertion. For instance, when someone says

> It is true that John is ill.
> John turns out to be ill.

he is *asserting* that the proposition "John is ill" is a true proposition, but he is not *presupposing* that it is a true proposition. Hence these sentences do not follow the factive paradigm:

> *John's being ill is true.
> *John's being ill turns out.
> *The fact of John's being ill is true.
> *The fact of John's being ill turns out.

The following sentences, on the other hand, are true instances of presupposition:

> It is odd that the door is closed.
> I regret that the door is closed.

The speaker of these sentences presupposes "the door is closed" and furthermore asserts something else about that presupposed fact. It is this semantically more complex structure involving presupposition that has the syntactic properties we are dealing with here.

---

[3]There are some exceptions to this second half of our generalization. Verbs like *know, realize*, though semantically factive, are syntactically non-factive, so that we cannot say *I know the fact that John is here, *I know John's being here*, whereas the propositional constructions are acceptable: *I know him to be here*. There are speakers for whom many of the syntactic and semantic distinctions we bring up do not exist at all. Professor Archibald Hill has kindly informed us that for him factive and non-factive predicates behave in most respects alike and that even the word *fact* in his speech has lost its literal meaning and can head clauses for which no presupposition of truth is made. We have chosen to describe a rather restrictive type of speech (that of C. K.) because it yields more insight into the syntactic-semantic problems with which we are concerned.

When factive predicates have first person subjects it can happen that the top sentence denies what the complement presupposes. Then the expected semantic anomaly results. Except in special situations where two egos are involved, as in the case of an actor describing his part, the following sentences are anomalous:

*I don't realize that he has gone away.
*I have no inkling that a surprise is in store for me.[4]

Factivity is only one instance of this very basic and consequential distinction. In formulating the semantic structure of sentences, or, what concerns us more directly here, the lexical entries for predicates, we must posit a special status for presuppositions, as opposed to what we are calling assertions. The speaker is said to "assert" a sentence plus all those propositions which follow from it by virtue of its meaning, not, e.g. through laws of mathematics or physics.[5] Presumably in a semantic theory assertions will be represented as the central or "core" meaning of a sentence — typically a complex proposition involving semantic components like S_1 cause S_2, S become, N want S — plus the propositions that follow from it by redundancy rules involving those components. The formulation of a simple example should help clarify the concepts of assertion and presupposition.

Mary cleaned the room.

[4]In some cases what at first sight looks like a strange meaning-shift accompanies negation with first person subjects. The following sentences can be given a non-factive interpretation which prevents the above kind of anomaly in them:

I'm not aware that he has gone away.
I don't know that this isn't our car.

It will not do to view these non-factive *that*-clauses as indirect questions:

*I don't know that he has gone away or not.

We advance the hypothesis that they are deliberative clauses, representing the same construction as clauses introduced *but that*:

I don't know but that this is our car.

This accords well with their meaning, and especially with the fact that deliberative *but that*-clauses (in the dialects that permit them at all) are similarly restricted to negative sentences with first person subjects.

*I know but that this is our car.
*John doesn't know but that this is our car.

[5]We prefer "assert" to "imply" because the latter suggests consequences beyond those based on knowledge of the language. This is not at all to say that linguistic knowledge is disjoint from other knowledge. We are trying to draw a distinction between two statuses: a defining proposition can be said to have in the definition of a predicate, or meaning of a sentence, and to describe some consequences of this distinction. This is a question of the semantic structure of words and can be discussed independently of the question of the relationship between the encyclopedia and the dictionary.

The dictionary contains a mapping between the following structures:

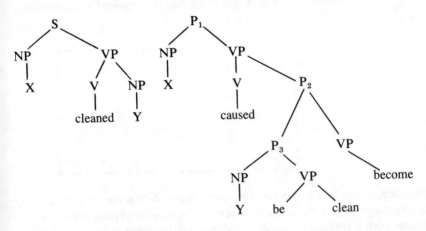

where S refers to the syntactic object "Sentence" and P to the semantic object "Proposition."

A redundancy rule states that the object of "cause" is itself asserted:

This rule yields the following set of assertions:

> X caused[6] Y to become clean.
> Y became clean.

(Why the conjunction of P_1 and P_2 is subordinated to P_0 will become clear below, especially in (3) and (5).)

Furthermore, there is a presupposition to the effect that the room was dirty before the event described in the sentence. This follows from "become,"

---

[6]Though we cannot go into the question here, it is clear that the tense of a sentence conveys information about the time of its presuppositions as well as of its assertions, direct and indirect. Thus tense (and likewise mood, cf. p. 326) is not an "operator" in the sense that negation and other topics discussed in this section are.

which presupposes that its complement has, up to the time of the change referred to by "become," not been true. This may be expressed as a redundancy rule:

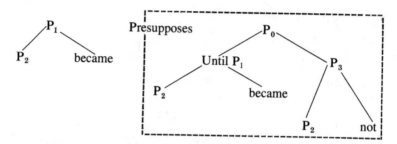

(Presuppositions will be enclosed in dotted lines. Within the context of a tree diagram representing the semantic structure of a sentence presuppositions which follow from a specific semantic component will be connected to it by a dotted line.) That this, like the factive component in *regret* or *admit,* is a presupposition rather than an assertion can be seen by applying the criteria in the following paragraphs.

1. Presuppositions are constant under negation. That is, when you negate a sentence you don't negate its presuppositions; rather, what is negated is what the positive sentence asserts. For example,

Mary didn't clean the room.

unlike its positive counterpart does not assert either that the room became clean, or, if it did, that it was through Mary's agency. On the other hand, negation does not affect the presupposition that it was or has been dirty. Similarly, these sentences with factive predicates (italicized)

It is not *odd* that the door is closed.
John doesn't *regret* that the door is closed.

presuppose, exactly as do their positive counterparts, that the door is closed.
In fact, if you want to deny a presupposition, you must do it explicitly:

Mary didn't <u>*clean*</u> the room; it wasn't dirty.
Legree didn't <u>*force*</u> them to work; they were willing to.
Abe didn't <u>*regret*</u> that he had forgotten; he had remembered.

The second clause casts the negative of the first into a different level; it's not the straightforward denial of an event or situation, but rather the denial of the appropriateness of the word in question (italicized and underlined above). Such negations sound best with the inappropriate word stressed.

2. Questioning, considered as an operation on a proposition **P**, indicates "I do not know whether **P**." When I ask

Are you *dismayed* that our money is gone?

I do not convey that I don't know whether it is gone but rather take that for granted and ask about your reaction.

(Note that to see the relation between factivity and questioning only yes-no questions are revealing. A question like

Who is aware that Ram eats meat?

already by virtue of questioning an argument of *aware*, rather than the proposition itself, presupposes a corresponding statement:

Someone is aware that Ram eats meat.

Thus, since presupposition is transitive, the *who*-question presupposes all that the *someone*-statement does.)

Other presuppositions are likewise constant under questioning. For instance: a verb might convey someone's evaluation of its complement as a presupposition. To say "they *deprived* him of a visit to his parents" presupposes that he wanted the visit (vs. "spare him a visit . . ."). The presupposition remains in "Have they deprived him of a . . .?" What the question indicates is "I don't know whether they have kept him from . . . ."

3. It must be emphasized that it is the *set* of assertions that is operated on by question and negation. To see this, compare

Mary didn't kiss John.
Mary didn't clean the house.

They have certain ambiguities which, as has often been noted, are systematic under negation. The first may be equivalent to any of the following more precise sentences:

Someone may have kissed John, but not Mary.
Mary may have kissed someone, but not John.
Mary may have done something, but not kiss John.
Mary may have done something to John, but not kiss him.

And the second:

Someone may have cleaned the house, but not Mary.
Mary may have cleaned something, but not the house.
Mary may have done something, but not clean the house.
Mary may have done something to the house, but not clean it.

All of these readings can be predicted on the basis of the constituent structure:

Roughly, each major constituent may be negated.
But the second sentence has still another reading:

Mary may have been cleaning the house, but it didn't get clean.

That extra reading has no counterpart in the other sentence. *Clean* is semantically more complex than *kiss* in that whereas *kiss* has only one assertion (press the lips against), *clean* has two, as we have seen above. How this affects the meaning of the negative sentence can be seen through a derivation:

(i)

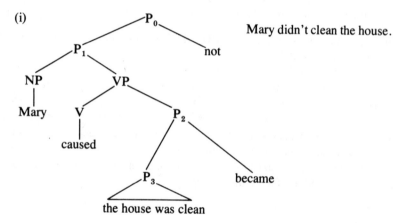

Mary didn't clean the house.

(ii) Application of redundancy rule on "cause":

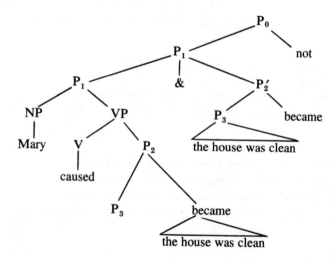

It's not the case that both Mary cleaned the house and the house is clean.

(iii) DeMorgan's Law yields

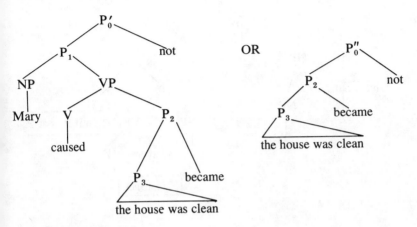

Either "Mary didn't clean the house" or "the house didn't get clean."

Thus to say *Mary didn't clean the house* is to make either of the two negative assertions in (iii). The remaining readings arise from distribution of *not* over the constituents of the lexicalized sentence.

Presumably the same factors account for the corresponding ambiguity of *Did Mary clean the house?*

4. If we take an imperative sentence like

(You) chase that thief!

to indicate something like

I want (you chase that thief)

then what "I want" doesn't include the presuppositions of S. For example, S presupposes that

That thief is evading you.

but that situation is hardly part of what "I want."

The factive complement in the following example is likewise presupposed independently of the demand:

Point it out to 006 that the transmitter will function poorly in a cave.

Assume the dictionary contains this mapping:

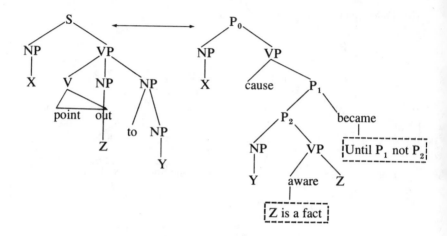

From the causative redundancy rule, which adds the assertion P_1, the definition of *point out*, and the fact that *want* distributes over subordinate conjuncts, it follows that the above command indicates

I want 006 to become aware that the transmitter . . .

However, it doesn't in any way convey

I want the transmitter to function poorly in a cave.

nor, of course, that

I want 006 not to have been aware . . .

5. We have been treating negation, questioning, and imperative as operations on propositions like implicit "higher sentences." Not surprisingly explicit "higher sentences" also tend to leave presuppositions constant while operating on assertions. Our general claim is that the assertions of a proposition (P_k) are made relative to that proposition within its context of dominating propositions. Presuppositions, on the other hand, are relative to the speaker. This is shown in figures 1 and 2. Figure 1 shows that the presuppositions of P_k are also presupposed by the whole proposition P_0. In Figure 2 we see that whatever P_0 asserts about P_k it also asserts about the *set* (see (3) above) of propositions that P_k asserts.

Figure 1

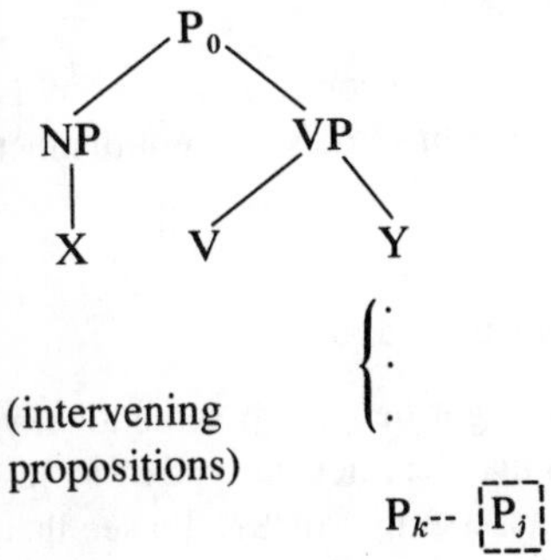

Figure 2

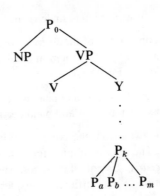

(intervening
propositions)

P_k-- P_j

Redundancy rule:
P_0 presupposes P_j

Redundancy rule:
P_0 asserts $\{P_a, P_b \ldots P_m\}$

Let us further exemplify this general claim:

> John appears to regret evicting his grandmother.

Since *appear* is not factive this sentence neither asserts nor presupposes

> John regrets evicting her.

However it does presuppose the complement of the embedded factive verb *regret*, as well as the presupposition of *evict* to the effect that he was her landlord.

It does not matter how deeply the factive complement (italicized) is embedded:

> Abe thinks it is possible that Ben is becoming ready to encourage Carl to acknowledge *that he had behaved churlishly*.

This claim holds for presuppositions other than factivity. We are not obliged to conclude from

> John refuses to remain a bachelor all his life.

that he plans to undergo demasculating surgery, since *bachelor* asserts *unmarried*, but only presupposes *male* and *adult*. Thus (ii) yields:

> John refuses to remain unmarried all his life.

but not

John refuses to remain male (adult) all his life.

6. A conjunction of the form S_1 *and* S_2 *too* serves to contrast an item in S_1 with one in S_2 by placing them in contexts which are in some sense not distinct from each other. For instance:

Tigers are ferocious and panthers are (ferocious) too.
*Tigers are ferocious and panthers are mild mannered too.

Abstracting away from the contrasting items, S_1 might be said to semantically include S_2. The important thing for us to notice is that the relevant type of inclusion is *assertion*. Essentially, S_2 corresponds to an assertion of S_1. To see that presupposition is not sufficient consider the following sentences. The second conjunct in each of the starred sentences corresponds to a presupposition of the first conjunct, while in the acceptable sentences there is an assertion relationship.

John deprived the mice of food and the frogs didn't get any either.
*John deprived the mice of food and the frogs didn't want any either.
John forced the rat to run a maze and the lizard did it too.
*John forced the rat to run a maze and the lizard didn't want to either.
Mary's refusal flabbergasted Ron, and he was surprised at Betty's refusal too.
*Mary's refusal flabbergasted Ron and Betty refused too.

III. A hypothesis

So far, we have presented a set of syntactic-semantic correlations without considering how they might be accounted for. We shall continue by analyzing these facts and others to be pointed out in the course of the discussion, in terms of a tentative explanatory hypothesis, by which the semantic difference between the factive and non-factive complement paradigms can be related to their syntactic differences, and most of the syntactic characteristics of each paradigm can be explained. The hypothesis which we should like to introduce is that presupposition of complements is reflected in their syntactic deep structure. Specifically, we shall explore the possibility that factive and nonfactive complements at a deeper level of representation differ as follows:[7]

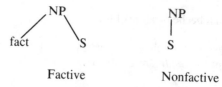

Factive   Nonfactive

[7]For further discussion of this point see additional notes on pp. 324–29.

If this interpretation is correct, then closest to the factive deep structure are sentences of the type

I regret the fact that John is ill.

The forms in the factive paradigm are derived by two optional transformations: formation of gerunds from *that*-clauses in position after nouns, and deletion of the head noun *fact*. (We do not pause to consider the general rules which take care of the detail involving *that* and *of*.) By gerund formation alone we get

I regret the fact of John's being ill.

Fact-deletion can apply to this derived structure, giving

I regret John's being ill.

If *fact*-deletion applies directly to the basic form, then the simple *that*-clause is formed:

I regret that John is ill.

Although this last factive sentence has the same superficial form as the non-factive

I believe that John is ill.

according to our analysis it differs radically from it in syntactic form, and the two sentences have different deep structures as diagrammed above. Simple *that*-clauses are ambiguous, and constitute the point of overlap (neutralization) of the factive and nonfactive paradigms.

If factive clauses have the deep structures proposed by us, these various surface forms in which factive clauses can appear become very easy to derive. That is one piece of support for our hypothesis. The remaining evidence can be grouped under three general headings:

1. syntactic insulation of factive clauses (section 4)
2. indifferent and ambiguous predicates (section 5)
3. pronominalization (section 6)

IV. Syntactic insulation of factive clauses

Let us first return in somewhat more detail to infinitive constructions, examining first the derivation of infinitives in general and then of the class of infinitive constructions which we mentioned as being characteristic of nonfactive predicates. Basic to our treatment of infinitives is the assumption that nonfinite verb forms in all languages are the basic, unmarked forms. Finite verbs, then, are always the result of person and number agreement between subject and verb, and nonfinite verbs, in particular, infinitives, come about when agreement does not apply. Infinitives arise regularly when the subject of an embedded sentence is removed by a transformation, or else placed into an oblique case, so that in either case agreement between subject and verb cannot take place. There are several ways in which the subject of an embedded sentence can be removed by a transformation. It can be deleted under identity with a noun phrase in the containing sentence, as in sentences like *I decided to go* and *I forced John to go* (cf. Rosenbaum 1967).

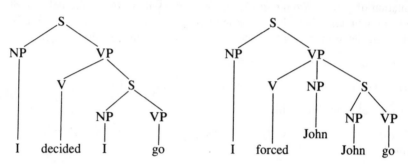

After prepositions, infinitives are automatically converted to gerunds, e.g. *I decided to go* vs. *I decided on going*; or *I forced John to do it* vs. *I forced John into doing it*. These infinitival gerunds should not be confused with the factive gerunds, with which they have in common nothing but their surface form.

A second way in which the subject of an embedded sentence can be removed by a transformation to yield infinitives is through raising of the subject of the embedded sentence into the containing sentence. The remaining verb phrase of the embedded sentence is then automatically left in infinitive form. This subject-raising transformation applies only to nonfactive complements, and yields the accusative and infinitive, and nominative and infinitive constructions:

He believes Bacon to be the real author.
This seems to be Hoyle's best book.

The operation of the subject-raising rule in object clauses can be diagrammed as follows:

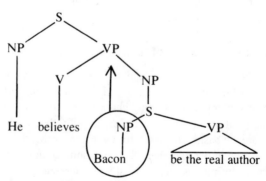

The circled noun phrase is raised into the upper sentence and becomes the surface object of its verb.[8]

We reject, then, as unsuccessful the traditional efforts to derive the uses of the infinitive from its being "partly a noun, partly a verb," or, perhaps, from some "basic meaning" supposedly shared by all occurrences of infinitives. We reject, also, the assumption of recent transformational work (cf. Rosenbaum 1967) that all infinitives are *"for-to"* constructions, and that they arise from a "complementizer placement" rule which inserts *for* and *to* before clauses on the basis of an arbitrary marking on their verbs. Instead, we claim that what infinitives share is only the single, relatively low-level syntactic property of having no surface subject.

Assuming that the subject-raising rule is the source of one particular type of infinitive complements, we return to the fact, mentioned earlier, that factive complements never yield these infinitive complements. We now press for an explanation. Why can one not say,

*He regrets Bacon to be the real author.
*This makes sense to be Hoyle's best book.

although the corresponding *that*-clauses are perfectly acceptable? It is highly unlikely that this could be explained directly by the *semantic* fact that these sentences are constructed with factive predicates. However, the deep structure which we have posited for factive complements makes a syntactic explanation possible.

Ross (1967) has found that transformations are subject to a general constraint, termed by him the Complex Noun Phrase Constraint, which blocks them from taking constituents out of a sentence S in the configuration

For example, elements in relative clauses are immune to questioning: *Mary* in *The boy who saw Mary came back* cannot be questioned to give *Who did the boy who saw come back?* The complex noun phrase constraint blocks this type of questioning because relative clauses stand in the illustrated configuration with their head noun.

This complex noun phrase constraint could explain why the subject-raising rule does not apply to factive clauses. This misapplication of the rule is excluded if, as we have assumed, factive clauses are associated with the head noun *fact*. If

[8]This subject-raising rule has figured in recent work under at least three names: pronoun replacement (Rosenbaum 1967); expletive replacement (Langendoen 1966); and *it*-replacement (Ross 1967). Unfortunately we have had to invent still another, for none of the current names fit the rule as we have reformulated it.

the optional transformation which drops this head noun applies later than the subject-raising transformation (and nothing seems to contradict that assumption), then the subjects of factive clauses cannot be raised. No special modification of the subject-raising rule is necessary to account for the limitation of infinitive complements to non-factive predicates.

Another movement transformation which is blocked in factive structures in the same way is NEG-raising (Klima 1964), a rule which optionally moves the element NEG(ATIVE) from an embedded sentence into the containing sentence, converting for example the sentences

It's likely that he won't lift a finger until it's too late.
I believe that he can't help doing things like that.

into the synonymous sentences

It's not likely that he will lift a finger until it's too late.
I don't believe that he can help doing things like that.

Since *lift a finger*, punctual *until*, and *can help* occur only in negative sentences, sentences like these prove that a rule of NEG-raising is necessary.

This rule of NEG-raising never applies in the factive cases. We do not get, for example

*It doesn't bother me that we will lift a finger until it's too late.

from

It bothers me that he won't lift a finger until it's too late.

or

*I don't regret that he can help doing things like that.

from

I regret that he can't help doing things like that.

Given the factive deep structure which we have proposed, the absence of such sentences is explained by the complex noun phrase constraint, which exempts structures having the formal properties of these factive deep structures from undergoing movement transformations.[9]

[9]We thought earlier that the oddity of questioning and relativization in some factive clauses was also due to the complex noun phrase constraint:

*How old is it strange that John is?
*I climbed the mountain which it is interesting that Goethe tried to climb.

Leroy Baker (1967) has shown that this idea was wrong, and that the oddity here is not due to the complex noun phrase constraint. Baker has been able to find a semantic formulation of the restriction on questioning which is fairly general and accurate. It appears now that questioning and relativization are rules which follow *fact*-deletion.

Factivity also erects a barrier against insertion. It has often been noticed that subordinate clauses in German are not in the subjunctive mood if the truth of the clause is presupposed by the speaker, and that sequence of tenses in English and French also depends partly on this condition. The facts are rather complicated, and to formulate them one must distinguish several functions of the present tense and bring in other conditions which interact with sequence of tenses and subjunctive insertion. But it is sufficient for our purposes to look at minimal pairs which show that one of the elements involved in this phenomenon is factivity. Let us assume that Bill takes it for granted that the earth is round. Then Bill might say:

John claimed that the earth was (*is) flat.

with obligatory sequence of tenses, but

John grasped that the earth is (was) round.

with optional sequence of tenses. The rule which changes a certain type of present tense into a past tense in an embedded sentence if the containing sentence is past, is obligatory in non-factives but optional in factives. The German subjunctive rule is one notch weaker: it is optional in non-factives and inapplicable in factives:

Er behauptet, dass die Erde flach sei (ist).
Er versteht, dass die Erde rund ist (*sei).

The reason why these changes are in part optional is not clear. The exact way in which they are limited by factivity cannot be determined without a far more detailed investigation of the facts than we have been able to undertake. Nevertheless, it is fairly likely that factivity will play a role in an eventual explanation of these phenomena.[10]

V. Indifferent and ambiguous predicates

So far, for clarity of exposition, only predicates which are either factive or nonfactive have been examined. For this set of cases, the factive and nonfactive

---

[10]This may be related to the fact that (factive) present gerunds can refer to a past state, but (nonfactive) present infinitives can not. Thus,

They resented his being away.

is ambiguous as to the time reference of the gerund, and on one prong of the ambiguity is synonymous with

They resented his having been away.

But in

They supposed him to be away.

the infinitive can only be understood as contemporaneous with the main verb, and the sentence can never be interpreted as synonymous with

They supposed him to have been away.

complement paradigms are in complementary distribution. But there are numerous predicates which take complements of both types. This is analogous to the fact that there are not only verbs which take concrete objects and verbs which take abstract objects but also verbs which take either kind. For example, *hit* requires concrete objects (*boy, table*), *clarify* requires abstract objects (*ideas, fact*), and *like* occurs indifferently with both. Just so we find verbs which occur indifferently with factive and nonfactive complements, e.g. *anticipate, acknowledge, suspect, report, remember, emphasize, announce, admit, deduce.* Such verbs have no specification in the lexicon as to whether their complements are factive. On a deeper level, their semantic representations include no specifications as to whether their complement sentences represent presuppositions by the speaker or not. Syntactically, these predicates participate in both complement paradigms.

It is striking evidence for our analysis that they provide minimal pairs for the subtle meaning difference between factive and nonfactive complements. Compare, for example, the two sentences

They reported the enemy to have suffered a decisive defeat.
They reported the enemy's having suffered a decisive defeat.

The second implies that the report was true in the speaker's opinion, while the first leaves open the possibility that the report was false. This is explained by our derivation of infinitives from nonfactives and gerunds from factives. Similarly compare

I remembered him to be bald (so I was surprised to see him with long hair).
I remembered his being bald (so I brought along a wig and disguised him).

Contrast *forget*, which differs from *remember* in that it necessarily presupposes the truth of its object. Although it is logically just as possible to forget a false notion as it is to remember one, language seems to allow for expressing only the latter. We cannot say

*I forgot that he was bald, which was a good thing since it turned out later that he wasn't after all.
*I forgot him to be bald.

There is another kind of case. Just as different meanings may accompany subjects or objects differing by a feature like concreteness, as in

The boy struck$_1$ me.
The idea struck$_2$ me.

so verbs may occur with factive and nonfactive complements in different meanings. Compare

a. I explained Adam's refusing to come to the phone.
b. I explained that he was watching his favorite TV show.

In (a), the subordinate clause refers to a proposition regarded as a fact. *Explain*, in this case, means "give reasons for." When the object is a *that*-clause, as in (b), it can be read as nonfactive, with *explain that S* understood as meaning "say that S to explain X." To account for the differences between (a) and (b), we might postulate two lexical entries for *explain* (not denying that they are related). In the entry appropriate to (a) there would be a presupposition that the subordinated proposition is true. This would require a factive complement (recall that the form of the complement has an associated interpretation) in the same way as the two verbs *strike*₁ and *strike*₂ would receive different kinds of subjects. The entry for (b) would have among its presuppositions that the speaker was not committing himself about the truth of the subordinated proposition, so that a factive complement would not fit. Thus, the meaning of the complement form is directly involved in explaining its occurrence with particular verbs.

VI. Pronominalization

The pronoun *it* serves as an optional reduction of *the fact*. It can stand directly before *that*-clauses in sentences with factive verbs:

> Bill resents it that people are always comparing him to Mozart.
> They didn't mind it that a crowd was beginning to gather in the street.

Although the difference is a delicate one, and not always clearcut, most speakers find *it* unacceptable in the comparable nonfactive cases:

> *Bill claims it that people are always comparing him to Mozart.
> *They supposed it that a crowd was beginning to gather in the street.

This *it*, a reduced form of *the fact*, should be distinguished from the expletive *it*, a semantically empty prop which is automatically introduced in the place of extraposed complements in sentences like

> It seems that both queens are trying to wriggle out of their commitments.
> It is obvious that Muriel has lost her marbles.

Rosenbaum (1967) tried to identify the two and to derive both from an *it* which he postulated in the deep structure of all noun clauses. This was in our opinion a mistake. In the first place, the two *it*'s have different distributions. Expletive *it* comes in regardless of whether a factive or non-factive clause is extraposed, and does not appear to be related to the lexical noun *fact*, as factive *it* is.

The relationship of factive *it* to the lexical noun *fact*, and its distinction from expletive *it*, is brought out rather clearly by a number of transformational processes. For example, the presence of factive *it* blocks the formation of relative clauses just as the lexical noun *fact* does:

> *This is the book which you reported it that John plagiarized.
> *This is the book which you reported the fact that John plagiarized.
> This is the book which you reported that John plagiarized.

But expletive *it* differs in permitting relativization:

> That's the one thing which it is obvious that he hadn't expected.
> *That's the one thing which the fact is obvious that he hadn't expected.

As Ross (1966) has shown, facts like these create seemingly insoluble problems for a system like Rosenbaum's, in which factive and expletive *it* are derived from the same source. We have not proposed an alternative in anything like sufficient detail, but it is fairly clear that a system of rules constructed along the general lines informally sketched out here, which makes exactly the required syntactic distinction, will not have inherent difficulties in dealing with these facts.

Direct comparison of factive *it* and expletive *it* shows the expected semantic difference. The comparison can be carried out with the verbs which are indifferent as to factivity:

> I had expected that there would be a big turnout (but only three people came).
> I had expected it that there would be a big turnout (but this is ridiculous — get more chairs).

The second sentence, with *it*, suggests that the expectation was fulfilled, whereas the first is neutral in that respect. On the other hand, expletive *it* adds no factive meaning, and the following sentence is ambiguous as between the factive and nonfactive interpretation:

> It was expected that there would be a big turnout.

This analysis makes the prediction that cases of *it* which cannot be derived from *fact* will present no obstacle to relativization. This is indeed the case:

> Goldbach's conjecture, which I take it that you all know . . .
> The report, which I will personally see to it that you get first thing in the morning . . .
> This secret, which I would hate it if anyone ever revealed . . .

On the other hand, it is not too clear where these *it's* do come from. Perhaps their source is the "vacuous extraposition" postulated by Rosenbaum (1967).[11]

The deep structures which we have posited for the two types of complements also explain the way in which they get pronominalized. In general, both factive and nonfactive clauses take the pro-form *it*:

> John supposed that Bill had done it, and Mary supposed it, too.
> John regretted that Bill had done it, and Mary regretted it, too.

---

[11]Dean (1967) has presented evidence from German and English that extraposition is the general source of expletive pronouns.

But the two differ in that only nonfactive clauses are pronominalized by *so*:

> John supposed that Bill had done it, and Mary supposed so, too.
> *John regretted that Bill had done it, and Mary regretted so, too.

These facts can be explained on the basis of the fairly plausible assumption that *it* is the pro-form of noun phrases, and *so* is the pro-form of sentences. Referring back to the deep structures given in section III, we see that the only node which exhaustively dominates factive complements is the node NP. For this reason the only pro-form for them is the pro-form for noun phrases, namely *it*. But nonfactive complements are exhaustively dominated by two nodes: NP and S. Accordingly, two pro-forms are available: the pro-form for noun phrases, *it*, and the pro-form for sentences, *so*.

VII. Emotives

In the above discussion we rejected Rosenbaum's derivation of infinitive complements like

> I believe John to have liked Anselm.
> I forced John to say "cheese."

from hypothetical underlying forms with *for-to*:

> *I believe for John to have liked Anselm.
> *I forced John for John to say "cheese."

This leaves us with the onus of explaining the *for-to* complements which actually occur on the surface:

> It bothers me for John to have hallucinations.
> I regret for you to be in this fix.

But once the spurious *for-to*'s are stripped away, it becomes clear that the remaining real cases occur with a semantically natural class of predicates. Across the distinction of factivity there cuts orthogonally another semantic distinction, which we term *emotivity*. Emotive complements are those to which the speaker expresses a subjective, emotional, or evaluative reaction. The class of predicates taking emotive complements includes the verbs of emotion of classical grammar, and Klima's affective predicates (Klima 1964), but is larger than either and includes in general all predicates which express the subjective value of a proposition rather than knowledge about it or its truth value. It is this class of predicates to which *for-to* complements are limited. The following list illustrates the wide range of meanings to be found and shows the cross-classification of emotivity and factivity:

	Emotive	*Non-emotive*
Factive Examples		
Subject clauses	important	well-known
	crazy	clear
	odd	(self-evident)
	relevant	goes without
	instructive	saying
	sad	
	suffice	
	bother	
	alarm	
	fascinate	
	nauseate	
	exhilarate	
	defy comment	
	surpass belief	
	a tragedy	
	no laughing matter	
Object clauses	regret	be aware (of)
	deplore	bear in mind
	resent	make clear
		forget
		take into account
Nonfactive Examples		
Subject clauses	improbable	probable
	unlikely	likely
	a pipedream	turn out
	nonsense	seem
future ⟶	⎰ urgent	imminent
	⎱ vital	in the works
Object clauses	⎛ intend	predict
	⎜ prefer	anticipate
future ⟶	⎨ reluctant	foresee
	⎜ anxious	
	⎜ willing	
	⎝ eager	
		say
		suppose
		conclude

We have proposed that infinitives are derived in complements whose verbs fail to undergo agreement with a subject. In the infinitives mentioned in section IV, agreement did not take place because the subject was in one or another way eliminated by a transformation. There is a second possible reason for non-agreement. This is that the subject is marked with an oblique case. There seem to be no instances, at least in the Indo-European languages, of verbs agreeing in person and number with anything else than nominative noun phrases. Good illustrations of this point are the German pairs

Ich werde betrogen   "I am cheated."
Mir wird geschmeichelt   "I am flattered."
Ich bin leicht zu betrügen   "I am easy to cheat."
Mir ist leicht zu schmeicheln   "I am easy to flatter."

Presumably the same syntactic processes underlie both sentences in each pair. The accusative object of *betrügen* is changed into a nominative, whereas the dative object of *schmeicheln* stays in the dative. But from the viewpoint of agreement, only the nominative counts as a surface subject.

As the source of *for* with the infinitive we assume a transformation which marks the subjects in complements of emotive predicates with *for*, the nonfinite verb form being a consequence of the oblique case of the subject.

We can here only list quickly some of the other syntactic properties which emotivity is connected to, giving an unfortunately oversimplified picture of a series of extremely complex and difficult problems. What follows are only suggestive remarks.

First of all, emotives may optionally contain the subjunctive marker *should*:

It's interesting that you should have said so.
*It's well-known that you should have said so.

(We do not of course mean the *should* of obligation or the *should* of future expectation, which are not limited to emotives.)

We assume that a future *should* is optionally deleted by a late rule, leaving a bare infinitive:

I'm anxious that he (should) be found.
It's urgent that he (should) be found.

Emotive complements can be identified by their ability to contain a class of exclamatory degree adverbs such as *at all* or (unstressed) *so, such*:

It's interesting that he came at all.
*It's well-known that he came at all.

Finally, it seems that one of the conditions which must be placed on relativization by *as* is that the clause be non-emotive although many other factors are certainly involved:

> *As is interesting, John is in India.
> As is well-known, John is in India.

VIII. Conclusions

Syntactic-semantic interrelationships of this kind form the basis of a system of deep structures and rules which account for the complement system of English, and other languages as well. The importance of a system successfully worked out along the general lines suggested above would lie in its ability to account not only for the syntactic structure of sentential complementation, but also for its semantic structure, and for the relationship between the two. Our analysis of presupposition in the complement system contributes a substantial instance of the relation between syntax and semantics, and enables us to correct an error which has been made in most past work on transformational syntax. The error is that different types of complements (*that*-clauses, gerunds, infinitives) have all been assumed to have the same deep structure, and hence to be .semantically equivalent.[12] We have seen that there is good reason to posit a number of different base structures, each mapped by transformations into a syntactic paradigm of semantically equivalent surface structures. The base structures differ semantically along at least two independent dimensions, which express the judgment of the speaker about the content of the complement sentence.

This approach to a theory of complementation is not only more adequate from a semantic point of view. Its purely syntactic advantages are equally significant. It eliminates the need for marking each verb for compatibility with each surface complement type, that is, for treating complementation as basically irregular and unpredictable. We account for the selection of complement types quite naturally by our proposal that there are several meaningful base structures, whose choice is in large part predictable from the meaning of each predicate. These base structures are subject to various transformations which yield surface structures in which the relation between form and meaning is considerably obscured.

FURTHER NOTES ON FACTIVE AND NONFACTIVE COMPLEMENTS

We have dealt with the syntactic repercussions of factivity in sentential complementation. This is really an artificially delimited topic (as almost all topics in linguistics necessarily are). Factivity is relevant to much else in syntax besides sentential complementation, and on the other hand, the structure of sentential

---

[12]The studies of Lees (1960) and Vendler (1964), however, contain many interesting semantic observations on sentential complementation and nominalization which still await formal description and explanation.

complementation is naturally governed by different semantic factors which interact with factivity. That is one source of the painful gaps in the above presentation which the reader will surely have noticed. We conclude by listing summarily a couple of possible additional applications of factivity, and some additional semantic factors which determine the form of complements, in order at least to hint at some ways in which the gaps can be filled, and to suggest what seem to us promising extensions of the approach we have taken.

1. There is a syntactic and semantic correspondence between *truth* and *specific reference*. The verbs which presuppose that their sentential object expresses a true proposition also presuppose that their nonsentential object refers to a specific thing. For example, in the sentences

> I ignored an ant on my plate.
> I imagined an ant on my plate.

the factive verb *ignore* presupposes that there was an ant on my plate, but the non-factive verb *imagine* does not. Perhaps this indicates that at some sufficiently abstract level of semantics, truth and specific reference are reducible to the same concept. Frege's speculations that the reference of a sentence is its truth value would thereby receive some confirmation.

Another indication that there is a correspondence between truth of propositions and specific reference of noun phrases is the following. We noted in Section I that extraposition is obligatory for nonfactive subject complements. Compare

> That John has come makes sense (factive).
> *That John has come seems (nonfactive).

where the second sentence must become

> It seems that John has come.

unless it undergoes subject-raising. This circumstance appears to reflect a more general tendency for sentence-initial clauses to get understood factively. For example, in saying

> The UPI reported that Smith had arrived.
> It was reported by the UPI that Smith had arrived.

the speaker takes no stand on the truth of the report. But

> That Smith had arrived was reported by the UPI.

normally conveys the meaning that the speaker assumes the report to be true. A non-factive interpretation of this sentence can be teased out in various ways, for example by laying contrastive stress on the agent phrase (*by the UPI, not the AP*). Still, the unforced sense is definitely factive. These examples are interesting because they suggest that the factive vs. nonfactive senses of the complement do not really correspond to the application of any particular transformation, but rather to the position of the complement in the surface structure. The interpretation can be nonfactive if both passive and extraposition have applied, or if neither of them has applied; if only the passive has applied, we get the factive interpretation. This is very hard to state in terms of a condition on transformations. It is much easier to say that the initial position itself of a clause is in such cases associated with a factive sense.

This is where the parallelism between truth and specific reference comes in. The problem with the well-known pairs like

Everyone in this room speaks two languages.
Two languages are spoken by everyone in this room.

is exactly that indefinite noun phrases such as *two languages* are understood as referring to specific objects when placed initially ("there are two languages such that . . ."). Again, it is not on the passive itself that the meaning depends. In the sentence

Two languages are familiar to everyone in this room.

the passive has not applied, but *two languages* is again understood as specific because of its initial position.

2. We also expect that factivity will clarify the structure of other types of subordinate clauses. We have in mind the difference between purpose clauses (nonfactive) and result clauses (factive), and different types of conditional and concessive clauses.

3. There are languages which distinguish factive and nonfactive moods in declarative sentences. For example, in Hidatsa (Matthews 1964) there is a factive mood whose use in a sentence implies that the speaker is certain that the sentence is true, and a range of other moods indicating hearsay, doubt, and other judgments of the speaker about the sentence. While this distinction is not overt in English, it seems to us that it may be sensed in an ambiguity of declarative sentences. Consider the statement

He's an idiot.

There is an ambiguity here which may be resolved in several ways. For example, the common question

Is that a fact or is that just your opinion?

(presumably unnecessary in Hidatsa) is directed exactly at disambiguating the statement. The corresponding *why*-question

Why is he an idiot?

may be answered in two very different ways, e.g.

    a. Because his brain lacks oxygen.
    b. Because he failed this simple test for the third time.

There are thus really two kinds of *why*-questions: requests for *explanation*, which presuppose the truth of the underlying sentence, and requests for *evidence*, which do not. The two may be paraphrased

    a. Why is it a fact that he is an idiot?
    b. Why do you think that he is an idiot?

4. Consider the sentences

    John's eating them would amaze me.
    I would like John's doing so.

These sentences do not at all presuppose that the proposition in the complement is true. This indicates a further complexity of the *fact* postulated in the deep structure of factive complements. Like verbs, or predicates in general, it appears to take various tenses or moods. Note that there correspond to the above sentences:

    If he were to eat them it would amaze me.
    I would like it if John were to do so.

These can also be construed as

    If it were a fact that he ate them it would amaze me.

A second oversimplification may be our assumption that sentences are embedded in their deep structure form. A case can be made for rejecting this customary approach in favor of one where different verbs take complements at different levels of representation. Consider direct quotation, which appears not to have been treated in generative grammar. The fundamental fact is that what one quotes are surface structures and not deep structures. That is, if John's words were "Mary saw Bill," then we can correctly report

    John said, "Mary saw Bill."

but we shall have misquoted him if we say

    John said, "Bill was seen by Mary."

If we set up the deep structure of both sentences simply as

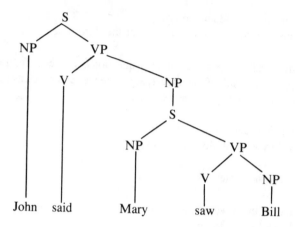

then we have not taken account of this fact. We should be forced to add to this deep structure the specification that the complement either must or cannot undergo the passive, depending on which of the sentences we are quoting. Since sentences of any complexity can be quoted, to whose deep structures the passive and other optional transformations may be applicable an indefinite number of times, it is not enough simply to mark the embedded deep structure of the quoted sentence as a whole for applicability of transformations. What has to be indicated according to this solution is the whole transformational history of the quoted sentence.

A more natural alternative is to let the surface structure itself of the quoted sentence be embedded. This would be the case in general for verbs taking direct quotes. Other classes of verbs would take their complements in different form. We then notice that the initial form of a complement can in general be selected at a linguistically functional level of representation in such a way that the truth value of the whole sentence will not be altered by any rules which are applicable to the complement. Assuming a generative semantics, the complements of verbs of knowing and believing are then semantic representations. From

John thinks that the McCavitys are a quarrelsome bunch of people.

it follows that

John thinks that the McCavitys like to pick a fight.

That is, one believes propositions and not sentences. Believing a proposition in fact commits one to believing what it implies: if you believe that Mary cleaned the room you must believe that the room was cleaned. (Verbs like *regret*, although their objects are also propositions, differ in this respect. If you regret that Mary cleaned the room you do not necessarily regret that the room was cleaned.)

At the other extreme would be cases of phonological complementation, illustrated by the context

John went "_____."

The object here must be some actual noise or a conventional rendering thereof such as *ouch* or *plop*.

A good many verbs can take complements at several levels. A verb like *scream*, which basically takes phonological complements, can be promoted to take direct quotes. *Say* seems to take both of these and propositions as well.

Are there verbs which require their complement sentences to be inserted in deep structure form (in the sense of Chomsky)? Such a verb X would have the property that

John Xed that Bill entered the house.

would imply that

John Xed that the house was entered by Bill.

but would not imply that

John Xed that Bill went into the house.

That is, the truth of the sentence would be preserved if the object clause underwent a different set of optional transformations, but not if it was replaced by a paraphrase with another deep structure source. It is an interesting question whether such verbs exist. We have not been able to find any. Unless further search turns up verbs of this kind, we shall have to conclude that, if the general idea proposed here is valid, the levels of semantics, surface structure, and phonology, but not the level of deep structure, can function as the initial representation of complements.

BIBLIOGRAPHY

BAKER, LEROY (1967). "A Class of Semantically Deviant Questions." Unpublished paper.

DEAN, JANET (1967). "Noun Phrase Complementation in English and German." Unpublished paper.

KLIMA, EDWARD S. (1964). "Negation in English." In Fodor and Katz, eds., *The Structure of Language*. Englewood Cliffs, N.J.: Prentice-Hall.

LANGENDOEN, D. T. (1966). "The Syntax of the English Expletive IT." *Georgetown University Monograph Series on Languages and Linguistics*, no. 19, pp. 207–16.

LEES, ROBERT B. (1960). *The Grammar of English Nominalizations*. The Hague: Mouton.

MATTHEWS, G. H. (1964). *Hidatsa Syntax*. The Hague: Mouton.

ROSENBAUM, P. S. (1967). *The Grammar of English Predicate Complement Constructions*. Cambridge, Mass.: M.I.T. Press.

Ross, John Robert. (1966). "Relativization in Extraposed Clauses (A Problem which Evidence is Presented that Help is Needed to Solve)." *Mathematical Linguistics and Automatic Translation*, Report no. NSF-17 to the National Science Foundation, Harvard University, Computation Laboratory.

——————. (1967). "Constraints on Variables in Syntax." Unpublished dissertation, M.I.T.

Vendler, Zeno (1964). *Nominalizations*. Mimeographed, University of Pennsylvania.

6 VARIATION IN LANGUAGE

Generative semantics has brought about a new focus on contexts and the communicative function of language in theoretical studies of grammar. This has always been the concern of scholars who have been primarily interested in usage, although their points of view have differed drastically over the centuries. In early studies within the framework of traditional grammar, formal usage and the literary language were viewed as superior. This attitude prevailed well into the twentieth century. By the 1940s, however, the findings of linguistics laid the basis for more liberal attitudes. Some scholars began to recognize the many varieties of language and their legitimate function in different social situations.

One of the first educators to adopt this point of view was John S. Kenyon, a professor of English at Hiram College, who served as a consulting editor for the Merriam-Webster dictionaries. In "Cultural Levels and Functional Varieties of English" (1948), he discusses the tendency to confuse cultural levels and styles. Cultural levels may be separated into the two classes of substandard and standard. On the other hand, functional varieties or styles, which do not depend on the cultural status of the users, range from the familiar to the formal; they include familiar conversation, private correspondence, formal conversation, familiar public address, formal platform or pulpit speech, public reading, public worship, expository writing, formal literary prose, and poetry. The different functional varieties of language are equally good for their respective uses. Kenyon points out that the tendency to confuse cultural level and functional variety has resulted in a misconception that colloquial language is something to be looked down upon.

The concept of functional variety was further developed by Martin Joos, a structuralist and a professor of linguistics at the University of Toronto. His ideas are set forth in his monograph *The Five Clocks* (1961), and in brief form in his article, "Homeostasis in English Usage" (1962), in which he points out that

331

linguistic usage is only part of the culture of a society and is in homeostatic equilibrium with the rest of the culture. Functional variety allows homeostatic equilibrium to be established in different social situations. Joos identifies five varieties or styles: intimate, the private language of family conversation; casual, used among friends and in working teams; consultative, the norm for coming to terms with strangers; formal, used for lecturing; and frozen or literary, the style for print or declamation. Authoritarians view only the formal and frozen styles as correct, whereas liberals recognize the entire linguistic spectrum.

Interest in the many varieties of English has resulted in serious studies of nonstandard dialects. A great deal of important work has been done by William Labov, a sociolinguist who works within the framework of transformational grammar. In *The Study of Nonstandard English* (1969), he points out that non-standard dialects are self-contained systems that follow their own sets of rules. These dialects are organized just as systematically as the standard forms of the language. If teachers are to teach standard English efficiently, they must under-stand the rules that are being followed by nonstandard speakers and be able to explain the alternative rules that operate in the standard form of the language. Differences exist in pronunciation, the tense system, the formation of negatives and questions, the use of auxiliaries, and the use of pronominal apposition. However, nonstandard dialects are not radically different systems from standard English but are closely related to it.

Labov has found that Kenyon's distinction between cultural levels and func-tional varieties of English actually does not hold up. Style and class stratification of language are not independent. The same variables that are used in style shift-ing also distinguish cultural or social levels of English. This is true for phonolog-ical variables such as pronunciation of *th*, *-ing*, and *r*, and for grammatical vari-ables such as pronominal apposition (My mother, she works there), the double negative (He isn't going nowhere), and the use of *ain't*. There is social stratifica-tion for each level of style, from casual to formal, but each group uses the same linguistic features and shows regular style shifting in the same direction.[1] Most people are not aware of their style shifting but tend to vary their speech uncon-sciously according to the social situation.

The ability to vary style and to recognize the social value of different forms is part of an individual's competence, just as much as is the knowledge of rules of grammar. Rules of appropriateness, conceptions of self and of others, mean-ings associated with particular forms and with the act of speaking, and knowl-edge of contexts are all brought to bear on speech.[2] Studies of sociolinguists suggest that the concept of competence should be broadened to include such fac-tors, and that the goals of linguistics should be broadened to include the study of language in its entire cultural setting.

[1]William Labov, *The Study of Nonstandard English* (Urbana, Ill.: NCTE, 1969), p. 22.
[2]Dell Hymes, *Foundations of Sociolinguistics* (Philadelphia: Univ. of Pennsylvania, 1974), p. 94.

Cultural Levels and Functional Varieties of English

JOHN S. KENYON

The word *level*, when used to indicate different styles of language, is a metaphor, suggesting higher or lower position and, like the terms *higher* and *lower*, figuratively implies "better" or "worse," "more desirable" or "less desirable," and similar comparative degrees of excellence or inferiority in language.

The application of the term *level* to those different styles of language that are not properly distinguished as better or worse, desirable or undesirable, creates a false impression. I confess myself guilty of this error along with some other writers. What are frequently grouped together in one class as different levels of language are often in reality false combinations of two distinct and incommensurable categories, namely, *cultural levels* and *functional varieties*.

Among *cultural levels* may be included, on the lower levels, illiterate speech, narrowly local dialect, ungrammatical speech and writing, excessive and unskillful slang, slovenly and careless vocabulary and construction, exceptional pronunciation, and, on the higher level, language used generally by the cultivated, clear, grammatical writing, and pronunciations used by the cultivated over wide areas. The different cultural levels may be summarized in the two general classes *substandard* and *standard*.

Among *functional varieties* not depending on cultural levels may be mentioned colloquial language, itself existing in different degrees of familiarity or formality, as, for example, familiar conversation, private correspondence, formal conversation, familiar public address; formal platform or pulpit speech, public reading, public worship; legal, scientific, and other expository writing; prose and poetic belles-lettres. The different functional varieties may roughly be grouped together in the two classes *familiar* and *formal* writing or speaking.

The term *level*, then, does not properly belong at all to functional varieties of speech — colloquial, familiar, formal, scientific, literary language. They are equally "good" for their respective functions, and as classifications do not depend on the cultural status of the users.

The two groupings *cultural levels* and *functional varieties* are not mutually exclusive categories. They are based on entirely separate principles of classification: *culture* and *function*. Although we are here principally concerned with the

(from *College English*, 10 (1948), 31–36.)

functional varieties of standard English (the highest cultural level), yet substandard English likewise has its functional varieties for its different occasions and purposes. Thus the functional variety colloquial English may occur on a substandard cultural level, but the term *colloquial* does not itself designate a cultural level. So the functional variety formal writing or speaking may occur on a lower or on a higher cultural level according to the social status of writer or speaker, and sometimes of reader or audience. It follows, for instance, that the colloquial language of cultivated people is on a higher cultural level than the formal speech of the semiliterate or than some inept literary writing.

Semiliterate formal speech is sometimes heard from radio speakers. I recently heard one such speaker solemnly announce, "Sun day will be Mother's Day." Because the speaker, in his ignorance of good English, thought he was making himself plainer by using the distorted pronunciation *sun day* instead of the standard pronunciation *sundy*, he was actually misunderstood by some listeners to be saying, "Some day will be Mother's Day." About forty years ago the great English phonetician Henry Sweet used this very example to show that "we cannot make words more distinct by disguising them."[1] He was referring to the use, as in this instance, of the full sound of vowels in unaccented syllables where standard English has obscure vowels. On the same page Sweet gives another example of the same blunder: "Thus in the sentence *I shall be at home from one to three* the substitution of *tuw* for *tǝ* [ǝ = the last sound in *sofa*] at once suggests a confusion between the preposition and the numeral." This was also verified on the radio. Not long ago I heard a radio speaker announce carefully, "This program will be heard again tomorrow from one two three." I have also recorded (among many others) the following such substandard forms from the radio: *presidEnt* for the standard form *prǝsident*, the days of the week ending in the full word *day* instead of the standard English syllable *-dy*, *ay man* for the correct *ǝ man*, *cahnsider* for *cǝnsider*, *tooday* for *tǝday*, *too go* for *tǝ go*, *Coalumbia* for *Cǝlumbia*, etc. This is merely one sort among many of substandard features in the formal speech of the semiliterate.

To begin my strictures at home, in *American Pronunciation* (9th ed., 4th printing, p. 17), I use the page heading "Levels of Speech." This should be "Functional Varieties of Standard Speech," for the reference is solely to the different uses of speech on the one cultivated level. Similarly, in the Kenyon-Knott *Pronouncing Dictionary of American English* (p. xvi, sec. 2), I carelessly speak of "levels of the colloquial" where I mean "styles of the colloquial," as three lines above. For though there are different cultural levels of colloquial English, the reference here is only to standard colloquial.

S. A. Leonard and H. Y. Moffett, in their study, "Current Definition of Levels in English Usage," say (p. 348): "The levels of English usage have been most clearly described in Dr. Murray's Preface [General Explanations, p. xvii] to the *New English Dictionary*.[2] I have varied his diagram a little in order to

---

[1] Henry Sweet, *The Sounds of English* (Oxford: Oxford Univ. Press, 1910), p. 78.
[2] S. A. Leonard and H. Y. Moffett, *English Journal*, 26, 5 (May, 1927), 345–59.

illustrate better the overlapping between the categories.'' It appears to me that Leonard and Moffett have so varied the diagram as to obscure Murray's intention. For he is not here primarily exhibiting levels of speech but is showing the ''Anglicity,'' or limits of the English vocabulary for the purposes of his dictionary. The only topical divisions of his diagram that imply a cultural level are ''slang'' and ''dialectal,'' and the only statement in his explanation of the diagram that could imply it is, ''Slang words ascend through colloquial use.'' This may imply that slang is on a lower cultural level than ''colloquial, literary, technical, scientific, foreign.'' We may also safely infer that Murray would place ''Dialectal'' on a lower level than colloquial and literary if he were here concerned with cultural levels. Murray's diagram rests consistently on the same basis of classification throughout (''Anglicity''), and he emphasizes that ''there is absolutely no defining line in any direction'' [from the central nucleus of colloquial and literary]. Moreover, Murray's exposition here concerns only vocabulary, with no consideration of the other features that enter so largely into ''levels'' of language — grammatical form and structure, pronunciation, spelling, and meaning — of styles, in short, only so far as they are affected by vocabulary. These he treats of elsewhere but without reference to levels.

It is not quite clear just how far Leonard and Moffett intend their grouping ''literary English,'' ''standard, cultivated, colloquial English,'' and ''naif, popular, or uncultivated English'' to be identical with what they call Murray's ''levels,'' his description of which they commend. But it is clear that they call their own grouping ''three levels of usage'' (p. 357) and classify them together as a single descending scale (cf. ''the low end of the scale,'' p. 358). The inevitable impression that the average reader receives from such an arrangement of the scale is: highest level, literary English; next lower level, colloquial English; lowest level, illiterate English; whereas, in fact, the first two ''levels'' are functional varieties of the one cultural level standard English, while the third (''illiterate or uncultivated,'' p. 358) is a cultural level.

Krapp has a chapter on ''The Levels of English Speech,'' in which he reveals some awareness of the confusion of cultural levels with functional varieties. He says:

> Among those who pay any heed at all to convention in social relationships, a difference of degree is implicit in all use of English. This difference of degree is usually thought of in terms of higher and lower, of upper levels of speech appropriate to certain occasions of more formal character, of lower levels existing, if not necessarily appropriate, among less elevated circumstances. These popular distinctions of level may be accepted without weighting them too heavily with significance in respect of good, better, and best in speech. A disputatious person might very well raise the question whether literary English, ordinarily regarded as being on a high level, is really any better than the spoken word, is really as good as the spoken word, warm with the breath of the living moment.[3]

[3]George Philip Krapp, *The Knowledge of English* (New York: Charles Scribners, 1927), pp. 55–76.

At the risk of having to own the hard impeachment of being disputatious, I must express the fear that the logical fallacy in treating of levels, which Krapp rather lightly waves aside, is having a serious effect on general ideas of speech levels, and especially of the significance of colloquial English in good usage. Krapp's grouping, frankly on a scale of "levels" throughout, constitutes a descending scale from the highest "Literary English," through "Formal Colloquial," "General Colloquial," "Popular English," to the lowest, "Vulgar English." Here the fallacy is obvious: Literary English, Formal Colloquial, and General Colloquial are not cultural levels but only functional varieties of English all on the one cultural level of standard English. The last two, Popular English and Vulgar English, belong in a different order of classification, cultural levels, without regard to function.

So in his succeeding discussion *level* sometimes means the one, sometimes the other; now a functional variety of standard English, and now a cultural level of substandard or of standard English. It is functional on page 58 ("a choice between two levels") and on page 60 ("level of general colloquial"), cultural on page 62 ("popular level" and "cultivated level") and on pages 63–64 ("popular level," "level of popular speech"), functional on page 64 ("general colloquial level"), cultural again on the same page ("popular level", "still lower level"), cultural on page 67 ("vulgar . . . level of speech," "applying the term 'vulgar' to it at certain levels"), cultural on page 68 ("its own [popular] level"), cultural and functional in the same phrase on page 68 ("speakers from the popular and the general colloquial level meet and mix"), and so on most confusingly to page 75.

The same kind of mixture of cultural levels and functional varieties is thrown into one apparently continuous scale by Kennedy: "There is the formal and dignified language of the scholarly or scientific address or paper . . . . The precision and stateliness of this uppermost level . . . is a necessary accompaniment of thinking on a high plane." Next in order he mentions colloquial speech, which he refers to as "the second level, . . . generally acceptable to people of education and refinement."[4] Clearly this is not a cultural level but a functional variety of standard English, like the "uppermost level." The third level is, however, a cultural one: "the latest slang," workmen's "technical slang and colloquialisms which other persons cannot comprehend," "grammatical solecisms." "The speech of this third level can fairly be ranked as lower in the social scale." His fourth level is also cultural: "At the bottom of the scale is the lingo, or cant, of criminals, hobos, and others of the lowest social levels."

Finally, Kennedy fixes the false mental image of a continuous and logically consistent descent from "the cold and lonely heights of formal and highly specialized scientific and scholarly language" to "the stupid and slovenly level of grammatical abuses and inane slang." In reality there is no cultural descent

---

[4]Arthur G. Kennedy, *Current English* (Boston: Little Brown Co., 1935), pp. 15–17.

until we reach his third "level," since "formal and dignified language" and "colloquial speech" are only functional varieties of English on the one cultural level of standard English.

In Perrin's excellent and useful *Index*, under the heading "Levels of Usage," he names "three principal levels": "Formal English" (likened to formal dress), "Informal English" (described as "the typical language of an educated person going about his everyday affairs"), and "Vulgate English."[5] From his descriptions it appears clearly that Formal and Informal English are functional varieties of standard English, while Vulgate is a substandard cultural level. A similar classification appears in his table on page 365.

On page 19, Perrin uses *level* apparently in the sense of functional variety, not of cultural level: "Fundamentally, good English is speaking or writing in the level of English that is appropriate to the particular situation that faces the speaker or writer. It means making a right choice among the levels of usage." His advice, however, involves two choices: 1) choice of a standard cultural level and 2) choice of the appropriate functional variety of that level.

A clear instance of the inconsistent use of the term *level* is found in Robert C. Pooley's *Teaching English Usage* (New York, 1946), chapter iii, "Levels in English Usage." He names five levels: 1) the illiterate level; 2) the homely level; 3) standard English, informal level; 4) standard English, formal level; and 5) the literary level. In (1) and (2) *level* has an altogether different meaning from that in (3), (4), and (5). In the first two *level* plainly means "cultural level"; in the last three it just as plainly means "functional variety of standard English," all three varieties being therefore on the one cultural level of standard English. So *level* in the two groups belongs to different orders of classification. All misunderstanding and wrong implication would be removed from this otherwise excellent treatment of levels if the last three groups were labeled "Standard English Level, Informal Variety"; "Standard English Level, Formal Variety"; and "Standard English Level, Literary Variety." Pooley's groups contain three cultural levels (illiterate, homely, standard) and three functional varieties of the standard cultural level (informal, formal, literary).

The misapplication to colloquial English of the term *level*, metaphorically appropriate only to cultural gradations, is especially misleading. We often read of English that is "on the colloquial level." For example, Krapp writes: *"Who do you mean? . . .* has passed into current spoken use and may be accepted on the colloquial level."[6] This implies that colloquial English is on a different cultural level from formal English (literary, scientific, etc.), and a too frequent assumption, owing to this and other misuses of the term *colloquial*, is that its cultural level is below that of formal English. This supposition, tacit or explicit, that

[5]Porter G. Perrin, *An Index to English* (Chicago: University of Chicago Press, 1930), pp. 364–65.
[6]George Philip Krapp, *A Comprehensive Guide to Good English* (New York: Charles Scribners, 1927), p. 641.

colloquial style is inferior to formal or literary style, leads inescapably to the absurd conclusion that, whenever scientists or literary artists turn from their formal writing to familiar conversation with their friends, they thereby degrade themselves to a lower social status.

This misuse of *level* encourages the fallacy frequently met with of contrasting colloquial with standard English, logically as fallacious as contrasting white men with tall men. For instance, Mencken writes: "I have no doubt *but* that . . . seems to be very firmly lodged in colloquial American, and even to have respectable standing in the standard speech."[7] This contrast, not always specifically stated, is often implied. For example, Kennedy writes: "Colloquial English is, properly defined, the language of conversation, and especially of familiar conversation. As such it may approximate the standard speech of the better class of English speakers, or it may drop to the level of the illiterate and careless speaker."[8] *May approximate* should be replaced by *may be on the level of*.

Similarly, on page 440: "Some measure words [are] still used colloquially without any ending in the plural . . .; but most of these are given the *s* ending in standard English usage." Here *standard* is confused with *formal*.

Kennedy (pp. 534, 616) several times contrasts colloquial English with "standard literary English." This implies that colloquial English is not standard, while literary English is. If he means to contrast standard colloquial with standard literary, well and good; but I fear that most readers would understand the contrast to be of colloquial with standard.

The term *colloquial* cannot properly designate a substandard cultural level of English. It designates a functional variety — that used chiefly in conversation — and in itself says nothing as to its cultural level, though this discussion, and the dictionary definitions, are chiefly concerned with cultivated colloquial, a functional variety of standard English. When writers of such standing as those I have mentioned slip into expressions that imply lower cultural status of colloquial English, it is not surprising that some teachers fall into the error. One teacher expressed the conviction that colloquialisms should not be represented as standard American speech. But the context of the statement indicated that its author was using colloquialism in the sense of "localism." I could hardly believe how frequent this gross error is, until I heard it from a well-known American broadcaster.

The best dictionaries, at least in their definitions, give no warrant for the various misuses of *colloquial, colloquially, colloquialism, colloquiality*. I urge the reader to study carefully the definitions in the *Oxford English Dictionary*, with its many apt examples from standard writers, and in *Webster's New International Dictionary, Second Edition*, with its quotations from George Lyman Kittredge. Kittredge's views on the standing of colloquial English are well

---

[7]H. L. Mencken, *The American Language*, 4th ed. (New York: Alfred A. Knopf, 1938), p. 203.

[8]Kennedy, *Current English*, p. 26.

known. It is said that somebody once asked him about the meaning of the label "Colloq." in dictionaries. He is reported to have replied, "I myself speak 'colloke' and often write it." I cannot verify the story, but it sounds authentic.

It seems to me inevitable that the frequent groupings of so-called "levels" such as "Literary, Colloquial, Illiterate," and the like, will lead the reader to suppose that just as Illiterate is culturally below Colloquial, so Colloquial is culturally below Literary. While I can scarcely hope that my humble remonstrance will reform all future writing on "levels of English," I believe that writers who confuse the meaning of the term *level* must accept some part of the responsibility for the popular misunderstanding of the true status of colloquial English; for I cannot avoid the belief that the popular idea of colloquial English as something to be looked down upon with disfavor is due in part to the failure of writers on the subject to distinguish between *cultural levels of English* and *functional varieties of standard English*.

Homeostasis in English Usage

MARTIN JOOS

The first word of my title is a newcomer to our vocabulary, not to be found in the first printings of what we have begun to call "the old Webster" — the 1934 *Webster's New International Dictionary, Second Edition* — but in later printings it is entered and defined in the Addenda. It is a good specimen of the sort of words that get into the vocabulary on what may be called the highest level, being deliberately created for technical purposes, typically to designate something not previously known in the real world, so that a new discovery or a new creation comes into the world accompanied by its newly invented name. Another such word is *transistor*. Some of these words, for example *transistor*, promptly become popular words; and then of course the public extends or otherwise alters their meaning to suit convenience: thus for a normal American today a *transistor* is primarily a portable radio, and only secondarily is it one of the half-dozen or preferably more mysterious widgets which are essential to the new gadget. This popular adjustment in meaning of the new word is still too recent to appear in what we now call "the new Webster" — the 1961 *Webster's Third New International Dictionary* — but we can depend on its appearing in the new dictionary's Addenda in due course.

This prompt adoption, with adjustments of meaning, is a typical instance of homeostasis in English usage. The word *homeostasis* itself was at first a medical word. It was invented as a name for that characteristic of an organism, notably a human or other animal body, according to which the organism maintains its own integrity and restores its own normal pattern of functioning, by means of internal readjustments, whenever it suffers a disturbance that is not fatal. For instance, *homeostasis* labels the process, and also the results of the process, by which the body-temperature is brought back to normal after over-heating or chilling. The word is of course not an explanation: it is only a label, and the homeostatic processes still have to be investigated and explained in detail.

The addition of *transistor* to the English vocabulary, and the alteration of its meaning, is the simplest example I can think of for illustrating the homeostasis of English usage. When the widget which it names was created, that sub-culture which consists of the natural scientists would have suffered intolerable inconveniences and occasional misunderstanding if the thing had had to be described every time it was mentioned; to prevent that, that is to facilitate and protect discussion, the new name was promptly invented. Now those people constitute only a tiny fraction of the population, and their decisions as to the meaning of the new word could not be binding on the population as a whole when the transistor radio

(from *College Composition and Communication* (October 1962), 18–22.)

appeared on the market. Could the public be expected to adopt the word in its technical sense? That would have been doing things the hard way, for it would have entailed learning a little electronic theory, if only sketchily. The public is wiser than that. One of the most important rules in the homeostasis of culture is to avoid new ideas whenever possible, or in other words to do as little thinking as possible. Obeýing this principle, the technical name "transistor radio" was of course interpreted as formed on the model of two-piece nouns like "girl friend." A girl friend is a girl; therefore a transistor radio is a transistor. This economical solution is typical of cultural homeostasis, which minimizes effort and softens cultural shock whenever possible. The fact that some transistor radios also contain other new widgets which resemble transistors but only have two terminals, so that they are technically solid-state diodes instead, is of no cultural importance to the public; that sort of thing is left to the repairmen, another sub-culture. On the other hand, the fact that a transistor radio does not need two separate batteries, one of them an expensive high-voltage battery, is of considerable cultural significance; accordingly, the man in the street will tell you that this radio is called "a transistor" because it uses only one cheap battery, or a few pen-light "batteries" as he calls those cells, for it was long ago settled that a cell is a battery for public convenience. For public convenience, you see, the man in the street has an indefeasible right to make *transistor* or *battery* mean whatever he likes; and the electronics people, you will find, do not object to this at all. Who does?

Besides the population as a whole, and the two sub-cultures consisting of natural scientists and repairmen respectively, there is another sub-culture concerned; rather, another personality-type whose functioning in the homeostasis of culture is of great importance to us in this CCCC* meeting. Before speaking of those other people, let me first speak of a culture in which they are reported to be absent. My Chinese friends tell me that in traditional Chinese culture it is not customary to make invidious distinctions among different Chinese usages; instead, coolie Chinese is regarded as just as respectable as scholarly Chinese, each being regarded as holding its proper place in the economy of Chinese culture. They tell me that no native Chinese word, pronunciation, or other detail of native Chinese usage, is conventionally called "incorrect." No doubt I have not entirely understood those statements of theirs, but in outline the case seems to be clear, and I hope to make it clear why that state of affairs is at least possible.

If it is possible, why isn't our American culture of this Chinese type with respect to matters of English usage? The reason is certainly to be found in the historical differences between the two cultures. The Chinese have always been their own masters in dealing with their own language. Behind "English" teaching, in contrast, there was the older tradition of Latin teaching. No, I am not going to repeat the story of schoolmasterly efforts to reform English usage on the model of Latin usage, for instance the doctrine that an English infinitive ought not to be split because it is physically impossible to split a Latin infinitive. My

*Conference on College Composition and Communication (ed).

point is much simpler than that, and more basic. Latin necessarily had to be taught in terms of "correct" and "incorrect" for obvious reasons. When "English teaching" began in the history of our schools, the teachers assumed that English also had to be taught in terms of "correct" and "incorrect" — how else, after all, could you teach any language? That is the point. English usages differ, as we all know. To those differences the principle was now applied that competing usages have to be sorted out into "correct" and "incorrect" usages, the "incorrect" ones of course in the majority because they were always in the majority when the Latin teacher was struggling with his pupils. That the sorting-out was often done according to Latin rules is a point of quite minor significance by comparison, and will not concern us further.

Now let me just postpone the rest of that dismal story for a while, while I return to the nature of cultural homeostasis and to the homeostasis of English usage. It is plain that usage is only a part of the culture, and is in homeostatic equilibrium with the rest of culture as well as within itself. Already, within the short distance that my argument has covered, it has become evident that the relation of usage to the rest of the culture provides criteria by which we can distinguish what I mean to call "dimensions" of usage. One such dimension has already emerged: the dimension which extends from the strictly technical or esoteric employment of such a word as *transistor*, through about three intermediate employments, all the way to the opposite extreme of strictly public or exoteric employment of the same word, where it means "needing only a few cheap pen-light batteries." Since I need to mention this particular dimension frequently, I invent a name for it, of course, say the dimension or scale of *tericism*, running, as just stated, from one extreme of *eso*tericism to the opposite extreme of *exo*tericism. The function of tericism in the economy or homeostasis of culture and usage is perfectly clear: it provides, at each point along the scale, precisely that meaning of the term *transistor* which is most useful and most convenient there.

The implications of this fact will become clearer when we consider a few other scales of usage. Four other scales have been listed in my monograph *The Five Clocks*, and two of them discussed rather fully there. (It would be nice to discover that there are just five scales, as well as five points on each scale, but I am not sure of that — at least not yet).

Most interesting to me, and consequently in my view most important among these scales, is what I call the scale or dimension of *style*, by which I mean what John S. Kenyon called "functional varieties" of usage. Let me just sketch the scale of style here; for a fuller treatment, see *The Five Clocks*.

At one extreme of the style scale is "intimate style," typically used between husband and wife in private. It is characterized by the employment of private jargon terms or family code-words presumed to be different from those used in other intimate groups, and by a sort of skeletonizing of sentences which often leaves nothing of the sentence but a melodious murmur. The second step on the style scale is "casual style," used among close friends and in working teams when there is no difficult information to be conveyed; it is marked by the use of slang and ellipsis. The third style is "consultative style," our norm for coming to terms with strangers who presumably speak the same language; it is therefore an entirely public style and is marked by devices for facilitating understanding and cooperation in temporary groupings, notably the standard listeners' insertions "yeah, unhunh, that's right, oh, I see, yes I know" and the "well" that means "now it's my turn to speak," and by the habit of supplying background information as needed, or even more than is needed. The fourth is "formal style," used for lecturing; it is marked by impersonality and thorough organization. The fifth style is what I have called "frozen style" for literary convenience; it is a style for print or declamation, and it is marked by depth of allusiveness and of appeal to the reader's total experience. Frozen style, which has also been called literary style, is diametrically opposed to formal style at least in the sense that formal style accomplishes its task by means of clarity, while frozen style accomplishes a quite different task by means of ambiguity. Some of us try to teach formal-style composition; nobody can teach frozen style: each writer has to invent his own, just as each family has to invent its own jargon. Thus, you see, the scale of styles closes into a circle.

The three central styles, namely casual, consultative, and formal style, are presumably the common property of all of us here at this CCCC meeting, besides which most of us are married and a few of us are literary workers. For my further argument, though, the three central styles will suffice.

It is obvious, I hope, that the scale of styles is not the same thing as the scale of tericism. The five steps of the one scale and the five steps of the other scale are in principle independent. If they were in practice entirely independent, there would be twenty-five combinations; actually, about fifteen combinations are used freely. If there were complete interdependence, only five combinations would be possible; fifteen is halfway between five and twenty-five, showing semi-independence; so that the two scales, tericity and style, deserve to be named separately, leaving their semi-dependence for later research and discussion for which there is no time here.

Each step on the tericism scale is marked by its own meanings for the word *transistor* and of course for thousands of other words. Conversely, each step on the style scale is marked by its favorite words and formulas, some of which are obviously nothing but labels for specific styles. For instance, "Come on!" is a label which distinguishes casual style from all other styles; the all-purpose preposition *on* "about, concerning, regarding, etc." is a specific marker of consultative style; the use of *may* "might, can" is a notorious label of formal style. When somebody says "I'd like to see you on a typewriter" he is asking for a consultation, of course in consultative style; you can't get a normal speaker of

English to use *may* in the same sentence with this *on*. The social convenience, not to say necessity, of this labeling technique is so evident that no further discussion is needed.

Now let us turn to another dimension or scale for measuring English usage. This will be the scale of *responsibility*, whose five steps are "bad, fair, good, better, best." Speakers use this scale to indicate how much responsibility they are willing to assume. The speaker who says *hisself* doesn't do it because he doesn't know the form *himself*: not to know it, he would have to be a hermit. He says *hisself* to signal the message "No responsibilities wanted!" At the opposite extreme, the speaker who uses the best English is telling us that he would like to be elected President of the United States. He is misguided, of course, if that is what he really wants; for the electorate prefers the middle of this scale, "good" usage, and instead makes a schoolteacher of the "best" speaker, or causes him to be appointed Ambassador to the United Nations. When I say "best" I do not, of course, mean the extreme of pedantry or genteelness: that belongs to still another scale, the scale of "breadth" which runs "popular, provincial, standard, puristic, genteel" and will presently be treated in a different pattern of discussion.

The relation of the breadth scale to all the rest is peculiar, in that it distinguishes types of culture by the different degrees of strength of the breadth scale in different cultures. Where the breadth scale has weak status, we find the liberalism of what I have called the Chinese type; where it is extremely strong, we find the absolutism of Arabic culture, where only the classical language is recognized as a language at all, so that *all* the language of practical life is categorized as "not the language"; in between, where the breadth scale has moderate strength, we find the schizophrenic American culture, torn between liberty and authority, the least happy of the three named.

Cultural schizophrenia is the natural matrix of contention, pulling and hauling, between advocates of liberalism and those of authoritarianism. In this contention, the authoritarians have an automatic advantage because their doctrine is simplistic. The authoritarian doctrine, looked at from the liberal or pluralistic point of view, takes on this appearance:

		Liberal		Authoritarian
Tericism	*Style*	*Responsibility*	*Breadth*	*Correctness*
esoteric	frozen	best	genteel	correct
careful	formal	better	puristic	
average	consultative	good	standard	
careless	casual	fair	provincial	incorrect
exoteric	intimate	bad	popular	

Another way of looking at the authoritarian doctrine is to call it not schizophrenia but drug-addiction. A culture like ours has its own sort of stable homeostasis, but this is the homeostasis of a drug-addict, who can function with his own kind of normality only as long as the supply of the drug is maintained. If he feels that the supply is in danger of being cut off or even reduced, he reacts promptly, more or less violently, and even irrationally. For example, we are at present witnessing a storm of violent and almost entirely irrational reaction to the appearance of the new dictionary, a reaction which is quite easy to understand if we compare it to the behavior of a drug-addict in the throes of withdrawal symptoms, though we must admit that it also exhibits some of the symptoms of cultural psychosis. In any case, the reaction itself is clearly part of the homeostasis of our culture, and we just have to live with it.

The Study of Nonstandard English

WILLIAM LABOV

CHAPTER II: THE NATURE OF LANGUAGE

It may seem altogether unnecessary to write very much about the nature of language in general, since all readers of this paper are speakers of one or several languages and have taught language or talked about it. Yet there are many oversimplified versions of what language is, of the "nothing but . . ." type, and some of these have indeed been encouraged by linguists. We hear that language is nothing but a series of sounds or words, a series of signals which succeed each other in linear fashion, or a succession of signs which unite in each a form and a referent. Such descriptions are far too superficial to account for the complex process of translating meanings or intentions into sound. The propositions we wish to convey are intricate and many-dimensional; our language must transform these into the linear series of symbols which can be spoken; our understanding of language must enable us to reconstruct this unfolded message into the replica of the original.

Let us consider such a sentence as *John wants to know how you like him*. As it is spoken, it consists of a chain of eight words in succession. But it conveys a complex message containing at least three distinct propositions. The dominant sentence is that *John wants something*. What is that something? It is *to know something else*. There is no immediate subject of *know* — it has been deleted by a regular rule — but it is plainly John who is *to know something else*. And that something else is *the extent to which*, or *how you like him*. We can suggest the complexity of this sentence by a diagram such as the following:

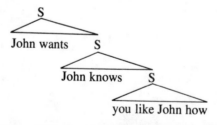

It might be possible for a language to glue these three propositions together by simple adjunction into something like *John wants John knows you like John how*. But we never hear anything like this; every school child is in control of a complex series of deletions, substitutions, and foregroundings which produce *John wants to know how you like him*. To produce this sentence he must at least

(from William Labov, *The Study of Nonstandard English*, Champaign, Ill.: NCTE, 1969, pp. 7–38.)

1. Attach the second sentence to the first as an infinitive with *for . . . to* as complementizer
   John wants for (John) to know . . .
2. Drop the second John as identical with the first
   John wants for . . . to know . . .
3. Drop the first half of the complementizer *for*
   John wants to know . . .
4. Bring the question word *how* in the third sentence to the front
   John wants to know how you like John . . .
5. Convert this *John* into the appropriate pronoun *him*.

One cannot overemphasize how abstract and complex the organization of language rules is. By "language rules" we do not mean the small number of rules that can be taught explicitly in school but rather the very large number which the child learns for himself before he comes to school. When the five-year-old first appears in kindergarten, he has learned a sizable number of individual words, a small set of articulations which he combines to make this larger number of words, and a very intricate syntax — far richer than anything we can now describe — which combines these words into sentences. Furthermore, the child knows many rules for the use of his language which we cannot yet even begin to formalize: how to answer questions, make objections, challenges, denials; how to tell stories and manufacture excuses.

What are the main features of language which the child must learn in school? He has of course an alphabetic code to learn, and there are a number of word forms which have to be adjusted to the standard shape: *brefekst* or *brekfust* has to become *breakfast*. There are many formal additions to his syntax which must eventually be made. For example, he must learn that whatever structures can be used for object noun phrases can also be used for subject noun phrases: it must be possible to say *How you like him is what John wants to know*, or even *The knowledge John wants to have is of how you like him*, but additions such as this may come very late if at all.

The child must also learn a number of alternative rules which do the same work as the rules he brought with him but in a slightly different way. *Who do you want?* and *It's me* are produced by his original rule that puts objective forms after the verb, subjective forms before; he will now be taught the rule that yields *Whom do you want?* and *It's I*, even if he does not use these in colloquial speech. *Ain't* must alternate with *isn't*, *hasn't* (or *didn't*); and the passive of *He got kicked* must alternate with *He was kicked*. In reading, he must also learn left to right visual patterning — for some children a new and difficult system — and a way of transferring information across the printed page instead of storing it in an auditory short-term memory.

In all these tasks, the child's underlying *competence* must be distinguished from his *performance*. This distinction, as elaborated by Chomsky, is sometimes overused to exclude the very data on nonstandard language which we will discuss below, but it applies with overpowering force to the classroom situation. Every good teacher knows that what a child says in class is determined by many factors besides his knowledge of English. His knowledge is an abstract, often unconscious pattern which may or may not be activated by the teacher's command or the test situation. Unfortunately, those who apply objective tests to measure the child's verbal capacity usually do not take this fundamental distinction into account and derive very misleading indices of children's linguistic skills.

We must also bear in mind the important distinction between production and perception. Not very long ago, linguists thought it might be possible to write a single grammar which would describe a person's capacity to produce and to understand language. But there is now a fair amount of evidence to show that a speaker's production and perception may not be symmetrical. The child's ability to understand language often outruns his ability to produce it, yet we often find the converse, too, as when children use words that are formally correct yet inappropriate in context.

The child continues to learn language after he enters school, but not all learning is dependent upon the classroom. Through reading he begins to learn the vast latinate vocabulary which provides the basis of the long-vowel-short-vowel correspondences: *decide - decision, telescope - telescopic*, and so on. He also will learn the social meaning of language differences: that there are sets of values clustering around language which are very different in his own peer group and in the adult world. He will acquire a rich set of rules for various speech occasions in which, as a small child, he was practically tongue-tied. For our purposes, it is important to note that he will also acquire a series of defensive manoeuvres which will enable him to present a dense, resistant front to the teacher's incessant test-questions and help him avoid commiting himself to the mistakes for which he will be penalized.

2.1. Three reasons for studying nonstandard language

Since language learning does take place outside of the classroom, and the six-year-old child does have great capacity for learning new language forms as he is exposed to them, it may be asked why it should be necessary for the teacher to understand more about the child's own vernacular. First, we can observe that automatic adjustment does *not* take place in all cases. Even the successful middle class student does not always master the teacher's grammatical forms; and in the urban ghettos we find very little adjustment to school forms. Students continue to write *I have live* after ten or twelve years in school; we will describe below failures in reading the *-ed* suffix which show no advance with years in school. Second, knowledge of the underlying structure of the nonstandard vernacular will allow the most efficient teaching. If the teacher knows the general difference between standard negative attraction and nonstandard negative concord, he can teach a hundred different standard forms with the simple instruction: *The nega-*

tive is attracted only to the first indefinite. Thus by this one rule we can make many corrections:

> He don't know nothing. → He doesn't know anything.
> Nobody don't like him. → Nobody likes him.
> Nobody hardly goes there. → Hardly anybody goes there.
> Can't nobody do it. → Nobody can do it.

Third, the vernacular must be understood because ignorance of it leads to serious conflict between student and teacher. Teachers in ghetto schools who continually insist that *i* and *e* sound different in *pin* and *pen* will only antagonize a great number of their students. The knowledge that *i* and *e* actually sound the same before *m* and *n* for most of their students (and "should" sound the same if they are normal speakers) will help avoid this destructive conflict. Teachers who insist that a child meant to say *He is tired* when he said *He tired* will achieve only bewilderment in the long run. Knowledge that *He tired* is the vernacular equivalent of the contracted form *He's tired* will save teacher and student from this frustration.

Granted that the teacher wishes to learn about the student's language, what methods are available for him to do so? Today, a great many linguists study English through their own intuitions; they operate "out of their own heads" in the sense that they believe they can ask and answer all the relevant questions themselves. But even if a teacher comes from the same background as his students, he will find that his grammar has changed, that he no longer has firm intuitions about whether he can say *Nobody don't know nothing about it* instead of *Nobody knows nothing about it*. He can of course sit down with a student and ask him all kinds of direct questions about his language, and there are linguists who do this. But one cannot draw directly upon the intuitions of the two major groups we are interested in, children and nonstandard speakers. Both are in contact with a superordinate or dominant dialect, and both will provide answers which reflect their awareness of this dialect as much as of their own. One can of course engage in long and indirect conversations with students, hoping that all of the forms of interest will sooner or later occur, and there are linguists who have attempted to study nonstandard dialects in this way. But these conversations usually teach the subject more of the investigator's language than the other way around. In general, one can say that whenever a speaker of a nonstandard dialect is in a subordinate position to a speaker of a standard dialect, the rules of his grammar will shift in an unpredictable manner towards the standard. The longer the contact, the stronger and more lasting is the shift. Thus adolescent speakers of a vernacular make very unreliable informants when they are questioned in a formal framework. The investigator must show considerable sociolinguistic sophistication to cope with such a situation, and indeed the teacher will also need to know a great deal about the social forces which affect linguistic behavior if he is to interpret his students' language.

2.2. Nonstandard dialects as "self-contained" systems

The traditional view of nonstandard speech as a set of isolated deviations from standard English is often countered by the opposite view: that nonstandard dialect should be studied as an isolated system in its own right, without any reference to standard English. It is argued that the system of grammatical forms of a dialect can only be understood through their internal relations. For example, nonstandard Negro English has one distinction which standard English does not have: there is an invariant form *be* in *He always be foolin' around* which marks habitual, general conditions, as opposed to the unmarked *is, am, are*, etc., which do not have any such special sense. It can be argued that the existence of this distinction changes the value of all other members of the grammatical system and that the entire paradigm of this dialect is therefore different from that of standard English. It is indeed important to find such relations within the meaningful set of grammatical distinctions, if they exist, because we can then *explain* rather than merely describe behavior. There are many co-occurrence rules which are purely descriptive — the particular dialect just happens to have X′ and Y′ where another has X and Y. We would like to know if a special nonstandard form X′ *requires* an equally nonstandard Y′ because of the way in which the nonstandard form cuts up the entire field of meaning. This would be a tremendous help in teaching, since we would be able to show what sets of standard rules have to be taught together to avoid confusing the student with a mixed, incoherent grammatical system.

The difficulty here is that linguistics has not made very much progress in the analysis of semantic systems. There is no method or procedure which leads to reliable or reproducible results — not even among those who agree on certain principles of grammatical theory. No one has yet written a complete grammar of a language — or even come close to accounting for all the morphological and syntactic rules of a language. And the situation is much more primitive in semantics; for example, the verbal system of standard English has been studied now for many centuries, yet there is no agreement at all on the meaning of the auxiliaries *have . . . ed* and *be . . . ing*. The meaning of *I have lived here*, as opposed to *I lived here*, has been explained as a) relevant to the present, b) past *in* the present, c) perfective, d) indefinite, e) causative, and so on. It is not only that there are many views; it is that in any given discussion no linguist has really found a method by which he can reasonably hope to persuade others that he is right. If this situation prevails where most of the investigators have complete access to the data, since they are native speakers of standard English, we must be more than cautious in claiming to understand the meaning of *I be here* as opposed to *I am here* in nonstandard Negro English, and even more cautious in claiming that the meaning of nonstandard *I'm here* therefore differs from standard *I'm here* because of the existence of the other form. Most teachers have learned to be cautious in accepting a grammarian's statement about the meaning of their own native forms, but they have no way of judging statements made about a dialect which they do not speak, and they are naturally prone to accept such statements on the authority of the writer.

There is, however, a great deal that we can do to show the internal relations in the nonstandard dialect as a system. There are a great many forms which seem different on the surface but can be explained as expressions of a single rule, or the absence of a single rule. We observe that in nonstandard Negro English it is common to say *a apple* rather than *an apple*. This is a grammatical fault from the point of view of standard speakers, and the school must teach *an apple* as the written, standard form. There is also a rather low-level, unimportant feature of pronunciation which is common to southern dialects: in *the apple*, the word *the* has the same pronunciation as in *the book* and does not rhyme with *be*. Finally, we can note that, in the South, educated white speakers keep the vocalic schwa which represents *r* in *four*, but nonstandard speakers tend to drop it (registered in dialect writing as *fo' o'clock*). When all these facts are put together, we can begin to explain the nonstandard *a apple* as part of a much broader pattern. There is a general rule of English which states that we do not pronounce two (phonetic) vowels in succession. Some kind of semi-consonantal glide or consonant comes in between: an *n* as in *an apple*, a "*y*" as in *the apple*, an *r* as in *four apples*. In each of these cases, this rule is not followed for nonstandard Negro English. A teacher may have more success in getting students to write *an apple* if he presents this general rule and connects up all of these things into a single rational pattern, even if some are not important in themselves. It will "make sense" to Negro speakers, since they do not drop *l* before a vowel, and many rules of their sound system show the effect of a following vowel.

There are many ways in which an understanding of the fundamental rules of the dialect will help to explain the surface facts. Some of the rules cited above are also important in explaining why nonstandard Negro speakers sometimes delete *is*, in *He is ready*, but almost always delete *are*, in *You are ready*; or why they say *they book* and *you book* but not *we book*. It does not always follow, though, that a grammatical explanation reveals the best method for teaching standard English.

Systematic analysis may also be helpful in connecting up the nonstandard form with the corresponding standard form and in this sense understanding the meaning of the nonstandard form. For example, nonstandard speakers say *Ain't nobody see it*. What is the nearest standard equivalent? We can connect this up with the standard negative "foregrounding" of *Scarcely did anybody see it*, or, even more clearly, the literary expression *Nor did anybody see it*. This foregrounding fits in with the general colloquial southern pattern with indefinite subjects: *Didn't anybody see it*, nonstandard *Didn't nobody see it*. In these cases, the auxiliary *didn't* is brought to the front of the sentence, like the *ain't* in the nonstandard sentence. But there is another possibility. We could connect up *Ain't nobody see it* with the sentence *It ain't nobody see it*, that is, "There isn't anybody who sees it"; the dummy *it* of nonstandard Negro English corresponds to standard *there*, and, like *there*, it can be dropped in casual speech. Such an explanation is the only one possible in the case of such nonstandard sentences as *Ain't nothin' went down*. This could not be derived from **Nothin' ain't went down*, a sentence type which never occurs. If someone uses one of these forms, it is important for the teacher to know what was intended, so that he can supply the standard equivalent. To do so, one must know a great deal about many underlying rules of the nonstandard dialect, and also a great deal about the rules of English in general.

2.3. Nonstandard English as a close relative of standard English

Differences between standard and nonstandard English are not as sharp as our first impressions would lead us to think. Consider, for example, the socially stratified marker of "pronominal apposition" — the use of a dependent pronoun in such sentences as

My oldest sister she worked at the bank.

Though most of us recognize this as a nonstandard pattern, it is not always realized that the "nonstandard" aspect is merely a slight difference in intonation. A standard speaker frequently says the same thing, with a slight break after the subject: *My oldest sister — she works at the bank, and she finds it very profitable*. There are many ways in which a greater awareness of the standard colloquial forms would help teachers interpret the nonstandard forms. Not only do standard speakers use pronominal apposition with the break noted above, but in casual speech they can also bring object noun phrases to the front, "foregrounding" them. For example, one can say

My oldest sister — she worked at the Citizens Bank in Passaic last year.
The Citizens Bank, in Passaic — my oldest sister worked there last year.
Passaic — my oldest sister worked at the Citizens Bank there last year.

Note that if the foregrounded noun phrase represents a locative — the "place where" — then its position is held by *there*, just as the persons are represented by pronouns. If we are dealing with a time element, it can be foregrounded without replacement in any dialect: *Last year, my older sister worked at the Citizens Bank in Passaic.*

It is most important for the teacher to understand the relation between standard and nonstandard and to recognize that nonstandard English is a system of rules, different from the standard but not necessarily inferior as a means of communication. All of the teacher's social instincts, past training, and even faith in his own education lead him to believe that other dialects of English are merely "mistakes" without any rhyme or rationale.

In this connection, it will be helpful to examine some of the most general grammatical differences between English dialects spoken in the United States. One could list a very large number of "mistakes," but when they are examined systematically the great majority appear to be examples of a small number of differences in the rules. The clearest analysis of these differences has been made by Edward Klima (1964). He considers first the dialect in which people say sentences like

Who could she see?
Who did he speak with?
He knew who he spoke with.
The leader who I saw left.
The leader who he spoke with left.

What is the difference between this dialect and standard English? The usual schoolbook answer is to say that these are well-known mistakes in the use of *who* for *whom*. But such a general statement does not add any clarity to the situation; nor does it help the student to learn standard English. The student often leaves the classroom with no more than an uneasy feeling that *who* is incorrect and *whom* is correct. This is the state of half-knowledge that leads to hypercorrect forms such as *Whom did you say is calling?* In the more extreme cases, *whom* is seen as the only acceptable, polite form of the pronoun. Thus a certain receptionist at a hospital switchboard regularly answers the telephone: "Whom?"

The nonstandard dialect we see here varies from standard English by one simple difference in the order of rules. The standard language marks the objective case — the difference between *who* and *whom* — in a sentence form which preserves the original subject-object relation:

Q - She could see WH-someone.

The WH-symbol marks the point to be questioned in this sentence. When cases are marked in this sentence, the pronoun before the verb receives the unmarked subjective case and the pronoun after the verb the marked objective case.

Q - She (subjective case) - could see -WH-someone
(objective case)

The combination of WH, indefinite pronoun, and objective case is to be realized later as *whom*. At a later point, a rule of WH-attraction is applied which brings the WH-word to the beginning of the sentence:

Q - Whom - she - could - see

and finally the Q-marker effects a reversal of the pronoun and auxiliary, yielding the final result:

Whom could she see?

Here the objective case of the pronoun refers to the underlying position of the questioned pronoun as object of the verb.

The nonstandard dialect also marks cases: *I, he, she, they* are subjective forms, and *me, him, her, them* are objective. But the case marking is done after, rather than before, the WH-attraction rule applies. We begin with the same meaningful structure, *Q - She could see WH-someone*, but the first rule to consider is WH-attraction:

Q - WH-someone - she - could - see

Now the rule of case marking applies. Since both pronouns are before the verb, they are both unmarked:

Q - WH-someone (unmarked) - she (unmarked) - could see.

Finally, the question flip-flop applies, and we have

Who could she see?

The same mechanism applies to all of the nonstandard forms given above.

We can briefly consider another nonstandard grammatical rule, that which yields *It's me* rather than *It's I*. The difference here lies again in the rule of case marking. As noted above, this rule marks pronouns which occur after verbs; but the copula is not included. The nonstandard grammar which gives us *It's me* differs from standard English in only one simple detail — the case-marking rule includes the verb *to be* as well as other verbs. It is certainly not true that this nonstandard grammar neglects the case-marking rule; on the contrary, it applies the rule more generally than standard English here. But the order of the rules is the same as that for the nonstandard grammar just discussed: we get *Who is he?* rather than *Whom is he?* Like the other verbs, the copula marks the pronoun only after WH-attraction has applied.

In all of the examples just given, we can observe a general tendency towards simplification in the nonstandard grammars. There is a strong tendency to simplify the surface objects — that is, the words which come before the verb. This is most obvious in pronominal apposition. The foregrounded part identifies the person talked about, *my oldest sister*; this person is then "given," and the "new" predication is made with a pronoun subject: *she worked at the Citizens Bank*.

A parallel tendency is seen in the nonstandard grammars which confine the objective marker to positions after the verb. But this tendency to simplify subjects is not confined to standard colloquial English. Sentences such as the following are perfectly grammatical but are seldom if ever found in ordinary speech:

For him to have broken his word so often was a shame.

Most often we find that the rule of "extraposition" has applied, moving the complex subject to the end of the sentence:

It was a shame for him to have broken his word so often.

In general, we find that nonstandard English dialects are not radically different systems from standard English but are instead closely related to it. These dialects show slightly different versions of the same rules, extending and modifying the grammatical processes which are common to all dialects of English.

Any analysis of the nonstandard dialect which pretends to ignore other dialects and the general rules of English will fail 1) because the nonstandard dialect is *not* an isolated system but a part of the sociolinguistic structure of English, and 2) because of the writer's knowledge of standard English. But it would be unrealistic to think that we can write anything but a superficial account of the dialect if we confine our thinking to this one subsystem and ignore whatever progress has been made in the understanding of English grammar.

This work will not attempt to give a systematic account of any one nonstandard dialect but rather will dwell upon the general principles which relate the nonstandard dialect to English as a whole — the knowledge which one must have in order to study a nonstandard language successfully. Much of this knowledge has been gained in the course of current studies of language in its wider social setting, an area sometimes called "sociolinguistics." In the next section we will present some of the findings, not as part of a separate or special kind of linguistics, but rather as principles which one needs for the realistic and accurate study of any language.

CHAPTER III: SOME SOCIOLINGUISTIC PRINCIPLES

Style shifting

One of the fundamental principles of sociolinguistic investigation might simply be stated as *There are no single-style speakers*. By this we mean that every speaker will show some variation in phonological and syntactic rules according to the immediate context in which he is speaking. We can demonstrate that such stylistic shifts are determined by a) the relations of the speaker, addressee, and audience, and particularly the relations of power or solidarity among them; b) the wider social context or "domain": school, job, home, neighborhood, church; c) the topic. One must add of course that the stylistic range and competence of the speaker may vary greatly. Children may have a very narrow range in both the choices open to them and the social contexts they respond to. Old men often show a narrow range in that their motivation for style shifting disappears along with their concern for power relationships.

We apply the principle stated above in a very concrete way when carrying out research with face-to-face interviews. We do not judge the absolute stylistic level of the speaker by some absolute standard of "casualness." We know that, as long as we are asking questions and receiving answers, the speaker is using a relatively "careful" or "consultative" style, and that he possesses a more "casual" or intimate style with which he argues with his friends or quarrels with his family. There are techniques for obtaining casual speech in an interview situation, but the soundest approach is to observe the speaker interacting with the peers who control his speech in everyday life when the observer is not there.

Well-developed social variables show a systematic range of style shifting which is correlated to the amount of attention paid to speech. We can easily observe such style shifting in certain long-standing variables which are common to almost all dialects of English. The *th* of *thing* and *that* can appear as a smooth fricative *"th"* sound, the standard variant; as a *"t"*-like sound lightly or strongly articulated; as a combination of these two; or as a zero as in *Gimme 'at*. For most Americans, the proportions of these forms are nicely blended and graded for each stylistic level — at different absolute levels for different social groups and different regions. Similarly, the alternation of *-ing* and *-in'* in unstressed syllables is a systematic stylistic variable for most Americans — again at different levels for different classes and regions.

At one time, the dialect areas of the eastern United States were sharply divided into *r*-less and *r*-pronouncing areas, according to whether consonantal *r* is pronounced in words like *car* and *card*. But in the last two decades the *r*-pronunciation of "general American" has become accepted as the standard of broadcast networks and of careful middle class pronunciation almost everywhere. As a result, we find that the new "prestige" pronunciation of *r* in final and preconsonantal position has become a sociolinguistic variable in the older *r*-less areas. Almost all younger and middle-aged speakers will show some style shifting with *r*, so that in the more formal styles they will use more *r* and in casual speech practically none at all.

The grammatical variables that show style shifting are quite well known in general, though we usually lack the exact knowledge of where and when these features are used to signal change of style. Some are well-established stereotypes, like *ain't*. Although dictionaries may vary in the way they label *ain't*, most native speakers are quite clear in their sociolinguistic approach to this word — in their social *evaluation* of the form. To make the point clear, imagine a community in which *ain't* is the formal style and in which people correct *isn't* to *ain't* when they are careful. Such a community would be very odd indeed — obviously not a part of the same American speech community in which we all live.

The "double negative" or negative concord is an important stylistic marker; it allows nonstandard speakers to express negatives in a particularly emphatic fashion by reduplicating the negative forms (*Nobody don't know about that*) and at the same time register their adherence to the nonstandard form which is stylistically opposed to the standard (*Nobody knows anything about that*).

The passive has two forms in English, which are closely allied but perhaps not equivalent in meaning. If we ask "What happened to him?" the answer can be "He got run over" or "He was run over." The colloquial form is clearly the former; nonstandard dialects depend almost entirely upon this *got*-passive, to the exclusion of the *be*-passive. As a result, the *be*-passive has acquired a standard, rather careful flavor which it would not have if there were no opposing forms.

In all these examples, we can easily demonstrate the meaning of the stylistic alternation by observing the direction of correction in false starts. In almost every interview, one will find speakers making corrections like "Nobody told him noth — anything about it." No matter how rare or how common such corrections may be, we find that they uniformly run in the same direction, since the more formal style is associated with a mental set in which greater attention is paid to speech and the less formal style with a casual and spontaneous use of language in which the minimum attention is given to the speech process.

It should be clear that the various sociolinguistic variables found in American English are rarely confined to one or the other dialect but usually wander from one end of the stylistic range to the other. There are some which are never used in standard literary or formal English; but as a rule we find that dialects differ primarily in the way in which they use these variables — that is, in the distribution of frequencies along the stylistic range. It would follow that writing a different grammar for each dialect is a wasteful and unnatural procedure; rather, it seems likely that the various dialects of English can be organized within a single pan-dialectal grammar. However, there are cases in which dialects differ sharply and abruptly from each other and use forms which appear to be meaningless or contradictory to those from other communities; this is particularly common with nonstandard Negro English, as we shall see, and in a number of ways this dialect appears to be a different "system." It may be that single grammars can only be written for dialects whose speakers are actually in contact with each other — dialects which are mutually intelligible in the clearest sense. This problem has not been resolved, but in general we can say that few sociolinguistic variables are confined to single dialects.

So far we have been speaking of monolingual style shifting. On the face of it, the shift to another language in bilingual situations seems to be a radically different step. Bilingual speakers do not think of Spanish as another "style" of English. However, there is a functional relation between different languages and different styles which cannot be overlooked. Research in stable bilingual communities indicates that one natural unit of study may be the "linguistic repertoire" of each speaker rather than individual languages; such repertoires may include a wide range of styles in one language and a narrow range in another. The sum total of styles and languages occupies a given range of situations or contexts in which the person interacts with others — linguistic "domains" such as home, neighborhood, job, church, store, school, and newspaper. A monolingual individual uses and understands a wide range of styles which are specialized for various domains; bilingual individuals rarely use both languages over all domains but rather show a comparable specialization of languages and uneven distribution of styles within these languages. When we encounter an individual in one particular domain, at home or in school, we can often tell from the range of style shifting in what domain he uses that language. For example, a first-generation Spanish-English bilingual may use a fairly formal Spanish — learned at school — in interviews; he may use a very colloquial Spanish at home; but in English he may have only a nonstandard dialect which he learned on the streets. A second-generation Spanish speaker may reverse this pattern, with Spanish confined to a very informal pattern used at home.

3.1. The social stratification of language

In 1948, John Kenyon introduced the distinction between *cultural levels* and *functional varieties* of English. He argued that we should recognize a colloquial standard and a formal nonstandard, as well as a formal standard and a colloquial nonstandard — in other words, that style and class stratification of language are actually independent. This would seem to be a common sense distinction, and it would obviously be useful and helpful if language were organized in this manner. Then, no matter how casually an educated person spoke, we would have no trouble in recognizing him as an educated person.

It is remarkable that this is not the case. In actual fact, the same variables which are used in style shifting also distinguish cultural or social levels of English. This is so for stable phonological variables such as *th*- and *-ing*; for such incoming prestige forms as *-r*; for the grammatical variables such as pronominal apposition, double negative, or even the use of *ain't*. If we plot the average values of these phonological variables for *both* style and social levels, we find such regular patterns as figures 1 and 2 for *th*- and *-ing*. The vertical axis is the proportion of the nonstandard variant used; the horizontal axis shows various styles, from casual speech to the reading of isolated words. Each point on this graph shows the average value of a group of speakers — a socioeconomic class in this case — in a particular style, and the lines connect all the values of (th) and (ing) for a given social group.

Note that at each style there is social stratification: whether we are listening to casual speech or to reading, it is clear that the social background of the speaker is reflected in his use of these variables. But each group also shows regular style shifting in the same direction; although these social groups are very different in one sense, they are all very similar in another sense: they all *use* the variable in the same way. Members of a speech community are not aware of this fact; their experience is limited to a) the whole range of speech styles used by their own family and friends, and b) the speech of a wide range of social classes in one or two styles. Thus the teacher hears the differences between middle class and working class children in classroom recitation but does not follow his students home and hear them at their ease among their own friends. He does not realize how similar the students are to him — how they fit into the same sociolinguistic structure which governs his own behavior. Instead, teachers like most of us tend to perceive the speech of others categorically: John always says *dese* and *dose*,

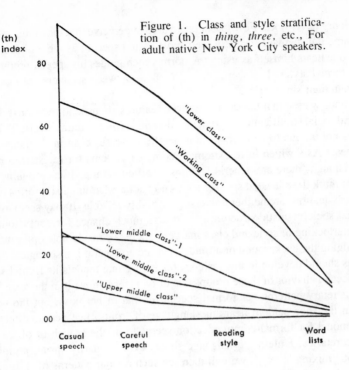

(th) index

Figure 1. Class and style stratification of (th) in *thing, three*, etc., For adult native New York City speakers.

80

60

40

"Lower class"

"Working class"

20

"Lower middle class"-1

"Lower middle class"-2

"Upper middle class"

00

Casual speech   Careful speech   Reading style   Word lists

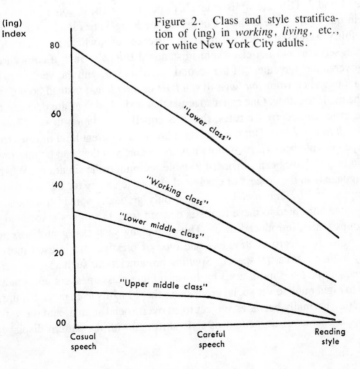

(ing) index

Figure 2. Class and style stratification of (ing) in *working, living*, etc., for white New York City adults.

80

60

"Lower class"

40

"Working class"

"Lower middle class"

20

"Upper middle class"

00

Casual speech   Careful speech   Reading style

but Henry never does. Few teachers are able to perceive that they themselves use the same nonstandard forms in their most casual speech; as we will see, almost everyone hears himself as using the norm which guides his speech production in most formal styles. In a word, the differences between speakers are more obvious than their similarities.

Thus we see that the same linguistic features are used to register style shifting and social stratification — functional varieties *and* cultural levels. This situation is not unique to English. It is generally the case, even in the languages of Southeast Asia which have extremely complex systems for registering respect. True enough, there are general features of articulation and voice quality which tend to mark the educated speaker for us no matter what linguistic forms he uses, but such qualities are neither universal nor highly reliable. It may seem astonishing that sociolinguistic structure provides so much chance for confusion; given this interlocking of style and class markers, there is considerable opportunity for misjudging the background or attitude of strangers. Yet it is also logical that languages should develop in this fashion, for each group models its formal style on the speech behavior of those groups one or two steps above it in the social scale. The secretary patterns her formal speech on that of her boss, but the working man in the shop seldom hears the language of front-office people directly; his chief model for formal communication seems to be the speech of office clerks and secretaries. Unless the language shows extraordinarily strong prohibitions against "mixing levels," we will then see such regular patterns of shifting as in figures 1 and 2. Discrete stylistic levels or codes do exist in some societies, and even in our own — the archaic English of the King James Bible, for example, has a fairly well-established set of co-occurrence rules which are used productively in sermons but not elsewhere in standard English. Such a co-occurrence rule governs the agreement of the second singular *thou* with the verb form *hast*: one cannot switch from *you have* to *you hast* or *thou have*; instead both changes must be made together. One can also argue that lexical choices are determined by similar strict co-occurrence rules, that it is equally a violation to say *Thou hast been swell to me, Lord*. But this violation breaks a different kind of rule (termed a "Type II" rule below); such violations *do* occur, and they can be interpreted.

So far, we have been considering stable sociolinguistic situations. Wherever the language is in the process of change, there is a tendency for the new forms to be adopted first by one social group and only gradually spread to others. The social value attributed to these forms is derived from the values associated with the groups which introduced them. Thus hip slang such as *dig* and *boss* introduced from the Negro ghettos has one type of prestige and is used most frequently in the most casual speech. Spelling pronunciations such as *often* with a *t* or *calm* with an *l* are introduced by lower middle class speakers and gradually spread to higher and lower social groups. As these linguistic changes mature, the new feature normally becomes subject to an overt social stigma, and the variable develops a characteristic pattern of style shifting, with the pattern displayed in figures 1 and 2. When the change goes to completion, the possibility of choice disappears, and with it the social value associated with the item. Today, the spelling pronunciation of *recognize* with a *g* is standard, and it has lost the over-careful, insecure character it must have had when it was first introduced. But incoming pronunciations such as *"perculator"* or *"esculator"* now stand at the other end of the spectrum. At any one time, social groups will differ in their attitude towards particular linguistic variables in process of change. For some, there is no problem in *It's I* vs. *It's me; Whom do you want?* vs. *Who do you want;* or *He does it as he should* vs. *He does it like he should.* For others, these are matters of paralyzing concern. The norms for pronouncing *vase* and *aunt* are now shifting, so that many people are baffled and embarrassed when they encounter these words in a text to be read aloud. Faced with two conflicting norms, speakers often find a meaningful use for both. As one woman said in an interview, "These little ones are my *vayses* [rhyming with mazes]; but these big ones are my *vahses* [rhyming with Roz's]."

The sharpness of the social stratification of language seems to vary with the degree of social mobility which exists in society as a whole. In London and its environs, we find that the use of initial *f-* for standard voiceless *th-* is a uniform characteristic of working class speech, but it is not heard in the standard speech of adults. Moreover, in their most careful, "posh" pronunciation, many working class speakers say *fings, free* and *frow* for *things, three* and *throw.* In the United States, we do not find such sharp stratification among white working class speakers: stops are common enough in *tings, tree* and *trēw*. But, as figures 1 and 2 show, even the lowest ranking social group has no difficulty in saying *things, three* and *throw* when reading word lists. We do find sharp social stratification between white and Negro speakers in the United States, where a pattern of caste rather than class differentiation has prevailed for a few centuries. We then can observe such differentiation between ethnic groups as the nonstandard Negro English difficulty with *-sps, -sts, -sks* clusters. Many Negro speakers literally cannot say *wasps, lists* or *desks*: these plurals are normally *wasses, lisses* and *desses,* forms which are quite unknown in the surrounding white community.

The ethnic stratification of society is thus reflected in linguistic patterns — sometimes partly independent of socioeconomic factors, sometimes closely interlocked with them. In New York City, the Jewish and Italian populations differ from each other in subtle ways as they both follow the general evolution of the vernacular. The Italians are far more forward in their raising of the vowel of *bad* to equal that of *beard;* the Jews, on the other hand, are somewhat more advanced in their tendency to raise the vowel of *law* to that of *lure.* In Phoenix, Arizona, the ongoing linguistic change which merges *cot* and *caught, Don* and *dawn,* is much more characteristic of the Anglo population than of the Negroes and Mexicans: the latter groups normally preserve this distinction between short *o* and long open *o*. In most urban ghetto areas, we find that the southern characteristic of merging *i* and *e* before nasals has become generalized among the Negro population so that Negroes of all geographic backgrounds neither make nor hear the difference between *pin* and *pen*, *Jim* and *gem*, while the surrounding white population still preserves the distinction. This is one of many examples of a feature of a southern regional dialect transported to an urban setting to become an ethnic and class marker.

When the ethnic group still preserves a foreign language for at least one social domain, we find clear traces of it in their English. Some foreign accents have high prestige in the United States — French is the most outstanding example — but usually not if there is a large immigrant group which speaks this language. Even where bilingual speakers use a fairly native English, they are limited in their stylistic range. Thus many who have learned English as a second language in their late teens will show an excellent, even native, careful style but no casual or intimate style at all.

Breaks in social communication between groups in society are reflected in the failure of certain linguistic items to cross the barrier between the groups. While certain kinds of slang pass freely and continuously from the Negro community into the white community, other grammatical and lexical items remain fixed, and we can witness *pluralistic ignorance* where neither perceives the actual situation: one group knows nothing about the form at all, and the other assumes that its use is quite general. Negro speakers have traditionally used *mother wit* as the equivalent of *common sense*, but no white speakers know this term except as an archaic and literary form. The Negro vernacular uses dummy *it* for *there*, saying *it's a difference; it's no one there; it's a policeman at the door*; but despite their long contact with Negro speakers in person and in dialect literature, the neighboring white speakers know nothing of this pattern.

The regular pattern of Figures 1 and 2 is that of a stable sociolinguistic marker. When the marker is in the process of change, we see patterns more like that of Figure 3, which shows the incoming prestige marker of *r*-pronunciation. The steepness of the lines is not the same for all groups: in particular, we observe that the lower middle class shows the sharpest shift towards *r*-pronunciation in formal styles, going even beyond the highest social group in this respect. This "hypercorrect" behavior, or "going one better," is quite characteristic of second-ranking groups in many communities. We find similar behavior in the *r*-pronunciation of such distant areas as Hillsboro, North Carolina, as well as New York City, and in overcorrect grammatical behavior as well as in pronunciation.

The sharpness of such style shifting is a direct reflection of the degree of linguistic insecurity felt by a particular group: that is, the tendency to shift away from the natural pattern of casual speech is proportionate to the recognition of an external standard of correctness. We can measure the strength of such feelings by various tests which reflect the extent to which people will say, "*That* is the correct way to say it, but *this* is the way *I* say it." Since American school teachers have traditionally been drawn from the lower middle class, the strong tendency

Figure 3.   Class stratification of (r) in *guard, car, beer, beard,* etc., for native New York City adults.

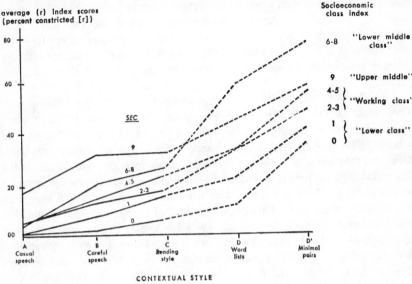

towards hypercorrect behavior which we see here must be reckoned with in designing any educational program. Along with linguistic insecurity and extreme range of style shifting, one encounters an extreme intolerance towards other dialects. For decades, educational leaders have asked teachers to regard the child's nonstandard language as "another" way of speaking, to recognize it as simply "different" from school language rather than condemning it as sloppy or illogical. But many teachers find it difficult to adopt this attitude, since they recognize in the child's language (perhaps unconsciously) the very pattern which they so sharply correct in themselves. It is extraordinary to witness how violently some people will express themselves on such apparently trivial points as the height of the vowel in *bad*. It is not uncommon for people to stigmatize a certain pronunciation by saying, "I would never hire a person who talked like *that*!" Such extreme reactions are quite common in our schools, and all teachers should be on the watch for them to the extent that they interfere with the process of education itself.

3.2.   Types of linguistic rules

In the last few pages, we have been concerned with a kind of linguistic behavior which has seldom been studied in the past: variable rules. There is no fixed instruction in English as to how we must pronounce the *th* of *then* in any given case; instead, there are several choices. But these choices are not in free variation. There is an important variable rule which tells us that those who pronounce *then* with a *d-* sound with a certain frequency are to be stigmatized as "uneducated" or "lower class." Anyone who does not know this rule is not a very good speaker of English. Rules of this sort — which we will designate Type III — are quite common in English. Despite the fact that they cannot be violated with any given pronunciation of a word, they are an important part of our linguistic competence.

The kinds of rules which are generally taught in school are a different sort. They state "Do not do this at all!" For example, "Don't say *ain't*!" But there is an added provision, usually unstated: "unless you want to fail" or "unless you want to be known as stupid or uneducated." These rules are cast in categorical form, but they are what we might call *semi-categorical:* they are written in the full knowledge that people do indeed make violations, and that one can interpret such violations. There is a ready-made label or interpretation which goes with the breaking of the rules. This labeling is not, of course, a simple matter, because some utterances of *ain't* are taken as jokes, others as slips, and still others as evidence of habitual violations. But in the school situation, each utterance of *ain't* is marked as a violation and reprimanded as such. We may call such rules Type II rules. When Type II rules are overtly violated, the violation is rare enough to be worth reporting: such violations are thus *reportable,* and an appropriate response to the report is "He did?" "He did say that?" If a school teacher were to use *ain't* in the middle of a grammar class, it would indeed make a story worth telling. It is common to find Type II rules at the beginning or at the end of a linguistic change in progress, where the form is rare enough to be noticed whenever it occurs. The broad *a* pronunciation of *aunt* and *bath* is almost extinct as a prestige form among white speakers in the middle Atlantic states. "Bahth" and "ahnt" survive as rare examples of adherence to an older prestige pattern and are frequently stigmatized as false attempts to impress the listener. They survive in another way which is characteristic of Type II rules: "I'm going to the bathroom," originally taken as humorous play on the notion of falsely impressing someone, now is becoming fossilized into a common and almost unconscious form of ritualized humor.

Most linguistic rules are of an altogether different character. They are automatic, deep-seated patterns of behavior which are not consciously recognized and are never violated. Rules for contraction of *is* form one such set of automatic rules among countless others, which we may call Type I. No one is taught in school the very complex conditions under which one can, if desired, contract *is* to *'s*: that one can do so in *He's here*, but not **Here he's*; in *He's ready*, but not **What he's is smart*. Such automatic rules exist in all forms of social behavior, but they are extremely hard to detect simply because they are never violated and one never thinks about them at all. For example, in asking someone for directions, one thinks about who to ask, and what polite forms to use, but never about whether one should introduce oneself. "Hello, I'm Bill Labov, where's Grand Central Station?" is a violation which never occurs. If one artificially constructs such a violation, people are simply confused; they cannot interpret it, and the most appropriate response is "Wha'?" Linguists have been discovering and formulating such Type I rules for many centuries, and most of our studies are concerned with them. They form the very backbone of linguistic structure; without them we would find it very difficult to speak at all. If English teachers indeed had the job of "teaching the child the Type I rules of English," it would be incredibly more difficult than the job which they actually do face, which is to instruct children in a small number of Type II rules and some basic vocabulary for talking about language. We can summarize this discussion of rule typology by the following chart:

Rule Type	How often rule operates	Violations	Response to violations	Example
I	100%	None in natural speech	Wha'?	Rules for when one can contract *is*: "He is" vs. *"He's."
II	95–99%	Rare and reportable	He did?	"Why you ain't never giving me no A's?"
III	5–95%	None by definition and unreportable	So what?	"He sure got an A" vs. "He surely got an A."

3.3. Linguistic norms

We have seen that sociolinguistic behavior shows social differentiation. Such behavior reflects a set of norms, beliefs, or subjective attitudes towards particular features and language in general. The regular stratification of behavior shown above has a subjective counterpart: uniform linguistic norms, in which all speakers of the community agree in their evaluation of the feature in question. In our society, these values are middle class norms, since the middle class is the dominant group in school, business, and mass communications. Certain linguistic forms, like the fricative *th* in *then*, the *-ing* in *working*, the *-ly* in *surely*, are considered more suitable for people holding certain kinds of jobs. One can set up a scale of jobs requiring more or less excellent speech which will obtain very general agreement, such as television announcer, school teacher, office manager, salesman, post office clerk, foreman, factory worker. The converse values are equally uniform: that nonstandard language like the *d*- in *den* (*then*), the *-in'* in *workin'* or the *never* in *Nobody never knows* are characteristic of "tough" guys who not only like to fight but come out on top. Those familiar with street culture know that there is in fact little correlation between toughness and the use of nonstandard language, but the stereotype seems to be well established. The fact that both values — job suitability and toughness — are clearest in the reports of middle class speakers suggests to us that both sets are in fact taught in school. If the teacher does in fact identify nonstandard language with the tougher elements in school, it seems inevitable that he will convey this notion to the students in the class and so gradually reinforce the values already present in the mass media.

The stability and uniformity of social values in respect to language are quite extraordinary. Social revolutions, such as those which have taken place in Eastern European countries, characteristically fail to overturn the sociolinguistic norms of the society; on the contrary, prohibitions against using vernacular forms in writing may grow even stricter. We can judge from impressionistic reports that this seems to be the case in the Soviet Union as well as Czechoslovakia. In our own society, we find that all social groups share the same set of norms in correct and public language. Radical and revolutionary figures do not use nonstandard grammar in public or in print: on the contrary, they endorse the rules of grammar as strictly as the conservative journals do. There has been a long tradition in the United States for politicians to appeal to the public with a sprinkling of the vernacular in their platform speeches. But such displays are confined rather strictly to certain set situations, and the same speakers insist on correct or even formal grammar in formal or solemn statements. The leaders of the black nationalist movement among the Negro people do not use nonstandard Negro English in their public speeches. Their grammar is essentially standard. Although there is a growing tendency to use fragments of vernacular language in public speeches, careful analysis shows that these are isolated elements; the basic grammar and phonology used is that of the middle class community, essentially that which is taught in school.

In highly stratified situations, where society is divided into two major groups, the values associated with the dominant group are assigned to the dominant language by all. Lambert and his colleages at McGill University have shown how regular are such unconscious evaluations in the French-English situation of Quebec, in the Arabic-Hebrew confrontation in Israel, and in other areas as well. When English Canadians heard the same person speaking Canadian French, on the one hand, and English, on the other, they unhesitatingly judged him to be more intelligent, more dependable, kinder, more ambitious, better looking and taller — when he spoke English. Common sense would tell us that French-Canadians would react in the opposite manner, but in fact they do not. Their judgments reflect almost the same set of unconscious values as the English-Canadians show. This overwhelming negative evaluation of Canadian French is a property of the society as a whole. It is an omnipresent stigma which has a strong effect on what happens in school as well as in other social contexts.

Such a uniform set of norms defines a speech community. People in the United States do not share the Canadian reaction to Canadian French. They do share a number of uniform values about nonstandard dialects, but they also differ considerably in their reaction to particular features, depending upon the underlying vernacular of the region. The short *a* of *mad, bad, glad*, is a crucial matter in New York City — in fact, it is probably the one feature of pronunciation which working class speakers pay most attention to in careful speech. In Philadelphia, the vowels are more strikingly different from the formal standard, but people don't care very much about it. A far more crucial issue for Philadelphia is the vowel of *go* and *road*. The Philadelphia and Pittsburgh vernacular forms have a centralized beginning, very similar to that of some high prestige British dialects. As a result, the Philadelphia vernacular forms sound elegant and cultivated to New York speakers, and the New York vernacular forms, with a lower, unrounded beginning, sound elegant and impressive to the Philadelphians. Conversely, the Philadelphians and the New Yorkers both despise their own vernacular forms. In general, it is an important sociolinguistic principle that *those who use the highest degree of a stigmatized form in their own casual speech are quickest to stigmatize it in the speech of others*. This principle has important consequences for the classroom situation. The teacher from the same community has the advantage that he can realistically detect and correct the most important nonstandard features of his students; but he has the disadvantage that he will react to these features in an extreme, sometimes unrealistic fashion. This is most relevant to questions of pronunciation. Grammatical norms are fairly uniform throughout the United States, and our chief sources of regional variation have to do with the pronunciation of vowels.

3.4. Differences between the sexes

In some societies there are striking differences between men's and women's speech, but in the United States we do not find widespread variation in the actual features of language used by the sexes. There are marginal examples: men are more apt to say *"Fill' er up"* than women are; men use more obscene language than women do — in public. But the major differences between the sexes are in the important areas of *attitudes* towards language. The sociolinguistic behavior of women is quite different from that of men because they respond to the commonly held normative values in a different way. Such differences appear in our earliest studies of sociolinguistic variables. In Fischer's 1958 study of the use of *-ing* and *-in'* in a New England village, we find that both boys and girls use both variants. But among the girls, ten out of twelve used more *-ing* than *-in'*, while among the boys, only five out of twelve did. In general, women are more sensitive to overt social correction and use more prestige forms than men. But this difference is not independent of social class. It is moderately true for the highest status group in a speech community, but the effect is far more striking in the *second highest* status group. Here the difference may appear in an extreme form. Below a certain point on the social scale, the effect is often reversed. Among lower class women who live at home, on welfare or without a regular occupation, we can observe less awareness of sociolinguistic norms and less response to them.

A typical pattern is that shown by men and women in their use of pronominal apposition — that is, *My brother, he's pretty good*. In Roger Shuy's sociolinguistic study of Detroit (1967), we find the following indices for the use of this nonstandard feature by men and women:

Status Group	I	II	III	IV
Men	5.0	19.3	23.1	25.0
Women	4.8	9.2	27.2	23.7

Men and women are practically the same for the highest status group. In the lower groups III and IV there are small differences with no clear direction. But in the second highest group there is a very great difference between men and women: women use less than half as much pronominal apposition as men.

When we examine the full spectrum of stylistic behavior for men and women, it appears that the crucial differences lie in the steeper slope of style shifting for women: in all but the lowest status group they may actually use more of a nonstandard form in their casual speech than men, but in formal styles they shift more rapidly and show an excess of hypercorrect behavior at that end of the scale. Furthermore, women respond in a much more extreme fashion to subjective reaction tests than men and are far more prone to stigmatize nonstandard usage. The overall picture of women's behavior fits in with the general sociolinguistic principle stated above — that those who use more nonstandard forms in their own casual speech will be most sensitive to those forms in the speech of others. The hypercorrect pattern of the second highest status group is accentuated in women. This is particularly important for the schools, since the majority of our teachers are women, and it is their reaction to nonstandard language with which we must be concerned in examining the educational applications of these findings.

3.5. Stages in the acquisition of standard English

In the sociolinguistic study of language learning, we can begin with the fundamental observation that *children do not speak like their parents*. This is indeed surprising, since we obviously learn to speak from our parents. If the child's parents speak English, and he grows up in the United States, he will certainly have English as his native language. Yet in almost every detail, his English will resemble that of his peers rather than that of his parents. We have as yet no thoroughgoing studies of the relation of parent, child, and peer group, yet all of the available evidence shows that this is the case. With a few exceptions, second-generation speakers in a given area will be as fully native as the third and fourth generations. As a rule, the child becomes a native speaker of a particular dialect between the ages of roughly four and thirteen. If the child moves into a new area at the age of ten or eleven, the chances are that he will never acquire the local pattern as completely as those who were born and raised in that area.

In some towns of northeastern New Jersey, for example, we find that adults do not equate *spirit* and *spear it*, nor do they rhyme *nearer* and *mirror* — that is, they do distinguish the vowels of *beat* and *bit* before intervocalic *r*. But the children in this area use the higher vowel of *beat* for both *nearer* and *mirror*, *mysterious* and *delirious*. In the middle class sections of the same region, most parents come from New York City and have an *r*-less vernacular, but almost all children are solidly *r*-pronouncing. Most parents are not aware of how systematically their children's speech differs from their own; if they do inquire, they will be surprised to find that there is no fixed relation between their own rules and those of their children. Instead, it is the local group of their children's peers which determines this generation's speech pattern. This is the case with rules of nonstandard urban dialects as well as the more neutral rules of regional dialects considered here.

The full force of peer group influence may not indeed appear in the speech of the six-year-old in the first grade. It is in the fourth and fifth grade, when the ten-year-old begins to come under the full influence of the preadolescent peer group, that we obtain the most consistent records of his dialect. It should also be pointed out that it is at this age that many school records show sharp downward trends, and this is not unconnected with the fact that peer groups present a more solid resistance to the schoolroom culture than any individual child can.

In the process of language learning, there are many sections of the vocabulary which are acquired quite late. It is possible that the underlying linguistic system used by a child will be different from that of adults if he has learned very little of the latinate vocabulary before the age of thirteen. Word alternations, such as microscope - microscopy, decide - decision, pérmit - permit, give the crucial evidence which supports and justifies the spelling system of English. We are badly lacking in any systematic studies of children's total vocabulary (active and passive) in the early grades; it is this vocabulary which provides the input to whatever linguistic insight the child has into English spelling, and this is the equipment which he brings to the task of learning to read.

At an even later stage the child acquires the sociolinguistic norms discussed in the preceding sections. Whereas the adult community shows almost complete agreement in responses to subjective reaction tests, adolescents are quite sketchy in their perceptions of these value systems. Children certainly know that there is a great difference between school language and home language, teacher language and their own language; but they know surprisingly little of the social significance of these differences. A conversation with a twelve-year-old may run like this:

"Have you ever heard anyone say *dese, dat,* and *dose*?"

"Yeh."

"What kind of person says that?"

"I don't know."

Anything that can be done within the educational process to accelerate the learning of these adult norms will certainly have an effect upon the desire to learn standard English.

If we map the acquisition of the adult sociolinguistic pattern in families with many children, we find that there is a steady upward movement with age. Families of all social levels follow the same general direction, in that older children show more style shifting and more sensitive subjective reactions than younger children. But there is regular class stratification in this area too. Middle class families start at a higher level and accelerate faster, so that middle class children may have a fully adult sociolinguistic system in their late teens. In college, these children will receive the most intensive training in the use of middle class formal language. On the other hand, working class families start at a lower level, and their children may not converge on the adult system until their thirties or forties. At this point, it is obviously too late for them to acquire productive control of prestige patterns: their performance will be erratic and unreliable, even though they are capable of judging the performance of others.

In general, we find that norms acquired later in life, especially after puberty, never achieve the automatic regularity of a Type I rule. A certain amount of audio-monitoring, or attention paid to speech, is necessary if any degree of consistency is to be achieved with such patterns. When the speaker is tired, or distracted, or unable to hear himself, this acquired or "superposed" pattern gives way in favor of the native vernacular acquired early in life. He may also stop monitoring his speech for the opposite reasons — when he is intensely excited, emotionally disturbed, or very much involved in the subject. It is an important sociolinguistic principle that *the most consistent and regular linguistic system of a speech community is that of the basic vernacular learned before puberty*. The overt social correction supplied in the schoolroom can never be as regular or far-reaching as the unconscious efforts of "change from below" within the system. It is almost a matter of accident which words rise to the level of social consciousness and become overt stereotypes to be corrected. The *o* of *coffee, chocolate* and *door* has moved to a very high *u*-like vowel in the vernacular of New York and Philadelphia, and it has finally become subject to the process of social correction. The *o* of *boy* and *Lloyd* is the same *o*, and it has moved to the same *u*-like vowel, but it is never corrected to a low vowel like the others.

Overt correction applied in the schoolroom is useful to the student in that it makes him aware of the distance between his speech and the standard language — in grammar and pronunciation. This correction cannot in itself teach him a new Type I rule; it most often gives him a variable Type III rule which he will use in formal situations. At best he may achieve a semi-categorical Type II control of this feature. There are many educated Negro speakers who were raised speaking nonstandard Negro English, which has no third-singular *s* and has obligatory negative concord as in *Nobody know nothin' about it*. In formal situations such speakers can supply all third-singular *s*'s and avoid negative concord. But this requires continual monitoring of their own speech. In relaxed and casual circumstances, the rules of their basic vernacular will reappear. It is certainly a good thing that this is the case, for a speaker who can no longer use the nonstandard vernacular of the neighborhood in which he was raised cannot return to that neighborhood as the same person.

We may consider the important question as to whether any speaker ever acquires complete control of both standard English and a nonstandard vernacular. So far, the answer to this question seems to be no. We have observed speakers who maintain perfect control of their original vernacular in casual speech and have variable control of standard rules in their casual speech. Educated black speakers will show, even in their casual speech, far more third-singular *s* than the vernacular; their negative concord will be quite variable; in a word, the Type I or Type II rules of the nonstandard dialect are now variable Type III rules for them. This does not stop them from communicating effectively with their old neighbors and friends. But it does mean that they are very poor informants on the fundamental rules of the vernacular. Teachers raised in ghetto areas cannot use themselves for reliable information on the original nonstandard rules. The knowledge of one system inevitably affects the other. The rules of standard English and its nonstandard relatives are so similar that they are bound to interact. Languages and dialects are not so carefully partitioned from each other in the speakers' heads that the right hand does not know what the left hand is doing.

3.6. Social differences in verbal skills

There is ample evidence to show that social classes differ in their use of language in ways that go beyond the use of stigmatized nonstandard forms. A number of studies show that middle class speakers use longer sentences, more subordinate clauses, and more learned vocabulary; they take a less personal verbal viewpoint than working class speakers. Our own studies of narratives of personal experience show that middle class speakers interrupt their narratives much more often to give evaluative statements, often cast in an impersonal style. Middle class speakers seem to excel in taking the viewpoint of the "generalized other."

There is also ample evidence to show that middle class children do better on a wide range of school tasks, in reading and mathematics, in achievement tests and nonverbal intelligence tests. In a word, they perform much better in school and do better at acquiring a number of important skills which they will need in later life. Everyone would like to see working class youth, especially Negro and Puerto Rican youth in the American urban ghettos, do as well.

There is, however, no automatic connection between these two sets of findings. Seeing these two correlations, many educators have immediately concluded that a third correlation exists: that working class children must be taught middle class verbal habits and be made to abandon the rules of their own dialect. Such a conclusion is without warrant, for we do not know at present how much of the middle class verbal pattern is functional and contributes to educational success and how much is not and does not.

The British social psychologist Basil Bernstein (1966) has devoted his attention to class differences in the use of language. He distinguishes a "restricted code" and an "elaborated code" which govern the selection of linguistic forms and suggests that working class speakers are confined to the former while middle class speakers have both. The chief characteristics of the "restricted code" may be summed up best in Bernstein's own language: speech is "fast, fluent, with reduced articulatory clues"; meanings are "discontinuous, dislocated, condensed and local"; there is a "low level of vocabulary and syntactic selection"; and most importantly, "the unique meaning of the person would tend to be implicit" (p. 62).

Bernstein's description of the restricted code is a good picture of the casual speech which we rely upon for our view of the basic vernacular of a language, with both working class and middle class subjects. The overall characteristic which he focuses on is greater or lesser *explicitness* — and in the formulation used earlier, more or less attention paid to the monitoring of speech. This is the style which is commonly used among those who share a great deal of common experience. The most explicit formal style is used in addressing a public audience or in writing, where we presuppose the minimum of shared information and experience.

Clearly, then, the verbal skills which characterize middle class speakers are in the area which we have been calling "school language" in an informal sense, which speakers confined to a nonstandard dialect plainly do not control. There is no reason to presuppose a deep semantic or logical difference between nonstandard dialects and such an elaborated style. Some aspect of the formal speech of middle class speakers may very well have value for the acquisition of knowledge and verbal problem solving. But before we train working class speakers to copy middle class speech patterns wholesale, it is worth asking just which aspects of this style are functional for learning and which are matters of prestige and fashion. The question must be answered before we can design an effective teaching program, and unfortunately we have not yet begun to answer it.

Working class speakers also excel at a wide range of verbal skills, including many not controlled by middle class speakers. In the urban ghettos, we find a number of speech events which demand great ingenuity, originality, and practice, such as the system of ritual insults known variously as *sounding, signifying, the dozens*, etc.; the display of occult knowledge sometimes known as *rifting*; the delivery, with subtle changes, of a large repertoire of oral epic poems known as *toasts* or *jokes*; and many other forms of verbal expertise quite unknown to teachers and middle class society in general. Most of these skills cannot be transferred wholesale to the school situation. Until now there has been no way of connecting excellence in the verbal activity of the vernacular culture with excellence in the verbal skills needed in school. Yet it seems plain that our educational techniques should draw upon these nonstandard vernacular skills to the better advantage of all concerned.